EUROPE

IN THE HIGH
MIDDLE AGES

THE PENGUIN HISTORY OF EUROPE
General Editor: David Cannadine

Simon Price: *Greek and Roman Europe*
Chris Wickham: *Early Medieval Europe*
William Chester Jordan: *Europe in the High Middle Ages**
Anthony Grafton: *Renaissance Europe*
Mark Greengrass: *Early Modern Europe*
T. C. W. Blanning: *Eighteenth-Century Europe*
Richard J. Evans: *Nineteenth-Century Europe*
Ian Kershaw: *Twentieth-Century Europe*

*published

William Chester Jordan

Europe

in the high

middle ages

PENGUIN HISTORY OF EUROPE

VIKING

VIKING
Published by the Penguin Group
Penguin Putnam Inc., 375 Hudson Street,
New York, New York 10014, U.S.A.
Penguin Books Ltd, 80 Strand,
London WC2R 0RL, England
Penguin Books Australia Ltd, 250 Camberwell Road, Camberwell,
Victoria 3124, Australia
Penguin Books Canada Ltd, 10 Alcorn Avenue,
Toronto, Ontario, Canada M4V 3B2
Penguin Books India (P) Ltd, 11 Community Centre, Panchsheel Park,
New Delhi – 110 017, India
Penguin Books (N.Z.) Ltd, Cnr Rosedale and Airborne Roads, Albany,
Auckland, New Zealand
Penguin Books (South Africa) (Pty) Ltd, 24 Sturdee Avenue,
Rosebank, Johannesburg 2196, South Africa

Penguin Books Ltd, Registered Offices:
Harmondsworth, Middlesex, England

First American edition
Published in 2003 by Viking Penguin,
a member of Penguin Putnam Inc.

1   3   5   7   9   10   8   6   4   2

Copyright © William Chester Jordan, 2001
All rights reserved

Maps drawn by Nigel Andrews

CIP data available

ISBN: 0-670-03202-6

This book is printed on acid-free paper. ∞

Printed in the United States of America
Set in PostScript Adobe Sabon

Contents

List of Illustrations	vii
List of Maps	ix
Acknowledgements	x
Note on Names	xi
Prologue	1

PART I: EUROPE IN THE ELEVENTH CENTURY

1	Christendom in the Year 1000	5
2	Mediterranean Europe	20
3	Northern, Celts and Anglo-Saxons	38
4	Francia/France	52
5	Central Europe	66

PART II: THE RENAISSANCE OF THE
TWELFTH CENTURY

6	The Investiture Controversy	85
7	The First Crusade	100
8	The World of Learning	113
9	Cultural Innovations of the Twelfth Century: Vernacular Literature and Architecture	129
10	Political Power and Its Contexts I	143
11	Political Power and Its Contexts II	161

PART III: THE THIRTEENTH CENTURY

12	Social Structures	181
13	The Pontificate of Innocent III and the Forth Lateran Council	194

CONTENTS

14 Learning   213
15 The Kingdoms of the North   226
16 Baltic and Central Europe   243
17 The Gothic World   259
18 Southern Europe   271

PART IV: CHRISTENDOM IN THE EARLY
FOURTEENTH CENTURY

19 Famine and Plague   289
20 Political and Social Violence   302
21 The Church in Crisis   314

Epilogue   327

APPENDIX: *Genealogical Tables*   329
References   344
Suggested Reading   348
Index   355

List of Illustrations

(Photographic acknowledgements are given in parentheses)

1 San Bartolomeo, Pantano, Pistoia, Italy. (Photo: © Scala)

2 Basilica of San Pietro, Moissac, Italy. (Photo: © Scala)

3 Autun Cathedral, France (Photo: © Corbis)

4 Durham Cathedral, England. (Photo: © Scala)

5 Basilica of Vézelay, France. (Photo: © Ludovic Maisant/Corbis)

6 San Millan, Castile, Spain. (Photo: © A.I.S.A.)

7 Basilica of Vézelay, France. (Photo: © Scala)

8 Rose window, Chartres Cathedral, Notre Dame, Paris. (Photo: © Corbis)

9 Gothic reliquary (National Gallery, Perugia, Italy) (Photo: © Scala)

10 Notre Dame, Paris, France (Photo: © Scala)

11 Bourges Cathedral, France. (Photo: © Scala)

12 World map, c. 1250 (Ms.Add.2861, fol.9, British Library, London). (Photo: © AKG London)

13 Krak des Chevaliers, Syria, c. 1142. (Photo: © AKG London)

14 Sainte-Chapelle, Paris. (Photo: © Scala)

15 Bourges Cathedral, France. (Photo: © AKG London/Eric Lessing)

16 Burgos Cathedral, Spain. (Photo: © Scala)

17 Westminster Abbey, London. (Photo: © AKG London/Robert O'Dea)

18 Tournai Cathedral, Belgium. (Photo: © Hutchison Library/Bernard Regent)

19 Wells Cathedral, England. (Photo: © Scala)

20 Virgin and Child, by Giovanni Pisano, Pisa, Italy. (Photo: © Scala)

21 Abraham and the Three Angels from the St Louis Psalter. (Biblio-teque Nationale de France). (Photo: © The Bridgeman Art Library)

22 Vignette from a Gothic manuscript (Santa Croce, Florence, Italy). (Photo © Scala)

23 King Solomon, from the 'Arsenal Bible' (Ms.5211, fol.307, Biblioteque de l'Arsenal, Paris/Biblioteque Nationale de France).

24 Crucifixion (Museum of Catalan Art, Barcelona). (Photo: © Scala)

25 Lewd marginalia from 'Le Voex du Paan' (Ms.24, fol.25v, Pierpont Library, New York). (Photo: © Scala)

List of Maps

1 Europe   6–7

2 Mediterranean Europe in the eleventh century   21

3 Northern Europe in the eleventh century   39

4 France in the eleventh century   53

5 Central Europe in the eleventh century   67

6 The First Crusade   101

7 Northern Europe in the twelfth century   144

8 Southern Europe (including Crusader States) in the twelfth century   162–3

9 The Fourth Crusade   198

10 England and France in the twelfth century   227

11 Scandinavia, Germany, Hungary and the Slavic lands in the thirteenth century   244

12 Later crusades   282

Acknowledgements

I wish to thank David Cannadine, the editor of the series, for inviting me to contribute the volume on the High Middle Ages. Ravindra Mirchandani, the original editor of the series at Penguin Press, was helpful in getting me started on the project. Simon Winder, who took his place, struck me from the first as a judicious and considerate person, one whom, I felt, I did not wish to disappoint, either by writing an entirely traditional book or being very late in completing it. In Princeton, Tina Enhoffer served as my research assistant, but she also read and assessed the individual chapters. Dr Adam Davis assembled the list of Suggested Reading. My colleagues Arno Mayer and Peter Brown gave me the benefit of their learned criticisms and suggestions, with regard to both style and content. I owe them a profound debt of gratitude.

I dedicate this book to the memory of my beloved sister, Ellen Marie.

Note on Names

Whenever possible I have adopted the usages of the *Dictionary of the Middle Ages*, ed. Joseph R. Strayer, 13 volumes (New York, 1982–1989) for personal and place names. In those relatively few instances where a person or place mentioned in this book does not appear in the *Dictionary* or where its usages seem idiosyncratic, I have adopted what I take to be the most common or sensible spelling in English-language texts.

EUROPE

IN THE HIGH

MIDDLE AGES

Prologue

The forty-seven-year-old Alsatian pilgrim, Bruno of Egisheim, who made his way more than 600 miles from Worms to Rome in 1049, had only recently become Pope Leo IX. In the cortege with this future saint, canonized in 1087, was a group of earnest and purposeful companions, including Abbot Hugh of Cluny and a still little-known Tuscan monk by the name of Hildebrand. These men and a few others like them had a conception of the universal Church and of a universal Christian society (Christendom) that they would impose imperfectly but in grimly determined stages and with enormous consequences on the princes and bishops of the Catholic faithful. In the person of the new pope, the conception was revealed principally through his unceasing efforts to eradicate simony, the purchase of ecclesiastical offices, a practice that placed local churches under the control of influential families and, thereby, permitted aristocrats of the period to exploit and impoverish local churches or to use them as pawns in their feuds.

The Frenchman Hugh of Cluny's contribution lay in the creation of a network of loyalties that transcended local ties. Under his abbacy, the great Burgundian abbey of Cluny became the pre-eminent monastic institution in the West, with innumerable daughter houses founded directly by its monks and with numerous other more ancient houses either reformed by its monks or inspired by the compelling Cluniac model to undertake their own reforms in close communion with it. From the magnificent church that he built at Cluny, the largest in Christendom until the Renaissance, St Hugh (he too would be canonized) helped to guide the fortunes of monks from Britain to Spain, and his prestige was such that princes and churchmen all over Catholic Europe begged his counsel and instruction.

The most controversial of the threesome would turn out to be Hildebrand, later Pope and St Gregory VII (1073–85). As pope the target of his wrath was the practice of lay investiture, the custom of allowing a prince to confer on a bishop the symbols of the latter's spiritual authority, a ring and a staff. The conferral or investiture of the ring symbolized the bishop's marriage to his diocese and therefore his spousal love of his people. Like natural marriage, this union was indissoluble in theory except by God or his vicar or substitute on earth, the pope. The staff represented the bishop's obligation and right to protect the Catholic faithful from within and without, to teach the faith and to beat back the wild dogs – schismatics, heretics and non-believers – who threatened to seduce the faithful from right belief. Only one part, but an important part, of the responsibility represented by the staff was the bishop's prerogative of excommunication, the formal exclusion of a baptized Christian from communion with the faithful of Christ. To Pope Gregory VII, lay investiture gave men outside the order of clerics inappropriate authority over the Church; it was as much an infringement of the liberty of the Church as simony was.

No scholar would now argue that the ideas of reform supported by these men appeared first with them, but the men themselves, united in their processional march to Rome in 1049, formed a loosely organized, yet resolute party to which many other ecclesiastics and lay people joined themselves in the decades to come. To describe the world out of which this reform party emerged is our first task.

PART I

EUROPE IN THE ELEVENTH CENTURY

I

Christendom in the Year 1000

Medieval European population can only be estimated from very incomplete data, but the sophisticated research techniques that demographers have developed to exploit these data, and the cautious nature of their conclusions in individual studies, give historians some confidence in their calculations. What their efforts suggest is that from the year 1000 until the Black Death struck in the mid-fourteenth century, the population of the continent increased from roughly thirty-five million to about eighty million.

By the end of the period, the most populous region, as defined by modern political boundaries, was France with roughly fifteen million inhabitants, although some scholars suggest that the number may have been as high as nineteen million. It had reached this peak from a starting point in the year 1000 of about five million. Not far behind were the Germanic-speaking regions of the continent, whose population grew from three or four million at the millennium to twelve to fourteen million by the early fourteenth century. Italy and England, two other regions on which demographers have done convincing work, saw growth from five million and two million respectively to eight or ten million, in the first case, and perhaps five million, in the second.

It is more difficult to estimate demographic change over this period for Iberia, modern Portugal and Spain, where the records are uneven owing to the disruptions brought on by the nearly incessant wars between Christian and Muslim principalities, but one estimate sees a net rise from about seven million at the millennium to nine million at its height before the Plague. It is equally difficult to make entirely persuasive estimates for the Scandinavian countries and parts of central and eastern Europe in the absence of the kinds of written records that exist for France, Germany, Italy, England and certain regions of Iberia. Nonetheless, impressionistic evidence suggests overall general increases of the

1. Europe

IRISH SEA

NORTH SEA

NORTH ATLANTIC OCEAN

Elbe

Oder

Thames

NORTHERN EURO

ENGLISH CHANNEL

Rhine

Seine

Loire

BAY OF BISCAY

HUNGARIAN PLAIN

Garonne

ALPS

Po

ADRIATIC

CANTABRIAN MOUNTAINS

Rhône

APENNINES

IBERIAN PENINSULA

Ebro

Tiber

CORSICA

Tagus

MESETA

Guadalquivir

BALEARIC ISLANDS

SARDINIA

SICILY

MEDITERR

STRAIT OF GIBRALTAR

MALTA

ATLAS MOUNTAINS

GULF OF SIRTE

magnitude discernible elsewhere, although not always at the same pace. By 1300, there seem to have been well over two million Scandinavians, consisting of 1.5 million Danes or Scandinavians under Danish royal authority, including many inhabitants of what is now southern Sweden, along with a half million Norwegians and a comparable number of Swedes. There were also at least five million Catholics living in Hungarian- and Slavic-speaking (Polish, Czech, Slovak, Croatian) regions of Europe by the time of the Black Death.

Population growth of this magnitude permitted greater specialization of labour and the expansion of rural markets. It encouraged the building of new towns along with the expansion of old ones and the creation among them of domestic and eventually international networks of trade. In short, it was a fundamental stimulus to economic growth. But how did population itself take off from the low levels of the first millennium? What made demographic increase on such a scale possible, especially given the crippling factors in the demographic mix: persistently high infant and child mortality, relatively high adult female mortality in childbirth, susceptibility to epidemic diseases that affected both adults and children, and recurrent food shortages, occasionally including widespread famine?

A reasonable case has been made for the prominence of a small number of factors in setting off population growth. The problem, however, remains the difficult one of cause and effect. Medieval historians have documented a transition from two-field to three-field agriculture in many regions in the eleventh century. In the simplest scenario a village that made the transition would have two-thirds of its plantable acreage growing crops at any one time in a three-field based regime, with one field fallow or resting in order to restore its fertility, whereas only one half would have been growing crops under the old arrangement. The increase in food and fodder production that was brought about would allow for improved nutrition for humans and animals, larger families and more work animals, along with more manure to fertilize gardens and some fields.

Of course, people cannot make the transition from two-field to three-field agriculture without pre-existing increases in the labour supply to do the additional work of planting and harvesting or at least without more intensive exploitation of under-utilized labourers. Moreover, there must be a sufficient number of animals and number and quality of tools to exploit such a massive increase in plantable acreage: more oxen and horses, more ploughs, more yokes and harnesses, more harrows and rakes, scythes and sickles, and wagons to cart and barns to store the more abundant harvests. The ability to fulfil these needs suggests the pre-existence of an extensive and specialized labour force composed of miners, smiths, carpenters and masons.

There is also the problem of technology. Oxen, castrated bulls, did most of the ploughing in the early period, but horses were stronger if they could be harnessed effectively. The horse collars of the early medieval period were crude; they ran the risk of choking the valuable animals. An inventor or inventors whose names will never be known to us appear to have perfected a non-strangulating horse collar around the millennium, and very slowly the technology diffused across Europe. The horse as plough animal could never displace the ox, for the latter had several advantages, including cheapness of initial purchase price, ability to tolerate poorer fodder, and high resistance to disease, all of which made it appropriate for some farms and on some estates. But the advantages that the horse added to the existing agricultural regime are universally regarded by scholars as instrumental in the improvement of crop production and carriage. The question remains: did the growth of population stimulate the perfection and diffusion of the new horse collar so that fields could be made to produce more abundantly or did the invention and dissemination of the new collar make possible the exploitation of fields whose abundant crops encouraged increases in population?

Even in the absence of the wide adoption of three-field farming and the improved efficiency of ploughing with horses, there were ways to increase harvests. Clearing new fertile lands, a process usually known as assarting, was the principal method. Assarting of the magnitude that medieval historians have documented in the period 1000 to 1300 required an enormous increase in the production of iron and an accompanying decline in its price. For iron was needed both for the tools to cut the trees of the seemingly endless hardwood forests of northern and central Europe and for the metal parts of the deep-cutting or heavy ploughs that farmers utilized to prepare the dense soils that were otherwise unworkable in the face of traditional ploughs. The heavy plough appears to have been invented long before the great age of assarting began in the High Middle Ages, but the widespread diffusion of the technology was made possible only by the millennial revolution in iron production. Once again, however, it may be doubted whether the assarting and the diffusion of the heavy plough initiated the steep growth in population after 1000, because the labour and general population requirements for effective assarting and for the creation of new villages were enormous from the beginning.

If no consensus has emerged on cause and effect, it remains true that population began a sustained rise in the first century of the new millennium. Few ordinary people had any impression of the general nature of this trend, or of the economic growth that accompanied it. In any one or two generations the shifts and innovations were so gradual, nearly glacial, that their fundamental potential to transform rural life would have gone almost wholly unperceived. Purchase of a new plough, putting a few more oxen out to pasture, a farmer's use of an unconventional new horse collar – events like these did not happen often and did not lead immediately to widespread change. Village life was cautious; decisions on major issues like how and what to plant were usually collective; and caution and consensus favoured conservatism. Survival was not to be put at risk by the promiscuous adoption of new techniques or by over-investment in animals that might die with inadequate winter fodder or by any other uncertain innovations.

Villagers of one settlement hearing for the first time of the creation of a new settlement in newly assarted woodlands also certainly knew that there were very likely few settlers who risked going there, that the new church was probably more plan than reality, that stumps still dotted the new fields and hindered ploughing and planting. Horses, oxen and tools were almost certainly in short supply there, even when lords and monasteries sponsored the new clearances, since they did not strip their existing holdings of equipment and sources of power. Assarting was long and difficult work; at times, it must have seemed frustratingly slow, almost pointless.

The reward of freedom perhaps helped more than anything else in sustaining the movement. Farmers who gave their time and labour to the creation of new settlements looked forward in a more or less distant future to improved economic status, but the act of clearing the habitat and colonizing the new settlement brought something more immediate; it conferred liberty on the colonizers, the *coloni*. Assarting made people free ('Rodung macht uns frei'); it elevated them from slavery and serfdom.

This fact is important in part because slaves were still a major component of society in the year 1000. Even in late eleventh-century England between 10 per cent and 30 per cent of some regional populations could be classified as slaves. These domestic and agricultural workers had no rights and no property in themselves or their labour. The tasks assigned such people varied from very heavy, like ploughing, to relatively light, like dairying, for example. But in theory the men and women themselves lived lives fully under the direct and unmediated personal authority of their owners.

Such arrangements could in practice and by custom confer benefits on slaves living in long-established and stable societies. Under such circumstances only the hope of economic advancement sweetened with the promise of an elevation of status, to freedom, would induce them to take the risk of abandoning settled patterns of life in order to try to create new villages, part of whose rents would increase the wealth and therefore power of the lords who sponsored the projects. Theory permitted the use of arbitrary force against slaves, but no essentially stateless world like that of eleventh-century western Europe mobilized the kind of power that would have been needed to achieve assarting on the scale experienced in eleventh- and twelfth-century Europe. Something more than force, like the guarantee of freedom, was needed.

For a number of reasons slavery, though still widespread in the eleventh century, was already dying out in lands under Latin Christian domination. New slaves were in increasingly short supply, in part because there was a strong ecclesiastical prohibition against enslaving Catholics. As pagans in Europe were successfully christianized, therefore, the pool of available slaves, except on the borderlands of Latin Christendom, dried up. Moreover, churchmen in general looked upon and encouraged lords' manumission of slaves as a virtuous act, and over time lords responded to the teaching by freeing their slaves. Those churchmen who owned slaves in the name of their churches were slower to manumit them, for certain kinds of church property, including slaves, were never supposed to be alienated. Consequently, even when slavery had largely disappeared on most northern European estates and in most households, a few churches continued to own slaves. Only after the status of these slaves was conflated with that of serfs, as we shall see, did slavery cease to exist.

Serfdom was the form of base dependency that replaced slavery. The precise nature of the restrictions on serfs varied from region to region and over time, but a law-abiding serf, unlike a slave, always had rights, including the right to due process if accused of a crime. Serfs became increasingly common in the settled lands of western Christendom in the late eleventh and twelfth century, in part because former slaves swelled the category, in part because debt and other factors induced free peasants to accept restrictions on their activities – in theory, perpetually, for servility was inherited. The promise of delivery from the burdens of serfdom on the individual and his or her lineage would soon induce large numbers of these people to join assarting teams in the High Middle Ages.

The burdens from which serfs sought delivery varied considerably, depending on local laws and practices. Many people classified as serfs possessed only restricted inheritance rights or none at all, except by custom; they were said to be under mainmort. Others could not move off their lord's estates or enjoy formariage, that is, marry serfs of different lords, let alone free people, without their lord's permission. Many owed labour services, corvées, specified according to the task or the duration of the work required, like reaping three days per week at harvest time, although lords might permit them to pay something as a substitute for providing these services. Men's and women's liability to other fixed levies, often known as tallages, but called by various names, were interpreted as further evidence of their debased, which is to say, servile status, even if custom and inflation would ultimately render the actual sums owed quite low. Debased status itself was a bar to men and women becoming monks and nuns and to men becoming priests.

All of these obligations were eradicated in the process of serfs assarting and settling a new village. Because of the investments of lords in the new infrastructure, other restrictions, like the obligation to use the lord's mills, ovens, grape presses and the like were imposed on the rustics, but over time a careful differentiation emerged between these non-debasing restrictions, known as banalities, and those more certainly carrying the stigma of serfdom.

In those parts of Latin Christendom where little assarting was going on, serfs at first had less opportunity to achieve free status in this period, but already in the eleventh and twelfth centuries the increase in the number of towns in these regions and the privileges accorded to new urban settlers were offering some rural migrants hope of improving both their economic condition and their legal status. However, before turning to this topic, summed up by the proverb 'Stadtluft macht uns frei' ('Town air makes us free'), more attention needs to be given to the masters of rural society.

The men and women who had the greatest power in rural society went by many names. It has already proved convenient to call them lords, but other words could serve. The French *seigneur* is a common substitute. Not all lords had the same power, of course, and the various words used to describe them sometimes reveal the differences. In the early eleventh century, the English word 'knight' and the originally Celtic word 'vassal' still suggested a servant, one who supports a superior lord but who is neither a simple rustic or peasant nor unequivocally a member of the social elite. The German *Ritter* (rider) and its French synonym, *chevalier*, along with other Romance language synonyms like Spanish *caballero* also emphasize implicitly or explicitly the equipment, the horse (Latin *caballus*), with which the knight fulfilled his military duties. And the generic Latin word *miles* put the stress on what the knight did in practice – fight.

It was only later, well into the twelfth century, that the occupation of the knight became synonymous with a more elevated status evoked in abstract nouns like knighthood and chivalry that reflect the deepening ritualization of the profession of arms. In some countries, like France, hereditary knighthood would become a token of nobility; in others, like England, this would not occur, but knighthood would still set a man and his family apart from the vast majority of the lower status population.

Above the knights in the rough and tumble status hierarchies of the early eleventh century were men called castellans and barons. As the word suggests, a castellan owned his own castle or had the command of another lord's castle delegated to him. The absence of effective central power in many regions in the eleventh century, like Poitou in western France, led to the proliferation of castles, a process known as encastellation, and an inevitable multiplication of the number of castellans and castle garrisons of knights. 'Baron' was a generic word for a man ordinarily of more importance, often possessing more than one castle, perhaps with a number of retainers, almost certainly with estates, including slaves in the earlier part of the period under consideration and serfs later on, that gave him, relatively speaking, enormous wealth, far in excess of that of simple knights and astronomical when compared with that of ordinary rustics.

Such power and wealth usually had jurisdictional rights attending them. Barons held courts for their tenants and for the knights who were their men. Sometimes these courts were the successors of public institutions established by Charlemagne and his heirs, but which, owing to the breakdown of Carolingian institutions in the West, particularly in the tenth century, had come to be possessed like private property. At other times, the courts were new, like the village courts established in and for assarted settlements.

The most elevated baronial families in rural society were those of viscounts, counts (earls in England), dukes and their equivalent like the marcher lords, so-called because they ruled marches, border principalities. These men were territorial princes whose titles, outside of England and Scandinavia, could often be traced to Carolingian grants, but who like other barons exercised their public responsibilities hereditarily and as if they were vested in themselves as of right. Often their power exceeded that of the kings and emperors to whom they nominally owed obedience. The duke of Normandy, to name one, was a mightier lord than the king of France in the eleventh century.

The ties that bound this heterogeneous group of men and families together were complex. Some swore oaths of allegiance and protection on a personal basis. A lord by such an oath could become the man (Latin *homo*) of another man, from which comes the word 'homage' to describe the bond and the ceremony: a great man would kneel before a greater man, have his clasped hands covered by the hands of his superior, and pledge to honour and support him. They would kiss on the lips to signify the closeness of the bond. Often the dependant would receive a piece of property whose income would help him give military support to his overlord. At its purest, homage would be done only once a lifetime and to only one person. It would be sworn indeed to the person to whom one would also give other deeply personal assurances, in technical language, *auxilia* or promises of aid, to ransom his body if he were captured in war and to honour his family by attending and contributing to the ceremonies that marked the great rites of passage for his children – the first marriage of his eldest daughter, the knighting of his eldest son.

Some oaths were less freighted. Men pledged themselves to be the faithful supporters of their superiors. They might enter into such relationships of fealty (from Latin *fidelitas*, fidelity) with several overlords, and they might confirm the oaths numerous times, although it could be argued that the fealty owed to the man to whom one had done homage took precedence over pledges to others and eventually that the fealty owed to a king had no equal. But these sensibilities, particularly the last, were still of little consequence around the year 1100. In the eleventh century the system of dependent relationships, if it can be called a system, had hardly achieved a stable shape.

What to label the lordship exercised over the lesser orders, and what to call the various arrangements and relationships among upper-class people themselves, have of recent years become a matter of angry scholarly contention. One word that has been used is 'feudalism', and it is the word that will be used here; yet, it can readily be acknowledged that to describe a regime, let alone a society, as feudal raises problems. Antiquaries and jurists of the seventeenth century who looked back on the Middle Ages saw particular significance in the property rights and jurisdictional characteristics of the fief (Latin *feudum*). But, in fact, fiefs were not important units of property everywhere and at all times. In many regions the word does not even appear before the mid-eleventh century. To talk about a 'feudal age', as some excellent scholars have done, before most regions in Latin Christendom had a clear concept of fief, has struck many critics as particularly bizarre. To describe a regime as feudal, based on a peculiar form of land tenure that was the prevailing form only in a small number of territories, like the Ile de France, the area around Paris, has also been mocked. Finally, the fact that the word 'feudalism' is used in many different ways has encouraged some scholars to belittle its analytical and descriptive value. It is a term, after all, that can simultaneously evoke either the economic exploitation of a dependent peasantry by *seigneurs*, its Marxist sense, or the corrupt political systems of some war-lord-dominated Third World countries.

Why, then, retain the term? It is because in the High Middle Ages the fief emerged as the form of landed property that symbolized the economic power of many aristocracies. There remained both allods, that is, unencumbered free holdings, and other forms of freehold or non-servile property. But a vast juridical literature emerged to describe and categorize fiefs in the High Middle Ages, and the vernacular literature of adventure written for the upper class and which seems to have expressed its mentality is obsessively concerned with the extent of fiefs, the inheritance of fiefs, and the relations among people holding fiefs of one another. These works, like the *Song of Raoul de Cambrai*, are largely twelfth-century and later productions, but they posit an eleventh-century world as obsessed as the twelfth century with fiefs. To this extent, many aristocracies conceived of themselves in a certain sense as a feudal order. And much of their power, prestige and authority was believed to stem from their rightful inheritance of fiefs.

All of this was somewhat strange, of course, since contemporary legal writers imagined fiefs as pieces of property or bundles of rights to which there were no inheritance rights. In this imaginary world, on the death of his father a vassal would approach his father's lord, seek to do homage, and, if successful, be invested with his father's fief. It was as if all that went before was irrelevant. The new vassal had no *right* of inheritance. He had to establish a personal relationship and hope for the best.

In practice, a sense of entitlement ran through the system. Almost from the moment we hear about fiefs, we hear about sons, typically eldest sons, expecting to receive those of their dead fathers. A son would pay relief, a sum of money due on the death of his father for permission to take possession of the fief. Until the sum was paid, it was assumed that the lord had the rarely enforced right of primer seisin or first possession to occupy the fief. There were still concerns about under-age or female 'heirs' (the word is apt, since it is clear that one is talking about heirship, legal theory notwithstanding). The lord, by right of wardship, might collect the revenues or some part of the revenues of the fief of the under-age vassal until he came of age, could perform military service and did homage. An heiress was certainly obliged to obtain permission from her lord for marriage, because it would be her husband who would have to fulfil the military service for which the fief had formally been granted to her father. Moreover, in a system in which honourable service was at the centre of relationships, dishonour was grounds for the legitimate reversion or escheat of a vassal's fief to his lord. Any attempt of a vassal to hand over possession of a fief to another person without a gift to his lord for the latter's permission, sometimes referred to as the fine on alienation, was also looked upon as a violation of the honour of the personal bonds that tied man to man. Nonetheless, despite all the caveats, the sense that under normal circumstances the eldest son or, in the absence of a son, the daughters of a fief-holder (co-heiresses) would succeed to the fief as an inheritance was in practice unquestioned.

*

Catholic Europe in the year 1000 was fundamentally an agrarian society. It would remain so until long after 1350, the date that marks the close of this book. The ties described above basically apply to this agrarian society. Nevertheless, there were towns in existence throughout the High Middle Ages. One may call them towns because, even though they varied enormously in numbers of inhabitants and some were smaller than large villages in this respect, they shared certain characteristics that set them off from rural settlements.

Relatively speaking, there was a greater density of population in towns than villages, although the line separating the two is necessarily arbitrary. Relatively, too, there was a more highly developed specialization and greater diversity of labour, especially, though by no means exclusively, of artisanal labour, in urban settlements. To be called a town, a settlement with a relatively high density of population and specialization of labour also requires an economy based on monetary exchange as opposed to barter, and one in which a sizeable proportion of income, again speaking relatively, comes from trade. The presence of a regulated periodic market did not define a town, for many a village had one, too. But a town without a periodic market is more or less unthinkable for the Middle Ages, which is not the case for a village. Finally, towns were distinguished, if not fully distinct, from large villages by a concentration of diverse monumental buildings – large churches, bell towers, warehouses, permanent market halls, guild halls, hospitals, town halls, and so on – although not every town had the full array of such buildings even by the end of the Middle Ages.

Some scholars would supplement the foregoing list of characteristics, for towns often had mints, special legal status and modes of landholding for the inhabitants, as well as autonomous criminal and civil court systems. One has even argued that an important criterion for the definition of a town is what might be called the existence of 'traffic jams' (Carlin, 1996, pp. 250–51) – the hustle and bustle of ox carts jostling against carriages, long lines of wagons bringing fruits and vegetables, raw materials and finished goods to markets, artisans' shops and warehouses, and the seemingly endless cavalcade of mounted men and women bearing messages, coming to shop, visit or attend meetings and clamouring at others on the street to make way. No traffic jams, no town.

However defined, towns around the year 1000 were few in number and very small in size in Catholic Europe; yet, by the early fourteenth century the number and size of urban settlements had increased exponentially. The Rhineland, which had no more than eight towns well into the twelfth century, boasted more than fifty in the thirteenth. Central Europe, which had but the thinnest sprinkling of settlements that might be deemed urban in the year 1000, witnessed the creation of 1,500 new towns from the eleventh century up until 1250 and 1,500 more in the fifty years or so after that. In southern Europe there was more continuity from earlier settlement patterns: growth came less from the creation of new towns, although new foundations were not uncommon, than from the flow of immigrants to old settlements.

Most of the early eleventh-century towns were weak in relation to the lords who ruled the countryside. In the majority of cases in the north, these lords controlled or owned the towns even though they did not typically live in them. Within the towns the agents of the lords' authority, men sometimes called reeves in England and provosts in France and Germanic-speaking areas, vied with bishops and other clergy for domination. The urban commercial element was ordinarily the weakest of the three contenders for power, but the relative weight of each party would change dramatically in favour of the merchants over the course of the High Middle Ages.

In the south, where traditions of urban oligarchic domination had not been completely effaced, merchants and senior craftsmen had a stronger say in town government. But here, too, there was a three-way struggle for power among the commercial oligarchy, the clergy and the lay lords, who more often than in the north actually had their principal residences in the towns. The outcome of these struggles would vary from region to region and over time. In the south, in northern Italy in particular, these struggles would dominate the political culture of the entire period from 1000 to 1350.

*

One term, 'Catholic', has already been used over and over again in these pages as if it had an obvious and unchanging meaning. There may be some core significance that a few conservative theologians would be willing to attribute to the term, but medieval historians have become less and less sure that this is permissible. With regard to behaviour, a typical Catholic in the year 1000, if anyone could be called typical, was a very different sort of person from one in 1100 or 1200 or 1300. What did a common villager or urban-dweller at the end of the first millennium know about the great mysteries of the Catholic faith – the Incarnation, the Passion and vicarious atonement; the trinity and unity of God; the sacraments, about which, like everything else among the doctrines, even the most learned and orthodox were and remained in subtle disagreement; the Resurrection and Ascension; the Second Coming and the Great Day of Judgement?

Indeed, the north in the year 1000 was only completing the missionary phase of Christian evangelization. Large numbers of Scandinavians and vast numbers of western Slavs had received baptism only because their rulers had ordered them to do so. There were still popular pagan sites of worship and many more modest shrines. Catholic priests and monks – the ecclesiastical elite – were in short supply, and parishes were recent establishments in these regions. The realization of the ideal of one or more church for every village was far in the future. No regular religious instruction or catechism could be executed under these conditions.

Preaching may not have been rare, but even in Southern Europe it was sporadic, as was attendance at church, taking communion, and obedience to ecclesiastical discipline, like the ban on Sunday labour. Liturgical practices had none of that apparent uniformity across the map of Europe that historians have sometimes imputed to the continent in the wake of the general reform of the church by the Fourth Lateran Council of 1215 and Franciscan and Dominican evangelization in the thirteenth century.

For most men and women, if not for the ecclesiastical elite, to be a Catholic in the year 1000 required little change in traditional behaviour, in part because there were so few people who were actively monitoring behaviour on behalf of that vague body so conveniently yet deceptively referred to under the monolithic label, the Church. Yet, all of this, like so much else in traditional Europe, was to change dramatically in the centuries we have come to call the High Middle Ages.

2

Mediterranean Europe

Certain scenes along the Mediterranean coast linger in the mind: salt-marsh grasses swaying under a too bright sky; aquatic birds in flocks, pairs or solo gliding through warm, humid air, restless until they settle along the lagoons to fish and preen. Not too far from where the sea laps the shore lie expanses of green fields that men and women have been tending for centuries. In the distant uplands, stands of oak and fir dominate the landscape. In the villages, from vines and from grove after grove of flowering fruit trees issue the fragrances of late spring and summer.

Virtually a tideless sea, the Mediterranean, along with its European hinterland, offered medieval fowlers, fishermen and mariners abundant opportunities. There was sport: aristocratic falconers loved to hunt the heronries, and rustics took hundreds of thousands, perhaps millions, of the estimated fifty billion migratory birds that annually leave their winter shelters in Africa to summer in Europe, making fatal stopovers on the northern shores of the Mediterranean. There was food in the sea as well, although its higher salinity made the population of fish less dense than in northern waters. And there were occasions for contact with peoples of different religions and cultures who were in port as emissaries, traders and slaves.

But the Mediterranean was also an untrustworthy companion. Winter storms could be savage, and mariners hesitated to sail in that season. Many of the continental harbours were inadequate for great vessels, partly because the gentle rising and falling of the sea was incapable of dissipating the quantities of silt disgorged by the sluggish rivers that fed it. In high summer the stench from the lagoons and the scourge of disease-bearing insects could make life loathsome. Now and again great, stiff winds blew in from the sea, freshened the air and swept the swarms of midges and biting flies from the air, but they also battered the poorly sheltered ships in their path.

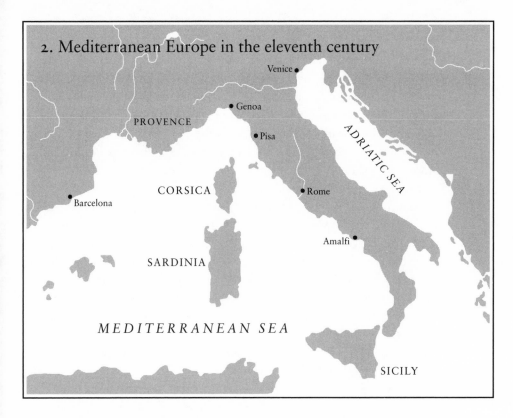

2. Mediterranean Europe in the eleventh century

Venice

Genoa

PROVENCE

Pisa

ADRIATIC SEA

CORSICA

Rome

Barcelona

Amalfi

SARDINIA

MEDITERRANEAN SEA

SICILY

High summer also brought drought. Rainfall in southern Europe does not compare to that in the north. The spring run-off from the mountain ranges produces innumerable rivulets that often become dry beds in their lower courses by late June or early July. By August parts of central Spain, southern France and southern Italy are desert-like in their ecology. Once verdant hills and hillocks take on an ashen grey look. Lizards delight in the revivifying heat of the morning sun and in lazing under the blazing midday sky; humans and their domestic herds and flocks languish in whatever shade they find. Fortunately, nearer the mountains – the Cantabrian and Pyrenees of Iberia, the Cevennes of southern France and the Apennines of the Italian boot – the lakes and streams often stay full, and the sprawling meadows nearby offer, or once did offer, plentiful pastures to enormous herds and flocks.

In the mountains themselves as well as on the islands and in numerous geographically sheltered regions of the south, the natural abundance of the land and the return from human agriculture were as varied as almost anywhere on earth. Sometimes human intervention was the key. Irrigation techniques introduced earlier but perfected by the Muslims had turned Valencia into a garden of earthly delights by the eleventh century. Elsewhere nature, less radically altered, produced similar benefits: the bewitchingly beautiful valleys of Sicily were among the most productive districts in eleventh-century Europe. On the continent, lush pastures attracted herders of the plains from great distances to Alpine and Pyrenean valleys in late spring, even if in other ways the mountains were forbidding and lonely and, as folk tales ceaselessly recount, more suitable for savage beasts and wild men than for Christians, civilized human beings.

The distinctive environments of the south gave a shape to daily life in innumerable ways. Midday summer heat turned the afternoon siesta into a ritual; even austere Benedictine monks were enjoined to read rather than work outside from Lent to October. The ubiquity of vines meant that where there was no effective religious ban wine was readily and cheaply produced, so that southerners – Christians and Jews, at least – were not constrained to drink only ale, cider and milk. The cultivation of the olive insured that animal fats would enjoy no near monopoly, as they did in the north, in providing oil used in cooking and manufacturing tasks, like softening hides.

Military and political history also set the south apart from the north. The long period of Roman imperial domination and Latin culture had left their impact on language far more effectively than the waves of invasions and migrations of Alans, Vandals and Goths in late Antiquity and the early Middle Ages. The bewildering array of Latin-based or Romance dialects of Iberia, France, Italy and the islands, like Sardo on Sardinia, for all their variety, formed a striking linguistic contrast to the Germanic speech of the far north. Men spoke of themselves in the south as being under Roman law, too. What they meant was that the procedures and, although to a far lesser degree, the substance of their contractual obligations to one another evoked principles and formulaic phrases that were recognizably the creations of ancient Imperial administrators.

Basque resistance in a small enclave of south-western Gaul and north-western Iberia, which from the ninth century onwards formed the kingdom of Navarre, had prevented the full victory of the Romance languages in south-western Europe. The apparent early victory of Romance speech in some south-easterly regions, like the Dalmatian coast, also turned out to be more ephemeral than real. But it was the Muslim conquest of Spain in 711 and of Sicily by 902 that, with the introduction of Arabic, presented the most significant linguistic competition for Romance. With the Muslim Arabs and waves of their non-Arab followers, like North African Berbers, came other cultural contributors to southern European life in the generations afterwards.

Islam itself afforded the greatest single cultural challenge. It offered an alternative religion to those of the Christian faith and to Jews as well. Adoption of it was made attractive partly because it gave access to the best jobs and to social respectability in regions dominated by Muslim rulers. Islam's doctrinal simplicity, compared to the doctrinal intricacies of Trinitarian Christianity, plus its incorporation of respect for Jesus and Mary, also perhaps persuaded a few irresolute Christians that conversion was not the sin the priests told them it was. To be sure, by the year 1000 the initial wave of Muslim conquests and Islamic diffusion in Europe was over, but the great retreat had not yet begun.

One of the most striking features of southern life in eleventh-century Europe was the presence of a strong urban culture, not entirely discontinuous with the ancient past. At Cordoba, for example, once the capital of a Roman imperial province, and in many other towns that had lost some of their antique lustre in Iberia, the Muslim conquerors encouraged urban life and culture with intense commitment. In Christian Europe, or at least in the south, a very varied but generally less robust urban landscape existed. Rome was a shadow of its former self. The ancient imperial capital of one million inhabitants was reduced to twenty thousand or so and must sometimes have seemed like a ghost town, with its cavernous monuments. But there were small prosperous Christian towns along the coast of southern Languedoc or Mediterranean France, as well as in Tuscany and Lombardy in Italy. At the head of the Adriatic Sea, Venice was also coming into prominence.

Already in the late tenth and eleventh centuries many of these towns were slipping away from the control of their traditional overlords, whether emperor, pope, resident bishop, or seigneur, and were renegotiating the terms of their dependency. The only major deviation from this pattern in Catholic principalities occurred in eleventh-century Sicily after the Christian reconquest, where a strong kingdom, building on Muslim institutions, was established and prevented the emergence of city-states.

The towns were mercantile centres for a wide variety of goods, in part because a striking feature of southern life was the cultivation and marketing of specialized commercial crops. By 1060 farmers were growing mulberry trees and harvesting the cocoons of silk worms on a vast scale in Sicily and Calabria in southern Italy for the silken cloth industry, centred from the tenth century in the northern Italian town of Lucca. There was also indigo production for the dyestuffs industry and some cane sugar production on plantations in southern Italy.

The diverse ethnic and religious mix of southern Europe has already been alluded to. Spain, except for a few relatively small Christian principalities in the Pyrenean north, was completely under Muslim domination from 711. The conquerors imposed their rule on a vast population of Christians and a substantial number of Jews. It is sometimes said that under Muslim rule, at least until the wars of Christian reconquest began in earnest, Christians, Jews and Muslims lived in a state of *convivencia*. Though always a minority throughout the period of their domination of the peninsula, the number of Muslims was steadily increasing from conversion and immigration. Confident of their continued hegemony, the argument goes, they lived amicably with Christians and Jews, even while denying them full rights. Yet all enjoyed freedom of religion, even if the religions of the conquered peoples were considered inferior to Islam. Architecture, poetry and other forms of cultural and intellectual expression in the subject communities borrowed freely from and adapted Arabic and Islamic motifs and tropes.

Recently this picture has been criticized as idealized or even as a more or less deliberate distortion imposed on the narrative of pre-Reconquest Spanish history by liberal and anti-clerical scholars writing in the modern period. Hating what Spain was perceived to have become – a priest-ridden, racialist, and economically and politically backward society when elsewhere in Europe 'Enlightenment' came to prevail – many nineteenth- and twentieth-century scholars imagined a time when the Church had little power, pureness of Christian blood or lineage was irrelevant and work and play among people of all faiths made for a prosperous and forward-looking society. But if *convivencia* of this sort is a myth, it remains true that the great fissures among the three religious communities in Spain were accompanied by less violence than we have come to associate with the later Middle Ages when the peninsula returned to more or less full Christian political domination.

Languedoc and Provence never went through a period of Muslim domination. The Muslim outposts established in the period of the conquest were ephemeral. Coastal and a few inland raids, some to a considerable distance northwards, it is true, continued until the eleventh century from seaboard bases on the continent, like Garde Frainet in

Provence, or from Muslim-dominated islands like the Balearics. Despite these raids, which, along with local in-fighting among Christian lords, made the political and economic development of Languedoc uneven, some generalizations are possible about the region from Toulouse to the Italian borderlands.

Largely a rural region, there were, nonetheless, in Languedoc and Provence a number of seaboard or nearby towns with diverse populations of natives, both Christians and substantial numbers of Jews. In peaceful times these towns – Narbonne, Arles, Marseilles being the most important – engaged in trade with North Africa, Spain, Italy and the Near East. In violent interludes many of their inhabitants turned to piracy. Inland towns were smaller and fewer in number. Toulouse was probably the most significant, perhaps the only significant one. Cities like Avignon, Orange and Valence, which were destined to play important roles in late medieval politics, were virtually backwaters in the eleventh century.

In the vast rural spaces of Languedoc and Provence the mostly Christian population (Jews there were few in number) consisted of the ancient amalgam of Gallo-Roman and Germanic peoples, but these had been supplemented with large numbers of Iberian Christian immigrants in the wake of the Muslim conquest and pacification of Spain. The central bond tying man to man in rural society was the personal tie of loyalty. At some point in the eleventh century, depending on the region, this might be expressed in the language of feudalism, but ties between the powerful (*potentes*) and the less powerful (*mediocres*) did not require homage and enfeoffment. The *potentes* and *mediocres* lorded over a population of *impotentes*: poor free farmers, serfs and slaves. These people were dependent in formal and informal ways on their social betters and suffered much, as did the clergy, from rural violence.

At the turn of the tenth/eleventh century this violence inspired a number of ecclesiastics and lay lords to articulate a programme of political and social justice, one that stressed the difference between righteous and unjustified war and between legitimate and illegitimate targets of violence and vengeance. At a series of ecclesiastical councils attended by local notables and crowds of *impotentes* and *pauperes* and in the presence of the holy relics of the saints brought from local churches, the leaders of this so-called Peace of God or Peace Movement issued regulations and set standards of conduct in war and tried to restrict fighting.

At the Council of Charroux in 989 the 'bishops, as well as clerics and monks, not to mention laypeople of both sexes' heard the archbishop of Bordeaux lead the higher clergy in solemnly cursing and excommunicating all those who ravaged churches, plundered the rustic poor or carried out sacrilegious attacks on priests. 'Many bodies of saints were also brought' to the council, which 'was adorned by frequent miracles through the presence of these saints'. A council held at Limoges in 994, and similarly enveloped in miracles, also issued a regional 'pact of peace and justice'. In the early eleventh century councils at Poitiers and Rouergue continued this work, because, as the record for Poitiers put it, 'Handsome indeed is the name of peace, and beautiful the belief in unity, which Christ ascending to heaven left to his disciples.' (Head and Landes, 1992, pp. 327–42, for all quotations.)

At the Council of Elne in Roussillon in 1027, held in the great meadow of Toulouges in order to accommodate the crush of clergy, aristocrats and the 'crowd of the faithful (not only men, but also women)', those presiding decreed many canons or rules typical of the Peace of God but also a truce (*treuga*) that restricted the periods of time when fighting could licitly take place. 'No one dwelling in the aforesaid county and diocese [of Roussillon] should assail any enemy of his from the ninth hour on Saturday to the first hour on Monday, so that everyone may render the honour owed to the Lord's day.' The Truce of God spread like the Peace of God, its canons often extending the periods when otherwise lawful fighting was permitted. By 1041 all of Languedoc seems to have been under a prohibition – not always honoured, to be sure – to refrain from violence each week 'from Wednesday evening to dawn the following Monday'.

Liturgical maledictions constituted one traditional practice monks used to enforce peace, and they were available for enforcing the Peace of God.

In the name of the Lord and the power of the Holy Spirit and the authority divinely granted bishops by blessed Peter, prince of the apostles, we separate them [malefactors] from the bosom of holy mother church and we condemn them with an anathema of perpetual malediction, that they might not have help from any man or contact with any Christian. May they be cursed in town and cursed in the fields. May their barns be cursed and may their bones be cursed. May the fruit of their loins be cursed as well as the fruit of their lands, their herds of cattle and their flocks of sheep. May they be cursed going in and coming out. May they be cursed at home and may they be fugitives outside their homes. May they drain out their bowels, like the faithless and unhappy Arius [the ancient heretic]. May there come upon them all those maledictions by which the Lord through Moses threatened transgressors of the divine law. (Little, 1993, p. 36.)

To the cursing of malefactors could be added the humiliation of saints' relics – taking them down from altars and placing them on the ground until the perpetrators of violence repented of their acts. But excommunication and, ultimately, interdiction, as the texts quoted suggest, were perhaps the most powerful weapons in churchmen's arsenal. Excommunication, cutting a man or woman off from the eternal life-giving sacraments of the church and making it a sin for their friends to have contact with them, and interdiction, the blanket suspension of ecclesiastical services in a region, were meant to strike fear into the hearts of disrupters of the peace as well as into the hearts of their supporters and innocent bystanders. Indeed, using these weapons put heavy pressure on communities to persuade malefactors of the error of their ways and the need to repent. The Peace and Truce of God may not have been entirely effective in Languedoc or anywhere else, but they betokened a major concern of the Catholic clergy and many lay aristocrats for stability and practical justice that would have its offspring in the re-emergence of strong secular government sanctioned by the Church.

*

So much for the region between the Atlantic and Provence; passing south-east over the Maritime Alps, one finds in Italy an almost entirely different political and economic environment. Northern Italy was already distinguished by the existence of a number of noteworthy towns. There was Venice on the Adriatic, and Genoa and Pisa along the north-western coast of the peninsula. The direct exploitation of the sea was always important to these cities, but they would also gain power and wealth through other means – commerce, the carrying trade, banking and manufacture. Venice provides an excellent example with which to begin.

Well situated on the gentle mud rises or islands, like the Rialto, at the centre of extensive lagoons between the mouths of the Adige river to the south and the Piave to the north, Venice nestled safe from both naval and land-based attack. It was technically a dependency of the Byzantine

Empire, but this was more theoretical than real: the city indeed had long enjoyed autonomy, in part owing to its location. An elected doge, from the Latin word for leader, *dux*, ruled the city, but he shared power with his councillors and an elected assembly, the senate.

Secure mercantile activity was essential for a city that exported salt produced from its lagoons, had an expanding glass industry, and marketed slaves, especially captives from Dalmatia on the eastern Adriatic coast. The carrying trade, whatever the goods, was also important to Venice's prosperity. The greatest and preferred market was Constantinople. Perhaps an estimate of the latter's population at five hundred thousand is rather too high, but several hundred thousand people lived within Constantinople's walls and suburbs, and there was no other town remotely like it in eleventh-century Europe. To assure access to Constantinople Venice had to create a substantial navy and clear the Adriatic of pirates or re-employ them as slave raiders, a task largely accomplished by Doge Pietro Orseolo II (983–1008).

Long-term mercantile success at Constantinople required trumping potential competitors. In nasty rivalries with other traders, Venetians managed to obtain extensive, if not absolutely unique, commercial privileges in the Byzantine Empire and, indeed, in Constantinople as early as 991. It also established political control over seaports like Zara and Traù (Trogir) on the north-eastern coast of the Adriatic. By the later eleventh century, because of the military aid which they gave to the Byzantines against the Norman invaders of southern Italy, a region claimed by the Byzantine emperor, Venetians were allowed to establish their own quarter in Constantinople and received exemption from customs duties in all Byzantine ports.

Among north Italian towns, Genoa and Pisa emerged as Venice's chief rivals. Genoa, at the base of the north-western Apennines, had a deep harbour but only a tiny hinterland, cut off as it was by the mountains. Its landward isolation coupled with its low level of production, with its inhabitants living largely from fishing and local food production, rather than from trade, contributed importantly to its autonomy. But during the central Middle Ages Genoa was an autonomous backwater. It became a major force in the western and central Mediterranean only in the late tenth century after a series of ferocious Muslim raids and incursions into the town early in the century had disrupted the traditional rhythms of the inhabitants' lives and prompted them to take concerted defensive and offensive action.

Like Venice, Genoa rescued its economic situation by systematically building a fleet, pursuing pirates, destroying pirate lairs, and by making opportune alliances with other towns, such as Pisa, that took the war against the Muslims to the latter's own strongholds. The years 1015 and 1016 saw a spectacular string of Genoese victories at sea against the Muslims and the clearing-out of Muslim enclaves in Sardinia as well. By the late eleventh century the Genoese, in league with the Pisans, who participated 'for the remission of [their] sins' (Riley-Smith, 1997, p. 51), were raiding North African Muslim redoubts like Al-Mahdiya, the chief city of Tunisia. These successes in turn allowed the Genoese to begin extending their commercial interests from the western and central Mediterranean eastward into regions where Venice was the pre-eminent Italian naval power.

If Pisa in alliance with Genoa carried out retaliatory attacks in the early eleventh century against the Muslims in Sardinia, as often as not the two towns were at each other's throats. Poorly sited at ten kilometres inland from its rather indifferent harbour, Pisa was an unlikely maritime rival. It lay on an ancient trade route still vibrant in the Middle Ages, and its fertile hinterland supported considerable grain production and the harvesting of timber for trade. In time, Florence, upriver on the Arno, would emerge as a major irritant and, finally, as a mortal adversary in Pisa's efforts at land-based expansion, but this hardly seemed likely in the early eleventh century. Pisans, in other words, chose to make their town into a maritime power despite other opportunities, and in the course of the eleventh century made serious inroads into the commercial networks of the central – and increasingly the eastern – Mediterranean, where they too, like the Genoese, were bound to come into conflict with the Venetians.

The urban revival in northern Italy, so striking in Genoa and Pisa, was more fragile in the central regions of the peninsula. Rome is a case in point. Within the city the fundamental presence was that of the papacy, but for much of the eleventh century the papacy was unprepossessing at best. Individual popes connected by blood or allied politically with powerful families in central Italy weighed in on one side or another in the incessant and violent feuds that plagued the heavily encastellated region.

The career of Pope Benedict IX is emblematic of the moral standing of the papacy at the time. He enjoyed, if that is quite the word, three pontificates, 1032–44, 1045 and 1047–8. Not even a teenager, it seems, when first elected, he ended his third stretch on the papal throne widely considered to be an illegitimate occupant of the papal see, one who at one time or another, depending on the source of the information, had accepted money to resign or had resigned in order to marry or had given up the papal throne because he felt shame at the dissipations of his personal life. Whatever the truth, the disgust in imperial German circles at the situation was so great, and the Holy Roman Emperor Henry III's determination to get control of affairs so firm, that at the Synod of Rome in 1046, Benedict's resignation was not just accepted but acknowledged by formal deposition. His final pontificate, which obviously came after this date, pitted him against the candidates whom the emperor favoured and whom we now call Popes Clement II (1046–7) and Damasus II (1048).

Benedict's deposition, the deposition of rival claimants and the election of bishops from German sees, like Clement II and Damasus II, were important steps in the more general reform of the papacy, a process that would make a still more decisive advance with the election of another German bishop, Leo IX, in 1049. But even in its unreformed state the papacy articulated some of the central ideological convictions of learned and powerful Christians. It was instrumental in keeping alive the dream of the recovery of the Holy Land and North Africa to Christian domination. Because of its possession of an enormous cache of relics of the saints, the papacy also encouraged pilgrimage from all over Christendom to the city of Rome. However poor and underpopulated Rome was, therefore, it still had the best claim of any Catholic city to be the capital of Latin Christendom and through the papacy's presence played a pivotal role in preserving and enhancing the sometimes fragile unifying structures and beliefs of western Christian society.

*

Western Christian society, Catholic Christianity, Latin Christendom – all these terms imply a distinction, in the first between western and eastern, in the second between Catholic and Orthodox and, in the third, between Latin and Greek. All these distinctions need to be made, but the cleavage between western and eastern Christianity was not yet unbridgeable. To this extent, the year 1054 has been over-emphasized.

In that year the representatives of the pope of Rome, during a delegation to the bishop or patriarch of Constantinople, excommunicated him. The patriarch responded by excommunicating the pope. Both sides defended their actions by bringing up real though, up to then, manageable disagreements they had had. The most famous, perhaps, is the Greek charge that the Latins had changed the Christian Creed by adding a clarifying phrase, *filioque*, in its Latin version. Western theologians insisted that the part of the creed that described the procession of the Holy Spirit needed expansion. The Holy Spirit proceeded from the Father 'and the Son', *filioque* in Latin. Greek views would later harden against the clarification as a matter of theology, but the primary objection at the time was that westerners had made a change without the consent of a general or ecumenical council of the church. The implication they most deeply resented was that the bishop of Rome's powers, which he claimed as an inheritance from St Peter the Apostle, whom Jesus had made the head of the Church and who was the first bishop of Rome, were sufficient to authorize the change.

It is certainly true that there were other differences in beliefs and practices in the two halves of Christendom. When Greeks celebrated communion they used bread that had been baked with yeast in it and had been allowed to rise. When Latins celebrated the same commemoration of Jesus's Last Supper with his apostles, they used unleavened bread. Nearly everywhere in the West worship was carried on in Latin and the exceptions were slowly being rooted out. In the East, Greek was perhaps the principal language of worship, but there were other strong traditions like Syriac and eventually Old Slavonic.

Nonetheless, all these differences taken together did not make a great divide, even if the events of 1054 constituted another step in that direction. Both sides knew they were members of the same body of Christ. Both recognized a common challenge in the Muslims. Both expected the differences to be worked out. The year 1204, when a crusader army sacked Constantinople and seized a large part of the Byzantine Empire, was more decisive than the year 1054 in the history of Catholic and Orthodox animosity, but this will be looked at in more detail in chapter 13.

If Rome and, to a lesser extent, the pope were symbols of Christian unity in the West, slightly south of Rome there was a port whose merchants and mariners were a major force in more materialistic ways in Europe. Much more than Genoa or Pisa, it was Amalfi, on the Gulf of Salerno between Salerno and the port of Naples, that was Venice's greatest challenger in the early eleventh century. Around the millennium, Amalfi's harbour, impaired subsequently by several major landslides, was still remarkably good. At times, also, its ships enjoyed important temporary technical advantages over other carriers. This was owing to their early adoption of the lateen or triangular sail which legend attributes to Amalfitan creation and to the later twelfth-century introduction of the magnetic compass, perhaps an Amalfitan invention or more likely an Arabic one that was quickly adopted by the Amalfitans.

It was the slave trade, Amalfi being a major player, that to a considerable extent made local merchants wealthy. These merchants in turn ruled an independent republic whose putative dependence on the Byzantine Empire, allegedly since the sixth century, was nominal. But the allegation can at least be taken as testimony of the substantial importance relations with Constantinople traditionally enjoyed in Amalfi's commercial policy.

Under the dynasty of Duke Sergius I, which extended from 958 until 1073, Amalfi achieved its greatest relative power before coming under the pressure and ultimately, in 1131, the domination of the Norman rulers of Sicily. It was in the period of its vigour in the tenth and eleventh centuries that Amalfitans established privileged trading depots at various seaports in the Byzantine Empire. It was in the same period that the town's magnificent cathedral was erected. Dedicated to St Andrew the Apostle, itself a nod to Byzantium, where the saint's relics were said to rest, the cathedral possesses an arresting black and white facing. It is also worthy of remark because of its magnificent bronze doors, said to have been wrought slightly before 1066 at Constantinople, an artistically striking connection to the eastern metropolis.

Amalfitan ships joined Genoese and Pisan vessels in the sack of Al-Mahdiya in 1087, but occasions for the town's ultimately enfeebling rivalries with the northern Italian maritime powers were perhaps more common than those for co-operation. The vibrant town did not go into a steep and steady decline but, like Gaeta, Bari and other potential contenders in southern Italy for domination of Mediterranean trade in the eleventh century, it faded before the relentless thrusts of the northerners. Ultimately, in 1135, Pisans would plunder Amalfi, effectively terminating all hopes that Amalfitans had for dominance in the southern and eastern Mediterranean.

*

The great arc of islands – Corsica, Sardinia and Sicily – that, together with the western coast of peninsular Italy, bounded the Tyrrhenian Sea also played an important role in the political and mercantile strategies of the emerging Mediterranean powers, a fact that has been too little acknowledged in general accounts. Corsica was never conquered by the Muslims, but it had endured wave after wave of invasions, raids and temporary occupation of small districts. The attacks and the attempts to preserve Muslim enclaves were military disasters for the invaders. A huge force was literally exterminated by the Corsicans and their Frankish allies in 810, but the raids continued until as late as the 930s, and Muslim piracy remained a threat thereafter.

Corsica was desirable, with its many small but excellent harbours, as a base for attacks elsewhere. It was also well watered and fertile. Its uplands (the island is largely mountainous) were covered by lush forests which could supply a shipbuilding industry. But more generally, Corsica also offered a hospitable environment in its piedmont and coastal plains where the dense verdure perfumed the air for leagues out to sea, giving rise to another of its names, the Scented Isle.

Resistance to the Muslims did not produce political unity among the mountain dwellers and the other inhabitants of Corsica. And Frankish power, which had been instrumental in helping to create island-wide alliances and prevent Corsica from falling to the Muslims, declined significantly in the Mediterranean during the tenth century. The early eleventh century therefore brought with it an era of competing lordships on the island, with violence becoming so destructive that a number of barons and representatives of important communities, in a manner not unlike that of the Peace Movement in Languedoc, came together soon after the millennium in a great assembly at a central location, the valley of Morosaglia, in order to work out ways to calm the situation.

The council's decisions had some effect in the north of the island in regularizing techniques of justice, although even in the north real centralization, partly owing to topography, was out of the question. In the south, feuding and seigneurial violence remained characteristic. One of the worst perpetrators of this violence was the family of the counts of Cinarca, who did not confine their aggression to other southerners. Their challenge to the newly established order of the north, however, did not go unmet. Around 1012 William, marquis of Massa, of the family later to be known and famous in literature as the Malaspina, was engaged to overthrow the Cinarca. By 1020 this task was effectively completed. Again, however, unity was impossible, or at least the Malaspina came to regard the relative autonomy of the many mountain lordships as acceptable as long as there was some recognition of mutual territorial integrity and, with that, a decline in political violence.

Only a few kilometres south of Corsica lies the coast of the equally mountainous and even larger island, Sardinia. Less well-endowed naturally than Corsica in terms of watercourses, access to wells and streams had been all the more contested for centuries. Since antiquity there had been recourse to *nuraghi*, small fort-like structures constructed of heavy rough-hewn stone blocks and shaped like upended and truncated cones, to protect strategic material and spiritual resources on Sardinia. Archaeologists have identified at least 6,000 such sites or ruins, most often located near springs and wells and ancestral tombs. Even the more ancient *nuraghi* remained defensible structures in the eleventh century for whatever forces occupied the island.

Although having few ports, Sardinia's harbours were good ones. So, as in the case of Corsica, Muslim raiders viewed Sardinia as a useful staging area for further military activity against Christendom. Their invasions began in 720, but, as with Corsica, they enjoyed very little long-term success against the rugged mountaineers and their allies. A few Muslim settlements were established, but a really major Islamic presence on the island dates only from about the year 1000, when the Muslim ruler of the Balearics managed to take Cagliari.

Sardinia is directly across the Tyrrhenian Sea from Rome, and the military danger was obvious. In 1004 Pope John XVIII urged the Christian powers to take back the Muslim enclave. Though Sardinia, like so many other Italian islands and peninsular regions, was nominally under Byzantine authority, it was Pisa and Genoa, as we have seen, rather than the Byzantines that joined forces to do so. By 1016 most of their work was complete, although Musat, the Muslim chieftain, seems to have held on tenuously until 1022. The last Muslim attempt to take the island ended in the rout of the invading forces at the gates of Cagliari in 1050. Relative unity in war did little, however, to undermine the autonomy of the mountain lordships. Sardinia, like Corsica, remained a politically divided and vulnerable land.

To discuss Sicily, the largest Mediterranean island, one has to address continental southern Italy as well, for both at the turn of the first millennium, but mainland southern Italy in particular, were of intense interest to the Byzantine authorities who claimed them. The Byzantines asserted, after all, that their empire, not the German concoction (the so-called Holy Roman Empire), was the true Roman Empire and heir to all its ancient territories. The theoretical claim found considerable practical support in the Italian situation in the opening decades of the eleventh century. Southern Italy was firmly under Byzantine control, and Greek worship and the Greek language flourished in many districts, like Calabria. Sicily *per se*, having been conquered by the Muslims, was outside the orbit of Byzantine power, but the Empire was primed for a rectification of this situation. The ruler largely responsible for the stability and, indeed, resurgence of Byzantine power in the central and eastern Mediterranean was Emperor Basil II (976–1025).

Byzantine victory in Sicily promised to be difficult, for the Islamic presence was well-established. From 827 to 902 Muslim forces had, piecemeal, carried out the conquest of Sicily, and during the tenth century Sicily was resolutely integrated into the wider Muslim world, although most of the minority of Jews and a great many Christians resisted the attractions of conversion to Islam. Besides the Byzantines, the rising naval powers of Amalfi and Pisa looked upon the prosperous island and its trade depots with longing. Scholars generally agree that Basil II, fresh from the destruction of his Bulgar enemies in the Balkans, would have moved first had it not been for his death in 1025.

Despite his death and also a series of messy succession struggles in the Byzantine Empire, Basil's dream began to play itself out in the 1030s in a series of raids and feints on Sicily near Messina. The Empire, however, could not make a concerted effort at recovery of the island, because of a new presence in central Mediterranean politics, that of the Normans. These northern freebooters, some of whom came to Italy as pilgrims, were enlisting in the service of local Italian potentates, including the pope, in the teens of the eleventh century. Their employers used them against two enemies – rival potentates and the Byzantines, who, under Basil II and his successors, had also been pressing to extend or reaffirm their authority in the central regions of the Italian peninsula.

Norman support was no guarantee of success, especially not against the well-organized forces of the Byzantine Empire. When Meles of Bari, a Lombard in revolt against the imperial administration in the south, used Normans for an attack on Apulia in 1017, the defeat he sustained at Byzantine hands was appalling. Moreover, employing Normans in raiding parties even when victory was secured created problems. Successful mercenaries had a nasty tendency to make demands of their employers. The duke of Naples had to grant Rainulf, one of the leaders of the Norman bands, the county of Aversa, slightly north of Naples, in exchange for aid against its Lombard prince. In various exchanges and as rewards or through threat and force, Normans continued to acquire territories and titles at the expense of local Lombard lords and Byzantine administrators. These successes in turn stimulated additional Norman immigration to Italy to share the spoils and make new acquisitions by selling their services for land or, if need be, by direct conquest on their own. As a result, by the time the decade of the 1050s came to an end a Norman lord ruled not only as count in Aversa, but as duke in Gaeta and as prince in Capua.

Robert Guiscard, a scion of a modest lordly family in Normandy, is the figure around which the most exciting tales of Norman derring-do in Italy and, eventually, Sicily whirl. Guiscard (the name means 'crafty') came to Italy in 1047, and from that moment and for the next several decades his was the principal military and political force in Italy and the central Mediterranean as a whole. He and his warriors were also among the most fearsome.

Guiscard hired himself out as a mercenary in Calabria and by dint of courage and persistence turned a series of kidnappings, military victories and opportune alliances against the Byzantines into a serious campaign to uncouple Calabria and indeed all of southern Italy from the Empire. In the event he managed to secure the title of count of the Normans. Among his enemies in his attempts at wider conquests in Italy was Pope Leo IX, whose army he annihilated in 1053. The amazing reversal in the aftermath of the pope's military defeat was Guiscard's entry into an explicit bond of fealty to the pope, ratified formally in 1059. The alliance with the papacy turned out to be an on–off affair. But despite papal misgivings, Guiscard would prove his usefulness over and over until his death in 1085.

Guiscard and his Normans longed to conquer Sicily. They began their work in earnest in 1061, and although there were occasional reversals, they stayed at the task for three decades until every Muslim redoubt succumbed, the last falling in 1091, only a few years after the count's death. The conquering armies by now were under the command of Roger, Guiscard's brother. Although the counts were only given formal recognition as kings during the rule of Guiscard's nephew, Roger II, in 1130, the newly recognized dynasty had exercised the equivalent of royal authority in southern Italy and Sicily (together the *Regno*) since the start of the conquest.

It was a hotchpotch that the Norman rulers governed: their subjects included some Jews and substantially larger numbers of Muslims, Greek Christians and Catholics. The Jews did not constitute a military threat and were tolerated, though discriminated against as religious dissenters. In a slow process that would not be complete until the thirteenth century, the Muslim presence would be reduced and finally eliminated. It was the fear and reality of revolt, with the possible support of North African allies, that on occasion encouraged the rulers to crack down on the Muslims. But it must be emphasized that Sicily remained an important centre of Muslim culture for more than a century. As for Greek Christians, there was more and more pressure over time on them to convert to the Latin rite. Again, however, the erosion of Greek Christianity was slow, partly because the Normans often needed to pay heed to the Byzantines' concerns over the fate of their co-religionists, and partly because the pressure to conform to Latin customs depended itself on the very gradual nature of the hardening of antagonism between the two branches of European Christianity.

The Normans rapidly adapted to the new environment in which they found themselves. They found it possible to take over almost intact or at least to restore the structure of Muslim administration after the conquest of Sicily. They largely ceased to be wanderers in search of booty, and settled down as eastern potentates in the island's great cities, like Palermo. And they lived exceedingly well off the revenues of trade and mercantile activity as well as from the income from vast estates and tribute that had made their Muslim predecessors wealthy. Sicily became one of the most effectively governed and surely among the richest kingdoms in Christendom. What a contrast this land of pomegranates and figs made with the northern lands from which the Normans had come.

3

Northmen, Celts and Anglo-Saxons

'They looked around them, whether they could see smoke or any sign that the land was inhabited, and they saw nothing . . . As they sailed from the land much snow fell upon the mountains, and therefore they called the land Snowland.' (Wright, 1965, pp. 346–7.)

SCANDINAVIA

Irish Christian hermits inhabited a few cells on the island of what the *Landnámabók*, the Old Norse description of settlements, in the quotation calls Snowland, more familiar now as Iceland, before the pagan Norse and other Scandinavians began to colonize the coasts and further inland in the late ninth century. The new population was never evenly distributed across the island, for the mountains, glaciers, high tableland, deep fissures and heat vents, the geysers and sulphur springs, as well as the volcanoes and lava flows, made the interior largely inhospitable. Continuing volcanic activity, especially from Mount Hekla, made the most climatically favoured lands of the south and west vulnerable to periodic devastation. Nonetheless, the coasts and adjacent zones offered the population, which at its height may have exceeded 60,000, a tolerable livelihood, when supplemented by trade. Men and women exploited the limited but rich meadowlands by raising cattle and sheep. Hunters snared birds and gathered their eggs, and fishermen brought in large catches, including whales and seals.

From Iceland the intrepid sailors made contact with Greenland in the early tenth century, settlements proper being established on the coast there later in the century, even as exploration continued. There is no doubt that Norsemen visited Labrador, Newfoundland and the coast of

3. Northern Europe in the eleventh century

GREENLAND

NORWEGIAN
SEA

ICELAND

NORTH ATLANTIC

OCEAN

SHETLAND

HEBRIDES   ORKNEY   NORWAY

SCOTLAND   SWEDEN

GULF
OF
BOTHNIA

IRELAND   NORTHUMBRIA

BALTIC
SEA

DENMARK

WALES   GREAT
          BRITAIN

CORNWALL   WESSEX

ENGLISH CHANNEL

North America; story-tellers celebrated their heroes' accomplishments
in a set of epic tales conventionally known as the Vinland Sagas. But
although the explorers also established small-scale settlements along the
coasts of these regions, these hamlets and camps turned out to be very
short-lived. The environment was not only harsh; it is probable that
there were serious and ultimately fatal clashes with indigenous peoples.

Colonization of Greenland was far more enduring. Small numbers of
later immigrants to the island brought with them Icelandic political
institutions and the Christian faith and, in the wake of the latter, an
ecclesiastical hierarchy. The settlers here, too, ran into grave problems.
The evidence is fairly strong that migratory peoples, *skraelings* as the
Norse settlers called them, had once occupied the western and southern
coasts. They would later return and destroy the Norse settlements on
the western coast of the island in the mid-fourteenth century. Those

along the southern and eastern coast survived for a longer time, and indeed communication between Greenland and Iceland, although somewhat irregular in frequency, did not cease until 1410. How long the remaining settlements stayed viable after contact was lost is a matter of scholarly debate, but one persuasive opinion holds that the complete disappearance of distinctively Norse villages and hamlets in Greenland did not take place before 1500.

Because of the only modestly successful colonization of Greenland, Iceland remained the most westerly major settlement of transplanted Europeans in the Middle Ages. There were no indigenous peoples to contend with on the island, but there were other difficulties for the inhabitants, especially an uncompromising environment that severely limited the production of grain, the medieval staple. Moreover, the low density of timberland, exacerbated by the periodic destruction of old forests by volcanic eruptions, created another major problem for communities utterly dependent on boats for personal travel and supply of goods. The building of sod houses and scrounging for driftwood helped make up but did not compensate fully for the lack of standing timber. Indeed, the low level of production of native grain and the relative lack of timber raise the question of why Scandinavians colonized Iceland with such determination in the first place.

The traditional scholarly explanation is that population pressure in Norway lay behind the waves of emigration from there, but in the absence of documentary material historians are dependent on late recorded traditions which *may* give some support to this explanation. Also, archaeological evidence has been marshalled, although, as is the case with so many other sources, data culled from archaeological digs is subject to various, frequently inconsistent, interpretations. No one really knows.

Late medieval Icelanders themselves thought they knew: they explained their migration in political terms. The story is that at the turn of the ninth/tenth centuries a strong lord by the name of Harald Fairhair struggled to create a united kingdom of Norway, but in so doing transgressed against the traditional rights of chieftains and their clans. Many of the clans submitted, but some left for the foggy and storm-ridden Faeroes, which were themselves later incorporated into the Norwegian kingdom. Others, who were determined to prevent the ascendancy of any single ruler, travelled further west to Iceland and settled there.

In Iceland, the pagan chieftains, who may have had cultic as well as political functions, organized a system of government that preserved the strong clans, affiliation to which was not based solely on blood ties but could be acquired through marriage, blood-brotherhood and ritual adoption. Slaves – captives from raiding and the children of already enslaved persons – were also kept. Irish female slaves fairly frequently became concubines of their male owners. Given a physical environment in which gang labour was out of the question, most slaves, male and female, including concubines, were household servants or workers who supplemented family farm labour. But Iceland was at no time a slave society in the technical meaning of that phrase, that is, a society whose economic viability depended absolutely on the existence of slave labour. Moreover, slavery as an institution gradually weakened as raids became less successful and, later, as Christian teaching undermined the justification of making other Christians, even war captives, slaves.

The preservation of strong clans and their relative independence in a loose confederation was made possible by a system that allotted power to local assemblies of chieftains and elders and to an Icelandic 'national' assembly, the Althing, of similar composition. (The Norse in Greenland established a comparable assembly.) The laws reflected the great men's desire for clan integrity and liberty of action, while at the same time they specified very carefully the proper grounds for and proper execution of feuds, the price Icelanders paid for their form of government, sometimes, if misleadingly, called democracy. The epic literature of high medieval Iceland, like the *Saga of Burnt Njal* and *Volsungssaga*, frequently focuses on the failure of the elaborate ties and the system of justice to control feuding.

The scene in the *Saga of Burnt Njal* in which Hildigunna induces her kinsman, Flosi, to seek vengeance has achieved classic status as an indication of the importance of vengeance to family and lineage honour. Even Christianity (for the story was written down and given a Christian overlay long after the events recorded supposedly occurred) is invoked in defence of the justice of the feud.

Hildigunna went back into the hall and unlocked her chest, and then she took out the cloak, Flosi's gift, and in it Hauskild had been slain, and there she had kept it, blood and all. Then she went back into the sitting-room with the cloak; she went up silently to Flosi. Flosi had just then eaten his full, and the board was cleared. Hildigunna threw the cloak over Flosi, and the gore rattled down all over him.

Then she spoke and said, 'This cloak, Flosi, thou gavest to Hauskild, and now I will give it back to thee; he was slain in it, and I call God and all good men to witness, that I adjure thee, by all might of thy Christ, and by thy manhood and bravery, to take vengeance for all those wounds which he had on his dead body, or else to be called every man's dastard.' (*Story of Burnt Njal*, 1911, pp. 208–9.)

Yet, despite the recurrent feuds, unity remained the treasured goal and ideal of Icelandic society. Every June, when the Althing met, the lawspeaker recited the laws from memory in a solemn ceremony meant to reinforce the cultural legacy of the chiefs' emigration from Norway and the distinctiveness of Icelandic identity. But political independence was precarious. To be sure, Icelanders and Vikings in general had a reputation as ruthless warriors, epitomized in the still only partly understood emblem of the berserker. The berserker seems to have been a warrior who wore a bear skin and was a consummate and ferocious fighter, oblivious to injury. Being able to calm a berserker was a sign of holiness. Whether these warriors were brought to this state of frenzy by getting high on hallucinogenic mushrooms remains a matter of dispute, perhaps more myth than fact.

Ferocity in combat, however achieved, was insufficient to maintain real political independence. In large part this was because Iceland's economy was untenable without imports. It was, therefore, dependent both on piracy, where equally ferocious warriors matched the Icelanders in courage and ruthlessness, and on Norway as a market for the coarse woollen cloth produced in some quantity on the island. It was in part profits from the export of cloth that made the purchase of grain for import possible.

Partly under the economic and political pressure arising from its dependency on Norway for trade, the law-making division of the Althing, the Lögrétta, adopted Christianity in the year 1000. Only five years before, in 995, a great Norse lord, Olaf Tryggvason, who had adopted Christianity while in exile in England, seized the Norwegian throne and imposed Christianity on the kingdom. Although Olaf was killed in the year 1000, the missionaries he sent to Iceland and the pressure he put on Icelandic chieftains to accept Christianity constituted his major contribution to the island's history.

The chieftains' conversion did not come without conditions, including the Icelanders' right to continue practices, like eating horsemeat, that were repugnant to the missionaries. In the long run, however, the conversion assured the incorporation of the Icelanders into the body of Christ. What might have become an isolated community or set of communities became part of Christendom. The peoples of Iceland also shared in, benefited from and contributed significantly to a common cultural world, characterized in part by the common themes of its heroic literatures, that included the British Isles and extended deep into the Scandinavian peninsula and even northern Germany.

Indeed, as we have seen, it was the peninsular kingdoms of Scandinavia – Norway especially, but also Denmark and Sweden – that furnished the bulk of the settlers in Iceland. These kingdoms had emerged by the millennium as political rivals in the north, but in the first half of the eleventh century Denmark was the dominant power and entered upon a period of imperial expansion. The Danish ruler, Sweyn Forkbeard (985–1014), led an invasion of England in the late tenth century and by the time of his death in 1014 had effectively displaced the native Anglo-Saxon dynasty in England, establishing his own in its place. His son, Cnut the Great, ruled both Denmark and England until his own death in 1035.

In Denmark, Cnut's rule was marked by persistent attempts to control clans and factions and to create something like central institutions, as already existed in England. His minting of royal coins is evidence both of the influence of English political practices on him (the striking of coins was a royal monopoly under the Anglo-Saxon kings) and of his desire to bind his Scandinavian kingdom together in creative ways. But if the relative cohesion established in Denmark by Cnut and his successors was genuine, the more general ascendancy of Denmark as an imperial power was brief. Danish rule in England ended in 1042 when the native dynasty returned to power under Edward the Confessor, in circumstances to be described later.

At its height, the Danish empire under Cnut extended well beyond Denmark and England. The great king also held sway over southern Norway. His Norwegian counterpart, Olaf II Haraldson (1015–28), managed to maintain a fragile independence in the coastal districts of Norway, north of the territories of direct Danish domination, and his ferocious efforts to maintain Norwegian Christianity in the teeth of pagan opposition would bring him recognition as a saint, but it was not until after Cnut's death that Norway's resistance to Danish expansion paid off and its kings were able to rule over and establish Christianity throughout a country whose geographical spread approximates that of the modern state.

Sweden, like Norway, presented the Danes with a difficult situation in the eleventh century. In the first place, the country was also deeply divided by religion, for Christianity had only recently been established in Sweden. The percentage of pagans adhering to the old religions, it is believed, was large, perhaps more than half the population, and Sweden's principal pagan sanctuary at Uppsala continued to function down to the late eleventh century. Animal sacrifice was certainly practised there, but scholars are unsure about the truth of contemporary allegations of human sacrifice. Whatever the case, pagan clans continually threatened the authority and power of the newly christianized monarchy, which refused to celebrate the sacred rites at Uppsala, on one occasion successfully expelling King Olof Eriksson (994–1022) to the region of West Gotland, which was under Danish domination. Events of the mid-eleventh century further complicated the situation, with civil and dynastic wars rendering Sweden ungovernable. It was only the hope of profiting from the growing volume of licit trade, as opposed to piracy, with the merchants of more thoroughly Christian kingdoms that began to have a damping effect on some forms of indigenous violence.

Moreover, Swedes became mercenaries like their Norman cousins, visiting and serving in, sometimes conquering Christian principalities. They maintained contacts with Swedes at home, and many returned from time to time with goods. The returnees tended to support the Christian kings against the pagan resistance, or at least it is supposed that they did. Steadily in the course of the eleventh century, pagan resistance was ground down and in its wake came the establishment of bishoprics and other elements of the infrastructure of Latin Christianity. By 1100 Sweden was a Christian country; paganism was of little or no importance.

THE BRITISH ISLES

A major objective of Scandinavian conquest and a prime target of raiding parties was the British Isles, especially Ireland and Great Britain. Although it is customary to write the history of the British Isles as the story of these two lands, we should recall that there were many other large islands and island groups that contributed enormously to religious, military, political and economic developments. During the eleventh century, in the extreme south, most of these islands, like the Isle of Wight off the southern coast and the Isle of Thanet in the Strait of Dover, were English in political allegiance and Anglo-Saxon in ethnic stock. Elsewhere, ethnically and culturally, the populations were either Celtic or Scandinavian; as a rule the more northerly they were, the more Scandinavian they tended to be. Most of these islanders were at one time or another perceived as serious threats by the settled populations of Ireland and Great Britain.

The island of Anglesey, for example, was the home base of the princes of Gwynedd, who were destined to lead the struggle to unify the Welsh and punish the English for their attempts at conquest. The Isle of Man, north of Anglesey, was a staging ground for Viking incursions into Ireland led by the Norse earls of Orkney, who had conquered the Celtic-speaking Manx inhabitants. Still further north, from island groups like the Hebrides and Shetlands as well as the Orkneys, Norse pirates targeted Celtic, Anglo-Saxon and peninsular Norwegian shipping until they were subdued by the Norwegian kings.

The bloody adventures of the northern islanders and of the seafarers of the Orkneys in particular were given epic expression in *Orkneyinga Saga*, composed originally in the twelfth century and supplemented thereafter. Led by an adventurer named Svein, the wily sailors in one scene from the saga sail

south of Scotland as far as the Isle of May where there was a monastery at the time with an abbot in charge named Baldvini. For seven days Svein and his companions lay weatherbound there, claiming to be Earl Rognvald's envoys on their way to see the King of the Scots. The monks doubted their story and suspected them of being robbers, so they sent to the mainland for help. As soon as Svein and his men realized this, they looted the monastery and boarded their ship.

But this was not all. The looters continued their expedition, finally arriving at the court of the king of the Scots. Laden, as they were, with finery (stolen, to be sure), they were welcomed as great men, entertained and feasted. In the end they even admitted to the king 'how they had plundered [the monastery] on the Isle of May'. Yet, in the heroic world of the north, still only partly Christian, this did not unsettle relations. Thereafter 'Svein and his men stayed for some time with the King of the

Scots and were granted fine hospitality' (*Orkneyinga Saga*, 1978, p. 137).

These and countless other pirates knew where the wealth was. Island monasteries, as the story suggests, were preferred targets, but there was even greater wealth on what various sagas call the mainland, usually meaning Great Britain or Ireland. Indeed, because of their size and resources Great Britain and Ireland have long commanded the lion's share not only of northern pirates' but of northern scholars' attention. And the preference for focusing on them has been reinforced by hindsight, that is, Great Britain's central and enduring importance in western European and world history and Ireland's central importance within British history during and since the Middle Ages. Consequently, no other lands of Scandinavian, Anglo-Saxon or Celtic settlement have ever attracted so much scholarly attention.

Traditional lordship in Celtic Ireland manifested itself in a balance of power among a wide assortment of petty kingdoms, but this balance had been under stress for two centuries before the millennium. Viking incursions had the effect of inducing the Irish to adjust their style of warfare, as, for example, by beginning to employ cavalry, and to abandon the already somewhat shaky adherence to the traditional political alliances among the petty kingdoms. These changes, in turn, escalated the violence of internecine rivalries, which in the short run permitted the Vikings to establish firmer control, including kingdoms of their own. The most famous and powerful of these Viking kingdoms had Dublin as its centre, but on the coasts as well as inland the invaders established other principalities, often with new Viking towns at their centres.

In the longer term, the internecine warfare of the Irish princes resulted in the emergence of a successful superpower among the native kingdoms, Dál Cais, north of Limerick. In the early eleventh century Brian Boru ruled Dál Cais and aspired to the high or paramount kingship of Ireland. At the battle of Clontarf (1014), although Brian fell, he defeated a coalition of Irish magnates in alliance with the Viking king of Dublin and other Scandinavian invaders from the Isle of Man and the Orkneys; and his successors, ruling an augmented kingdom from Munster in the south-west, maintained the ascendancy of his dynasty over several others in the years that followed.

Their success hardly created unity in Ireland, but it did provide a relatively well-organized countervailing weight to the Scandinavian military threat. At the same time the Scandinavian lordships on the island were formally abandoning paganism for Christianity. Doing so under the influence of English and continental missionaries, they introduced, on the Roman model, territorial dioceses with powerful bishops, contrary to the customary Irish practice in which bishops enjoyed less authority than abbots. Native Irish reluctance to institute territorial dioceses, a form of ecclesiastical organization that, if brought under rulers' control, would have strengthened their ability to govern, was one factor that contributed to the tenuous cohesion of the native principalities.

The Celtic regions (Scotland, Cornwall and Wales) of Ireland's neighbouring island, Britain, had similarly tangled political and dynastic histories. The Scots were deeply divided by clan and geography, the highlands and mountains of the north and west of their land contrasting sharply with the topography of the less elevated regions of the country, which included large marshy districts. The low level of productive resources, including plantable acreage, made the country poor and less attractive than England or Ireland to invaders, although there were permanent Norse settlements at Caithness in the extreme north. In part it was material scarcities that gave rise to persistent and widespread banditry and feuds.

By 1034 a single dynasty, represented in Duncan I (1034–40), claimed rule over all of Scotland. How effectively this claim translated into governance remains a matter of bitter scholarly dispute, for stability was not a characteristic of the monarchy in the eleventh century. Duncan was slain by Macbeth (1040–57), who was himself a mortal victim of Malcolm III, Duncan's son. How unified the kingdom was in any other respect is also a matter of sharp contention. The Scottish Church, established in the early Middle Ages, contributed to a sense of unity, but it was hampered in doing so by the structural weaknesses, including itinerant bishops, it shared with the Irish Church.

Wales, too, lacked cohesiveness in the eleventh century, and like Scotland, the lie of the land, which was mountainous in the north and west, contributed to the absence of unity, a unity which in the Welsh case does seem to have been a cultural ideal. Viking raids were destructive, as were raids by the English, and they reduced productivity. But in a curious way the negative consequences of this raiding received some compensation in the recognition by the Welsh of their own vulnerability and need for political and military renewal. They also drew on a quasi-legendary tradition of Welsh cultural achievements and aspirations to unity in the tenth century under Hywel the Good (c.910–c.950), in whose time the bishopric of St David's claimed primacy within the Welsh

Church. The cult of David, a fifth-century evangelizing saint, became the spiritual focus of Welsh devotion and pilgrimage and helped underpin appeals to Welsh political unity. To Hywel have also been attributed innovations like national coinage and the proclamation and inscription of national laws.

Whatever the inspirational force of these traditions, the battlefield prowess of one Gruffydd ap Llywelyn was crucial in furthering political and military renewal in Wales. In 1039, from his power base in the north of the country, Gruffydd emerged as the leading Welsh prince. He steadily extended his power southward against rival princelings and carried on raids against the English, thus in many quarters increasing his prestige. By 1055 or so he was master of most of Wales, but, in the absence of other changes, brute force and terror hardly laid a firm foundation for continued stability. As in Ireland, the institutional structures needed to preserve unity were still weak, if not absolutely absent, at the time of Gruffydd's death in 1063 at the hands of Welsh rivals, who killed him while he was in retreat from an English counter-attack.

Cornwall, unlike Scotland and Wales, was wholly dominated by England. Partly this was due to the fact that no significant natural barriers existed to determined penetration by the more numerous English and their armies. To be sure, a distinctively Cornish culture survived down to the early modern period, as evidenced by the existence of late medieval miracle plays in the Cornish language and by the fact that the spoken language did not die out until the eighteenth century. Nonetheless, unlike their Welsh neighbours, Cornishmen never seriously challenged English political authority after the initial conquest of their homeland in the eighth century.

*

As should now be clear, economically the most productive, demographically the most populous, and militarily the strongest of the political divisions of Britain was the array of territories that came to be called England (the usage of the word in this, its wide geographical and political meaning, seems only to date from the period of Danish conquest). Despite the imposition of Danish rule in the early eleventh century, the conquerors' settlements never spread much beyond the north, the so-called Danelaw. Moreover, the longest reigning and most impressive of the Danish rulers, Cnut the Great, admired and preserved the modes of governance that he found in place in Old English society.

Cnut, like his Anglo-Saxon predecessors, governed through appointed officials who supervised the courts, markets, local defence and collection of revenue. The most important of these officials, those administering the largest districts or shires, were the sheriffs, but the shires were divided into smaller units, called either hundreds, each remotely a unit of a hundred homesteads, or, in the Danelaw, wapentakes, that is, 'weapon-takes', a term that evokes their role as military districts. Each of these units was administered by a royal official known as a reeve.

The Anglo-Saxons in the eleventh century also followed what had by then become the centuries-old Christian practice of anointing the new king, transforming him, as clerical opinion would have it, into *Christus Domini*, the anointed of the lord. This conferred authority, but also in ideological terms implicitly invoked a set of moral guidelines that in theory limited the Crown's authority. The king, for example, took a coronation oath in which he pledged to protect the people and defend the Church. At the same time, the king controlled the English Church in many ways, especially by appointing important abbots and all bishops, including the chief bishop or primate, the archbishop of Canterbury. Moreover, the bishops were often selected from experienced priests of the royal chapel who, besides saying mass, wrote the king's letters and orders or writs, preserved the laws in writing, and made records of land transactions for the Crown. In the famous words of one historian, the Anglo-Saxon church was 'an integral part of the State'. (Sayles, 1961, p. 192.)

Ideally, the king was to act in harmony with the legitimate interests of the upper class, expressed through the *witan*, the great council of the wise. The *witan* was purely aristocratic, comprising various members of the royal family and of the Anglo-Saxon and Anglo-Danish noble families, as well as bishops and abbots of major monasteries. Its total membership at any one time was typically between thirty and forty. It met two or three times per year, but also whenever a new king needed to be chosen, war had to be declared or peace formally concluded.

When the *witan* met as a judicial body it was known as the *witenage-mot*, the moot or court of the wise ones. It stated the customary laws or deemed the dooms, as it was put, formulating them in such a way as to make it appear in this deeply tradition-affirming society that law was discovered rather than created. Most historians insist nonetheless that these putative acts of discovery were the equivalent of legislation.

As the use of the word 'court' implies, the *witenagemot* was also the forum for the adjudication of disputes among the high-born or of other conflicts that, unresolved, might threaten the well-being of the kingdom. The work of the court followed long-established customs known to the *witan* and specialists in the law, and lower courts often followed similar practices. Convicted criminals were obliged to compensate the victim or his or her family according to the rank of the injured party, the *wergild*, or the nature of the injury, the *bot*. All this work was guided by the general desire both to forestall feuds, although properly declared feuds were legitimate, and to maintain the king's peace, a multivalent concept which extended from the most general sense of harmony (Old English, *frith*) to the specific immunities and protection offered by the king to particular places (OE *mund*) or particular people (OE *grith*).

Most people, of course, rarely transgressed the king's peace or came into contact with the highest institutions of royal governance, except in periods of great crisis. National politics in ordinary times meant little to them even if they were free and still less if they were enslaved, a category that exceeded 10 per cent of the total population in some regions of the country. For free and slave alike, life was lived principally in and circumscribed by the concerns of innumerable individual hamlets and villages. While the Danish peace persisted, this situation was not likely to change: generations of Anglo-Saxon and Anglo-Danish lords, from the exalted rank of earls down to that of thegns, exploited their estates and the labourers on their estates with rigour and with relative impunity.

Until 1042, under Cnut and his two sons, the *pax danica* was firm. Indeed, England emerged as the most stable part of the Danish empire and was certainly more successfully administered by its kings than the other Scandinavian and Celtic kingdoms were by theirs. The year 1042, however, brought a crisis in the succession. One relative of Cnut fighting in Norway made a claim for the throne, but was unable to bring forces to bear to make the claim effective. Two descendants of the old Wessex line of Anglo-Saxon kings also made claims. The first of these was living in exile in Hungary, too distant at the time to act effectively in England. The other, with the encouragement of the duke of Normandy, in whose territories he was living in exile, and with the support in England of a powerful earl, Godwin of Wessex, was selected by the *witan* and crowned king as Edward.

Known to posterity as Edward the Confessor, the new king was a well-meaning man who lived in a holy non-sexual union with his wife. He was already Normanized by his long sojourn in Normandy. He spoke French and made French, instead of English, the language of his household. The traditional portrait is that Edward was a weak king who could not control the earls, especially Godwin, and that the effectiveness of royal governance went down abruptly during his rule. Other scholars disagree. But all recognize that Edward and Godwin, along with Godwin's son, Harold, came to distrust one another. The situation degenerated throughout the reign, only to be resolved at the king's death in 1066, when a disputed succession precipitated an event, the Norman Conquest of England, that would forever change the constellation of power in the north (see chapter 10).

4

Francia/France

Everywhere in northern Europe in the eleventh century violence was characteristic of political life. This is not to suggest that violence was constant or that every outbreak was intensely destructive to human life or property. Much of the violence practised by elites against other elites is now regarded as being of a ritual character. At the knightly level and upwards, people of roughly the same economic and social standing faced off in confrontations meant as much to demonstrate power and courage as to reinforce boundaries in both a territorial and a conceptual sense. Men – and here we are talking principally about men – needed to know their place, where they could exercise authority, and whom they could exploit and to what degree.

The limits were occasionally being redefined, as by the emergence of movements like the Peace and Truce of God, and thus, in a curious way, force or the ritual show of force was required to confirm the new limits. Yet, one thing is certain. However much new tendencies within Christian society like the Peace Movement stimulated the reconfiguration of political forces, there was as yet in the eleventh century little reduction in the absolute number of actors who claimed rights to the legitimate use of force.

This fact helps explain why in France and Germany, although there were long traditions of centralizing, if never fully centralized, royal authority, centrifugal forces always seemed poised to destroy every semblance of unity. In each case, there was a constant struggle to hold the polity together, and in each case the struggle was only partly successful. Nonetheless, containment of the forces of disunity was more successful in Germany than in France even though new polities on the German borderlands, the Hungarian and Polish kingdoms, complicated the situation which the German emperor confronted. The uncertain conversion of the people of these new kingdoms to Catholic Christianity

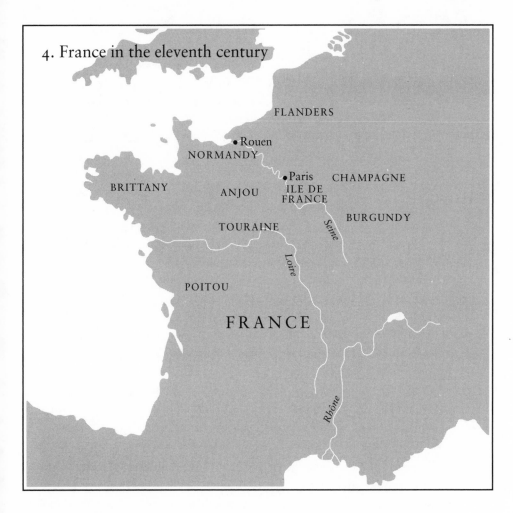

4. France in the eleventh century

FLANDERS

• Rouen
NORMANDY

• Paris   CHAMPAGNE
ILE DE
FRANCE

BRITTANY   ANJOU

BURGUNDY

TOURAINE   *Seine*

Loire

POITOU

FRANCE

Rhône

created further problems in international politics. In this chapter we
consider the political situation of France; in chapter 5 that of central
Europe.

*

Francia, the kingdom of France, was more an abstract concept than
a reality of governance in the early eleventh century. Not even its
geographical extent is easy to describe, because the Crown claimed
suzerain authority over territories at a great distance from its heartland,
which was in and around the Parisian basin. Indeed, the legacy of
France's late Carolingian history – devolution of authority, erosion of
military power, economic regression – had turned the realm into a
congeries of self-governing principalities, some well managed, others
poorly, but almost always in bitter rivalry. It was the lands directly

under the king's fiscal exploitation, the royal demesne, rather than the kingdom as a whole, that really defined the sphere of his governance.

Despite their best efforts, however, scholars know very little about the quality and extent of governance of royal demesne lands in this period or even about the governors themselves. The three early Capetian kings of France, Hugh Capet (987–96), from whose nickname eighteenth-century writers coined the name of the dynasty, Robert the Pious (996–1031) and Henry I (1031–60), displaced (according to their supporters) or usurped (according to their detractors) the claim of the Carolingian dynasty to the throne. They were successful in part because they survived at all, let alone for such a long time, and managed to pass on the kingship to their eldest sons.

They achieved this, in part, by stressing the honour of the Crown. Kingship mattered in that an elaborate ideology justified its existence. The king of the Franks, to use the formal title of the French ruler, was lionized by ecclesiastical supporters as a new David and a new Solomon and as the Lord's anointed. The kingly office, bestowed at his coronation, no doubt bore many of the trappings of imperial authority. We do not know as much as we might like to know about the coronation ceremonies, however. We can argue back from twelfth- and thirteenth-century records and imagine the new king inoiled at the magnificent cathedral of Reims with chrism said to have been sent from heaven in the mouth of a dove for the baptism of Clovis, the first Christian king of the Franks, in the fifth century. We can envision the new David girded with Charlemagne's sword as a sign of his military prowess and carrying a baton topped by an ivory sculpture of a hand (the *main de justice*) to represent his Solomonic and Christ-like persona as the Just Judge. And we can picture the new king as a miracle worker after the coronation, healing the repellent skin disease, scrofula, by the mere touch of his fleshly hand and the making of the sign of the cross on the victim.

Unfortunately, many of these ceremonies are almost certainly not early eleventh-century rites. Touching for scrofula was not practised either as an immediate post-coronation rite or regularly at other times until more than a century after the accession of Hugh Capet, although the publicists of Robert the Pious believed he had used the miraculous power, and there is some indication that some ritual of miraculous touching, however infrequently it occurred, was already regarded as a custom in the reign of King Philip I (1060–1108). As to other matters, the record is equally spotty and inconclusive about eleventh-century practice. Reims cathedral was not fixed as the coronation site until 1129. The first mention of the miraculous chrism does not occur until 1131; it is scarcely credible that this oil would have gone unremarked if it had been used in eleventh-century coronations.

The point is that an eleventh-century core of religious ceremonies, including coronation, acclamation and related rites of kingship, needed repeatedly to be 'enhanced' as part of an ongoing and self-serving celebration of Capetian kingship. It was not until the thirteenth century that the Capetian rites of kingship surpassed those of other Catholic dynasties in brilliance and, to a large extent, in the bold claims they embodied.

While their ecclesiastical supporters were enriching the coronation ceremony, they were also of necessity stressing the Capetians' personal virtue, as opposed to their birthright, as justification for rule, for it proved impossible in the short run to suppress the accusation that the new rulers were usurpers. Robert the Pious's reign was crucial here. Despite irregularities in his personal life, especially his liaison with a cousin, a union regarded technically as incestuous and therefore condemned by the pope, Robert managed to inspire a strong cadre of supporters. (His eventual submission to papal discipline by his renunciation of his cousin certainly helped.) His devotional practices gave him a monkish reputation, as did his support of the Cluniac reformers, of the Peace of God, and of the faith against the alleged perfidies of Jews and heretics, some of the latter of whom he caused to be executed by fire. Thus, it is no accident that Robert was the first Capetian alleged to have had thaumaturgic powers.

The new dynasty also practised a politically stabilizing form of anticipatory succession which they maintained until the late twelfth century. Lords in some other principalities, such as Normandy, practised very similar forms of succession. In the case of the Capetians, the eldest son was associated with his father, was crowned in his father's lifetime, and at least formally ruled as co-king until his father's death, after which he was crowned a second time. Robert the Pious, indeed, was associated with his father, Hugh, from the very beginning of Hugh's reign. This method of inheritance was not only a preventative against disputed successions, but also, depending on the characters of the senior and junior kings, helped the younger men get considerable experience of ruling.

Despite their best efforts to represent themselves as chosen by God to rule, the Capetian kings found political rivals everywhere in the fertile landscape of northern France. Much of the time and effort of the eleventh- and indeed twelfth-century kings was spent on the nasty work of bringing these rivals – barons and men of lesser status who controlled strongly fortified castles in the Parisian basin itself – into submission. They found their justification for doing so in part from the royal claim, repeated in every coronation oath, to protect the Church, which translated in practice into coming to the defence of the scores of individual churches and monasteries which were among the principal objects of depredation by local lords.

The vineyards, grain fields, sheep flocks and array of dairy and orchard farms that dotted the lush countryside and were held in dependence by monastic, episcopal and lay lords in the Ile de France were tempting targets to plunderers and brigands. And it must be said that except for the spring floods that turned the many rivers of the region into formidable barriers to raiders and to more serious invaders as well, the villages and agricultural lands of northern France, nestled as they were in a gentle landscape, enjoyed little natural protection. When peace prevailed, this meant that the countryside was open to easy communication and economic penetration across political boundaries. The same rivers that, swollen and choked with debris, endangered farmland and villages provided in normal weather and tranquil times extensive and effective means of transportation of goods. The Ile de France was almost inevitably a hub of trade and mercantile activity, and great cities – none greater than Paris – were growing up despite the recurrent political disorder.

Elsewhere the disorder was both more and less crippling. In Brittany political authority was in shambles from internecine strife and from continual pressure from the counts of Anjou and from the dukes of Normandy, both of whom sought, more or less successfully, to dominate the Breton regions bordering their principalities. This two-fold pressure from Anjou on the east and Normandy on the north-east of the province meant that only the western Celtic-speaking regions of Brittany were spared 'foreign' invasion. Not surprisingly, these were by far the poorest regions of the province, although there were numerous relatively prosperous fishing villages hard by the sea, and many Bretons made tolerable livings from trade and piracy.

Of the two principalities putting most pressure on Breton political autonomy, namely, Anjou and Normandy, Anjou displayed the more aggressive character. Watered by delightful rivers and blessed with a lovely climate and rich soil, its bounty provided the counts with the surplus revenue they needed for military action against their enemies and rivals. Throughout the first half of the eleventh century the counts annexed major adjacent territories. Annexation by marriage may have been the preferred strategy; it cost less (there were limits to the counts' wealth) and was usually less risky in the short run, but the appetites of the counts, two of whom, Fulk Nerra and Geoffrey Martel, are legendary for their expansionist desires, could not be fully whetted except by outright conquest. Besides the borderlands of Brittany as far as Nantes, over which they exercised and maintained control from the tenth century onwards, the counts expanded their domains southward into Poitou and Touraine, incorporating the capital of the latter, Tours, into the Angevin patrimony by the mid-century. These enormous territorial gains were secured by the construction of a large number of stone castles, which were staging points both for disciplinary action against rebellious subjects and for strikes at foreign invaders.

Fulk's countship (987–1040) was marked by brutality. Monkish chronicle sources may exaggerate just how brutal he was, but his three pilgrimages to Jerusalem testify not merely to his piety but also to his recognition that his behaviour on and off the battlefield failed to live up to the moral standards of Christian rulership then being articulated and could only be redeemed by the penitential act of pilgrimage. His son and successor, Geoffrey Martel (1040–60), was probably less brutal, but brutal enough. In any case he was equally effective in keeping the vast array of Angevin territories in submission. He never let the castellans achieve anything like political independence, and at every opportunity he carefully reinforced what were sometimes local lords' rather vague notions of the nature of their dependence on him as overlord. Under Geoffrey, the Angevin principality probably became the most powerful in western France.

Equally martial in its political culture, though still remarkably stable in the first two decades of the eleventh century, was Normandy under Duke Richard II (996–1026). Inheriting a province whose Scandinavian conquerors had settled down as free farmers to exploit the rich land increasingly famous for its dairy products, fruit and grains, he ruled with benign self-confidence. He was not only a competent ruler but also a major player, more so than the Angevin counts, in international politics. Some sort of commercial tie with England was almost inevitable.

Normandy and particularly its capital, the port of Rouen, constituted a natural entrepôt for the exchange of English for French goods. Moreover, through his sister, Emma, Richard was the brother-in-law of the Anglo-Saxon king, Aethelred II, the Unready (d. 1016). To be sure, Aethelred's line, the house of Wessex, was superseded in England in the wake of the Danish conquest, but since Emma was, by Aethelred, also the mother of a son, the dukes nurtured their own hopes of a restoration of the Wessex line. These hopes were realized when that son returned from exile in Normandy after the collapse of Danish rule in 1042 to assume the crown in England as Edward (the Confessor).

Duke Richard was also responsible for bringing a zealous Lombard aristocrat and churchman, one Guilermo of Volpiano and usually known in English-language books as William of Volpiano, to Normandy. Guilermo came from a successful career in Dijon in the duchy of Burgundy, where as a Cluniac monk and abbot of Saint-Bénigne of Dijon, he was known as a great reformer of the moral and material fabric of the church. Besides the renewal of the spiritual life of Saint-Bénigne, to Guilermo of Volpiano is attributed the inspiration for the rotunda of the majestic abbey church there, which was built on the model of that of the Holy Sepulchre in Jerusalem.

Guilermo of Volpiano did his job in Normandy extremely well, reestablishing the once important abbey of Fécamp, which had been destroyed by the duke's pagan Viking ancestors, and instituting reformed monastic chapters on the Cluniac model in other monasteries in the territories most closely tied to Richard. Most of the new foundations, more than twenty-five in the next two or three decades, were owed directly to the duke's or his near kin's patronage. This close relationship between the dukes and the churches helped undergird the duchy's political cohesion, which in turn benefited ideologically from the celebratory mythology that passed for history among the writers who recorded the settlement and achievements of the Normans. The fact that the highest levels of the aristocracy were kindred of the ducal family and recognized that the security of their property depended on his good will further strengthened the unity of the province. Consequently, in Normandy, neither encastellation nor unrestrained feud or private war rose to levels visible elsewhere, such as in Brittany. By and large, the castles that were constructed in Normandy, like those in Anjou, were defensive centres and staging points for the duke's retainers.

Grave problems arose when one of Richard's successors, Robert I (1028–35), designated an illegitimate infant son as his heir. Soon afterwards Robert died while on pilgrimage to the Holy Land, itself evidence, like the pilgrimages of the Angevin counts, of the increasing centrality in northern Europe of the holy city of Jerusalem to the devotional life of the age. Only seven years old at the time of his accession, the child whom Robert left behind was for many years in no position to rule, but in 1047, as an adolescent, he dared to assert his authority and by doing so provoked a rebellion from those subjects who had become accustomed to the looser rule of the prince's minority. Thanks to the opposition of King Henry I of France, the rebellion faltered, and the young man, William by name, survived and came effectively into personal rule. Almost immediately he retaliated against his enemies, expanding his influence militarily into the west of the duchy, where opposition to him had been strongest, and into the neighbouring provinces of Maine and Brittany as well, from which some of his opponents had launched raids or sought support.

Duke William's relations with Flanders, his northern neighbour, were more irenic. Under Counts Baldwin IV (989–1035) and Baldwin V (1035–67), whose daughter William married, Flanders entered upon that phase of its history that would make it one of the wealthiest regions in northern Europe. Benefiting from its navigable rivers – the Meuse, the Scheldt and the lower Rhine – and from its coastal harbours, economic life in Flanders was almost intimately connected to trade. But land reclamation on an immense scale, largely brought about by dyking, also made possible increased grain and animal production to support the burgeoning populations of big trading towns like Ghent, Ypres and Bruges.

If the trading centres of Flanders were growing in power, they did not yet offer any significant challenge to the count's rule. That came from other lords, particularly the German emperor, Henry II, against whom Baldwin IV had to defend himself and his lands by force shortly after the turn of the millennium. The eventual outcome of their struggle was recognition on the count's part that he held some of his territories directly from the emperor. This collection of lands, known as imperial Flanders, needs to be differentiated from those lands held of the French king, French Flanders, in order to understand the complexities of international relations involving the county in the centuries to come.

This political division only very imperfectly replicated the linguistic division of French (Walloon) and Germanic (Flemish) in the count's territories, but that linguistic division was also the basis of a rivalry among the count's subjects that had deleterious consequences for the effectiveness of his and his successors' rule. It did not help matters of governance that Baldwin's son chafed under his father's dominion and rebelled in 1028, or that the son was ineffective himself as a warrior after he came into the countship in his own right in 1035. Only by skilful negotiation, including an alliance with the dukes of Normandy, did he preserve and extend his patrimony and thus safeguard the opportunity to improve modes of governance in Flanders during his thirty-year countship.

The power of the French king was certainly inferior to that of the duke of Normandy and potentially to that of the count of Flanders during most of the eleventh century, but the princes who seemed to the Crown potentially even more ominous rivals were the rulers of another collection of lands, usually called Blois-Champagne. It was Count Eudes II (d. 1037) who amassed the lands of this great agglomeration of fiefs. His possession of Blois was uncontested from the beginning of the eleventh century, but the legality of his claim to the inheritance of Champagne was less clear. At Eudes's request, Bishop Fulbert of Chartres, one of the greatest scholars of the age, put together a compelling dossier in the count's favour, arguing for the legitimacy of Eudes's inheritance of extensive territories in Champagne in 1021 through his grandmother.

At the core of Fulbert's argument, besides the legalities, was the avowal he made of Eudes's unshakable fidelity as a royal vassal, a valuable pledge in a world where personal loyalty counted so much in being able to confront one's enemies effectively. On this subject the bishop could wax eloquent. 'He who swears fealty to his lord,' he writes,

ought always to have these six things in mind: what is harmless, safe, honourable, useful, easy, possible. Harmless, in that he should not do his lord bodily harm; safe in that he should not betray his secrets or defences; honourable, in that he should not weaken his rights of justice or other matters that pertain to his honour; useful, in that he should not attack his possessions; easy or possible in that he should not hinder his lord in doing good . . . or make difficulties in what is possible for his lord to do. (Strayer, 1965, p. 113.)

Fulbert's successful assertion of Eudes's rights in Champagne and of his loyalty to the Crown was followed by the count's marriage in 1030 to the heiress of Sancerre, as a result of which the collection of lands owing him allegiance either directly or through his wife were linked together geographically. With Champagne, ideal for growing grain, and other lands, like the Sancerre patrimony, equally ideal for growing vines, the count's wealth was enormous. It was augmented over time to his and his successors' benefit by the emergence of Champagne in particular as a great mercantile centre whose international commercial fairs became legendary. Eudes seemed on the verge of forging a principality that virtually surrounded the royal domain lands and exceeded them in wealth. For the Capetians, the domains of the counts of Blois-Champagne were worth keeping a very close watch on.

The one other principality that was sufficiently large, cohesive and wealthy to play a major role in politics, at least on the scale of that played by Anjou, Normandy, Flanders and Blois-Champagne, was Burgundy. In fact, there were two Burgundys – the county, which was east of the Sâone and in imperial territory, and the duchy of the same name, which was west of the river and in Francia proper. The duchy was an especially fertile land of small farms and larger estates, and there was a vibrant trade in the wines grown there, which were already fabled for their fine quality. The county of Burgundy, on the other hand, remained heavily wooded, and far less developed commercially.

A count of Mâcon, one Otto-Guillaume, who claimed the countship of Burgundy, the imperial fief, but died in 1027 without fully realizing his claim, had tried to expand his power westward into the more prosperous duchy, but here he was thwarted by the Capetians in the person of King Robert the Pious. Although the count's heirs continued to be powerful lords in the imperial territories adjacent to the duchy of Burgundy, the French king invested his own son with the duchy *per se* and on that son's accession to the Crown in 1031 as King Henry I, the latter bestowed it on his younger brother. He thus created a line of Capetian dukes of Burgundy known in the centuries to come for their loyalty to the royal house.

*

It is certainly true that the politics of northern France cannot be understood apart from the shifting rivalries and alliances among the various princes who emerged as more or less independent rulers in the eleventh century. Although the king could claim a paramount status, this was, as we have seen, more theoretical than practical in the early part of the century. His power – indeed, his survival as a great territorial lord – depended on timely alliances with other princes and his capacity to exploit rivalries among these princes. There is no doubt that the Capetian kings were fairly good at doing both these things by the middle of the eleventh century, but they were not noticeably superior in their political savvy to the dukes of Normandy, who would emerge as their most powerful and persistent rivals over the next 150 years.

Outside the narrow political context of princely rivalries there is another context that helps explain the frenzied struggle for power among the great lords of Francia. It has already been pointed out that northern France was richly endowed in resources. Trading centres of notable importance were growing up in the towns of Champagne, as well as in Paris, Rouen, and in the Loire valley towns of the counts of Anjou. Jewish traders and merchants were moving into these centres, itself testimony of the towns' economic vitality. Grain was grown in abundance throughout most of the rural regions, and the wines produced from the grapes were coveted in France and elsewhere. It was also in the north that there emerged a very concerted effort to harness water power to the daily tasks of life, especially the grinding of grain at water mills. Village after village exploited the streams and rivers with a mill and mill pond, the latter providing fish also for local populations.

Besides grain, fruit and wine, northern France soon became known for the raising of flocks and therefore the production of wool and for the raising of industrial crops like flax for linen cloth and woad for dyestuffs. With its extensive, though heavily exploited woodlands, still another resource in the form of pasturage for pigs, lumber for building, wood for fuel, and charcoal for making steel added to the wealth of the rulers and their subjects. War itself had a productive aspect in that it stimulated certain forms of artisanship, like the production of metal weapons and armour, that could be reoriented in peacetime to the manufacture of ploughshares, hoes, harrows and axes. The woodlands in turn yielded – or began to yield – to further efforts at clearance.

Thus, according to one calculus, it may be argued that rival princes in northern France were attempting to expand their lands not merely because it gave them masculine prestige, but also because it made economic sense to do so. It was an ironically depressing truth, however, that their very attempts – by interrupting rural workers' production, by making villagers homeless through savage acts of arson, and by destroying productive resources like mills and forges – put brakes on what might have been a yet more spectacular economic take-off, one even more beneficial to them.

In hindsight scholars can tell that the slow process that would bring most petty lords under control and would give the Crown superior access to the resources just described started around the mid-eleventh century in the reign of King Henry I (1031–60) and continued in the even longer reign of his son Philip I (1060–1108). The remarkable length of the individual Capetian reigns contributed to the stability that was required to pursue a consistent policy. And the desire to magnify the stature of the dynasty was manifested not simply in the evolving coronation rituals, but also in opportune marriages. Philip I was called Philip, a Greek name, not because the apostle Philip's name was a common choice in the West (it was not), but because it was so in the East, and that is where his mother, Anne, came from.

A Russian princess, the daughter of the ruler of the great principality of Kiev, Anne had been a very desirable match in that the family of which she was a part was recognized as one of the most important in Europe. Her father, Prince Iaroslav the Wise (1019–54), ruled an immense congeries of territories in eastern Europe and seemed single-handedly to be holding back the steppe barbarians. He may even have flirted with aligning the young Russian church with the Roman rather than the Orthodox obedience, for he was no slavish sycophant of Constantinople. But he failed in his attempt to take Constantinople by military force late in his reign and thereafter remained at peace with the Eastern Empire. Despite this setback he continued to command respect and fear until the day he died.

Evidence of the family's prestige, as suggested above, abounds in the marriage alliances. Iaroslav himself wed a Swedish princess, while one sister made a match with the king of Poland and the other with a high-ranking member of the Byzantine nobility. Iaroslav's six children, three boys and three girls, all married high European nobility: the three girls the kings of France (Anne), Hungary and Norway respectively. The allegiances – marital and implicitly political – testify to the increasing 'europeanization' of Christian elites in the eleventh century, a hallmark of aristocratic life for centuries to come.

King Henry I, with young Philip, his son by Anne, as nominal co-ruler the last two years of his reign, kept up the pressure on the petty lords within the Ile de France, but increasingly fell foul of the Norman duke, William, whose reign he had earlier helped secure. Henry twice, unsuccessfully, invaded Normandy. The important point was not the failure perhaps, so much as the pattern. The Crown was beginning to take a more active role against the really great princes in the kingdom.

Unfortunately, when Henry died Philip was still very young, only seven or eight. His father had foreseen the likely precariousness of the situation for his son and had arranged for the count of Flanders to act as regent of the kingdom, a brilliant move in that it put Philip under the protection of a powerful man who was also the father-in-law of the Norman duke. It thus placed a moral obstacle in the way of Duke William avenging the attacks that Henry I had launched against Normandy a few years before.

Philip I continued his father's policies when he reached adulthood. For much of his reign he did so successfully, and to Philip are often attributed innovations like the institution of provosts: officers, more or less territorially based, often in a town, who were to oversee the collection of royal revenues and carry out other administrative duties. Increasingly, too, one finds evidence of more systematic organization of the central administration, with a few officials emerging as the principal administrators of genuine departments of government. Again, it is not far-fetched to see Philip's hand at work in this development.

Like his counterparts elsewhere in Europe, however, Philip did not fully understand or ultimately endorse all the currents of change that were convulsing the Church towards the end of the eleventh century (see chapter 6), and his confusion, alternating as it did with hostility to any change that might limit his authority, led to disputes with ecclesiastics. No dispute was as bitter or put as much of a break on the aggrandizing policies of the Crown vis-à-vis the territorial lords as Philip's renunciation of his wife, Bertha, and his remarriage, or bigamous marriage, as censorious ecclesiastics would have it, to Bertrade de Montfort in 1092: excommunication, then absolution, then another excommunication for backsliding, another absolution, and on and on for a dozen years, while the king himself seems to have become more and more morose, lethargic about governing, and generally unfit for rule.

The dignity of the Crown was saved through the luck of Capetian associative kingship; Philip's son Louis began to take up the slack, in what by then seemed a traditional manner, and pressed on with the work of territorial consolidation (suppressing lordlings' petty acts of violence) and expansion, if not by conquest, then by purchase, as with the viscounty of Bourges in 1101. Most importantly, the son was not irredeemably tainted in churchmen's eyes by his father's sins. The eleventh century, on balance, therefore, must be counted as a success for the Capetians and for those who saw in the Capetian monarchy the best hope of creating a lasting internal peace for France.

5

Central Europe

Neither of the principal central European monarchies, Germany and Hungary, was entirely stable in the eleventh century, and they differed considerably from each other. Nonetheless, insofar as centralization is a proper standard of comparison, they stood in sharp contrast to the politically splintered kingdom of France, as we saw in the last chapter. Of course, it may be argued that centralization is not an appropriate or important marker of difference, that the similarities among all three kingdoms in economic and social organization were much more significant than variations in nascent 'state formation'. But this argument is dubious at best. Ordinary people in the towns and villages of all the northern continental countries of Christendom had much in common in terms of the way they exploited the land, organized workplaces, and responded to the demands of lordship. But levels of violence which differed significantly in the three kingdoms deeply affected these arrangements, and the perceived threat of paganism on the borders, in Germany's case, or within and on the borders (Hungary's), undermines facile attempts by scholars to homogenize everyday life across the map.

GERMANY

Germany's Ottonian or Saxon dynasty projected itself as the rightful guardian of the legacy of Charlemagne; and as Holy Roman emperor, from 962, the head of the dynasty ruled extensive territories in Italy, claimed a universal lordship in Christendom, and enjoyed a special theocratic status recognized as such by many prominent churchmen. He garnered economic support for his rule from extensive rural estates

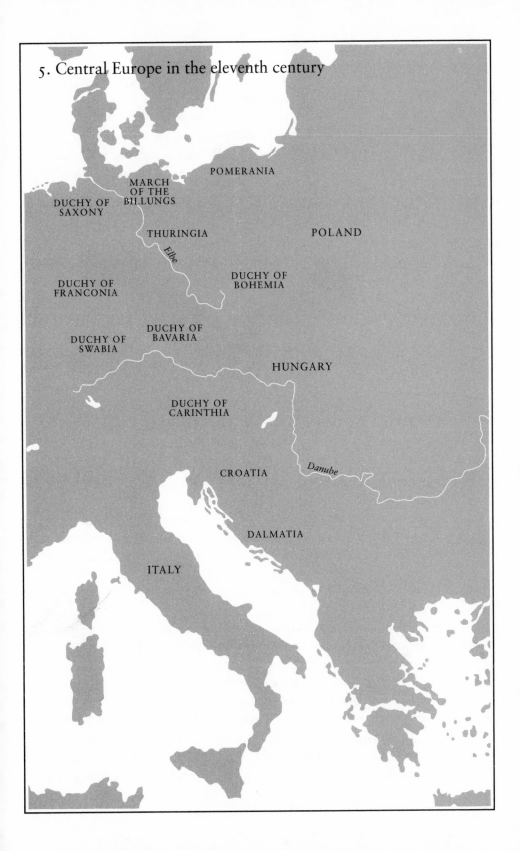

5. Central Europe in the eleventh century

under his direct lordship in Germany and from various taxes and levies in the towns and cities of the empire.

The German king who had assumed the imperial title in 962 and who gave his name to the Saxon dynastic lineage was Otto I the Great (936–73). The heartland of his realms, even after his coronation as emperor, was Germany or, more precisely, the Germanic-speaking areas of Europe, including much of present-day Belgium, the Netherlands and Luxembourg, France east of the Meuse and the Rhône, and Switzerland. In the early eleventh century there may have been only four million or so inhabitants of this 'Greater Germany', despite the fact that geographically it was the largest kingdom in Christendom. (For comparison, England, which was territorially less than a quarter the size of Greater Germany, had a population of one to two million in the mid-eleventh century.)

Vast districts, particularly in the central and southern parts of the realm, were heavily forested and/or mountainous, but it was only later that the mountains yielded up some of their vast wealth to the princes and princelings in the form of silver. Levels of agricultural exploitation and the intensity of mining remained low in large parts of the country. More prosperous areas of the realm were to be found in the towns and the cities of the Rhineland, which were on the verge of a spectacular period of demographic and economic growth, and in Flanders, although here the prosperity benefited the count much more than the German king.

Unlike in the more southerly areas of Germany, agricultural settlements in the northern plain were already expanding apace as rustics, sometimes in the employ of monasteries, undertook the clearance of forests, marshes, and kettle and moraine (lands marked with pits and boulders by the receding glaciers of aeons past). At times the expansion in size and numbers of German villages came not at the expense of wilderness, but from the conquest of Slavic settlements and expulsion of the Slavic population. The further east from the Elbe, as a rule, the more tentative, even precarious, was the German presence and the stiffer the Slavic resistance. Lords exercised a sometimes brutal rule in these troublous border or marcher regions – the March of the Billungs, the March of Thuringia (east of Thuringia proper), the Ostmark (Austria) and Carinthia, among others.

The Ottonian patrimony – the region of the greatest concentration of direct royal rights and of the Crown's most productive estates and most lucrative fiscal rights – was concentrated in the north in Saxony and Franconia, but the rulers sought, in part through the surrogate powers of the Church, to extend their influence and multiply their rights in the southern part of the country as well. By claiming protection over the Church the monarchs were asserting rights and power in regions in Germany far distant from the patrimony. By investing the bishops directly with their episcopal and temporal authority, the kings were implying a personal dependency owed by the episcopate that was tantamount to the bonds of loyalty and fidelity that tied the ranks of the nobility to them. By endowing the Church with large estates, sometimes from lands confiscated from fractious barons (for the growth of Ottonian monarchy was not uncontested), the rulers expected the prelates to be willing and able to put military forces in the field in support of the Crown's ambitions.

Much more fascinating than internal consolidation of authority in Germany, at least in a long tradition of modern scholarship, has been the Ottonians' territorial ambitions. Otto I's aspirations in this regard, as his taking of the imperial title suggests, focused largely on Italy, but in the mid-960s he also saw opportunities for the enhancement of his territorial base on the disturbed eastern border of German settlement. There, Slavic and German or, put another way, pagan and Catholic rivalry grew exceptionally fierce. Otto I had no illusions about the Slavic threat or qualms about how to deal with it, and skirmishes with tribes living between regions of dense German settlement and Poland were common. Indeed, German expansion eastward came largely at the expense of these tribes.

Poland was a powerful presence further east. And because the Poles, unlike some other Slavic ethnic groups, possessed the kind of political and military institutions under their leader Mieszko (962–92) that permitted them to raise substantial forces, relations between Poland and other central European polities were more formal. War was always possible, and war between Germans and Poles occasionally took place. But in the tenth century, at least, relations on balance between Germany and Poland were stable and reasonably good.

The Poles' own situation was complicated in the long run by the absence, except for extensive marshlands separating them from the Russians, of any very effective natural defences before the millennium. This absence continued to be characteristic of the principality's boundaries until well into the eleventh century, when expansion south reached beyond Krakow to the Carpathians, but even these mountains offered a defensive line only for one part of Poland's lengthy borders. Moreover, Poland's marshes and its mountains faced enemies east and south not west, where German power was concentrated. Again, however, there was an underlying reason to hope for continued good relations, for Mieszko's marriage to a Bohemian Christian princess and his subsequent embrace of the Catholic faith in 966 opened up the possibility of strong bonds of fraternity with other Christian princes.

Otto the Great spent the greatest effort in the last years of his life in trying to make imperial authority in Italy a reality. His son, Otto II (973–83), continued the effort. The second Otto had married a Byzantine princess, and it was probably as a result of his Byzantine connections that he chose to be called Imperator Augustus Romanorum (Emperor Augustus of the Romans) and tried to achieve the kind of control over the ancient imperial capital, Rome, that would add lustre to his claim. But his dreams of uniting Italy under his imperial dominion ended when Muslims inflicted a crushing defeat on his army in 982 in Calabria in southern Italy. Thereafter, even though Muslim ascendancy was ephemeral on the Italian mainland, German imperial authority was confined to central and northern Italy.

The dream of imperial hegemony was not forgotten or abandoned. Otto II's son, the third Otto (983–1002), was only three years old when his father died, and his succession owed much to the ability of his Greek mother, Theophano, who became regent. The boy himself appears to have been fascinated by things Byzantine and imperial, and when he came into his own continued to augment the trappings of German imperial rule. The palace he caused to be constructed in Rome evoked this dream, and by temporarily bending the bitter factions in the city to his will, he went a long way towards fulfilling his father's hope that control of Rome would enhance the imperial stature of the sovereign and renew the Roman Empire (*renovatio imperii romanorum*). Otto III also tried to rule in the Byzantine manner, by adopting ceremonies and rites from the Eastern imperial court as his own.

The emperor promoted his claim to universal rulership by an array of titles he appropriated to himself. To be styled 'servant of Jesus Christ' and 'servant of the apostles' was nothing less than to claim equality with the pope, the 'heir of St Peter the Apostle', the 'vicar of Christ [*or* of God]', the 'servant of the servants of God' – all pontifical titles that went back to the seventh century or before. Otto III aimed at a collaborative co-dominium with the pope over the bodies and souls of all the faithful of Christ.

Along with the trappings of imperial rulership went policies meant to enlarge the ecclesiastical compass of the emperor's power. And here the views of a substantial number of zealous missionary churchmen who sought the Slavs' conversion and risked martyrdom for it (St Adalbert of Prague got his wish in 997 at the hands of the pagan Prussians) played a major role in Otto III's thinking. The situation with regard to Poland is a case in point. Despite Mieszko of Poland's conversion in 966, ferocious wars between Germany and Poland occurred in the reign of Otto II, to the Germans' serious disadvantage. It was the pious young emperor Otto III who remade the eastern policy when he came into his own.

Otto III seems to have imagined himself standing above petty rivalries in order to pursue a higher goal of Christian unity. That goal, which he affirmed with many of his ecclesiastical advisers, like the future martyr Adalbert, implied that the primary duty of a Christian emperor was to spread the Catholic faith. To this end, supporting Mieszko in his efforts to convert the Polish population at large took pride of place over the military confrontations in his predecessor's reign that threatened to delay or even put in jeopardy the full christianization of Poland. Otto III had a mystical streak. His zeal for conversion found its natural expression in an almost priestly solicitation for the Poles and their spiritual health. By ecclesiastical standards his was a noble dream, of sorts, but it provoked a conservative reaction in Germany that took strength from the lack of direction after the young emperor's early death and from the fact that this reaction cohered with the sentiments of Otto's successor, a collateral heir from the Bavarian branch of the royal family, Henry II (1002–24).

Part of Henry's hesitation in pursuing Otto's goal was the uncertain character of his governance in Germany itself, the territory that continued to provide the bulk of royal income from estates and various fiscal rights. Despite all the creative efforts of the Ottonian monarchs, many of the powers that might have been thought to inhere in the king-emperor as of right in Italy remained in the hands of local potentates, who in good times, as reckoned by the Crown, were kept in check by the monarchs and their retainers ceaselessly on the move in displays of their authority. The relationships of power between the Crown and these potentates was not seen, by the former, as written in stone; the eleventh-century German kings – Henry II was no exception – persisted in trying to reconfigure conditions more in their favour.

In Germany itself, their principal rivals, as they would have seen them, were the dukes, who, though clearly in a subordinate relationship to the Crown because of its political and military successes in the tenth century, remained powerful. An older historiography describes the tension between the magnates and the Crown as intractable and at the very centre of German politics. It makes of the magnates, by trivializing differences among them, a more coherent opposition than they were or than they were considered to be at the time by the Crown. But the existence of rivalries between Crown and magnates, which was quite real, did not mean that there was no community of interests. Both Crown and magnates had a monumental stake in social peace, and magnates accepted – to varying degrees – the claims of the Crown to spiritual leadership. Moreover, both magnates and Crown recognized that there had to be a fixed set of hierarchical relations and obligations among them.

Power, legitimately exercised, depended on some mutual recognition of the proper spheres of influence of various potentates. But the distribution of power, as already remarked, was not set in stone. In those troubled borderlands with the Slavs new German families rose to prominence, as they carved out villages and estates, while other families fell. The ups and downs of the Billungs and collateral branches of that lineage in the so-called March of the Billungs, east of Saxony proper, are revelatory. Favoured by the king, the Billungs displaced an old ducal family that opposed the Ottonians. Accumulating properties, they became local magnates of great power, whose interests then sometimes ran counter to the centralizing practices of the Crown. Rival factions within the family, sensing opportunities in the instability, vied for authority in an ever-changing mix of characters violently seeking power.

Many families had less violent histories, but all sought to augment their resources. Some by preference invested their resources in the founding of new monasteries, thus anchoring their power in the prestige of nurturing the Catholic faith and in the material benefits that accrued from the economic growth that these monasteries brought from the introduction of new or enhanced modes of exploitation in the (sometimes undeveloped, sometimes newly conquered) lands given over to them. The founding of monastic establishments under aristocratic patronage in Germany was nothing short of a revolution in the eleventh century. By the end of the century hundreds of new houses were in existence; indeed, the number of monasteries appears to have tripled.

If it is wrong, then, to see the rivalry of the magnates and the Crown as always dominating the mental universe of German princes, and if it is equally wrong to think of the rivalry as unmitigated in its intensity and uniform in its character, it remains the case that German history in the eleventh century exhibits a number of flashpoints when the unity of the German kingdom seemed to be threatened. And it was the vested interests of the magnates in competition with the vested interests of the Crown that made these moments of social tension so dangerous.

External uncertainties, like the perceived threat of Poland, only complicated matters further. Henry II may have believed that his military confrontation with Poland spoke to German aristocratic sentiment more approvingly than Otto III's morally noble pacific policies, but he underestimated the Poles' capacity to resist the imperial onslaught. In a series of three wars, in fact, the Poles established their independence; in 1025, almost surely with papal approval and with the objections of Henry II laid to rest with his death the year before, Poland became a kingdom under Mieszko's eldest son, Boleslaw. Unfortunately for the Poles, Boleslaw died a few months later, in June of 1025, and was succeeded by a younger son whose claim was disputed. Poland descended into anarchy, a usurper renounced the royal title, and lordly violence coupled with a peasant rebellion led to a pagan revival. In the event, the imperial authorities succeeded in bringing their influence to bear by supporting the royal line of Casimir I (1034–58), known as the Restorer because he fostered the rechristianization of Poland. But Polish–German tension remained a major factor in the international politics of northern Europe and would have significant effects on the internal histories of both kingdoms in the decades to come. Of course, this story is intimately related to another, the great struggle between the emperors and the popes over the nature of royal and papal power, the Investiture Controversy, and may best be considered in that context (see chapter 6).

HUNGARY

A steppe people who spoke an Ugrian or central Asiatic language, the Magyars had definitively abandoned their nomadic ways after Otto the Great's effective defeat of their forces in 955 at the battle of the Lechfeld, a site on the River Lech, a tributary of the Danube, in the very shadow of the ancient city of Augsburg (a Roman foundation). Unlike the small and rather more typical raiding parties, the army that the soon-to-be Roman emperor Otto I crushed was huge and assembled from the full array of Magyar tribes. The clan chiefs had concluded, no doubt from the predictions of their shamans, that fortune would bless their enterprise. The 'luckless' Magyars were therefore deeply disturbed by the defeat, for in the mental universe of the nomadic steppe peoples, fortune was like a god or goddess. To lose and to lose so decisively was similar to becoming bereft of the mandate of heaven. And there were no easy major victories to be had in the aftermath of the defeat to recover the luck. To the south-east of the Hungarian plain the Byzantines might be bested in a skirmish here or there, but their own material defences were generally strong and they maintained defensive alliances that helped keep the Magyars at bay. They also, through bribery, managed to sow dissension among the chieftains of the various Magyar tribes.

The Magyars, the name of one clan among many, had long occupied the Hungarian plain, an appellation that derives from another name the tribesmen bore, Onogur. This became the core territory of their settlement, and to some extent maps nicely onto the modern map of Europe as the small country of Hungary. But the medieval kingdom, at its height, was far larger, overspreading additional areas now belonging to Slovakia, Ukraine, Rumania and Croatia. Much of the land, the great plain, was very suitable for agriculture and horse culture, but it was ringed by mountains like the Carpathians and the Balkans that provided some natural defences for the agricultural pursuits of the newly settled population, whose size was still less than one million in the early eleventh century. And there were natural resources, like salt, from which steady income could be obtained by clan chieftains to supplement the wealth from crops and raising horses.

The Hungarian monarchy was not that much younger than the empire of Charlemagne which the Ottonians claimed as their lineage, since the Árpádian dynasty, chieftains of a clan that came to dominate Magyar society, dates from at least 875. However, as noted, the territorial character and early geographical limits of the realm were confirmed by military defeat only with the battle of Lechfeld, and the monarchy took on Christian trappings later still. An usurper, Stephen I (St Stephen [997–1038]), the first fully Christian king, was consecrated in a ceremony on 1 January 1001 or perhaps a week earlier, on Christmas Day 1000, with a crown and other regalia, including a lance, sent from Rome that came with the joint blessing of the German emperor and the pope.

The Hungarian rule of succession, on the death of a grand prince, favoured the oldest closely related prince, not necessarily the grand prince's own offspring. Stephen, the son of Grand Prince Geza and the Transylvanian princess, Sarolt, known as 'The White Lady', nonetheless seized power from Koppány, his older pagan kinsman, and in the aftermath proved himself to be a gifted ruler whose personal devotion to Latin Christianity far exceeded his father's nominal regard for the religion. Stephen was nearly unmatched – for the time and in so recently converted a kingdom – in his feverish effort to establish the essential institutional underpinnings of the Catholic faith. Esztergom, the site of the coronation, became, with papal permission, an archbishop's see, and four more bishoprics were established by 1010. The king typically employed Latin prelates brought from abroad and therefore absolutely dependent on his goodwill to rule the new sees and the major monasteries. As in Anglo-Saxon England, the church in Hungary became an integral part of the state.

Politically, Stephen moved against rivals, some of whom were pagan, some Orthodox Christians, but all of whom opposed both his attachment to papally sponsored evangelization in Hungary and his broader plans for consolidation of his power and the Church's, which required widespread confiscations of property. These confiscations followed Stephen's usurpation but instituted long-standing plans of his pagan predecessors to consolidate tribal lands under their control. In a series of savage campaigns (1003–8), including one that put an end to the deposed Koppány (he was pitilessly hacked to death, possibly at the grisly insistence of Stephen's mother, Sarol the White Lady), Stephen silenced the opposition. For twenty years afterwards he was virtually without open opponents inside Hungary.

Stephen's borders were less secure. To be sure, his relations with the Empire seemed stable and pacific enough. His wife, Gisela, was the daughter of Henry, the duke of Bavaria, and the sister of Emperor Henry II. The royal couple chose to name their son and putative heir Imre, the Hungarian version of Henry, as a symbolic reminder of their tie to the imperial family. Moreover, five years after their marriage in 995, Stephen, as we have seen, received his crown with imperial acquiescence. Nevertheless, disputes with a subsequent emperor, Conrad II, undermined relations between the two countries and provoked the latter to invade Hungary in 1030.

To the north-east and east, military pressure both from Poland and from pagan Pecheneg tribesmen threatened the borderlands of the kingdom. In the case of Poland, the intermittent fighting was part and parcel of attempts on the part of the Polish princes to escape imperial control and expand their influence towards Bohemia and southwards, where they came into conflict with the Hungarians. In the case of the Pechenegs, the situation was even more complicated.

The Pechenegs, a confederation of Turkic-speaking tribes, had come across the Eurasian steppe more than a century before the christianization of Hungary, and indeed had accompanied the nomadic and pagan Magyars as allies. They fought skirmishes and wars with any number of their neighbours – nomadic and sedentary alike – including the Khazars, a heterogeneous mix of peoples of Iranian and Turkic origin, who created a kingdom whose ruling family converted to Judaism. But they also fought the Byzantines and the Russians as well. By the early eleventh century, while Stephen ruled in Hungary and partly because of the pressures of other military forces on them further east, the Pechenegs made inroads into the relatively newly acquired Transylvanian provinces of Stephen's kingdom, provinces which the king had seized early in his reign from Prince Gyula, one of his Orthodox Christian uncles.

Despite the continuing border troubles, it is fair to say that within the heartland of Hungary, much of Stephen's reign was a period of remarkable peace, and even an anxious and bitter peace such as that imposed by his iron hand encouraged the flourishing of administrative institutions and of culture in a more general sense. Territorial governments were carefully put in place, and in each, whether on the borders or in the heartland, a careful allotment of landed property was made to the Crown's advantage, while also rewarding the king's loyal subjects with whatever confiscated lands were available. Each of the territorial governments was supervised by a count in matters judicial, commercial (fairs), fiscal (estate management), and – especially in the border territories – military. As in Normandy and Anjou in contemporary northwestern Europe, the castles that served as the administrative and defensive centres of all of these territories were held directly by the ruler.

With government came the normative texts of governance. One of the earliest 'Mirrors of Princes' – handbooks on ideal rulership which would emerge as a major genre of political writing all over Europe in the next three centuries – seems to date from or soon after Stephen's reign. Stephen issued codes of laws, or codes were quickly attributed to him, that rival those of the Anglo-Saxons in their comprehensiveness, with protections for the Church, elaborate requirements of *wergild* and other forms of punishment, and penalties for witches and wizards. Like Cnut of Denmark, who adopted from Anglo-Saxon practice the minting of royal coins as a mode of unification in Denmark, Stephen also introduced royal coins as an assertion of his status as ruler of all Hungary.

Meanwhile, the king continued to endow bishoprics and monasteries, calling on reformers from the West, like the monks from the German monastery at Gorze, to help direct the effort. He encouraged the establishment of parishes and the building of parish churches. His chief subjects supported the nascent church with their own endowments both in imitation of the Crown's policies and because of their own deepening commitment to Catholic Christianity. Northern European pilgrims and, later, crusaders found the land route through Hungary to points east to their liking, and Stephen and his successors supported the pilgrimage movement, including the foundation of pilgrim hostels as far distant as Rome and Jerusalem, with as much fervour as they increasingly did many other forms of Catholic devotion. Odilo, the abbot of Cluny, expressed the gratitude of Christendom ('almost the whole world') in a letter to King Stephen: 'Almost the whole world speaks of how great the passion in your soul is in honour of our divine religion, especially those who returned from the tomb of Our Lord bear witness to you' (Gyorffy, 1994, p. 89).

As in all eleventh-century kingdoms and lesser principalities, it was the succession that would test the institutions and traditions of unity and cohesion that founders like King Stephen initiated. It remained unclear how great the potential for a pagan revival and the devolution of power in Hungary was. The chieftains' and counts' commitment to Catholic Christianity was encouraging but still recent. The commitment of ordinary men and women would be a completely open question if the pressure for christianization emanating from the Crown were to relax. Castles that provided nodes of monarchical control in the countryside under Stephen could easily become centres of independent authority if royal governance faltered. To this extent, everything appeared to rest on the shoulders of Imre, Stephen's son. If Imre, who seems to have shared his father's vision of the Catholic kingdom, had lived, stability might have been maintained. But Imre died in a hunting accident in 1031, and the last years of Stephen's life were tainted by lingering illness, mourning for Imre, and brooding over whom he should name as heir.

His suspicions of his nearer kinsmen motivated him to name Peter Orseolo, the son of the doge of Venice and his own nephew, as his successor, a choice that prompted rather than averted a succession crisis. Twice deposed, Peter could never provide effective leadership, and various factions within the royal family vied for power over the next several decades. Such strife precipitated both principled and opportunistic intervention by other territorial lords, notably the German emperors, who now had familial ties with so many of the Hungarian noble class. But these interventions, meant to protect German territorial and imperial family interests, never brought a decisive end to internal conflicts. They merely escalated the level of violence.

Two major popular rebellions also revealed deep social fissures in the country. The first, in 1046, was a pagan and new-Christian uprising against the fiscal obligations laid on the laity by Stephen and his ecclesiastical advisers. Its savagery was manifested by the execution of a number of high churchmen. The second, in 1061, is not considered primarily a pagan revival, for the successful repression of the rebels of 1046 had broken the back of the pagan party in Hungary. Instead, those sources that tell us what little we know about the rebellion of 1061 speak of it as an uprising of peasants, rural folk under the heavy obligations that necessarily came from supporting military defence, paying for the Church, and giving up so much of their surplus to lords and administrators. This rebellion was also put down, but it revealed the profound and enduring social cleavages of Hungarian society.

Hungary did not emerge from the kind of civil strife characterized by dynastic warfare and popular rebellion effectively until well after the mid-eleventh century. When it did so, however, it turned out that Stephen's work had been well done. The infrastructure of christianization remained in place: parishes were still served in most areas by parish priests, even if their property had been violated. Despite the evidence of pagan strength in 1046, the majority of Hungarians do seem sincerely to have accepted the Catholic faith even by that date. Despite the rebellion of 1061 and the social fissures it laid bare, later kings drew on Stephen's legacy to articulate a strong ideology of Hungarian unity and specialness. Under King Ladislas I (1077–95) efforts were made to reform the laws and improve economic life. Ladislas was effective, too, in rallying his people against the Cumans and other pagan steppe barbarians who threatened them. Under him and his successor King Coloman (1095–1116), Hungary also embarked on a successful period of territorial expansion into Croatia, eventually annexing the whole country. By the year 1100 it appeared that the luck, now in Christian rather than pagan form, had returned to the Magyar peoples of Hungary.

CODA

In the north of Europe as in the south, as we have observed in these first few chapters, common bonds of Catholic Christianity established the existence of an entity that for convenience one can call Latin Christendom, but the ties that bound the many cultures in the many polities of eleventh-century Europe were tenuous and fragile. Large parts of the north lurched back and forth from Christianity to paganism or threatened to do so. In the south it was not self-evident that Muslim power had begun a steady decline or that Byzantine power would inevitably recede in the central Mediterranean. For most of the period papal claims to spiritual overlordship, though not hollow, were undermined by scandals and subservience to the dominant issues of Italian familial and territorial politics.

All this changed in the next few decades. The world of Latin Christendom began to be remade in earnest. The radical nature of the transformation, 'the reformation of the twelfth century', as it has been called (Constable, 1996), is addressed in the next section.

PART II

THE RENAISSANCE OF
THE TWELFTH CENTURY

The phrase 'Renaissance of the twelfth century' achieved currency as a result of the work of Charles Homer Haskins, an American medievalist who used it as the title for a book describing the revival of learned Latin culture in the period 1050 to 1250. Haskins devoted little space to material culture, politics or vernacular literature but was well aware of the monumental changes that were occurring in these areas as well. He chose the word 'renaissance' partly to emphasize the renewed interest in the sophistication of Latin poetry and prose, an interest that harked back to a still earlier revival in the Carolingian period of the eighth and ninth centuries. But partly he wanted to make the polemical point that the Italian Renaissance was not quite so extraordinary as many of its enthusiasts who disparaged the Middle Ages made out. It was an appropriate and opportune moment (1927) to set out this argument.

Its polemical resonance now considerably softened, the phrase 'Renaissance of the twelfth century' – if we accept the breadth of the dating favoured by Haskins, acknowledge the new as well as the renewed in the period, and factor in reforms in religious life and vernacular culture – is an apt description of the era we shall now be exploring.

6

The Investiture Controversy

Emperor Henry III (1039–56) was responsible for the election of his kinsman, Bruno of Egisheim, as Pope Leo IX in 1049, and his intention was clear. He would support Leo's efforts to reform the clergy in order to root out the vice of simony and the practice of clerical marriage and concubinage. Scholars have sometimes seen these as matters of internal reform. Clerics were to put their own house in order, but the emperor, it is frequently alleged, had neither the expectation nor the wish that they should modify the traditional arrangements between secular and spiritual authorities in doing so.

This does not make sense, or, rather, it beggars logic. The emperor was a sincere reformer and devout Catholic who desired the purification of the Church as an institution. He also wanted to ensure that his customary relations with the upper clergy, where these fitted his vision of a right-ordered Christendom, should continue in place. Where customs and habits transgressed this vision, he wanted them abolished. In part he supported the struggle against simony and clerical marriage and concubinage in order to weaken the grip of Roman and other Italian families on ecclesiastical offices, offices which they treated like heritable property and which gave them inordinate territorial power, at least in comparison with that of imperial officials.

The problem was how far a campaign of this sort should go. Should it have as its aim the suppression of all lay control of the Church, even that of the emperor or of any anointed or, for that matter, unanointed prince? Were such rulers – by God's grace His governors on earth – laymen at all? 'The powers that be are ordained of God,' the Apostle Paul had written (Romans 13:1). If the apostle could say this of the pagan rulers with whom he was concerned, how much more appropriate was it to the Christian kings who succeeded them and many of whom were anointed with holy oil like priests on the head, breast, shoulders and brachial joints at the time of their coronation or inauguration? Such men were transformed, at least in theory. They became new Davids, new Solomons, indeed, by unction, new Christs (*christus* means anointed one). 'We thus have to recognize' the king, wrote one anonymous author, as 'a *twin person*, one descending from nature, the other from grace . . . One through which, by the condition of nature, he conformed with other men: another through which, by the eminence of [his] deification and by the power of the sacrament [of consecration], he excelled all others. Concerning one personality, he was, by nature, an individual man: concerning his other personality, he was, by grace, a *Christus*, that is, a God-man' (Kantorowicz, 1957, p. 46).

Some of the theorists asserted that, like Christ, the candidate for Christian rulership became both king and priest, after grace leaped into him at his anointment during the coronation ceremony. The coronation was therefore an essentially religious act, a sacrament or vehicle of grace – or nearly so. Occasions for crown-wearing in the lifetime of the monarch were religious rites performed on the higher Christian feast days, like Christmas, Easter and Pentecost (the anniversary of the descent of the Holy Spirit to the apostles and the foundation of the Church). The praises of Christ (*laudes Christi*) were appropriate for the praises of the king (*laudes regiae*). Specific liturgical practices, like the chanting of *laudes regiae* in the king's presence and for him during the worship service played exquisitely upon the analogy '*Christus vincit! Christus regnat! Christus imperat!*' ('Christ conquers! Christ reigns! Christ commands!') What powers could be denied God's representative on earth, anointed like Christ, both king and priest? 'Fear God; honour the king' (1 Peter 2:17). The medieval political theology described here, which draws heavily on the biblical texts quoted, has sometimes been characterized as liturgical kingship, because of its presentation in sources that describe or prescribe the practices of Christian worship.

In the early stages of reform, down to Henry III's death in 1056, the implications of this theory for the king's authority and power within the Church were less repugnant to ecclesiastical reformers than they became later. Indeed, the struggle for reform did not properly become the 'Investiture Controversy' until the reforming party within the Church insisted that the emperor's authority, though always exceptional in comparison to that of other lay rulers (he claimed, after all, to be the successor to Charlemagne), was essentially and irredeemably laical with regard to the Church.

This consensus, even among radical reformers, emerged gradually. The bitter fight between Emperor Henry IV (1056–1106) and Pope Gregory VII (1073–85) provided the most important political context for the articulation of the radicals' views, even if that fight also in the interim blocked the translation of the papal programme into practice. Only in the early twelfth century, and indeed in conflict with still another emperor, Henry V (1106–25), did the papal reform party partly succeed in its campaign, with consequences that helped shape the course of imperial and papal history for centuries.

*

By the time Emperor Henry III died in 1056 he had, to all intents and purposes, appointed the four most recent popes. All had served him loyally in the German Church, and all are regarded as reformers, although they did not necessarily favour the same reforms, pursue them with the same single-mindedness of purpose or always act in ways that suited other reformers. Leo IX (1049–54), for instance, received other reformers' praise for his actions against simony and his denunciations of clerical service at arms, but many reformers, like the austere hermit and from 1057 Cardinal Peter Damian, found repugnant his willingness to lead papal forces in 1053 in a military campaign against the Normans in southern Italy. That the pope was taken prisoner, albeit swiftly released, only made his conduct the more scandalous. Nonetheless, there was real continuity between the pontificates of Leo IX, his two immediate predecessors, and his successor, and this continuity owed a great deal to the reforming vision, guidance and zeal of Emperor Henry III.

Thus, when Henry died there was bound to be an impact of more or less significance on the history of the papacy, but the fact that the emperor's successor, Henry IV, was a boy of six made the transition particularly stressful. For Henry III, as one can surmise from what has already been written, had been determined to control aristocratic forces not only in Italy but in Germany as well. His treatment of Duke Godfrey of Lorraine in 1044 is instructive. The duke, angered at being granted only Upper Lorraine rather than the entire duchy of Lorraine, rebelled against the emperor in that year, but was checked militarily and then, as punishment, was denied Upper Lorraine as well.

Even while the old emperor lived there were dangers from the chastened baron, who rebelled again in 1047 and continued to stir up trouble in Italy, where he took up residence in the early 1050s. In the wake of the emperor's death, aristocratic forces grew bolder. It was the paramount duty of the succession of regents for the young emperor to do as much as possible to prevent or contain the aristocratic reaction. As the power base of the monarchy was rooted in the dynastic holdings around Goslar in Germany, inevitably most of the attention of those who wanted the monarchy to survive was focused on preserving that power base in Germany. In the event, the reform party at Rome was forced to fend for itself.

The reformers used the imperial crisis as an opportunity to ensure the continuity of their programme, unfettered by the fortunes of imperial authority. They did so by articulating arguments in favour of the independence of papal elections and then issuing an authoritative decree to this effect in 1059 at the Synod of Rome. The assembled clergy vested the right of election in the cardinals, the Church's chief dignitaries after the pope. As a corporation this group, still very small in the eleventh century, came to be known as the college of cardinals.

Faced, like the imperial regents, with an aristocracy trying to reassert its powers, the papal reform party also formulated more radical statements of the independence of the Church from lay authority. It was in the year of the decrees on papal election by cardinals (1059) that the papacy denounced laymen's ceremonial investiture of clerics with churches, a denunciation reiterated in 1063. Clearly encouraging these moves was Hildebrand, the future Pope Gregory VII, along with other clergy. But these general denunciations and prohibitions, important as they certainly were, paled in comparison to the reformers' efforts to impose their own candidate on the archiepiscopal see of Milan in northern Italy.

Perhaps control of Milan was not the one and only key to the domination of northern Italy, but it was certainly one of the more important. The city had enormous dignity as the historic bishopric of the great church father of antiquity, Ambrose. It commanded additional prestige inasmuch as its archbishop was the prelate who crowned the German king as king of Italy with the iron crown of Lombardy. And, in simple geographical terms, Milan was in the very heart of northern Italy's most fertile and productive region, a fact that inspired wave after wave of invaders in the earlier Middle Ages to try to bring the city under their sway.

It was the Ottonian rulers of Germany who had most recently subdued the city, doing so in alliance with the archbishop, on whom the trappings of Carolingian authority rested. The process had not been easy: ethnic hostility between Germans and Italians was alarming. The old Lombard capital, Pavia, was a hotbed of resistance to Ottonian authority, although it too was brought into submission in the course of time. The support of the archbishop of Milan, who was allowed to develop an extensive network of military dependents (*capitanei*) on church lands in the hinterland of the city, was considered essential to the security of imperial power in northern Italy and a necessary counterweight to Pavia. But the archbishops of the early eleventh century, though the emperors' loyal partisans, were also notorious simoniacs.

Under Emperor Henry II (1002–24) and without a reformer on the papal throne, this situation did not present a crisis, but matters degenerated late in the reign of Emperor Conrad II (1024–39). The usefulness of the archbishop depended on his capacity to control the region around Milan in the emperor's interest. A revolt in 1035 while the incumbent, Archbishop Aribert, was on an imperial mission threw that capacity into doubt. The rebels were minor lords who chafed under the domination and condescension of the archbishop's *capitanei*. Their representatives tried to persuade the emperor that his archbishop was exploiting and exacerbating the ethnic conflicts between Germans and Italians, to the Germans' detriment. Whatever Conrad's real feelings about these charges, he clearly believed that it was necessary to soften the distinction between the highly privileged *capitanei* and the lesser lords who were in rebellion, and he did so in a decree of 1037 that granted the latter the rights of nobles.

Archbishop Aribert defied the proclamation and in retaliation put together an anti-imperial party intent on preserving the *status quo ante*. The early days of the reign of Henry III saw tentative gestures meant to defuse the crisis, but the whole situation exploded in 1042 when mercantile and artisanal groups in Milan expelled the archbishop and his anti-imperial retainers from the city.

A compromise worked out in 1044 did not last. Politics in Milan was a bizarre cacophony of clashing forces: the townsmen in a sworn commune or conspiracy opposed the again resident archbishop and his noble supporters, and the spectre of imperial intercession hovered in the wings. During all of this time, it needs to be recalled, the emperor remained convinced that the key to the domination of northern Italy lay in restoring and maintaining some sort of workable alliance between himself and the archbishop. A pliant and dependable archbishop was a necessity.

In fact, the situation degenerated further under Aribert's successor, Guido of Velate, who became archbishop in 1045, a year before the first of the German-sponsored reform popes ascended the papal throne. Archbishop Guido was a simoniac of the old school, and he faced determined opposition from so-called *patarini* who, inspired by the reformers' programme, preached against simony as well as clerical marriage and concubinage in Milan. The word *patarini*, 'ragpickers', was an epithet applied to these local reformers by their opponents. Unwilling to see either the compromise of 1044, with its restrictions on the archbishop, or the ragpickers' programme bear fruit, the simoniacal Guido found himself and his noble and ecclesiastical supporters and their forces at odds with the communards, lesser nobles and the defenders of the *patarini* in a horrifying eruption of violence.

After the death of Emperor Henry III in 1056, the hope of an arbitrated settlement brokered by the Crown or the imperial regents steadily diminished. Instead, it was the pope who sent a delegation of reform-minded clerics, including Hildebrand and the Milanese bishop of Lucca, Anselm of Baggio, to arbitrate the dispute. The truce they negotiated was always tenuous and internal violence flared from time to time. To what extent Archbishop Guido had a hand in the violence is in dispute, but he chafed from the reformers' condemnation of him as a simoniac and may not have been displeased when the leader of the *patarini* was killed in 1066. Guido resigned the archbishopric the next year, on first impression a statesmanlike gesture, but he did so in the time-honoured way. He sold it to a would-be aspirant to whom Emperor Henry IV, still coming into his own after the regency, had no objection. When the emperor officially confirmed the transfer of power, there was anger among reformers in Milan and in Rome who had believed that they could rely on the emperor to oppose simony, but no argument could persuade Henry to withdraw his support of his new archbishop. In an open act of defiance in 1072, reform clergy and people in Milan thus elected an archbishop on their own. And the same Anselm of Baggio, since 1061 Pope Alexander II, who had been a negotiator between the factions in Milan and had continuously laboured to have the emperor come over to the reformers' view on the Milanese see, ratified the reformers' choice.

It was not for Alexander but for his successor, Gregory VII (1073–85), to see the situation enter a still more dangerous phase: civil war in

Milan, the killing of the new head of the *patarini*, and the emperor's refusal to give in to the reformers' demands. Indeed, the emperor's decision to replace the simoniac incumbent with an imperial appointee rather than with the reform candidate was perceived more as a challenge than as a gesture of reconciliation.

The new pope, who had been swept into office on a wave of enthusiasm for ecclesiastical liberty and renewal, but in a perhaps not procedurally canonical election, a fact that would be of enormous significance later on, began to articulate a fuller programme of reform. In December 1074 he had already forbidden married priests in Germany to perform the sacraments, and in February of 1075 he prohibited lay investiture. The emperor, in alliance with the majority of German bishops, most of whom owed their offices to him, denounced the papal decrees. Sometime during the year 1075 clerks at the papal court drew up the *Dictatus Papae*, a list of privileges and powers attributed to popes in ancient and early medieval documents.

Though hardly an official pronouncement, the *Dictatus* may be read as the expression of a revolutionary challenge to the existing political and ecclesiastical order. The document asserts, among other things, that 'only the pope might use imperial insignia', that 'all princes must kiss the feet of the pope and his alone', and that 'it is licit for the pope to depose emperors' (Cowdrey, 1998, pp. 504–7). Perhaps with this reading in mind Gregory sent a letter on 8 December 1075 demanding that the emperor do penance or face removal for opposing the papal decrees.

Henry IV reacted by putting even greater pressure on the bishops in Germany, and with the willing co-operation of some of their rank, he denounced Gregory on 27 January as a false monk and declared his procedurally dubious election as pope null and void. Perhaps more a threat than an intention to convoke dissident prelates to elect a new pope, the imperial response could not be taken lightly, since emperors had so often made and unmade popes in the recent past. Gregory chose to stand firm, and only a matter of a few weeks later, during Lent 1076, he excommunicated Henry IV, thus cutting him off from the Catholic sacraments and making it a sin for others to support him.

It was not absolutely certain until June, except perhaps in Gregory's mind, that this excommunication had any genuine hope of success. On the twenty-ninth of that month, an ironically appropriate date as the Feast of the Apostles Peter and Paul, the patron saints of the Holy See, those German bishops who were still supporting Henry retaliated by excommunicating the pope. The good news for Gregory was that several German bishops dissented from this course of action and defected, not necessarily with enthusiasm, to the papal cause or at least to neutrality. Moreover, many of Henry's political adversaries seized the opportunity to justify their taking up of arms against him as an unholy king.

The autumn of 1076 was given over to jockeying for position, with the emperor coming to recognize that his position was becoming an increasingly vulnerable one. If civil war came, it would decisively undermine his authority in Germany and Italy in the short run, even if, in the end, he overcame his opponents. Moreover, victory over the opposition in war was only a probable, not necessarily an inevitable, first step towards re-establishing the kind of control of or working relationship with the Roman pope that had functioned so well in the reign of his father. In imperial circles, therefore, the thrust of opinion was in favour of averting full-scale military confrontation by reaching some sort of compromise with the pope.

While Gregory VII was at Canossa in the Tuscan Alps in the winter of 1077, Henry IV arrived and played the role of the penitent pilgrim. For three days in late January he appeared barefoot in the snow, begging forgiveness. Shrewd politics might have demanded a different reaction from Gregory, but the pope seemed genuinely to have been moved by the emperor's gesture and received him back into the fold of the Catholic faithful as a repentant sinner. In so doing he undermined the justification for revolt that many disgruntled German aristocrats had invoked against their unholy king. Nevertheless, some magnates joined together to set up their own king in opposition to Henry. Civil war was inevitable.

Hostility from Poland at this critical juncture was a further destabilizing factor in Germany. Since Casimir the Restorer's death in 1058, and building on the relative stability Casimir had brought to the still very weak state he ruled, Poland's new prince, Boleslaw II, the Bold, had striven to recover the glory of the late tenth and early eleventh centuries, when Polish forces had more than matched those of their German imperial adversaries. By the 1070s he had successfully regained some lost territories, brutally brought several important noble families into a tenuous dependence on him, and with ruthless determination strengthened the Church to prevent another pagan revival. The Investiture Controversy provided him an opportunity as well. Boleslaw supported Pope Gregory VII, who in turn gave papal sanction to Boleslaw's coronation as king on Christmas Day 1076.

Neither the Germans nor the disgruntled Poles, who resented their king's efforts to strengthen the Crown at their expense, were willing to tolerate Boleslaw's policies. The history of Poland in the last quarter of the eleventh century is a sorry mess of German threats, civil war, including the deposition and exile of Boleslaw II in 1079, and a series of disputed successions and partitions among claimants to the throne. Finally some semblance of order was restored and stiff resistance was put up to the German military threat under the old king's nephew and namesake, Boleslaw III, the Wry-Mouthed (1097–1138).

Nonetheless, Polish support of the pope's position in the crucial late 1070s at least lifted the reform party's mood while the spirit of peace generated by events at Canossa was fading. Despite Pope Gregory VII's initial neutrality in the German civil war in the aftermath of his dramatic absolution of and apparent reconciliation with Emperor Henry IV, the fundamental issues that divided pope and emperor were not resolved. Quite soon after the poignant scenes at Canossa, imperial–papal relations degenerated once more. The pope felt obliged to renew his excommunication of the emperor and his denunciations of the imperial party, thereby giving fresh life to the coalition of the emperor's enemies. In retaliation the emperor sent military forces against Gregory while at the same time he supported the election of his own candidate as Pope Clement III to replace the 'false monk', Hildebrand. Gregory fled Rome and died in 1085, still unvindicated. It is said that he quoted a verse from Psalms 44:7 (45:7), one repeated in Hebrews 1, as his death approached: 'Thou lovest righteousness, and hatest wickedness: therefore God, thy God, hath anointed thee with the oil of gladness above thy fellows.' On Gregory's lips the triumphant verse became tragic: 'I have loved righteousness and hated wickedness; therefore I die in exile.'

*

Reform was not defined only by the changing, albeit contested, status of the papacy and the clergy. Reform movements, like that of the *patarini* and the Peace and Truce of God, achieved something approaching a popular level. There is no need to separate these genuinely widespread reform impulses, as one historian has done, from elite clergymen's attempts to reform the papacy. Moreover, it is a caricature to say that papal reform was merely a mode of aggrandizement of pontifical authority or that the later phases of the Peace Movement pitted people against clergy, as the clergy allegedly manipulated the desire for peace into a forced recognition of their rights over rustics (Moore, 1996, pp. 24, 33).

Yet it remains the case that the successes and failures of popular reform had their own history. Gregory's failure – as his death in exile would have appeared in 1085 – and the uncertainty whether other kings, like Philip I of France or Ladislas I of Hungary, would obey the decrees on lay investiture did not undermine other forces for spiritual renewal in Christendom. The older orders of monks, like those bound more or less tightly to Cluny, in Burgundy, or to Gorze, on the Moselle, responded to these forces by re-emphasizing or recovering traditional forms of devotion and discipline. Other groups of clergy, known generally as canons, adopted modified but stricter rules of common life in their houses. Houses of Augustinian (or Austin) canons constitute the most famous and probably most widespread example of this development. But what has seemed most remarkable to scholars are two other developments.

First, there is the sheer increase in the number of houses in the century following the onset of the Investiture Controversy. We know that thousands of new men's houses were founded, although scholars are still combing the records to try to get at a definitive figure. Getting a definitive figure for nunneries is even more difficult, given the quality of the documentation. But a conventional estimate sees a fourfold increase in the number of nunneries between 1070 and 1170. In a tiny region like the Sénonais, encompassing the northern French town of Sens and its hinterland, a traveller in 1170 would have admired the great old churches and abbeys, some, like the Benedictine monastery of Saint-Pierre-le-Vif, dating from the period of the original christianization of the Franks. In the landscape of 1070 these churches stood like great, immobile and isolated giants. In 1170 a dazzling array of new foundations transformed this landscape. One could not walk down a country road in the Sénonais without seeing a spire or roof-top cross testifying to the material manifestation of twelfth-century devotion.

The second development that strikes historians powerfully and one that is not unrelated to the increase in overall numbers of monasteries and nunneries is the proliferation of entirely new orders, including the Carthusians, Cistercians and Premonstratensians. Now, in all or almost all cases the new orders stressed organizational austerity and personal asceticism. And all responded to and, in turn, encouraged the cult of the Virgin Mary, devotion to whom was undergoing revolutionary development and expansion. This devotion drew on ancient precedents, but, in synchrony with a contemporary shift in emphasis towards commemorating the human nature of Jesus, including his infancy and his bodily vulnerability, the sentimentalization of the relationship between the Virgin and her son received a strong impetus.

The twelfth century would see a proliferation of stories of the Virgin and her concerns for ordinary people, including her miraculous interventions in their lives and the protection of their faith and morals against the dangers of heresy, fornication and Judaism. It would also see the rise to prominence of other forms of art and devotion that stressed her intercessory role: an explosion of prayers and hymns in her honour, including the 'Ave Maria' or 'Hail Mary', the prayer spoken with the rosary beads (Mary was figuratively the rose) popularized at the turn of the twelfth/thirteenth century by still another new order, the Dominicans (see chapter 13), and culminating in the mid-thirteenth century 'Stabat Mater', a moving hymn that recounted the Virgin's agony in watching her son die on the Cross.

The first house of Carthusians, La Grande Chartreuse, was founded in 1084 by St Bruno with the support of the local bishop of Grenoble. The Alpine setting, the site of Bruno's foundation, replicated the isolation and the emphasis on self-reliance in material matters of the desert fathers, the early monks of the Christian church.

Here [Bruno wrote] we strive for that vision by whose clear gaze the bridegroom is wounded with love, and by whose cleanness and purity God is discerned. Here we practise a working leisure and are stilled in quiet activity. Here God provides his athletes with the desired reward for the labour of combat – a peace which the world does not know, and joy in the Holy Spirit (Mursell, 1988, p. 256).

Like the establishments of those ancient athletes of God, the Egyptian monks, Carthusian houses retained many features which made them seem more like associations of hermits than tightly regimented corporations. The men who entered the order tended to be mature; their decision to accept monastic life was deeply considered. They craved solitude, in general avoided contact with 'the world', and silence was much encouraged and practised. Without entirely rejecting collective activities, they severely limited them in number. Even the lay workers on their estates were obliged to accept the status of *conversi*, converts, of a sort, to the religious regimen. Or perhaps it would be more accurate to say that they sought the status of convert, for they too were men who desired to turn their back on the world, although because of either their lack of education or their sense of their own limitations they did not feel justified in taking full monastic vows. The reputation of Carthusian monks for holiness spread widely. The severely austere life they practised, however, inhibited the proliferation of new houses.

The Cistercians, whose first foundation, Cîteaux in Burgundy, dates from 1098, dedicated every one of their churches to the Virgin. Stressing, like the Carthusians, their desire to reproduce the isolated life of the earliest Christian monks, they too deliberately sited their first monasteries in out-of-the-way places, performed manual labour to clear the lands, and practised forms of devotion that avoided the ornateness of traditional worship. Their churches, ornaments and vestments were plain; gold and polychromatic artifacts were shunned. The habit or monastic dress they wore was pure white (hence the name, 'White Monks') with only a short black cape worn as a wide, soft scapular or shoulder covering.

The Cistercians' infiltration across the European landscape was more pronounced than that of the Carthusians, partly because of the less isolating nature of their living arrangements, partly because of their relative willingness to take younger recruits than the Carthusians did, and partly because, in the person of Bernard of Clairvaux, their most celebrated member, the fame of the order attracted recruits. By the year 1150 there were well over 300 affiliated houses planted across the map of Christendom, most with *conversi* who worked with and for the monks in clearing lands, growing crops, and herding flocks of sheep.

The attraction of the Cistercians' austere piety cut across gender lines. Women, one male ecclesiastical observer wrote in about 1150, 'of their own free will embraced violently, nay joyfully, the Order of Cîteaux, which many robust men and youths fear to enter. Laying aside all linen garments and furs, they wore only woollen tunics. They did not only women's work, such as spinning and weaving, but they went out and worked the fields, digging, cutting down and uprooting the forest with axe and mattock, tearing up thorns and briars, labouring assiduously with their hands and seeking their food in silence. Imitating in all things the monks of Clairvaux, they proved the truth of the Lord's saying, that to the believer all things are possible' (Evergates, 1999, p. 105). In 1150 this was genuinely *imitation*. The Cistercian leadership opposed the creation of a female division of the order, although grudgingly and under continuing papal pressure they later allowed houses of nuns (along with their *convers[a]e*, female servants) to affiliate. These, like all the houses of the order, were subject to rigorous regular investigations called visitations, intended to ensure the moral integrity of the monks, nuns, *conversi* and *converse*.

The order of Premonstratensian canons had a more complicated history. Founded around 1120 by St Norbert of Xanten, a man who had had a spiritual awakening from a life of worldly concerns, it adopted a modified form of the Augustinian rule and right from the beginning welcomed clergy, laymen and laywomen. These flocked in numbers to Norbert, a charismatic preacher, whose career took him from Prémontré in northern France, where he established the first community, to Magdeburg, where he died while serving as archbishop. Norbert's method was to whip up local enthusiasm and then establish a house for men in close proximity to another for women, with both sexes worshipping together in the same church. After his death in 1134, this form of organization petered out, and the prominent presence of canonesses faded as well. Nonetheless, the Premonstratensians were always more in the world than their Carthusian and Cistercian counterparts, ministering especially to the needs of the poor.

*

The religious ferment and the diversity of impulses represented by the movements for renewal in the older orders and the proliferation of newer ones, of which the Carthusians, Cistercians and Premonstratensians are only three of many, testify to the intensity of interest in revivifying the Church as a whole. In this sense, the unresolved conflicts of the Investiture Controversy continued to prick the consciences of principled clergy and lay persons. The violence associated with the Controversy only served to underline the need to reach a settlement as expeditiously as possible. But the conflicts seemed for a long time to defy resolution.

With Pope Gregory VII's death in 1085, the upper hand temporarily lay with Emperor Henry IV, but he and the anti-pope he supported met their match in the reformist claimant to the pontifical throne, Urban II (1088–99), who began an energetic campaign to promote the Gregorian position. But Urban was not Gregory VII's immediate successor. That honour fell to a man of immense European stature, Desiderius, the abbot of Montecassino, perhaps the most prestigious monastery in all of western Christendom, the monastery of St Benedict himself, the chief force in the establishment of monasticism in Europe. Taking the name Victor III, the great abbot had not been fated to wear the papal tiara for long, but on his sickbed he gave his blessing to a Frenchman in his mid-sixties who had held various important ecclesiastical posts, including archdeacon of Reims, prior of the abbey of Cluny and, under Gregory VII, cardinal-bishop of Ostia.

As Urban II, this new pope embarked on an extraordinary series of travels meant to rally the cause. He ventured to Rome, left, later returned, travelled, holding councils at various times all through France and Italy as part of his efforts. It was at one of these councils, at Clermont in 1095, that he gave the first of a series of sermons on the theme of sending military aid to Christians troubled by Muslims in the East, which ushered in the crusades (see chapter 7). He also enlisted the support of the wisest man of Christendom, St Bruno, the pope's former teacher and the founder of the Carthusian order, who travelled to Rome during Urban's pontificate to serve as an adviser. Finally, the pope capitalized on the support of the powerful north Italian heiress, Matilda of Tuscany, an ardent supporter of reform, by arranging a marriage between her and Duke Welf of Bavaria, one of Henry IV's principal enemies.

Emperor Henry IV, despite the prestige of his opposition, stood firm in his support of the imperial investiture of bishops and in his insistence that the popes elected under his aegis were the true pontiffs. The two sides' mutual unwillingness to compromise, despite many false starts, thus condemned Germany to years more of strife. Pope Urban's death in 1099 might have been an opportunity for settlement, but it was soon followed by news of the crusaders' conquest of Jerusalem, a miraculous sign to some that Urban II, the declarer of the crusade, embodied the true line of popes. Still, Henry IV would not yield.

By 1104, the emperor's son had had enough. Following in the footsteps of an elder brother who had revolted in the 1090s but died in 1101, he decided to take up arms against his father, whose intransigence he saw as jeopardizing both his inheritance and the traditions of authority of the German Crown. He undoubtedly thought there might be grounds, if his father were deposed, for some sort of compromise with the reformers. He therefore took matters into his own hands and forced his father to abdicate. Soon after, in 1106, the old emperor died. With Henry V's assumption of full power, there arose renewed hope for peace, but he quickly discovered that he had overestimated the degree to which the reformers were willing to reduce their demands. Strife and violence continued.

It was not until sixteen years later, in 1122, at a concordat reached at the Rhineland city of Worms that a formal settlement was reached. It was ambiguous, skirted some issues and avoided others altogether. This has caused some scholars to conclude that the settlement was one that turned its back on the genuine hopes of Gregory VII and Urban II. The emperor's influence in episcopal elections was preserved, after all; he could even decide disputed elections. Was it a sufficient concession that he renounced his right to the formal investiture of bishops with the signs of their spiritual authority or that, henceforward, the administration of the oil of consecration for a king was to follow a separate protocol from that for bishops? (No more would kings be anointed on their heads nor would they be anointed with chrism, the specially sanctified oil now reserved for ecclesiastical rites.) If the compromise was a rebuke to the most radical vision of the liberty of the Church, on at least one point its implications were firm, and this was of enormous significance. A king, even an emperor, was a layman. The liberty of the Church – the reformers' battle cry – was far from fulfilled, but in 1122 it was no will of the wisp.

7

The First Crusade

There was curiously little pacifism in the High Middle Ages. St Augustine, already by the fourth century, had formulated a theory of just war (*bellum justum*), and subsequent clerics interwove his theory into a wider ideology of Christian kingship. The ideal Christian king tried to avoid war or, if war was unavoidable, tried to find honourable ways to re-establish peace ('Blessed are the peacemakers: for they shall be called the children of God', Matthew 5:9). The Christian prince whose lands were invaded without legitimate reason or whose subjects were imperilled by the forces of a rival prince or by rebellion would necessarily use war as an instrument of policy and could do so legitimately.

War had rules – in time this elaborate set of rules became known as chivalry. In the late eleventh century, it was widely accepted in elite circles that non-combatants were not licit targets, unless they were spies or harboured or supplied the enemy. Under special protection were those considered as the most vulnerable non-combatants: women and children in general, but especially widows and orphans, as well as priests, monks, nuns, the aged and the infirm.

The just wars of the biblical past, for which the book of Joshua provided textual proof, openly received the blessing of God. Had He not made the sun stand still so that Joshua's victory might be assured? (Joshua 10:12). In the most extreme statement of the case, it was said that wars against non-believers who had attacked the people of God were waged by the direct will of God. Apart from direct illumination from the Almighty, how better to determine the will of God than to have a priest, preferably the high priest, sanctify the war?

Jesus's rebuke to Peter, who tried to defend him when he was being taken prisoner in the Garden of Gethsemane on the eve of his crucifixion, was the proof here: 'Put up thy sword into the sheath' (Matthew 26:52). The sword of physical retribution was not to be wielded by the spiritual

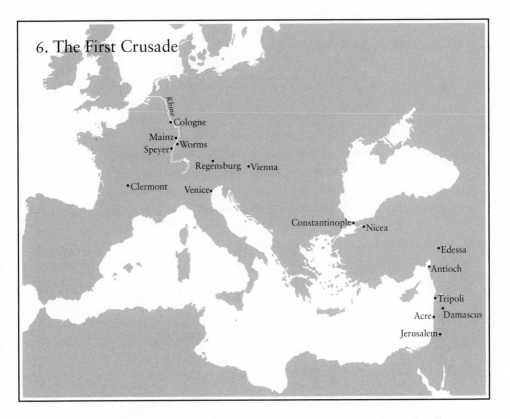

6. The First Crusade

descendants of St Peter – the clergy – but lordship over the sword still remained with the clergy: 'Put up *thy* sword.' It therefore rested with the Church, according to some ecclesiastical theorists, to determine how and under what conditions secular rulers could legitimately unsheathe and wield the sword of physical retribution. This was not in conflict with the older 'doctrine of the two swords' – one, spiritual (humiliation, malediction, excommunication, interdict), to be employed by the Church to coerce open but recalcitrant sinners; the other, temporal (physical force), to be employed by secular rulers. Rather, it clarified the traditional doctrine of the two swords by explaining the Church's superintendence of temporal authority.

There was a centuries-old liturgy of war that emphasized certain other aspects of the intimate relationship between the clergy and righteous military violence. Ideally there was general fasting before battles were waged, and the clergy present in the entourage of the army celebrated votive masses, asking for victory and promising eternal devotion to God. The priests blessed the commanders and their troops and gave sermons of exhortation, the spiritual equivalent of the secular commanders' harangues. They led the faithful in hymns and responsive readings like

Psalm 20 (Vulgate 19), with the famous verse, 'Some trust in chariots, and some in horses: but we will remember the name of the Lord our God. They are brought down and fallen: but we are risen, and stand upright.'

Also drawing on the stories in the biblical Book of Joshua of the conquest of the Promised Land, the clergy and the commanders commemorated victory, suggestive if not self-evident testimony, when and if it came, of the justness of their cause. They did so in part by following the example of the ancient Hebrews, who, *at God's command*, despoiled their beaten enemies during the conquest of the Promised Land (e.g., Joshua 8: 26–27). They also obliged the army to hear mass, to rededicate itself to the vows of devotion with which the soldiers had prepared for battle, and to honour the weapons of war in the cult of military relics.

So, already in the eleventh century elite thinkers and other high-born people knew what a just war was and how it should be fought, even if they did not live up to their ideals. The Peace and Truce of God had done much to disseminate and popularize some of these ideals, but a particular set of events in the late eleventh century helped to create a more remarkable type of just and holy war – the crusade.

There was, it has been argued, a significant strain of millenarian feeling in eleventh-century western European society. This was perhaps slightly more characteristic of the earlier part of the century, but it may be that millennial and apocalyptic movements of a more or less popular character were in train throughout the century. The idea of a decisive colossal confrontation between the forces of good and the servants of evil was at the prophetic centre of several of these movements.

Jerusalem and its liberation, and more particularly the deliverance of the Holy Sepulchre, the Tomb of Christ, from pagan domination, loomed large in apocalyptic discourse. (In the eleventh and into the twelfth century Christians in northern Europe tended to regard Muslims as pagans.) Jerusalem was being used as a first name for girls in the West (Riley-Smith, 1997, p. 33), evidence of the penetration of its image into popular consciousness; and pilgrimages to Jerusalem from the West, relatively uncommon from the seventh to the tenth century, began to increase in frequency in the tenth. They became fairly common in the eleventh and also on occasion enormously large. In 1054, one band of such pilgrims numbered 3,000. Seven thousand Germans are said to have joined together to make the Jerusalem pilgrimage in 1064–5.

Reports of various Muslim victories over Near Eastern and Spanish

Christians and of the gestures that sometimes followed fuelled the smouldering hatred and desire for vengeance by western Catholics. In October
1086, the Muslim victors at the battle of Sagrajas in Spain had the heads
of the Christian victims gathered up into wagons and in a gruesome
procession the wagons made their way down the peninsula and thence
through North Africa with their rotting trophies. Pope Gregory VII
himself, a decade or so before, seems to have envisaged the papacy's
retainers, the *fideles* of St Peter, as a possible army, to be accompanied
by him, for delivering eastern Christians from the onslaught of their
Muslim enemies and also for redeeming Jerusalem. Because of the Investiture Controversy and perhaps lingering doubts about the appropriate-
ness of direct papal involvement in fighting, the fantasy never became
reality, and important features of genuine crusade ideology, such as the
penitential vow of the troops, were lacking in his vision, but Gregory's
musings helped inspire and sustain other images of a just war of liberation in reform circles.

After his election in 1088, and being obliged to vie with the imperial
anti-pope Clement III for backing, Pope Urban II cast about for support
in numerous ways. In part owing to the Peace Movement a close relationship had emerged between local aristocracies and a number of powerful
monasteries, especially in France. Focusing on prayer – the prayers of
the monks for the ancestors and living members of these aristocratic
lineages – the relationship implicitly and sometimes explicitly raised the
hope of these aristocrats' salvation because of the good work they did
in protecting the monastic life, the highest form of the Christian life
and, by extension, Christendom in general. In practice, protection was
ordinarily achieved by persuasion or the threat of force rather than by
the actual use of force against would-be malefactors. But when persuasion and threats failed, the application of force against those who
attacked monks and other vulnerable Christians was believed to be
righteous in itself.

Force in the service of retributive justice (the *bellum justum*) was
carefully distinguished from the fury and chaos attending 'petty' disputes
among lords, the acts of internecine violence (*guerrae*, the origin of our
modern word 'war') that had plagued the Central Middle Ages and
helped excite the Peace Movement in the first place and which were still
thickly woven into the fabric of social life in the late eleventh century.
But Urban II or one of his advisers, drawing on the legacy of Gregory
VII and inspired by pleas for help from eastern Christians, took another

decisive step in the development of the idea of the crusade. The same lords who protected monks could protect Christendom east and west by directing their violence against the Muslim invaders and conquerors of the eastern Mediterranean, including the Holy Land.

There is some uncertainty as to the rewards the pope promised these would-be soldiers in his famous sermon at the Council of Clermont in southern France on 27 November 1095. But there is no doubt that the idea of fighting to regain the Holy Sepulchre or to help fellow Christians in the east was in the air and met a genuinely enthusiastic response. Although the mutual excommunications of pope and patriarch of Constantinople in 1054, emphasized so much in traditional interpretations, had exacerbated tensions between the western and eastern churches, they had not set them in malignant combat or reduced all mutual feelings of respect to nothing.

At the Council of Clermont shouts went up of 'God wills it! God wills it!' in response to the pope's words. He appealed to lords and lordlings to put aside their petty strife, which would lead them to hell, and instead to take up the Cross, to offer their lives to save threatened Christians. Would there be sin in killing their enemies in what was clearly conceived of as a just and holy war? No. Would there be remission of sins in some wider sense, a wiping clean of the slate or immediate entrance into paradise if one died in the effort? The pope might have been carried away and uttered ambiguous words on this occasion or on any of the many subsequent occasions on which he gave similar speeches in favour of an expedition to the east. Certainly some of his audience that first day and many others later on believed that faithfully fighting in such an expedition would be rewarded with full forgiveness of all past sins and that death in such fighting was equivalent to martyrdom. Although learned churchmen understood and stressed the penitential nature of crusading, they were far more insistent on the limited nature of the forgiveness that joining or dying on a crusade might entail.

The pope recognized from the moment he addressed the crowds in Clermont that he had touched a well-spring of militant devotion. He continued in future sermons to make the same plea and to urge those lords who responded to make firm plans for an expedition in the spring of 1096. It may well be that some of the enthusiasm at subsequent councils and rallies in late 1095 and early 1096 was scripted, with supporters of the pope's plan strategically planted in the crowds to get the chanting of 'God wills it!' started. It may also be the case that the genuine enthusiasm of the moment sometimes ebbed in the weeks that followed, as lords came to recognize the dangers and expense of the long and otherwise unpredictable journey they were going on. Fear of dying in a far-off place when one's expectation had been to be buried in the choir of the family church, or at least in Christian soil, troubled their souls. It would later be stipulated that the flesh could be buried but the bones of dead crusaders had to be brought back for separate burial in their native lands.

All these apprehensions notwithstanding, the crusading movement, once started, grew exponentially in territories like France, the southern Low Countries, and those parts of Italy where the legitimacy of Urban's pontificate was recognized. And, given its later successes, attributed to the intervention of God (He simply worked *through* the Franks), it raised disturbing questions about the evident lack of imperial sponsorship for the project. Emperor Henry IV was well aware of this, for at one point he offered to join the crusade himself. But as he would not yield on the point of lay investiture, his offer came to nothing.

Pope Urban II encouraged those who took the vow to prepare conscientiously, and the principal leaders, including many Flemish, Rhineland, northern French and Provençal barons – though in the end no king – ultimately settled on 15 August 1096, the Feast of the Assumption of the Blessed Virgin, as the date of departure. However, it was difficult to co-ordinate and control efforts that were taking place all over northwestern Europe, and what is sometimes known as the Peasants' Crusade or Popular Crusade – the expeditions of several dispersed groups under the leadership of various itinerant preachers and knights – set off in the late spring. A small group at Rouen in Normandy helped set the violent and almost anarchic tone of these early expeditions by massacring several Jews in the city. Another of these groups, somewhat better commanded by a knight known as Walter the Penniless (Sansavoir), left France and travelled through Germany and Hungary, making it to the outskirts of Constantinople by July. A third group, led by the charismatic preacher, Peter the Hermit, arrived there by the end of July, but on their way these poorly disciplined troops provoked any number of bloody and, for them, humbling skirmishes with Hungarian and Byzantine soldiers.

Many of the earliest crusaders never made it, even to Constantinople. The disorder and depredations of one group, whose leader was a priest by the name of Gottschalk, provoked the Hungarians, through whose lands they were marching, to destroy them. An otherwise unknown preacher named Volkmar led his followers to a similar fate in Nitra on the Hungarian border with Bohemia, but only after they had violently attacked the Jews of Prague. The most notorious of the bands was led by the Swabian Count Emich of Flonheim. He and his followers, inspired in part by the desire to loot but mainly, it seems, to force the Jews' conversion, carried out a series of violent attacks in the Rhineland, repercussions from which would reach down the centuries.

Before they left Germany on their way to the east and were themselves cut down by Hungarian forces, Emich's men and other bands ravaged the Jewish communities of Speyer, Worms, Mainz, Cologne, Trier, Metz and Regensburg. In some cases, like Mainz, the entire Jewish population of these towns was annihilated; at others (Regensburg is an example) nearly every Jew was forced to convert to Christianity. Even where Christian authorities, especially bishops, intervened to protect the Jews, the situation continued to be ferociously dangerous. Occasionally, for example, Jews were dispersed into the countryside to prevent the crusaders from besieging them *en masse*, but search parties hunted down the refugees in villages and hamlets. On other occasions, churchmen promised protection at the price of conversion. Most arresting, perhaps, was that in several places Jewish resistance to the crusaders' demands for conversion assumed the form of voluntary suicide. Many Jewish women led the way, urging the men of their communities to take their own lives rather than convert. Parents also slaughtered their children as a supreme act of devotion.

There had been rare instances of mass suicide earlier in the history of Judaism, but in 1096 and later years rabbis were troubled as to the moral legitimacy of the suicides. In the end, they came to accept them and subsequent ones as legitimate responses to the threat of forced conversion, and generations of poets would celebrate the heroism of the martyr suicides and the martyred children. Many of their names would be inscribed in memorial lists. The poetry celebrating their sacrifice entered the liturgy of the synagogue, so that the memory of the events of 1096 and of the martyrs and victims in later crusades and at other crises would never be forgotten.

> Oh, how the children cried aloud!
> Trembling, they see their brothers slaughtered;
> the mother binding her son, lest he profane the sacrifice by shuddering;
> the father making the ritual blessing to sanctify the slaughter.

Compassionate women strangle their own children;
pure virgins shriek bitterly;
brides kiss their bridegrooms farewell –
and all rush eagerly to be slaughtered.

Almighty Lord, dwelling on high,
in days of old the angels cried out to You to put a halt to one sacrifice.
And now, so many are bound and slaughtered –
why do they not clamour over my infants?

(Carmi, 1981, pp. 372–3)

Relations between Christians and Jews were affected in at least one other way by the horrendous incidents of 1096. A fissure developed in the Jewish community between those who seem to have developed a more restricted understanding of proper Jewish life and those who went back to the way of life they knew before. It is probably unfair to see the movement or sect attributed to these *hasidim* or pietists of the Rhineland only as a reaction to the crusade massacres, but that slaughter must have had an enormous impact in sustaining the rigorous beliefs of those survivors who insisted on a more pious way of living and an even greater avoidance of social and religious contamination by contact with non-pious Jews, let alone Christians. The sect disappeared in time; its ideas, embedded in an important body of texts, especially the *Sefer Hasidim* ('Book of the Pious'), have repeatedly inspired revival movements among European Jews.

*

Although most of the contingents of the Peasants' Crusade never reached Constantinople, those commanded by Walter the Penniless and Peter the Hermit did. The Byzantine emperor, Alexius, and his commanders were suspicious of these rag-tag troops and, rather than have them bivouac for a protracted length of time on the outskirts of the imperial capital, they transported them across the straits to Asia Minor on 6 August. There the crusaders split into several groups, largely along linguistic lines. A few early raids were successful, but a large band of German crusaders was isolated and defeated near Nicea and forced to convert to Islam and be deported eastwards or, if they refused, to die. By 21 October, the main body of crusaders, chastened by the slaughter of their comrades but still not co-ordinating their operations competently, and with relatively ineffective military intelligence, came face to face with overwhelming Turkish forces and were annihilated.

Meanwhile, back in Europe, the Princely Crusade was in the final stages of preparation. Powerful aristocrats commanded the various units, and in each case the commander knew that his retinue had honed their skills in battles at home. Long-standing and strong personal loyalties bound many of the units as well. It is a myth that the crusaders were composed of landless young knights; they tended to be mature and experienced men who left considerable properties behind. The prominence of loyalty among these warriors did not mean that there was always harmony within the units or that the various units themselves co-ordinated their efforts effectively. Nevertheless, there was a military ethos that informed the Princely Crusade in a way that it did not the Peasants' Crusade. Moreover, the new units were relatively better supplied than their predecessors. Partly this was because the great aristocrats had much more cash and credit at their disposal to buy equipment and other supplies. Partly, however, it was a matter of timing: having departed at a later date, the new crusaders had more liberty to plan, while also having the opportunity to benefit from the harvests of 1096.

The chief princes and their crusader retinues began to arrive in Constantinople in November and continued to arrive until May 1097, and were steadily ferried across the Bosporus in anticipation of engagement. Most of the commanders promised that, if they were successful, those lands they conquered which had once been part of the Byzantine Empire would revert to the Empire, a necessary concession if Byzantine troops were to complement their efforts, as in fact they did for a time. According to the best estimates, the crusade could count on more than 40,000 troops.

This enormous army appeared at Nicea on 19 June and overawed the Turkish garrison, which surrendered to the Byzantines. A week later, the crusaders set out for the interior and on 1 July defeated additional Turkish forces at Dorylaeum. Forty-eight hours later they resumed their march, traversing city after city of interior Asia Minor in the weeks that followed, but eventually encountering another major Turkish force at Ereghli in early September. Here, too, the crusading army crushed their enemies and sent the remnants packing.

Two of the leading commanders, Baldwin of Boulogne and a mercurial baron, Tancred, the son of Robert Guiscard, then took contingents eastwards and south-eastwards, where they accomplished the reconquest of the coastal cities of Anatolia, including Tarsus, which they knew as St Paul's birthplace. Baldwin followed up this success with the conquest of Edessa and, after supplanting its Armenian prince, he set up the first crusader principality there. Pressure was then put on the temperamental Tancred to rejoin the main crusader army, which was engaged in the long siege of Antioch from 21 October 1097 until June 1098.

The successful conclusion of the siege, with only the Muslim garrison of the citadel still holding out, led to the occupation of Antioch, but a few days later a large number of Turkish reinforcements arrived and surrounded the occupied city. At this point, a Byzantine army in reserve a few miles from Antioch and under the direct command of Emperor Alexius might have saved the situation, but the emperor's military intelligence overstated the size of the Turkish forces and the significance of their early successes. The Byzantines therefore withdrew.

Out of this desperate situation arose the first great sequence of events that would mark the crusade – in the crusaders' minds at least – as undeniably God's work. Visionaries among the besieged claimed to have received comfort and inspiration personally from Jesus. The Blessed Virgin's appearance was reported, as were the appearances of St Andrew and St Peter. And, miracle of miracles, thanks to a poor peasant, a lance was found under the floor of the Cathedral of Antioch which was said to be, though not everyone at first credited the tale, the lance with which the centurion had stabbed the dead Christ on the Cross (John 19:34). The Holy Lance, regarded as a relic, was interpreted as a sign for the crusaders to abandon the relative safety of Antioch's defences and confront the Turks directly. On 28 June, they did just that. Completely surprised and unnerved by the crusaders' daring, the Turks fled. Equally surprised by the failure of the Muslim army, the citadel garrison, which until that moment had courageously held out, also surrendered to the crusaders. Antioch, where the followers of Jesus were first called Christians, was now entirely in crusader hands.

The crusaders believed that such success, like finding the Holy Lance itself, was a sign from God, but success also bred strife. The treachery of the Byzantine emperor, as some of the crusaders conceived it, relieved them of the necessity of honouring their promise to return all conquered lands to his authority. Other commanders demurred at forswearing their solemn oaths. Presently disease afflicted the army, felling some of its most gifted commanders and decimating the ranks. But despite this, the bickering persisted: as they continued to debate future plans, what was and was not pleasing to God became painfully and dangerously uncertain.

By January 1099 many of the rank and file were rallying around lesser lords, who intended to bring order to the army by compelling dissident commanders, by force if necessary, to put aside their disagreements and resume the march. Force was necessary, it turned out (in the guise of an attack on the fortifications of Raymond of Saint-Gilles, who favoured holding to the agreement with the Byzantines), but it was followed by a sobering rededication to the expedition. By February most of what was left of the army was on the move, traversing Lebanon and reaching Palestine in May. On 6 June Tancred conquered Bethlehem, the birthplace of Jesus, and on 7 June the bulk of the army began the siege of Jerusalem. There were now approximately 15,000 troops left to do so.

They moved more quickly than they had at Antioch to end the siege, storming the city on 15 July. The frenzy of the assault and the slaughter were of epic proportions, as the crusaders took control.

Many of the Saracens [Muslims] who had climbed to the top of the Temple of Solomon in their flights were shot to death with arrows and fell headlong from the roof. Nearly ten thousand were beheaded in this Temple. If you had been there your feet would have been stained to the ankles in the blood of the slain. What shall I say? None of them were left alive. Neither women nor children were spared. (Fulcher of Chartres, 1969, pp. 121–2).

A week later the victors elected Godfrey of Bouillon as ruler – not king – of Jerusalem: Jesus was king. But they had learned something from the experience at Antioch. The Muslims would undoubtedly send another force to try to retake Jerusalem, and indeed an enormous Egyptian force invaded Palestine in August. But on the twelfth of the month, crusader forces surprised the Egyptians near Ascalon, on the Mediterranean coast about fifty miles west of the Holy City, and utterly destroyed them.

The First Crusade had reached its emotional high point, and it is customary to claim that the crusade more or less ended at this moment. The setting up of principalities and the evolution of political and religious life proceeded apace, but these hardly appeared to be aspects of the crusade itself. In fact, the crusade was far from over. For the next twenty years, men streamed into the Holy Land and fought any number of actions in the extraordinary attempt to stabilize, expand and territorially consolidate the Crusader States. These actions were the necessary coda of the more spectacular conquest of Jerusalem and are properly considered part of the First Crusade. What this almost continuous warfare ensured was that the political institutions and social arrangements of the Crusader States would be skewed. What has sometimes been said of Spain in the era of the Reconquest (see chapter 11) can be said even more accurately of the Crusader States: they constituted a society organized almost solely according to the exigencies of war.

One of the more distinctive features of this society was the presence of military orders, well-organized associations of devout Christians who cared for and provided protection for pilgrims, nursed the sick, and ultimately took an active part in the military defence of the Crusader States. Groups of people dedicated to the nursing of pilgrims probably existed before 1099, but there were dramatic increases in the numbers of Christian pilgrims to the Holy City from the time of the Christian reconquest onwards. Pilgrims to Jerusalem characteristically, if not exclusively, were aged or sick; they came to the city not for miraculous cures but in order to die where Christ had died. It was in part due to the pressure of such numbers that the people ministering to them organized themselves into formal orders. The earliest of these seems to have been the Order of St John of Jerusalem, known more familiarly as the Hospitallers. The Order of the Temple of Solomon or Knights Templars came into being in 1119–20, originally to guard the pilgrimage routes.

The Hospitallers ran the great pilgrim hospital in the Holy City, sometimes employing Jewish and Muslim physicians to help minister to the sick. The hospital accepted both Muslims and Jews who needed care. Orphans of war and abandoned children were taken in and put in the charge of female nurses; when they came of age they were invited to join the Order. But, as was typical of the military orders, the Hospitallers, while never losing their original function, came more and more to be identified as a fighting force. The Order's great hospital, perhaps 1,000 beds or more, was often filled with the wounded from its own battles.

The military orders, in their mature form, came to be composed of knights who took monastic vows and vowed celibacy, priests who carried out the spiritual functions of the order, sergeants from lesser social backgrounds, and nuns who helped nurse women and children and who prayed for the success of the Christian mission. They were international orders who owed direct obedience to the pope and were supported by houses established throughout Europe which both sent funds to the orders in the Holy Land and provided venues for the retirement of older members of the orders. Their work, in the heroic age following the conquest of Jerusalem, was deeply admired. To St Bernard, who wrote in praise of the Templars, they represented a new order of Christian knighthood. King Alfonso I of Navarre and Aragon (d. 1131) wanted to give one-third of his kingdom to the Hospitallers to carry on their work.

*

The news in Christendom of the fall of Jerusalem and the good work of devoted Christians confirmed, more than almost anything else could, the spirit of renewal that had been articulated in the efforts at papal and popular reform. Of the crusaders who lived and returned home to Europe, few came back rich, and the difficult local conditions that had arisen on their estates during their absence often demanded extraordinary efforts at peacekeeping and restoration on their part. All of these men had lost kinsmen and good friends in great numbers in the deserts and plains of the Near East. Nonetheless, those who returned relished recalling their adventures – stories of their suffering and courage that grew in the retelling into wondrous tales of inspiration for generations to come.

Those who had failed to go on the expedition felt all the more need to prove themselves as time went by. But the specialness of having gone on the First Crusade was never lost. Families assiduously preserved the memory of the participation of their ancestors. Other families who could not count an ancestor on the expedition found it difficult to explain why this was so, since nobility and the defence of Christendom were so closely related in the aristocratic imagination. As time passed, some of these lineages 'invented' ancestral participants in the First Crusade by clever misreadings, whether deliberate or inadvertent, of original chronicle reports (Murray, 1998, pp. 38–54). Surely, it might be said, if the family of so-and-so had gone off to war in the East with a great entourage, and this family was closely connected to one's own, then it was only natural and right to suppose that in that entourage one's own kinfolk could be numbered. To have served Christendom in this, allegedly the most righteous of its wars, was the crowning achievement of nobility.

8

The World of Learning

Concurrently with success abroad in the First Crusade, western cultural ideals and practices began to undergo a long period of renewal and creativity in Europe. The roots of these developments were classical, although like almost everything else connected to intellectual developments in the twelfth century, they owed much to the stimulus provided by the great and more recent conflict over investiture between the popes and the German emperors.

Familiarity and critical engagement with classical Roman and, to a far lesser extent, ancient Greek learning in Latin translation was characteristic of the entire Middle Ages, even the early Middle Ages, despite the disruptive social and political changes in the period before the eleventh century. Yet many thinkers' respect for the natural and moral philosophy of pagan antiquity was partial at best. Any number of ethical principles, such as suicide as an honourable response to shame, defended by classical thinkers and recorded in the texts that were their legacy to the early and central Middle Ages were at variance with Christian doctrine. Moreover, a great many texts that would have demonstrated the diversity of classical thought and revealed strands in it more compatible with Christian belief were simply not available in the monastic libraries of the early medieval West.

There were, for example, many references in available treatises, commentaries and anthologies to a large number of Plato's Dialogues, and something was known of their content from what Neoplatonists and the Church fathers, like Augustine, had written. But only the *Timaeus* was available (and then not fully) in a Latin translation before the High Middle Ages. Now, the *Timaeus*, as even the modern casual reader of Plato's works quickly realizes, is very odd if only because of Socrates's extremely muted role and its almost lyric quality. The *Timaeus*'s myth of creation offers a stark contrast to traditional medieval Christians' understanding of creation; after all, it describes the creation of the Olympian pantheon and a cosmos in which man's place is tiny. Yet, partly because passages of the Dialogue's story stress the creator's goodness and the goodness and beauty of his creation (no matter what he created), and partly because of a general sense expressed by the Church fathers that Plato anticipated fundamental Christian beliefs ('If these men [Plato is mentioned by name] could live their lives again,' Augustine wrote in *Of True Religion*, 'they would become Christians'), the *Timaeus* became popular among monastic readers and its dialogue form among writers.

Christian thinkers also domesticated the available content of Plato's works, made it palatable by allegorizing it, as ancient authors themselves often did; questions of its literal truth as a description of the world were thus put to one side. *Nous*, a favourite Greek philosophical term for the creative intellect, could be glossed or interpreted allegorically, as it was by the twelfth-century philosopher, Bernard Silvester, as the Christian God in the act of creation. In his words, *Nous* is 'the consummate and profound reason of God, . . . [and] the knowledge and judgement of that divine will in the disposition of things' (Bernardus Silvestris, 1973, p. 69).

In biography and Latin poetry, there had been a recovery of classical styles, even in Charlemagne's time. Neither in the Carolingian Renaissance nor in the more widespread and profounder recovery in the Renaissance of the twelfth century was the imitation of Roman stylistic and rhetorical practices slavish. Although Suetonius's *Lives of the Twelve Caesars* of the second century provided a model for royal biography and also influenced hagiography, there were radical departures from the classical model in both of these genres, particularly the admission of the miraculous and a deliberate emphasis on conversion experiences, from the evil to the good life or the good to the better life.

In Latin poetry, classical conceits had also been eagerly assimilated in the Carolingian Renaissance. The whole range of these, like the most complex metrical phrasing, continued to be taught as academic exercises and even employed on occasion in the verse of the twelfth century. But new ways of poetical writing or new emphases on conceits less favoured in antiquity often displaced classical practices. These included the use of assonance or vocalic, non-consonantal rhymes; *rana* (frog) and *papa* (pope) are assonantally rhymed. Poets delighted in fuller rhymes, too, such as *accipis* (you take) with *precipis* (you order) or *meus fundus/ totus mundus* (my money/the whole world), and complex end-of-line rhyme schemes and extravagant alliteration virtually unknown or shunned in Ovid's and Virgil's world.

The twelfth century saw major achievements in the development and redaction of law, medicine, history writing, and more. All owed something to the classical past or to the Carolingian interpretation of that past. But no intellectual endeavour survived the Renaissance of the twelfth century unchanged manifestly by its creative impulses.

THE INSTITUTIONAL SETTINGS

Traditional Benedictine monks who had preserved, adapted and critiqued classical texts in their monasteries for hundreds of years continued to make a major contribution to intellectual life in the twelfth century. Their efforts were supplemented by those of monks in the newer orders. As these new orders expressly stressed poverty in monastic life, simplicity in worship, manual work, and devotion to the Virgin, the works of scholarship, meditation and devotion that emerged from them tended to have distinct emphases, somewhat different from those of their Benedictine counterparts. But too much can be made of the contrast. Worse still, some scholars make it seem as if everything interesting and creative was emerging from Cistercians and other reformers, like the friars of the early thirteenth century (see chapter 14), or even that learning in the Benedictine monasteries – these institutions having fulfilled their task of preserving the classical heritage – was withering away. This is an unfair assertion, as any list of major Benedictine authors of the twelfth century would confirm. In the genre of history alone, the Benedictines reigned supreme. The Benedictine monks of Saint-Denis wrote the official histories of the kings of France; the Benedictine monks of St Albans did more or less the same thing for the kings of England, starting in the middle of the period under discussion.

One thing the expansion of new orders did do, however, was to encourage the proliferation of knowledge. Each new monastery, canonry and nunnery needed books: a bible or bibles; the statutes of the order; workbooks that recorded estates, rents and contractual obligations; liturgical and devotional books, such as the breviary with the canon of the mass, hymnals and saints' lives; and, naturally, some of the standard interpretative manuals, especially books that explained Christian doctrine. Everywhere a Carthusian or Cistercian house was established books had to be bought or borrowed in order to be copied; the establishment of libraries was mandated in the statutes of the orders.

As time passed, even the tiniest libraries of the smallest houses expanded in size, for new standard reference works emerged, and the monks tried to get them for their collections. Not every monastic librarian or scribe could purchase or copy every important book. But some books seemed absolutely essential. To defend one's house in court cases, an abbot employed a lawyer or procurator, but some familiarity with ecclesiastical law was important for at least some of the monks themselves. When Gratian's *Concordance of Discordant Canons* began to displace a wide variety of competing legal texts during and after the 1140s and became the fundamental legal code of the Church, librarian after librarian saw the wisdom of securing a copy. Soon after Peter Lombard finished his *Sentences*, a summa or comprehensive summation of Christian doctrine in four books in the mid-twelfth century, it became the standard account in schools. It behoved ecclesiastical librarians to secure a copy or epitome for their collections.

Some libraries were already or soon became real research centres. Fulda, in Germany, set the standard by being able to put 2,000 volumes at the service of scholars. Cluny in the twelfth century was in the process of building up a library of almost 1,000 books, including a Latin translation of the Qur'an (the Muslim holy book), important letter collections, and philosophical and theological tracts. And equally to the point, a number of newer monasteries were becoming research centres. The Cistercians, confronted by inconsistencies in the various manuscripts of the Vulgate, organized a team to establish the biblical text with certainty. From this effort emerged an improved text, known as the Cistercian Bible. Although the rate of proliferation of Cistercian monasteries exceeded the ability of scribes in the early twelfth century to make copies of this bible, the actual work of creation required the amassing of a large number of Latin Vulgate manuscripts and other works in the library of Cîteaux.

Perhaps even more impressive than the growth of monastic libraries, however, was the establishment of libraries and a book production system in the major European cities and towns. In some cases the libraries were associated with houses of canons, like the Augustinian abbey of St-Victor of Paris, but each cathedral was also supposed to have a school and, thus, books.

Occasionally these schools achieved great renown because of the eminence of their teachers or students. The cathedral school of Chartres will forever be associated with the bishop, John of Salisbury, the author of a great treatise on political theory, the *Policraticus*, an attempt to understand the relation of ecclesiastical and secular authority. The abbey of St-Victor of Paris brought a host of great scholars to prominence, mostly theologians, including Hugh, Andrew and Richard, all known as 'of St-Victor', although by birth probably a German, an Englishman and a Scot respectively. It may have been from among their circle that the standard interpretation of the Bible, its *Glossa Ordinaria*, arose. It was certainly they, in particular Andrew of St-Victor, who spearheaded the effort to understand the Old Testament by consulting Jewish sages, although the enterprise came in for virulent criticism from some of the canons. The Victorines also wrote massive tomes on the sacraments, education, devotion, mystical union and the liturgy.

The schools of Paris, of course, achieved renown and notoriety in part through the career of Peter Abelard, who came to the city around the year 1100, made a reputation as a brilliant and arrogant scholar, and was hired by an influential cathedral canon, Fulbert, to tutor the canon's niece, Heloise. Abelard publicly and imprudently disparaged other teachers by referring to what he regarded as their intellectual inferiority to himself, and he also seduced and impregnated his youthful pupil, Heloise. Provoking criticism for these actions, he trod a very difficult path. Heloise's uncle thought he had an agreement with Abelard to live in a conventional marriage with his niece. But it was she who objected. Suspecting betrayal by Abelard, Fulbert and his friends revenged themselves by castrating him. All Paris was saddened – if we accept the victim's own description of the reaction to the attack in his *History of My Calamities* – but Abelard went on to acknowledge, 'how just a judgement of God had struck me in the parts of the body with which I had sinned, and how just a reprisal had been taken by the very man I had myself betrayed' (Abelard, 1974, p. 75).

Abelard's career was not over. He kept in touch with Heloise in a series of letters and gave her all sorts of advice, even as she slowly and painfully reconciled herself to the failure of their romance. She seems to have given their baby, baptized Astrolabe after a new navigation instrument of the period, to other family members to be raised while she became a nun at a little monastery in Champagne, known as the Paraclete or Comforter, a name for the Holy Spirit. It had been refurbished as a convent after having once served as Abelard's own refuge from strife and as a venue for his continued teaching. Although Abelard himself was never a very able administrator in the monastic institutions in which, thanks to his fame, he soon won offices, he continued to write poetry and philosophical and theological treatises.

A century earlier, Abelard's works and those of other masters might have had a very restricted distribution. They would have been copied occasionally and lent from one monastery or cathedral library to another. Word of mouth would also have propagated and distorted their views. Of course, to some extent, this situation remained in place, but there were a great many more monasteries and canonries in Abelard's time than there were a century before, which allowed the views of some of these thinkers wider dissemination. The fame of the schools in which they taught also stimulated distribution of their works. But perhaps most important, a specialized commercial book trade was emerging in the major urban centres of learning in order to service the hordes of students who needed to buy or borrow cheap books. With the rise of this trade, it is possible for the first time to speak formally of 'publica-tion'; book learning came to displace the emulation of charismatic figures as the central process of education, although the adulation of Abelard in some circles shows the persistence of the older style in the newer environment. Yet it was acknowledged among his opponents that the real danger of Abelard's allegedly indiscreet, if not heretical, teachings ('they replace light with darkness') was that they now spread so rapidly. '[T]hey pass from one race to another, and from one kingdom to another'; they 'cross oceans, they leap over the Alps . . .; they spread through the provinces and the kingdoms' (Jaeger, 1994, p. 239). Ultim-ately Abelard would be forced to give up writing and witness many of his ideas and books spurned by the authorities, but the promulgation of his ideas could not be suppressed.

Leavening the world of learning in several late twelfth-century towns were universities, emerging often, if not always, from an existing school or schools and under some degree of ecclesiastical control. Even though students started young, often as young teenagers, and had a reputation for rowdiness, they usually enjoyed special jurisdictional immunities, in part because they were considered members of or potential members of the clergy. One of the first universities was founded in Bologna in Italy. There the corporation (the meaning of the word *universitas*) comprised the students, not the *magistri* (masters, teachers), who existed sometimes in an uneasy relationship with the institution. Universities were not only corporations; they were academies of general study (*studia generalia*). Masters taught the entire seven liberal arts – the *trivium* (grammar, rhetoric and dialectic) and the more advanced *quadrivium* (music, arithmetic, geometry and astronomy) – as well as even more advanced professional subjects.

Although a very wide curriculum was always available, some universities were best known for particular subjects. Bologna was most famous for its law school. The situation was similar for the University of Montpellier, also a comprehensive academic institution, but most famous for its law school and school of medicine. Rivalling both these institutions in importance, except in legal education, from which it was officially restricted, was the University of Paris. Chartered by the French king only in the year 1200, it had functioned *de facto* as a corporation of masters for several decades before this. It had several faculties but was renowned for the study of theology. Oxford and then Cambridge emerged as *studia generalia* in the early thirteenth century, and became major centres of natural philosophy and theology.

Several other universities came into existence and flourished, sometimes only briefly, in the twelfth and first half of the thirteenth century, but it is remarkable that no university took root in Germany or in Spain, one false start in the latter notwithstanding, until much later, indeed towards the end of the Middle Ages. This did not prevent Spain and Germany from contributing significantly to the intellectual revolution of the twelfth century through the other institutions that, as we have seen, were centres of learning: monasteries (old, reformed and new), friaries (the German ones nurtured some of the most distinguished scholars, like Albert the Great and Thomas Aquinas), cathedral schools, and, perhaps especially in Castile and Aragon, aristocratic courts. What the absence of universities in Spain and Germany did mean was that relatively substantial numbers of Spaniards and Germans who wanted to attend university went to places like Bologna and Paris, thereby giving the institutions an enhanced international flavour and contributing to the cosmopolitanism of elite clerical culture.

The institutions discussed, from university to local school, were primarily male and always Christian. It is reasonable to ask, then, whether women or Jews had a 'Renaissance of the twelfth century'. Heloise's education already suggests that some of the currents of twelfth-century intellectual developments could have an effect on elite women's lives.

Traditional learning in the nunneries also seems to have taken on a lustre in the twelfth century, although perhaps historians have inferred lustre from the mere existence of texts, small in quantity compared to the number coming from male institutions but a real plethora when measured against the legacy of women's writing from earlier centuries. However that may be, we shall encounter outstanding contributions from women in medicine, story-writing and poetry, even if the institutional settings in which they were educated continued to be limited, by and large, to households for personal tutoring or to convent schools.

As for Jews, traditional schools of an elementary nature and for higher education were hoary with age. Students usually met in private houses under the discipleship of a master or in a building specifically dedicated to instruction. Famous masters attracted students from great distances, a pattern that was analogous to the charismatic attraction of disciples to Christian masters like Abelard. It was possible to cross linguistic lines, because the language of instruction at the highest level was Hebrew, and every adult Jewish male, unless he was mentally deficient, had at least some Hebrew. Many had a great deal.

Again, whether it is possible to speak of a Renaissance of the twelfth century, as opposed to simply an exceptional series of towering figures, is debatable. There were extraordinary intellectual giants, such as Rabbi Solomon ben Isaac (Rashi) of Troyes in Champagne at the very opening of the period. One of the greatest biblical exegetes who ever lived, his interpretations, mediated to be sure, were to have an important influence on Andrew of St-Victor. Another such figure is Rabbi Moses ben Maimon (Rambam or Maimonides), who, although his entire career was spent in countries under Islamic rule, had a profound influence on the Christian theological tradition in the late twelfth and thirteenth centuries. To be sure, some of the methodological approaches of Jewish writers show fairly strong resemblances to those in use among Christians, but both groups, directly, indirectly or remotely, were often borrowing from the same Aristotelian, Platonic and Neoplatonic sources. Nonetheless, in some areas the contact between Christians and Jewish thinkers was immediate and stimulating on both sides. Discussions of biblical exegesis led to polemics of a high level on both sides, and the translations of philosophical texts, to which repeated reference will be made, heralded an intellectual revolution.

It is not surprising that the intellectual ferment in the academies, urban centres, some nunneries and Jewish schools had its counterpart in the princely and aristocratic courts, like those in Spain. They, too, amassed libraries and attracted scholars, who sometimes doubled as advisers, administrators and publicists for the princes. The libraries were perhaps more likely to have a substantial component of secular and vernacular literature than that found in the libraries of monasteries, canonries or cathedrals. And considerable amounts of history-writing were undertaken, among which were family histories commissioned by local lords, redacted in the vernacular and intended to celebrate their lineages.

CURRICULUM AND SCHOLARSHIP

The Christian schools developed a distinctive style of study which takes its name – scholasticism – from the Latin word for school, *schola*. Early scholasticism entailed a rigorous approach to moral, theological and philosophical issues based on the rules of logic enunciated in Aristotle's works, known either through the medium of his sixth-century epitomizer and interpreter Boethius or, increasingly in the period under discussion, directly from new translations of the philosopher's treatises. These new translations largely came about through the collaborative efforts of Christian, Jewish and Muslim scholars in Spain and Sicily. Consequently, Aristotle's works sometimes came into the schools garbled. It did not help that the original Greek manuscripts were usually no more than late copies of Aristotle's students' notes of his philosophical discourses; students' notes often leave much to be desired. Distortions crept in thereafter through faulty Hebrew or Arabic translations of this Greek material. Whatever Aristotle really taught, his doctrines ran a final risk of distortion in their retranslation from Arabic and Hebrew into Latin.

And yet, despite the occasional inane passage, the body of material that Latin scholars came into contact with was enormously impressive. Aristotle seemed to have spoken with authority about nearly everything. As St Paul was 'The Apostle', St Augustine 'The Theologian', Emperor Justinian 'The Jurist' (see below), so Aristotle became 'The Philosopher'. Unhappily, however, the philosopher was a pagan – a very, very smart pagan, to be sure, a pagan platonized by some early interpreters, but a pagan nonetheless. It behoved Christian scholars to make Aristotle their own, just as they had made Plato theirs. This meant incorporating as much as possible of Aristotelian thinking into their own understanding of the world, and, when rejecting some of his teaching, like the eternity of the world (how could the world, created at a moment in time by the Christian God, be eternal?), explaining how and why the philosopher went wrong and doing so with the very tools that he had provided in his logical works.

They employed dialectical reasoning in their discussions, another distinctive aspect of the scholastic method. For each problem a thesis might be stated, some contention whose truth had to be tested, and authorities were often marshalled in favour of the thesis. Its opposite or antithesis would then be stated, with the available authorities marshalled in its favour. The scholar's job was to arrive at the truth, a synthesis that either harmonized the evident contradiction between thesis and antithesis or led to the rejection or modification of one or the other.

The methods by which this resolution was achieved were multiple. Most famously, of course, resolution was accomplished through the rigorous use of the tools of Aristotelian logic, especially deductive logic. At other times, a scholar might show that an apparent contradiction was illusory because the plain meaning of words in the thesis or antithesis did not correspond to the philosophical or theological meanings of the words: there are three persons in the Trinity, but the Trinity is a unity, one God. The statements, perhaps baffling on the surface, become less so – or so medieval theologians insisted – if one realized that in specialized theological language 'person' translated Greek *hypostasis*, often rendered as 'manifestation', although to even venture this suggestion would have provoked other theologians to continue the discussion, querying 'manifestation' and making other suggestions (was it 'substance' or 'essence'?), and so forth.

Or, to cite another example, one might consider the word 'man'. Man is a categorical term. We recognize certain individuals as fitting into the category (Socrates, for example). But what was the ontological status of 'man', a universal in medieval philosophical language? Were universals real? Or were they simply names (Latin *nomina*, hence the name of the philosophical position, nominalism)? There is no value in oversimplifying: there were many different types of realisms (that is, arguments in favour of the view that universals were real), and there were many kinds of nominalists (those who denied the reality of universals, but tried nonetheless to describe the precise character of their status). But imagine a debate on the ontological status of universals in relation to God and the three persons of the Trinity. One of Abelard's most vehement and controversial arguments revolved around just this issue.

This philosophizing could be a dangerous business. Failure to resolve matters in doctrinally and morally acceptable ways provoked acerbic criticism. Abelard felt the sting again when in the *Sic et Non* ('Yes and No') he refused to resolve apparently contradictory assertions from sacred authorities. Moreover, applying scholastic methods to the dissection of theological truths, even to defend them, angered some churchmen. The Trinity was one of the central mysteries of the Catholic faith; it neither needed explanation nor could be explained. Clarification of the language of Trinitarian theology was certainly permissible, even encouraged. But even moderate clerics denied that the goal of clarification was a licence for vain curiosity about, say, the relations of power among the three persons of the Trinity. This was one part of St Bernard of Clairvaux's denunciation of Abelard.

Catholic Christianity, nevertheless, was a doctrinally complex religion that seemed to demand high-powered philosophical defence, as the entirely orthodox Richard of St Victor eloquently pointed out in the introduction to his brilliant treatise on the Trinity. The equally orthodox St Anselm, an Italian who became prior of a Norman abbey and then archbishop of Canterbury in England, valued faith above all things, but faith sought understanding. One believes in God on faith, but reason may stimulate or reinforce belief. A reformer opposed to lay investiture, an ascetic who denounced the vices of his age, twice in exile from his archbishopric because of arguments with his king, Anselm could have used the example of his holy life, his long suffering and dedication to principle, as a kind of evidence of the reality of the Christian God (why would he suffer, except that he had faith, the highest form of knowledge, that his Redeemer lived?). But Anselm was also a philosopher involved, like Abelard and Richard of St-Victor, in the feverish debate on the nature of the Trinity. He did not shy away from other subjects that we might now regard as perilous minefields.

Perhaps Anselm is most famous for a formulation to be found in a work of his entitled *Proslogion*. After defining God as a being than which no greater can exist, he insists that even those who deny God's existence know the meaning of the word God when they deny His existence. Otherwise their denial would be incoherent. Therefore, God exists in the mind of the one who denies His existence. But it is possible for the denier to think of God existing apart from the mind in the real world. Of course, this is a contradiction, since real existence is greater than mental existence, and the real God would be greater than the denied (idea of) God, who has already been imagined as that than which nothing greater can be conceived. The contradiction can only be resolved if the real God and the God denied are the same. If one exists, the other must. Even the 'fool [who] hath said in his heart, There is no God' (Psalms 14:1), therefore, has a concept of Him, than which nothing greater can exist, and having this concept demonstrates the existence of God.

One sometimes calls this the 'ontological proof' of the existence of God. It seems to be a seventeenth-century name for it. Others have been less kind. 'Slippery' is a word that comes to mind. Why is having a concept of God in the mind equivalent to God existing in the mind? Why must real, that is, extra-mental, existence be superior to 'mere' mental existence, even if this was a belief common to medieval thinkers? Why – logically – must it be so? And how can arguing from a definition of an entity prove the existence of the entity anyway? Finally, even if one grants the logic of Anselm's argument, does it not lead to absurdities? An opponent pointed out that the perfect sea isle must exist or else one could imagine one more perfect, which would be a contradiction, since there are no degrees of perfection. Anselm brusquely responded that God's existence is necessarily included in the definition of His perfection – which is not the case with a sea isle. But neither Anselm's nor his supporters' efforts succeeded in silencing objections; the ontological proof, sometimes modified, to be sure, would be the subject of violent controversy, passionate support and equally passionate ridicule, down through the philosophical revolution of the early modern period.

Like philosophy and theology, another very advanced discipline which was to find a niche in the universities was academic medicine. In a world so heavily influenced by the intellectual paradigm of the *Timaeus*, where the little world (microcosm) of the individual organism mirrored the greater (macrocosm), understanding the body – medical knowledge – was deemed crucial to understanding the universe. Many important medical treatises that came out of the monastic tradition reflect this overarching philosophical concern, admixed, of course, with rather more straightforward therapeutic concerns. This is the tradition within which the work of the nun, Hildegard of Bingen, who wrote on nearly everything, would have to be placed.

The most famous medical centre, at Salerno in Italy, was neither a monastery nor a university, but an anomalous kind of institution where medicine was always touted as a practical not merely discursive art. The penetration of medicine into the university curriculum occurred because of the existence of texts, scrupulously glossed at Salerno, that could also be subjected to technical scholastic analysis. The texts were rich and difficult, partly because of the same problems of transmission through multiple translation and interpretation that we have seen before. But the texts, flawed as they were, incorporated a long southern European tradition of learning. The central ancient works were the *Aphorisms* and the *Prognostics*, attributed to Hippocrates, and another body of texts which went under various names and were attributed to Galen. These were supplemented by translations of Arabic works.

A wide variety of other influences also helped produce more distinctively Salernitan texts, like the gynaecological works attributed to the woman physician Trotula which would spread across the map of Europe in translation. She (or the man or men writing under her name) advised practitioners, in one passage, to help a pregnant woman carrying a dead foetus to deliver quickly by the application of pepper powder under and into her nose. The sneezing generated would help contract the muscles, forcing the would-be mother to deliver. (*Medieval Woman's Guide*, 1981, p. 139). Advice like this, which seemed to come from a person whose expertise on the female body was rooted in her being a female herself, was widely sought after. Male practitioners could ground their authority over the female body in their knowledge of Trotula's works.

The central concepts in medicine revolved around diagnostic signs. Disease was seen in part as a divergence from a normalcy, varying from person to person but defined by essential characteristics and balances. Each healthy person enjoyed a different balance of hot and cold, wet and dry temperaments or, in the technical language of the texts, complexions. Balance should also extend to the four fluids that served the organism, blood, phlegm, black bile and yellow bile. Imbalances could be identified by fevers, runny noses, coughs, spitting up of blood, dark urine, white urine, swelling, skin discoloration, lesions, stench, putrefaction, and the like, in other words, by what common sense still regards as signs of illness. Balance might be restored, where it was possible to be restored, by environmental change, drugs, stones (lithotherapy) or surgery.

This concept of balance helped make medicine, outside of its therapeutic application, an attractive analytical subject. It was possible to bring to bear a large part of the conceptual baggage of scholastic discourse in dealing with questions of balance. To this extent, academic doctors could draw upon the kinds of arguments that other scholastics were making in their moral analysis of, say, justice. Notions of retributive justice implied some theory of comparability and equilibrium. And both philosophers and academic specialists in the law subjected the problem of retributive justice to intense scholastic analysis.

In the history of medieval legal learning, where some of this discourse on justice was developing, the formative events were, first, the reacquaintance of scholars in the eleventh century with the original texts of the Roman law as put together at Emperor Justinian's order in the sixth century; second, as one might expect, the Investiture Controversy; and, third, the founding of the law school at Bologna. It has been argued recently, with passion, that both the pre-history of the recovery of the Justinianic corpus and the existence of other Italian institutions besides Bologna were more important in the development of academic law than scholars have given them credit for. Be that as it may, the traditional picture is one of new texts stimulating the narrow world of legal scholarship at what was a momentous time of political and religious change. The texts included the *Digest*, a collection of ancient legal opinions, often of a very pithy nature. There were also the *Code* (the standing laws of the Empire at the time of compilation), the *Novels* (new laws subsequent to the *Code*), and the *Institutes* (the textbook which students in late antiquity were to use to study the law).

The Bolognese and masters at other institutions glossed these texts, the laws of the *civitas* and *imperium* of Rome. The texts seemed particularly seductive in their comprehensiveness, their engrossing picture of ancient imperial authority, and the elegance of their maxims, each of which was usually referred to by its opening or key words. For example, *Digna vox* or *Lex digna* ('Worthy voice' or 'Worthy law') referred to a passage in the *Code* (1.14.4), 'It is the worthy voice of the majesty of the ruler that the prince professes himself bound to the law, inasmuch as our authority [that of the fourth-century co-emperors, Theodosius and Valentinian, who issued the decree] depends upon the authority of the law. And truly, greater than the imperium is the submission of the principate to the laws' (Kantorowicz, 1957, p. 104).

A statement like the one quoted, if regarded as normative, could have played into the hands of contemporary anti-imperial jurists, men who supported the church and who argued that the emperor, in their case the German emperor, had transgressed the law by investing bishops and therefore abrogated his right to authority. But other maxims, especially if they were found in the *Digest*, which came to be regarded as a repository of almost inspired wisdom, appeared to trump this view. The *Digest* (1.4.1) insists, in the so-called *Lex regia* ('Royal law'), for example, that 'what pleases the prince has the force of law'. Since Emperor Justinian himself, 'The Jurist' in the reverential speech of medieval interpreters, declared that his compilers had tried to eliminate all inconsistencies in the body of legal knowledge and opinions they brought together, medieval masters were stimulated to try to harmonize apparently divergent sentiments, like the *Lex digna* and *Lex regia*, when they encountered them.

The masters of Roman law, or civilians, as they are also known, expounded their various views principally in lectures, that is, in academic readings of their interpretations to their students. The environment was one of the most erudite, productive and provocative in western history. Those who glossed or harmonized what seemed to be pro-imperial positions, like the famous Master Irnerius (probably a latinization of the German name, Werner), sometimes incurred papal wrath. Irnerius was excommunicated in 1119. Those who teased out rather less exalted pictures of imperial authority suffered the hostility of the other side.

Nonetheless, the dialogue, however freighted with political consequences, went on among the professors and students. Glosses accumulated and eventually masters came along who tried to produce summas of these interpretations. One such summa, that written by Master Accursius, would become standard: his *Glossa Ordinaria* to the Roman law was published in the early thirteenth century. But even such a comprehensive work as Accursius's only stimulated more dialogue, more glosses, more summas and more controversy.

At Bologna and elsewhere in northern Italy, and eventually elsewhere in Europe, parallel studies were going on. The counterparts to the civilians – those who studied Roman law – were the canonists, those who developed and glossed the law of the Church. In part stimulated by the dissension arising out of the Investiture Controversy, churchmen had ransacked available texts for relevant discussions of clerical and secular authority. What did the Bible say about authority? What had the church fathers said? Early papal letters and the decrees of councils? Even ancient imperial and royal edicts?

The need to put all this together comprehensibly and comprehensively inspired Gratian's work, the *Concordance of Discordant Canons*, also known as the *Decretum*, and the method the author chose to do so, a dialectical engagement, would have long-lasting influence. For like Justinian of six centuries before, this monk, of whom we know almost nothing, wanted to resolve the discordances or contradictions in the canons or laws that he assembled. The papacy found the result to its liking and approved the book. On its framework a greater and greater legal structure was created. Many of Gratian's declarations were challenged over time. New and perhaps profounder masters, like Huguccio at the end of the twelfth century, emerged and redacted their opinions, but always at the core of the Corpus of the Canon Law, as it came to be known, was Gratian's *Decretum*.

*

The description offered in this chapter hardly exhausts, even in the sketchiest way, the achievements of twelfth-century scholars or the environments within which they accomplished these achievements. But it should give something of the flavour of intellectual life – its creativity, excitement, even dangers – in the most elite circles and at the most elite institutions. The Renaissance of the twelfth century had still wider ramifications, however, and it is to these, in the domain of the arts, that we shall now turn.

9

Cultural Innovations of the Twelfth Century: Vernacular Literature and Architecture

The cultural developments of the long twelfth century, 1050–1250, were so many and so remarkable that it is difficult to say which was the most characteristic of the period. Certainly, achievements in the arts have done much to define the age for future generations. When moderns think of the European Middle Ages, they conjure *chansons de geste*, like the *Song of Roland*, romantic heros like Sir Lancelot, beautiful illuminated manuscripts, German minnesingers and their melodies, or perhaps most compellingly the cathedrals and the music and ceremonies that filled these great churches.

VERNACULAR LITERATURE

Vernacular literature existed in an almost agonistic relationship with Latin writing, which, given the prestige of the latter as the language of the Vulgate Bible, maintained its position as the preferred medium for a large number of genres, especially for official and academic writing. The universal Church also found one of its most effective means of governance in its ability to communicate across linguistic boundaries through the common language of the liturgy and clerical education. Nonetheless, the vernaculars occupied what turned out to be an ever-expanding niche by colonizing new literary genres and by being adopted for older ones. The audience for vernacular writing and recitation was both larger and less strictly clerical in composition than the one to which Latin catered. And even in a few of those areas in which Latin seemed secure, like official documentation, some regional vernaculars, like Castilian in Castile and Flemish in Flanders, began to make inroads before the period we have been calling the 'Renaissance of the twelfth century' came to an end.

Among the most remarkable of the new genres was the *chanson de geste*, which as its name implies was a long poem or song dealing with some heroic action, a *geste*, usually but not invariably located in the distant past. The deeds of Charlemagne and his close companions, like Hruodland (Roland in French), made particularly attractive themes. Around such deeds songs had undoubtedly been sung for a long time in the various vernaculars. One can compare the Spanish tradition of singing the praises of the eleventh-century adventurer, El Cid, and his struggles with the Muslims long before the epic poem *El Cantar de mio Cid* was put to parchment. Whether these songs (we might liken them to modern ballads) were then stitched together in the epic poems we call the *chansons de geste* may be doubted; the poems are more coherent than this would imply. But it seems fairly certain that individual authors, though they usually remain anonymous to us, drew inspiration and raw material from any number of short songs and stories, as well as from what could be found in learned histories, in order to create their epic *chansons*.

The reference to learned histories in the last paragraph should remind us that the *chansons*, even if they achieved a certain popularity in aristocratic circles, were not themselves simple folk tales, but the creations of learned men, perhaps clerics. These poems were long; even the short ones, like the *Song of Roland*, ran to about 4,000 lines. The poets used complex forms in which to express their thoughts. A common pattern was to have lines of ten syllables in length, each of which would have a breath or pause (caesura) after the fourth or sixth syllable. But some poets favoured an eight-syllable line.

The earliest *chansons*, again like the *Roland*, whose manuscript tradition does not go back before 1138, consistently use assonance. By the end of the twelfth century, however, fuller rhyme began to displace assonance. Sections of the poems, sometimes called *laisses*, are difficult to characterize. It is not the case, for example, that a fourteen-line *laisse* will pick up one sub-theme or one action, and the next, say, twelve-line *laisse* will then move the poem forward to a different sub-theme or action. There is much overlap between and among *laisses*. On the other hand, unified by its assonance and sometimes followed by a refrain or other marker, such as the *Roland*'s cryptic AOI, whose meaning is lost, a *laisse* does have a kind of poetic integrity and is certainly an aid to memory. As modern investigation of epic story-telling traditions suggests, bards can memorize immensely long poems and yet, having done so, can impart to them their own distinctive style by modifying rhymes, changing well-known words, pausing in unexpected places, and even adding or subtracting from the traditional story in response to the reactions of their audience. If, as seems likely, the deeds of Charlemagne and Roland were spoken or chanted around crusader campfires, among other places, particular moments of poignancy in the tales would have been stressed on different occasions, in response at least in part to the recent experiences of the crusaders.

It has also been argued with vigour that poems of this sort served to introduce aristocratic boys to the culture of heroism which they were expected to sustain throughout their whole adult lives. A word on the 'epic blow' will help clarify this assertion. The epic blow is a mounted hero's downstroke of his sword by which, in the *chanson de geste* tradition, he inflicts horrifying injury on his opponent. The hero's sword may be described as cleaving the helmet, the skull and brain, the teeth, the shoulders and the torso of the enemy, indeed going right through him to cleave his steed as well. Any adult warrior would know that this was impossible and that glancing (sideways) blows were the preferred form of using the sword while mounted. A boy, who had never yet been blooded in war, might well have none of this knowledge; the amazing picture of the epic blow would have seized his imagination. He would have wanted to be the hero – or so the argument goes – and he would have understood that it was his duty to achieve that status.

This is not to say that these elaborate poems were only intended for boys. As today, men who have been in war still enjoy good and even bad action movies in which the heroes achieve totally impossible, indeed superhuman feats. Nor is it to argue that women and girls were excluded from the audience or failed to enjoy the poems. Presumably they accepted the culture of heroism into which their sons, brothers and husbands had been or had to be socialized. Perhaps, too, like the men and boys they were easily moved by scenes like the death of Roland or the occasional word portrait of a woman caught by the terrifying events described in the *chansons*. Few people can come upon the horrific scene of the burning of the nuns of Origny in the *Song of Raoul de Cambrai* and remain unmoved. Even the knights themselves, as depicted in the *chanson*, 'could not help weeping for pity' (Raoul de Cambrai, 1936, pp. 43–44). All of which is to say that the *chansons de geste* served multiple purposes in medieval culture.

The *chansons* whetted the appetite for heroism. There was plenty of time to introduce boys and young men to the 'realism' of war. In northern Europe the invention of the tournament is a case in point. These started out as real mêlées, two large groups of knights that, seemingly ruleless or under the sanction of very few rules, beat each other up until one side gave in or was declared the winner. These were dangerous blood sports; the description of some, slightly fictionalized, became themselves episodes in epic stories. However, it was not long before the old mêlées were refashioned into the highly rule-bound and ritualized tournaments that moderns imagine they always were, individual jousts between beplumed human opponents, often separated by a low wall, or the tilting at non-human targets as a show of skill, all in front of an audience of great knights and beautifully attired aristocratic ladies.

In addition to the epic poetry of heroism, the period produced an abundance of much shorter vernacular work, including fables and *lais* (short rhymed tales) and lyrical and love poems. The most famous fable collection, amounting to 102 stories and existing in more than a score of manuscripts, was composed by a woman, Marie de France, who flourished in the latter half of the twelfth century, and was the author not only of fables but of *lais* and a long, profoundly allusive 2,000-line fiction on St Patrick and the persuasive power of Purgatory to transform sinners' ways of life, the *Espurgatoire Saint Patrice*.

Much has been conjectured and almost nothing is known of Marie's origin except that she was French and had noble, even royal patrons. Her fables are brought together from several sources, although she adds numerous touches of her own, effectively making many of them new creations. They are didactic stories, whose allegories are capable of wide interpretation, constrained, however, by the morals the author provides. The themes are traditional: the evils of exploitation, abuse of power, pride, injustice. Yet they reinforce social norms; they do not subvert them. Power justly resides in an implicit or allegorized aristocratic elite. What is bad is not this siting of power, but its misuse by those who otherwise deserve having the power.

Contemporary with Marie de France, and writing perhaps in England, where she too may have written, was the Jewish author, Berechiah ha-Nakdan, Berechiah the Punctuator. The collection of stories he put together was in Hebrew, therefore not strictly speaking in the vernacular which Jews spoke in common with their Christian neighbours. It is known as the *Mishle shu'alim* or 'Fox Fables'. Many of these use the same storylines as those found in Marie de France's tales, and only one of Berechiah's stories, it has been argued, is entirely, that is separately, Jewish in origin, a fact that testifies to at least one facet of literary taste shared by Jew and Christian in literature of this period.

Marie de France, as mentioned above, was also the author of *lais*, each line of which is ordinarily eight syllables in length. The plots for these brief and succinct narratives were drawn ostensibly from Breton lore and were apparently creative adaptations of sung short stories. They share themes with the heroic genres, blending tales of prowess and affection in a short space. Like the fables they are thoroughly, though delicately, moralized. A reader or listener would have come away with a clear basis for rational behaviour, a reason (*reisun*) for moral action.

Some 2,500 or so pieces of lyrical and love poetry have survived in the Provençal language alone. They, too, like the epics, served multiple purposes in medieval culture. Many of them (just for a moment concentrating on the Provençal material) were composed for the consumption of aristocratic courts and were meant to be sung by troubadours and jongleurs in performance. Some, a small but significant minority, were written by women, The vast majority of them, however, assume the male authorial voice. Many are in praise of the Virgin, and a fair number of others, which describe a knight's love for a distant, idealized lady, employ metaphors that clearly evoke Marian devotion.

Other love poems, however, seem more secular, and these have provoked lively controversies. A group of poems and songs known as *pastourelles* constitutes one such set of works. The first *pastourelle* seems to have been written in the early twelfth century by a singer and composer named Marcabru, a confessedly low-born Gascon hanger-on at aristocratic courts in Spain and southern France. The early *pastourelles* describe knights who spy innocent, if pert, shepherdesses whom they take for sexual pleasure and then abandon. Modern readers have sometimes interpreted these as both a reflection and an endorsement of male aristocratic predatory behaviour. But this is questionable (Paden, 1998). A reflection of behaviour they certainly are not, at least if we concentrate simply on the treatment of shepherdesses. Some knights were certainly guilty of rape, but not of shepherdesses, for the simple reason that the medieval world had almost none; shepherding was a male monopoly. One could still argue that the shepherdess stood for all innocent and unprotected women, but a problem would remain as to whether the poems endorse or celebrate the knights' behaviour. The cluster of associations with idealized shepherdesses in other literary texts, like the life of St Margaret of Antioch, suggests that the medieval listener was supposed to censure the knights' actions. Later *pastourelles* forestall some of the problems of interpretation in that they dampen the violence; sometimes they do little more than describe knights who have stopped to observe idyllic scenes of shepherdesses and other country folk at play.

Equally controversial are the love poems that have often been situated along with romances in the so-called 'courtly love' tradition. Courtly love purportedly describes the championing by medieval aristocratic men and women of an ideal of adulterous love. That is to say, medieval aristocrats allegedly valued adulterous love as more genuine than the sentiments binding married couples in that aristocratic world of arranged marriages. Although scholars have never been limited to using terms that were current in the periods they study, it is a bit disconcerting to learn that the phrase 'courtly love', characterizing such a radical world view of an otherwise devout aristocracy, was invented in the nineteenth century during the Romantic revival. The Romantic revival was a period of general mythologizing about the Middle Ages. It was Romantics who imagined medieval people gripped by the 'Terrors of the Year 1000', with virtually no proof that they knew the dating system that made it the year 1000 or, if they did know the date, cared about it or its supposed terrors at all. (Serious students of millenarian feeling, of which there certainly was some around the year 1000, continue to be burdened by the backlash against Romantic exaggerations.) It was also Romantics building on the Enlightenment critique of feudalism who popularized the notion that medieval feudal lords had the right to sleep with their serfs' brides on their wedding nights, which universalizes almost the rarest of abusive practices.

The scholars who invented the term 'courtly love' were hardly unschooled dreamers. They judged that they had good grounds for believing courtly love was characteristic of medieval aristocratic culture, for there is a longing for unrequited love expressed in many texts of the period. The closest medieval term to courtly love may be *fin'amors* and actually means something like 'unblemished love' – love which, because it cannot or should not be fulfilled, achieves a certain purity and poignancy. Of course, in the poetry and more so in the romances, good stories demand conflict, the conflict, in this case, between accepted Christian prescriptions and the weight of emotional life. In these fictions, failure occurs repeatedly. Adultery undermines purity. Depicting it allows the authors to celebrate the joys of (even illicit) consummated love, but adultery in itself does not compete with decency as an ideal. And there is much more parodic intent in the literary sources which have usually been marshalled in defence of the existence of courtly love than the defenders of the term ordinarily acknowledge. But the debate still rages.

Romance, as noted above, has also been placed in the courtly love tradition, a positioning that has engendered the same vigorous opposition. Romance was a new poetic genre, the medieval version of the modern novel, although not every literary scholar would endorse this comparison. In any case, romance emerged in the first decades of the twelfth century. Romance authors, like Chrétien de Troyes, drew abundantly on folk legends, especially, as in the case of the verse *lais*, those originating in the Celtic lands or flourishing in them, wherever they may have originated. To these Celtic stories, often with King Arthur at the centre or in the background, were added material drawn from the love poetry, emerging ideas about ideal knighthood, and ethical material or at least ideas drawn from the Bible and classical texts.

Sometimes the borrowing from the classical tradition was wholesale, although there were always peculiarly medieval christianizing twists. The author of the twelfth-century version of Virgil's *Aeneid*, the *Enéas*, will not allow the melancholy Dido to be unforgiving (unchristian) with regard to her heartless treatment at Aeneas's hands when he abandons her to found Rome. She utters no curse as in Virgil's original. Instead, the reader is treated to an ideal Christian-like Dido who wishes her callous lover and his city of the future god-speed.

Very brave and wise was I until love gave me rage, and I would have been lucky had he not come to my land – the Trojan who betrayed me, for whose love I lose my life. . . . I pardon him here my death; and in the name of agreement and peace, I kiss the garments on his bed. I pardon you, Sir Eneas. (Cormier, 1973, pp. 86–7)

It was people's struggles to achieve virtue even in terrifying ethical dilemmas that ordinarily provided the moving force to the sub-plots and overall plots of the stories.

It is very difficult, however, to generalize about romances. Medieval writers recognized the genre by its characteristic formal features, but as to content, they acknowledged a multitude of themes. The Troy legends or ancient matter in general and the Arthurian legends (the matter of Britain), of which the Grail legends were a subset, were two important categories. There were also romances set in more or less contemporary settings. And there was, finally, the *Romance of the Rose*, the work of two French authors (Jean de Meun finished Guillaume de Lorris's poem), which was a didactic and heavily allegorical work with a number of decidedly misogynistic themes.

The characteristic feature of these *romans*, a name attested already by 1150, was their vernacular language. The French may have set the standard, but composition in other vernaculars soon followed. These novels in other languages either developed plots already common in French romances, like that of the tragic love story of Tristan and Isolde or the heroic quest for the Holy Grail, or they created entirely new plot lines based on local legends. The German *Nibelungenlied*, which reworks strange tales of love, jealousy and wandering adventures associated with early Burgundian aristocrats and their consorts, is an example of the latter.

With a few exceptions, the standard presentation in the earlier romances took poetic form. Rhymed lines of eight syllables were typical, although by no means unique to romance. Later on, prose began to displace rhyme. What seems clear is that whether in rhyme or in prose, romance differed from the other vernacular genres discussed, except possibly fables, in that it was meant to be read or recited, never sung. These highly polished novels also frequently proclaimed their authorship in their prologues, which is certainly not the case with the *chansons de geste* but is sometimes a feature of shorter poems and songs.

All told, then, it can be said that there was an explosion of vernacular literature in the twelfth century. Of course, the foregoing discussion has hardly covered all aspects of this phenomenon. The immense outpouring of sagas and poetic material in the Germanic languages of the north is a case in point. Not quite romances or *chansons de geste*, the sagas in particular nonetheless shared some features with them, including representation of the past as heroic. In most cases, the audience for the new genres of poetic and prose composition were aristocratic men and women, although the audiences for the sagas, including, as they probably did, wealthy farmers, may have been wider in social composition from the beginning. In France, it was the courts, like those of the count of Champagne and the duke of Aquitaine, that were especially favoured venues for authors of poems and romances to seek patrons and to have their works sung and read. Here, too, because the themes of the poems and stories these authors wrote were in part drawn from those circulating already, there was no hard and fast division between aristocratic and 'popular' culture. Moreover, some singers and story-tellers were really street-corner performance artists who added juggling and acrobatics to their bag of tricks in the emerging urban cultures of Latin Europe. Whether low-born folk or high-born folk down on their luck, they provided a link between the culture of the aristocratic courts and that of the bourgeois and villager.

ARCHITECTURE

Part of the deeply moving transformation of medieval religious devotion, namely, the growth of pilgrimage to the principal sites of Rome, Canterbury, Cologne, Compostela and the Holy Land, is reflected in the romance tradition discussed above. The quest for the Holy Grail, most notably, draws on and develops themes of pilgrimage and unites these with episodes of righteous violence. The ideal knight, the knight of chivalry, is in some sense a crusader; his violence is necessary and altogether virtuous; he is on a pilgrimage, metaphorical or real, which has as its goal his eternal salvation.

There were thousands of shrines that pilgrims could visit, sites where they could venerate the relics of saints or drink miracle-working waters. Some of these were nothing more than roadside crosses, maybe with tiny statues, catering to occasional passers-by and local villagers. But some had achieved regional importance and were lucky enough to be located near major roads that ran from great cities or already flourishing pilgrimage sites to other famous shrines. If they did enjoy favourable locations on major pilgrimage routes, it is likely that, over time, such shrines benefited from pilgrims' offerings as well as from local and regional aristocratic patronage, which helped to expand or rebuild churches to accommodate the pilgrim worshippers. Nearby there would also grow up pilgrims' hostels; at the more attractive international shrines perhaps more than one hostel might exist, each of which catered to a different linguistic group of travellers. One of King Stephen of Hungary's main devotional acts was the founding of pilgrims' hostels.

A relatively small number of the original pilgrimage churches survive in their eleventh- and twelfth-century form or with eleventh- and early twelfth-century elements still intact. Almost none of the other buildings do. Nonetheless, it is fairly certain that the hostels and an array of other structures shared with the churches a common architectural style. That style is known as Romanesque, from the fact that it incorporated and developed several features common to ancient Roman architecture.

Romanesque was distinguished by relatively massive masonry construction and also by the use of rounded arches. According to engineering studies, the rounded arch is structurally weaker than the pointed arch characteristic of Gothic buildings and so Romanesque walls had to support a higher proportion of the weight than the simple pointed roof. This, in turn, dictated the construction of heavy walls and only a limited number of windows (see Figure 1). There is sometimes, indeed, a fortress-like quality to some of these churches, which could be used to advantage. The Anglo-Norman version of Romanesque, characteristic of some building in England after the Norman Conquest and most vivid in Durham Cathedral (see Figure 4), served as an imposing symbol of authority to the conquered English in the north as well as a warning to the Scots. But it goes too far to write, as one popular textbook did, that 'the Norman cathedrals [in England] show us the huddling together of wretches crazed by fear of the outside world, its murder and rapine', while High Gothic, on the contrary, 'express[es] the relation of free men in a free world, bound together by the love of God' (Harvey, 1961, p. 44).

Rounded arches framed the portals in Romanesque buildings. Above the portals of some of the most famous Romanesque churches were half-circles of relief sculpture, the tympana (see Figures 2 and 3). Despite the vivid scenes depicted in the tympana, like the Last Judgement or Christ in majesty or the marriage feast at Cana, exterior decoration of Romanesque churches was otherwise relatively simple. Of course, the emphasis here has to be on the word relatively, and as usual the comparison is with High Gothic. Nonetheless, some examples of Italian Romanesque on the pilgrimage route through sun-drenched Tuscany to Rome have rich sculptural façades, many of them depicting scenes from the life of Christ, including the favourite pilgrimage and crusader-art scene, Jesus's triumphal entry into Jerusalem on the first Palm Sunday.

The sculpture in and on Romanesque churches employed straighter lines than would become characteristic in the Gothic period (see Figure

5). This, too, has given rise to invidious comparisons with Gothic. Romanesque sculpture in traditional interpretations is said to be lacking in expressiveness or to have an air of gravity about it which crosses the boundary into an almost depressing solemnity.

Romanesque churches as a whole have also been categorized as ponderous and gloomy, an impression strengthened by their relative lack of height, compared with that of High Gothic churches, and the limited amount of interior light from their typically few and small round windows (see Figure 6). It is true, on the latter point, that in the absence of artificial light most Romanesque churches were dark, but so were even most tall well-windowed Gothic churches, at least until yellow glass began to be used in preference to multicoloured stained glass in the very late Middle Ages. But the important point is that artificial light was available. Oil lamps and numerous, often silver, candelabras adorned churches; the lamp- and candle-light played on the metallic objects of devotion, especially reliquaries, and on the walls. The walls seem often to have been adorned with narrative paintings or with various set biblical and hagiographical scenes which were meant to be illuminated by the lamp- and candle-light. It has been a real scholarly effort to try to recover something of the content of these marvellous paintings from the very few fragments that have come down to us. During the various processions and ceremonies, additional great candles or tapers filled the church with supplemental light that bathed the sanctuary and reflected off the pillars and ribbed vaulting of the interior (see Figure 7). Here and there scenes drawn from (christianized) myth and even local folklore – as it were, vernacular art – would be illuminated for the delighted eyes of the worshippers. Combined with the chant that reverberated in the veritable echo chambers that the sanctuaries constituted and the heavy aroma of incense, a worshipper's impression must have been striking.

None of this is to say that contemporaries were unwilling to modify or experiment while remaining loyal to Romanesque design and composition. Architectural historians recognize that some features of what would emerge as the new and more fashionable cosmopolitan style, Gothic, were already being employed in some Romanesque buildings. Even so, some builders did break more decisively with the past. It is still generally accepted that this occurred, in terms of the emergence of Gothic as a distinct and more than embryonic style, during the remodelling of the abbey church of St-Denis, north of Paris, dedicated in 1140. The breakthrough will forever be associated with the heroic efforts of Abbot Suger, who found the existing church too small and cramped and spared no effort to enhance it. He was in a fine position to do so. The chief adviser of King Louis VI, a confidant of Louis VII and regent of the kingdom during the latter's absence on crusade, Suger was also the head of the most important royal monastery in France. It was there that much of the regalia of the monarchy was treasured, like the oriflamme, the royal battle flag. It was there that the official history of the Crown and kingdom was inscribed. And it was the abbey church that became the royal necropolis, at least for the male dynasts. In the event, Suger's remodelling of St-Denis turned out to be a virtual rebuilding of the church.

However, the church at St-Denis now is not Suger's church; there were subsequent rebuilding campaigns. Thus, much of what we know about Suger's new church is based on the putative remnants of the twelfth-century building, Suger's own description of the abbey and its treasures, and the learned but imaginative mental reconstructions of generations of art and architectural historians. One other thing ought to be borne in mind: Gothic did not come into the world fully developed. The categories known as Early Gothic, High Gothic and Late Gothic encompass a vast number of differences within each period. Indeed, it is with some misgivings that these terms are retained at all; some scholars would like to get rid of High Gothic in particular, with its implication of a perfected style, especially since there are other words and phrases that more accurately describe the edifices: *rayonnant* (meaning 'radiating out'), for example, for the late twelfth- and thirteenth-century buildings for which the radiant rose window is a key motif (see Figure 8). For convention's sake, we will adopt the more traditional usages here.

Early Gothic is not known for particularly tall buildings or for the rose window, which are much more characteristic of thirteenth-century or High Gothic. Nor is Early or even High Gothic characterized by the elaborate vaulting known as fan vaulting or, as we have seen, plain yellow glass; these are features of Late Gothic. Common to all Gothic buildings, however, are pointed arches, complex cross-vaulting and relatively large windows. Sculptural façades are elaborate, and the sculptural figures themselves often have more decisively curved bodies than in Romanesque sculpture, although Romanesque styles continued to flourish alongside the newer Gothic ones.

By the 1190s, when the High Gothic period may be said to have begun with the commencement of the construction of Chartres Cathedral (although the centrality of Chartres as a model monument was exaggerated by the Romantics), builders both incorporated and refined older ideas and introduced new ones. Height became an obsession in some quarters, but this preoccuption does not define High Gothic (that is, it is not High because many of the buildings were themselves lofty). Nevertheless, it is striking to a modern observer how the passion for height manifested itself not only in the interior elevation of some of the great cathedrals but also in the desire to augment their façades with great towers or spires. To sustain walls of such height, the pointed arch alone was insufficient. Buttressing was already known before the Gothic period, but flying buttresses intended to deflect the weight of the roof away from the walls became more and more common in monumental buildings (see Figures 9 and 10).

Who paid for these edifices and for the other treasures of Gothic art, like the richly illuminated manuscripts for liturgical use, stained glass windows, golden and bejewelled reliquaries (see Figure 11) that adorned the sanctuaries and which were often cast in the form of miniature Gothic churches? In France, where the style started, the answer is relatively easy to give. To some extent worshippers' oblations provided the money. But since many of the greatest buildings were cathedral churches and therefore located in towns, rich bourgeois patrons were also major donors. Guilds, for instance, frequently endowed windows that allegorically celebrated or commemorated their crafts. But the greatest patrons continued to be the aristocracy and the Crown. Aristocrats richly endowed rural churches and urban churches that were close to the seat of their power. The Crown favoured Paris and the churches of numerous other cities as well as a number of great rural monasteries. So much did the building campaigns come to depend on noble and royal largesse that the construction teams which travelled around the country would shrink in number or disband entirely when large numbers of nobles or the king withdrew financing in order to accomplish some other important task, like launching a crusade.

As the Gothic style spread far beyond France, indeed throughout Christendom, similar modes of financing were adopted in other regions. It is probably the case, however, that the mix among donors varied from place to place. In Italy the cities, because of the erosion of imperial power, had been thrown on their own resources. In many of them the dominant voice in the construction of urban monuments was that of the non-noble patriciate, even though aristocrats more often lived in towns in Italy than in northern France. Economic considerations shaped but did not entirely determine what elements of Gothic less wealthy communities could support: there is many a Gothic church in Europe that has a rose window and no spires or small spires and no rose.

Whatever the sources of the funds, even the small buildings put enormous demands on the coffers of medieval communities. Interruptions of building campaigns could leave unfinished buildings – from cathedrals to parish churches – dangerously liable to decay. Resumed campaigns, five, ten or fifty years after suspension, had both to compensate for the damage and respond to new demands from donors and patrons and to new styles. Were spires still *in*? The asymmetric character of so many of the buildings that have survived to our own day testifies to this. So we see one tower where two were once planned; two towers but in different styles; vacant tympana; different strata of stone; apparently strange intrusions of 'foreign' styles or artifacts brought back from the East by a crusader-turned-donor who insisted on their incorporation into the building, and so on. Yet, in the end, despite the difficulty in bringing the projects to completion (some, like Cologne, were not completed until the nineteenth century), the wondrous array of Gothic monuments stands as extraordinary testimony to the dynamism and capacity for creative accomplishment of medieval society in the long Renaissance of the twelfth century.

I O

Political Power and its Contexts I

The impact of the Investiture Controversy on Germany was incalculable. Germany would produce strong kings and king-emperors in the future, but in every case they would be confronted by political situations of immense complexity: seemingly intractable Italian problems, new and debilitating confrontations with the papacy, and what was perhaps the most serious issue when viewed from the perspective of the kings' quest for unrivalled political authority and power, a suspicious aristocracy in Germany itself. All of these issues, it can plausibly be argued, took on extreme forms because of the legacy of the struggle over lay investiture. Add to them a continuously difficult situation on the northern, eastern and southern frontiers with Scandinavians, Balts, Slavs and Hungarians, and it may seem remarkable that the German monarchy survived at all.

It did survive, and it did so in part because the kings were willing to compromise. For recognition of its rights in governance, the aristocracy was mollified without being entirely satisfied. Germany became characterized by 'particularism', an enduring state of political division. Government effectively took place at a level below that of the central (royal/imperial) administration, falling instead to local princes of various ranks – from dukes, marcher lords and counts to bishops who had the powers and title of counts.

Whether the institutions of any particular region were in the control of the Crown or a territorial lord, the administrators were likely to be men known as *ministeriales*, people mostly of servile origin who carried out the routine and not so routine tasks of governance. They might administer castles, like petty nobles in other countries, or they could serve as estate managers. Some had judicial functions. Some tutored noble children in the arts of courtesy and book learning. Others were captains of military contingents, knights in all but legal status, commanding free-born knights. Probably, the extreme reliance on servile

7. Northern Europe in the twelfth century

men for functions typically carried out by free men in other countries has to do with two factors, foremost the prevalence of allodial (duty-free) property among free men in Germany. Without pre-existing ties of dependency, free men in Germany were unwilling to be *bound* to do the kinds of tasks they conventionally performed in France and England.

Second, in the absence of the kind of ties of dependence within the upper class found in many other places in Europe, lords, including prelates and the king himself, had the opportunity of creating an administrative elite in Germany that was absolutely dependent on them, or as dependent as possible. Serfs met the requirement. Jews did so, too, but the religious issue, particularly the Church's condemnation of the presence of Jews in superordinate positions, complicated the question of the employment of Jews and made recourse to them relatively infrequent, even in more cosmopolitan southern Europe with its large numbers of Jews.

All the powers in Germany, royal, ecclesiastical and baronial, had recourse to *ministeriales*. There were problems, of course. Serfs having the power of knights had to grin and bear it if they were looked down on outside of Germany, as, for example, when they went on a diplomatic mission. But within Germany they expected to be treated with more respect than agricultural labourers of the same status. They expected to have greater rights of inheritance in their property than the servile agricultural population did. And so it went. The result, although it was a long time coming, was a gradual amalgamation of the *ministeriales* in the later Middle Ages with the non-servile knightly class. What else could have occurred with a servile class that included men like Werner of Bolland, a *ministerialis* who had seventeen castles and 1,100 armed men dependent on him?

Lords' utilization of *ministeriales* as the administrators of their households and estates may have given a certain efficiency to their governance and created an intensely loyal administration. It did not contribute to overall German unity. Of course, there was nothing inevitable about the durability of the more or less loose confederation of principalities that emerged in Germany. The balance between the princes and the kings could shift. To a large extent, the efforts of the two sides to effect an alteration in their relative power is what the political history of the twelfth century is all about. In the end, a truly decisive and long-term shift in favour of the Crown, like that which gave rise to the royal authoritarianism that typified France in the late twelfth and thirteenth centuries, never occurred. That 'failure' would someday be looked upon – rightly or wrongly – as a major factor in the instability associated with German state-building in the modern period.

The very working-out of some sort of balance of power between local and central authorities was punctuated by civil wars. In 1125, only three years after the Concordat of Worms brought an end to the Investiture Controversy, Emperor Henry V died without heirs. He had designated his nephew, Frederick of Staufen, the duke of Swabia, as his successor, but influential churchmen and certain lay aristocratic elements desired to confirm the reality of German elective monarchy and, of course, their effective control of it. They elected Lothar III. The Staufen (or Hohenstaufen) candidate went to war to defend his claim. When, later, Lothar III wanted to transfer his title by hereditary right, he lost the support of many of his adherents, some of whom turned to the Hohenstaufen claimant, by then Conrad III, in retribution. Thus it continued, a dismal and depressing story of political intrigue and factionalism, as well as conflicting principles of appropriate succession, until the emergence of a strong Hohenstaufen ruler in the person of Frederick I Barbarossa (1152–90).

The new king, coming to the throne as he did after many decades of chaos, recognized the need to radically rethink royal policies. In the royal *ministeriales* he had an instrument at hand to govern the royal territories and at least to represent his interests loyally in areas where his fiscal and judicial rights were less dense. He came to depend on them utterly, assembling large military contingents from among them, using them in Italy and on crusade, and raising the status of some individuals to the rank of the high nobility. Markward of Anweiler, one of these, will be encountered later, but his example is worth mentioning now. Possibly because he needed the cachet of free status outside of Germany, Markward was nominally delivered from his servility and was granted ducal rank in the late twelfth century. This *ministerialis* soon reached the pinnacle of his career. Sicily having come into Hohenstaufen hands, he was entrusted with the regency of that kingdom, when Emperor Henry VI, Frederick Barbarossa's son, died in 1197 (see chapter 13).

Despite the role the *ministeriales* played in strengthening the monarch's rule, Frederick Barbarossa realized that he needed to persuade the aristocrats or some significant selection of them to tie their fortunes to the success of the monarchy. To this end he elevated the cream of the nobility to princely rank and began a process of enforcing the ranked subordination of the rest in what is usually called a feudal hierarchy. But there were several aspects of his programme, with regard both to the princes and to his overall strategic vision, that in the long run produced results that he probably would have abhorred.

First, the princes were clearly granted more powers of governance than existed in contemporary principalities. England went through a period of 'unlaw' in the years 1135 to 1154 when the aristocratic members of society began to carve out great lordships and when even royal towns made tentative claims to autonomy, but the re-establishment of royal authority in 1154 put the brakes on and indeed turned back these developments in England. France was steadily advancing, from the Crown's viewpoint, in circumscribing the powers of lesser lords and never abandoned its effective overlordship of its growing towns; by the end of the twelfth and beginning of the thirteenth century it would be pulling the reins in on the last remnants of its over-mighty subjects. Barbarossa, like his contemporaries, imagined a partnership between the throne and the nobility (he was less interested in the towns or in the progress of German colonization into Slavdom, for that matter), but the balance of power did not favour him as it began to favour other monarchs in northern Europe.

Second, the king's dependence on the great princes in Germany implied that they would have to be assured at all costs that their collective position would be maintained. Therefore, for example, when Henry the Lion, the duke of Saxony, was juridically deprived of his fiefs in 1180 for failing to answer an imperial military summons, Frederick seized the fiefs but did not retain them as royal domain property. He felt compelled to enfeoff other important magnates with them. The obvious comparison, though it occurred a few decades later, is the behaviour of Philip II Augustus of France after the confiscation of Normandy, Maine, Anjou and other fiefs from their Plantagenet lord. They were immediately assimilated into the royal domain; Philip *became* duke of Normandy, count of Maine, etc.

Third and finally, Barbarossa's strategic vision always included northern Italy, which in turn meant expending resources against hostile alliances among some of the Italian communes, which had become zealous defenders of their liberties, and against the papacy, which remained deeply suspicious of the German king-emperor. The disputes with the papacy were very complicated. They went back to a series of misunderstandings and broken promises about the amount of support Frederick would give the popes in their attempt to establish effective rule in Rome. The papacy's suspicion was deepened by the evident attempts Frederick was making to exercise control over the German clergy to the detriment, his opponents alleged, of the liberty of the Church. When Frederick encouraged a schism, the election of a pro-Hohenstaufen pope in opposition to the canonically elected Alexander III (1159–81), the liberty of the Church seemed even more precarious, and battlelines were drawn. Frederick's repeated military failures, relieved by a few but no very decisive victories, rendered his efforts to consolidate his rule in Germany ever more difficult. When reconciliation was ultimately achieved with the pope (1177) and the Italian towns in rebellion against the emperor (1183), Frederick was a prematurely old man. The great saviour of Germany had accomplished at best a very partial act of salvation.

A last chance for the emperor to wrap his office and himself in the dignity and honours of Christian rulership occurred in 1187. Jerusalem fell to Saladin in that year and a shock wave ran through Christendom. Frederick took the cross, but the Third Crusade (see chapter 11) was a personal disaster for him. The march through Europe and the privations in Asia Minor were horrendous. The old warrior, nearly seventy, drowned while leading the military avant-garde over the River Gök Su on 10 June 1190. In popular lore his name carries no force in the mythology of the Third Crusade; that honour would go to the English king who mounted an expedition, Richard the Lionhearted.

*

The kingdom that Richard the Lionhearted ruled was utterly different from Barbarossa's Germany. If particularism is a word that has been used to categorize and belittle the allegedly limited achievements of the German kings in the twelfth century, 'constitutionalism' has been employed to praise English developments with the same benefit of hindsight and the same curse of teleology. Since constitutional government came to be lauded in the liberalizing movements of the nineteenth century and since it seemed to coexist comfortably with stability and power in England and the British Empire, scholars looked back to the medieval past to find the roots of British or more specifically English political strength. How had there emerged notions that there exists a fundamental set of laws that not even the monarch is above and that to change the laws requires the consent of the political nation?

These scholars imagined a gradual and profoundly progressive accretion of constitutionalist elements in English history. Nineteenth-century expansion of the electorate could not have been possible without the emergence of party government in the eighteenth, the constitutional constraints on the Stuart kings in the seventeenth, the Reformation through Parliament in the early sixteenth, the development of representation in Parliament in the thirteenth or, finally, the invention of the common law in the twelfth. This complacent picture of constitutional development has been recognized by insightful scholars as deeply flawed right from the beginning. Nonetheless, those who painted the picture were right to see the invention of the common law as a paramount achievement of the twelfth-century kings. In fact, the context out of which it arose was extremely complex and conflict-ridden.

The recovery of the English throne from the Danes by Edward the Confessor in 1042 did not assure the continuity of native English rule on the island. Edward himself, as pointed out in chapter 3, lived a chaste marriage; he produced no heirs of his own. Moreover, although they were instrumental in helping re-establish the dynasty, the earl of Wessex, Godwin, and his son and successor, Harold Godwinson, developed an antagonistic relationship with the king. Who would succeed Edward the Confessor became the crucial question. There were still Scandinavian claimants. In addition, while Harold Godwinson was in Normandy under difficult circumstances, he acknowledged that Edward's own choice, Duke William of Normandy, should succeed to the throne upon the king's death. Whether the promise was coerced has long been debated, but that Harold made the promise is certain.

In 1066 Edward died, and Harold Godwinson seized the throne. Soon afterwards he was confronted with a Scandinavian invasion which he marched north to meet. He could scarcely celebrate his magnificent victory, for he received intelligence that Duke William of Normandy was launching his own invasion in the south. After a forced march of more than 200 miles, Harold's army met William's on the battlefield. It was a see-saw affair, but the victor at the Battle of Hastings, and in consequence the new ruler of England, was Duke William, forever afterwards known as William the Conqueror (1066–87).

As a result of the deaths of so many English nobles at Hastings and in localized and regional rebellions thereafter (for William's rule was not uncontested), the Norman conquerors effectively replaced the native Anglo-Saxon and Anglo-Danish ruling class in England. Steadily, too, Normans or other continentals came to replace the leading prelates in the Church, as the native Anglo-Saxons retired or died. For example, William's archbishop of Canterbury, Lanfranc, a distinguished writer, was an Italian who had been prior of the ducal abbey of Bec in Normandy. Another addition to the increasingly cosmopolitan mix in England were Jews, immigrants from Rouen mostly, never more than about 5,000 resident in the kingdom at their demographic peak a century or so later, but, as it would turn out, important in English history far beyond their tiny numbers.

Several thousand Norman men in Church and state dominated at least two million Anglo-Saxons and Anglo-Danes. They could do so only by a judicious use of conciliation and, when conciliation failed, terror. English law would be respected, although the new king's clarifications of the limits of its application to the Normans allowed him to adjust its content. Thus, he introduced trial by combat, a Norman procedure, as a new mode of proof in land disputes and direct accusations of felonies. He protected his Normans from retribution by the introduction of the murder fine. Knowing that the killing of a Norman might incur a fine on an entire community, communities had a vested interest in controlling hotheads.

William was aware that there was a wide variety of forms of resistance to his rule, even though he consistently argued the legitimacy of his accession. He realized that local landholders who had obligations to their former Anglo-Saxon and Anglo-Danish lords would try to hide those obligations from him and their other new Norman lords or at least get out of the ones they thought unjust. In 1085, William therefore authorized a systematic survey of royal rights. Although it was never completed, possibly because of the king's death in 1087 while putting down an uprising in the county of Maine on the continent, it was nevertheless the most comprehensive investigation of a medieval principality yet undertaken and has survived in what we know as Domesday Book. It allowed William and his immediate successors to know more about their realm than perhaps any other rulers in western Europe.

When William died in 1087, he was succeeded in England by his second son, William II Rufus, and in Normandy by his eldest son, Robert, presumably because what he had inherited (Normandy) had to go to his eldest son, but what he acquired apart from inheritance (England) could go to whom he wanted. This explanation has been much disputed, however, particularly since notions of primogeniture, the pre-eminent rights of the eldest son, were so primitive at the time.

In any case, William Rufus did succeed his father in England and ruled with equal vigour. During the papal schism of the Investiture Controversy, Rufus hedged his bets, but Lanfranc's successor as archbishop of Canterbury, the Italian theologian and philosopher, Anselm, who had also been prior and abbot of the ducal abbey of Bec, supported the reformers in the person of Pope Urban II. The titanic struggle between the two men, Rufus and Anselm, over whose right it was to determine the legitimate pope, together with the strong control the king still had over the English Church, provoked the archbishop to go into exile in opposition to his king.

William Rufus ruled in Normandy as well as England after his elder brother joined the First Crusade. When Robert returned, he intended to take the duchy back into his own hands, and, after the childless William's accidental death by an arrow while hunting, Robert also expected to become king of England. In this he was thwarted by his still younger brother, Henry, who was in the hunting party and immediately departed the accident scene, seized the royal treasure and had himself crowned king as Henry I (1100–35). The civil war which ensued between Robert and Henry turned decisively in Henry's favour in 1106, making Henry the more or less undisputed ruler of both England and Normandy from that date.

Under Henry's rule the ethnic division in England between Normans and Anglo-Saxons and Anglo-Danes became less marked, and the institutions of government achieved a certain cohesiveness. The financial administration of the kingdom became especially sophisticated through the creation of what was known as the exchequer, a centralized office where the accounts of the sheriffs were audited and from which expenditures were authorized. There seems also to have been some attempt to keep an eye on the execution of justice in the provinces by sending representatives of the king's court on tours of inspection and adjudication from time to time. Ecclesiastical problems continued. Anselm gladly returned after William Rufus's death. Henry I vilified his brother's memory in order to enhance his own stature and represented himself as the welcomer of the exiled archbishop and the protector of the Church. But Anselm was as prickly as ever. When it came to the issue of lay investiture in England, he drew the line, desiring Henry I to abandon rights that the popes were also demanding the emperors cede on the continent. Henry resisted. Anselm resumed his exile, which, in the event, encouraged Henry to yield.

However, the main problem after the effective end of the war with Robert in 1106 was not financial, judicial or ecclesiastical, but the royal succession. Henry had two legitimate children, a boy and a girl. The girl, Matilda, would become Emperor Henry V's widow and is often therefore called by courtesy Empress Matilda, after the highest rank she achieved in life. When Matilda's brother died, the king arranged to have the aristocracy twice promise to accept his daughter as his successor. In fact, in 1135, when Henry I did die, they reneged on their promise to accept rule by a woman and embraced in her place Stephen of Blois, William the Conqueror's grandson by his daughter Adele. The result was another civil war, this time between the forces of Stephen and of the widow Matilda, now remarried to Geoffroy, the count of Anjou.

The civil war, or anarchy, as it is often called, lasted from 1135 until 1153. Much of the time the continental domains were in the hands of Matilda's forces, although there were occasions when she extended her power strongly in England itself. Increasingly she turned the initiative over to her son, also named Henry. When a settlement was reached in 1153, it was decided that on Stephen's death Henry would accede to the throne as Henry II. In the next year Stephen died, and Henry II (1154–89) thereupon united in his person the rulership of England, Normandy, Maine and, on account of his inheritance from his father, the county of Anjou and its dependencies. Through his wife, Eleanor of Aquitaine, he ruled Poitou and most of south-western France by courtesy as well. In 1154 the Angevin Empire was born.

It is to Henry II that we owe many significant developments in English government, none more important than the 'invention' of the common law. The legacy of the anarchy or unlaw period was such that the king had two major problems to face: the re-establishment of order and the assurance of a smooth succession. Within two years he had successfully disarmed most of the armed companies that had flourished during the civil war. He had also caused as many as 2,000 small fortified sites that had been constructed without royal licence to be razed to the ground.

The king also began to investigate abuses by the sheriffs and other problems of the royal administration. In 1164, he authorized a series of inquiries in the provinces into the extent of crime. Who was suspected and of what? Those indicted by these groups of local good men, grand juries, were to be taken into custody, if they could be found, and tried by ordeal. Even if they were found innocent, they were exiled due to the ill-repute into which they had fallen. If those indicted could not be apprehended, royal justices – circuit judges who were sent out to hear the findings of the grand juries and supervise the trials – would solemnly outlaw them, that is, withdraw the protection of the law from them.

In 1166, Henry II followed this up with a series of inquiries, also undertaken by circuit judges, into any recent (*novel*) violent dispossessions (*disseisins*) of landholders from their lands. The judges were to ask local juries what occupants of land were believed to have committed disseisins of free men from their free holdings 'unjustly and without the judgment' of a court. Those whom the juries indicated were then evicted and fined. Later, in the mid-1170s, any dispossessed freeman could seek a writ from the royal chancery to initiate a court case against the alleged dispossessor. The circuit judges, when they came around to hear cases of *novel disseisins*, would seek verdicts from local juries in order to adjudicate the cases. Of course, they would be deciding only possessory rights, not whether one or the other parties had the better proprietary right to the property. The creation of the writ of *novel disseisin* and many similar writs was intended to bring judicial action to bear to forestall or quickly end violence.

In this way, England came to have a system of royal justice, the common law, which embodied a set of principles and procedures that, if not unique, was perhaps more highly developed in England than elsewhere. One of the most important principles has been encapsulated in the phrase, 'the beatitude of seisin'. Peaceful seisin or possession was blessed; it would be protected against violent redress. Violent redress met its match in the royal forum that offered the dispossessed party the writ of *novel disseisin*. If one had a legitimate claim against a man in long and peaceful seisin, on the other hand, the proper mode of proceeding was a formal challenge of his proprietary right to the property, and the mode of resolution was a court case whose mode of proof was trial by battle. Yet, by the late 1170s, one could opt for trial by jury instead of trial by battle in these civil or property cases as well.

Trial by jury, therefore, emerged as a standard procedure and principle of the common law as well. Of course, in the twelfth century, it still meant only that people involved in civil actions had recourse, in many cases obligatorily, in others voluntarily, to juries. It did not mean that all civil actions were necessarily tried by jury. On the criminal side of the law, even though grand juries came to be used regularly to indict criminals, it was still possible to make a direct personal accusation. Moreover, actual trials of the alleged felons proceeded either by battle, in the case of a direct personal accusation, or by ordeal, in the case of grand jury indictment.

One of the reasons there were so many and such profound innovations in judicial matters that dealt with crimes and violent dispossessions of property was that the rulership of Henry II was constantly being tested. On the continent, every dispute with the French, who were both envious and resentful of Henry's power, usually led to some sort of military confrontation. And it did not help matters that Henry's power in the south-west came through his wife, whose marriage to the French king Louis VII had been annulled. But Henry was also ill-served by various 'disloyal' subjects, including this same wife and his sons by her, who resented his domineering treatment of them and sometimes raised rebellion against him. Finally, and somewhat unexpectedly, there was also a small but influential group of ecclesiastics who felt that the king abused the Church. William II Rufus and Henry I came into conflict with St Anselm; Henry II confronted Thomas Becket.

Becket was a well-educated young man to whom the king took an immediate liking early in his reign. It is quite clear that Becket had an ascetic streak that Henry took little or no notice of, however. He made Becket his chancellor and with his help began the process of stabilizing royal governance. When the old archbishop of Canterbury died in 1162, Henry persuaded Becket, who was not even a priest at the time, to accept the office. Immediately following his ordination to the priesthood he became archbishop.

Undoubtedly Henry II expected matters to go smoothly. He would work with Becket as the Conqueror had worked with Lanfranc to bring order to England, and more specifically to the Church. But Becket the archbishop was not the same man as Becket the boon companion or chancellor. He did not take his new duty to be subservience to the king but obedience to God. The nastiest issue – the issue that shattered Henry and Becket's friendship – concerned 'criminous clerks'.

A churchman or clerk who was accused of a felony was tried in a Church court and, if convicted, punished by the Church. William the Conqueror had regularized or confirmed this privilege soon after the conquest. Since the Church did not practise capital punishment or other blood punishments like mutilation, the convicted clerk often had a relatively easy imprisonment in an ecclesiastical prison as retribution for his crime. Henry wanted his officials to have at least some presence at the ecclesiastical trials, and he certainly wished the defrocked clerk to suffer the same punishment a layman would suffer. But Becket construed this and similar changes in the relations between Church and State to be unwarranted incursions on the liberty of the Church.

The English episcopate itself was divided, but even some of Henry's supporters disliked his methods. He had his officials make accusations of bribery with regard to Becket's actions as chancellor. The charges, even if they had a grain of truth, were clearly opportunistic. Becket, like Anselm more than a half-century before, went into exile, but although he became the French King Louis VII's close friend, he did not have the pope's unequivocal support. The latter had his hands full with Frederick Barbarossa and would have preferred a calmly negotiated settlement of the disputes in England.

It was noted above that Henry II's two principal goals were to stabilize the governance of his principalities and assure a smooth succession. His success at the former, as we have seen, was mixed, despite the important legacy of the common law in England. His initial effort at the latter was positively disastrous, for while Becket was in exile, the king decided to have his eldest son crowned as co-king. In France this had been the Capetian way of doing things since 987, and their successions had all been relatively smooth. The problem in England was that the crowning of a king was the prerogative of the archbishop of Canterbury. In the absence of the exiled archbishop, Henry chose the archbishop of York to do the job. Becket fulminated. The pope supported him. Thus, the very device that had been designed to assure the succession threatened to turn influential public opinion against Henry and jeopardize the succession. After a formal reconciliation with Becket while in Normandy to defuse the crisis, Henry permitted his former friend to return to England.

Becket did so and straightaway set about to excommunicate all those who had taken part in the 'false' coronation. When Henry got word he raged against the archbishop; and four of his household knights left Normandy, believing they were doing the king's will, and went to England and murdered Becket. The sustained outpouring of grief was astounding, although in part it was due to the fact that some of the finest and most respected men in the high intellectual circles of Europe, men like John of Salisbury, knew and admired Becket and actively propagated his memory and later his cult. Within a few years Becket was canonized, his tomb at Canterbury became the major pilgrimage site in England, and Henry II was obliged to undergo public penance for his indirect responsibility for the act of murder. He also strategically retreated on issues like that of criminous clerks for which Becket had endured exile and suffered martyrdom. But the final irony was that the young co-king was not only disloyal and rebelled against his father but also predeceased him. The relatively smooth succession in 1189 would bring Richard the Lionhearted to the throne, a king who spent no more than six months of his ten-year reign in England and who would make his name as a great crusader rather than as a great administrator and law-giver. The proof of King Henry II's accomplishments is usually taken to be the fact that government functioned so smoothly after his death, even with the new king's extended absences.

*

A significant portion of the time that Richard was absent from England was because his co-crusader and adversary, King Philip II Augustus of France, connived with the duke of Austria to have Richard locked up and held for ransom on his return trip from the Holy Land after the Third Crusade. Philip found Richard, who gloried in his crusader credentials, personally insufferable, and he hated the fact that one man, who was not himself, controlled so much of the kingdom of France.

A catch-all phrase to describe this kingdom or the political ideology of its rulers might be 'sacred monarchy'. Its secular expression was 'authoritarianism'. Again, as in the other kingdoms discussed here, Enlightenment and post-Enlightenment historians choosing such a phrase to describe the emerging medieval kingdom of France were trying to explain what they regarded as the distinctive nature of government and civil society in their own or recent times. France of the *ancien régime* was typically categorized as absolutist, a term now somewhat in disfavour, given early modern limits on the technologies of power. To explain its alleged absolutism, nonetheless, historians took care to emphasize those aspects of its medieval history which celebrated the sacredness of its ruler and his authoritarian rule.

There was more than a grain of truth in their focus on sacrality, for despite many other reasons for loyalty to the Crown, such as feudal notions of paying honour to one's overlord, loyalty was incessantly said to be owed because of the special character of the monarch. Ideas that were still unevenly integrated in the eleventh and early twelfth centuries came to coalesce into a fully fledged ideology in the late twelfth and thirteenth. Repetition had persuasive force. Every king was now said to be crowned with oil from heaven; every king could and did heal scrofula by touch; every king went on crusade, some went twice.

King Louis VI (1108–37) had assumed most of the authority of the Crown in the waning years of the reign of his father, depressed and ineffective as the latter was in the wake of his dispute with the papacy over his bigamous marriage (see chapter 4). Louis struggled hard to keep control over the nobility and entrusted a great deal of authority to the high household officials, like the chancellor, in doing so. The chancellor, however, Etienne Garlande, put together his own party, which the Crown came to regard as a threat. In the event, Louis removed Garlande and turned to a monk, later abbot of Saint-Denis, Suger, who became his chief counsellor.

With Suger's eager and able support, efforts to subjugate the nobility of the royal domain proceeded apace, and Suger and many other ideologues continued to lay stress on the quasi-sacred character of the French Crown and, increasingly, the special character of 'sweet France'. The contemporary text, *The Song of Roland*, repeatedly uses this phrase, which captures something of the holiness of the land and the special qualities of the people, two other themes that increasingly came to be articulated. The golden lily or fleur-de-lys was not uniquely the symbol of France, but more so than in any other kingdom it was an artifact of royal propaganda. France was as pure as the lily.

It is hard to know how important this self-aggrandizing propaganda was, especially for those who saw the king as a usurper of their prerogatives or as an interferer in what had once been their customary games, including banditry. But Louis VI had a long reign, almost thirty years, and longevity counted for something. Castellans and other barons in the royal domain got used to a government that ruled actively. Generations of nobles came of age never having known the weak state of the early eleventh century.

Yet it was a different case with the great principalities outside the royal domain. They paid lip service to the paramountcy of the king, but they had few qualms about meeting him on a battlefield. Here, too, though, it looked as if change might be in the air. First, in the year before his father's death, Louis VII (1138–80) made a very advantageous marriage to Eleanor of Aquitaine, the heiress to the south-west, which appeared to promise an enormous territorial increase in the royal domain and a tipping of the military balance among the princes in the king's favour. Second, Louis VII, leaving the able Suger as regent, went on the

Second Crusade. Since no kings had gone on the First Crusade, the French Crown increased its international prestige enormously.

These two choices, the marriage to Eleanor and Louis VII's decision to go on crusade, both of which held so much promise, backfired. Something happened on the crusade in 1147 that estranged the royal couple and their marriage was annulled in 1152. Worse, Eleanor remarried two months later, this time to Henry, soon to become Henry II of England (1154). Together with his holdings in England, Normandy, Maine, Anjou and Touraine, his possession of Poitou and Aquitaine by this marriage placed almost all of western France in his hands. The decision to go on the Second Crusade, that other promising choice, lost much of its lustre when the expedition failed so miserably (see chapter 11). Future French kings would maintain the tradition of crusading; they believed in the wars and they recognized that even if they failed, there was dignity in taking the vow. But the dismal outcome of the Second Crusade, in particular, was deeply distressing to Louis VII.

Much of Louis VII's time was taken up after the annulment of his marriage with trying to keep Henry II's Angevin empire at bay. Fortunately for the French, as we have seen, Henry had his own problems. Eleanor and Henry's sons by Eleanor turned against him one after the other and kept his domains in turmoil. The Becket controversy and the subsequent murder added to the trouble.

Louis VII had become very friendly with Becket during his exile in France. In 1179, a few years after Becket's canonization, the ailing king even asked and received permission to visit England and pray at the saint's tomb for his son's recovery from a serious illness. Philip was Louis VII's only son, from his third marriage, and his birth thirteen years before had been greeted by a troubled country with enormous satisfaction, since it promised a smooth succession. When the old king returned from his pilgrimage to Canterbury, he was delighted that the boy was on the way back to full health and had him crowned in the Capetian manner as co-king soon after. A year later, on his father's death, Philip took full power at his second coronation. He was the last heir ever to serve as co-king in the lifetime of his predecessor; the principle of primogenitary succession was now firmly established in France.

Philip II Augustus was as obsessed as his father had been with assuring firm rulership in the royal domain, augmenting his territories where possible, and, most of all, keeping the Angevin pre-eminence in France in check. Henry II died in 1189 and was succeeded by Richard I the Lionhearted. Both Richard and Philip took the cross in order to participate in the Third Crusade of 1190. Philip used the opportunity of the period of preparations to strengthen the institutions of governance, by carefully delineating the responsibilities of provincial officials, *baillis*, whose job was to exercise the royal authority at the regional level and to supervise the enforcement of the full array of royal rights by other officials, like provosts, at subordinate levels.

He spent very little time on crusade. Indeed, he returned so quickly that it was considered something of a scandal. But as far as he was concerned he had fulfilled his vow. What he did in the next few years was to augment the revenues of the kingdom by exercising a quite draconian fiscal lordship, through lucrative wardships and other feudal rights especially. But he also found another target in the Jews. Back in 1182 he had expelled several thousand Jews from the royal domain (roughly the Ile de France) and seized their property because he believed that they were exploiting his subjects with their money-lending practices and might also be guilty of killing Christian boys in secret re-enactments of Jesus's crucifixion. In 1191, immediately upon his return from crusade, he personally led a raid on a settlement of Jews living on baronial lands outside the royal domain. His justification was that these Jews had escaped punishment for killing one of his men. Every male Jewish adult was cut down, eighty in all. Yet, seven years later, in 1198, Philip had a change of heart with regard to Jewish settlement in the royal lands and let those return who wanted to do so. Many did, although until the very end of Philip's reign, the Jews were subjected to periodic confiscatory taxation of their wealth.

Philip II was known as 'Augustus' because he augmented the territory of the royal domain. While Richard the Lionhearted lived and faced him militarily, Philip at best held his own, at worst suffered occasional, though temporary, humiliations. When Richard died childless in 1199, his younger brother John became king. John displaced his nephew, Arthur of Brittany, the son of an older deceased brother. Widely regarded as Arthur's murderer, John would, as we shall see in later chapters, have a very troubled reign. For Philip, of course, the opportunity came in the year 1200, when John offended one of his vassals by kidnapping the latter's young fiancée and marrying her. The vassal soon appealed to Philip as his overlord to rectify the situation. John refused to submit to judgement, and his fiefs in France were declared forfeit in 1202.

Twelve years later, in 1214, the English king's best efforts to undo the disasters that followed the forfeiture went up in smoke at the Battle of Bouvines. This battle confirmed what had essentially been the case since Philip's initial successful campaigns (in 1204) to enforce the forfeiture. The French Crown had decisively shifted the balance of power among the princes in its favour with the incorporation of all the lands of the old Angevin empire north of the Loire, including Normandy in particular, into the royal domain.

Did the French king have designs south of the Loire? The judgement of forfeiture issued against King John in 1202 applied to all his French lands (except perhaps in Aquitaine, since he held those only by courtesy until his mother Eleanor died in 1204). Philip did not want to over-extend himself militarily after 1204 and mopping-up operations only lasted until 1206 or so. It was clear, however, that a real opportunity opened up when Pope Innocent III announced the Albigensian Crusade against the Cathar heretics and their supporters in southern France in 1208 (see chapter 13). Philip encouraged the crusaders but he did not lead the expedition or contribute very much material or financial support. Perhaps his decision here was strategic and goes back to his fear of over-extending himself. Whatever the cause, the kingdom of France, meaning the north, entered a long period of peace after the Battle of Bouvines in 1214. The canny old king died in 1223. There was some vain talk of trying to get the lukewarm crusader canonized, a recommendation at which, understandably, the Church baulked.

11

Political Power and its Contexts II

Northern Europe's great powers were fighting among themselves or, in the case of Germany, against the papacy for most of the twelfth century. In the south – to the west and to the east – the perennial enemy was Islam. For Iberia and the Crusader States, indeed, the struggle between Christians and Muslims generally defined the nature of political life. Little or nothing was left unaffected by the encounter. In the central areas of the Mediterranean, by contrast, Islam was a presence to be reckoned with militarily, as the Sicilian kings were aware, but many contacts were less fraught with violence, and many other problems would have seemed more central to political life in continental Italy proper. The discussion that follows begins with the western Mediterranean and moves eastwards from there.

PORTUGAL AND SPAIN

In the year 852 a Christian ascetic and hermit by the name of Isaac, who was disappointed by the way his co-religionists accepted the Muslim conquest of Spain and were leaving the religion of their parents for Islam, appeared in the streets of Cordoba, the resplendent capital of Islamic Spain, from his rural retreat and publicly reviled Muhammad as a false prophet. The crime was punishable by death. Perhaps Isaac did not realize the potential consequences of what he had done, the authorities thought. If he were told, he would surely stop and go back where he came from. But Isaac did know, and he did not stop. His execution followed.

At first, Christian prelates made little of Isaac's sacrifice, but then other Christians began to follow his example. To conservative Christians

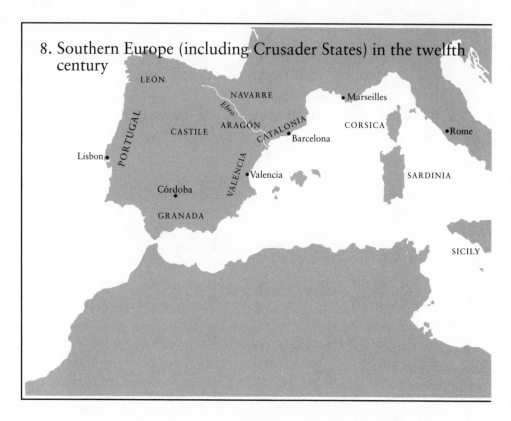

8. Southern Europe (including Crusader States) in the twelfth century

LEÓN

NAVARRE

Marseilles

PORTUGAL

Ebro

CASTILE

ARAGÓN

CATALONIA

CORSICA

Rome

Lisbon

VALENCIA

Barcelona

Valencia

SARDINIA

Córdoba

GRANADA

SICILY

these were not martyrs, but suicides; their acts constituted a sin against the spirit of God. Yet by the year 859 the number of these martyrs/ suicides had reached forty-four, the last being the priest Eulogius, whose writings exalted the victims. Something about their courage touched other Spanish Christians, even some of the critics of the practice. Conversion from Christianity to Islam did not immediately abate in Iberia in the wake of the Cordoban martyrs; indeed, in the short run the acts of defiance may have been counter-productive, inspiring waffling Christians to leave the faith rather than endure the increasing wrath of Islamic authorities, who resented that their prophet was being publicly mocked.

It took time, in other words, for the memory of the Cordoban sacrifices to do its work among ordinary Christian believers, but the tension between adherents of the two largest faiths of the Iberian peninsula was never far from the surface after the martyrdoms. At the heart of Spanish political history from Eulogius's death until 1492 was the question of the Islamic political presence. Not until the eleventh century, however, did the small unconquered Christian principalities in the extreme north of the peninsula begin in earnest the series of counter-attacks that would lead to the reconquest of Iberia.

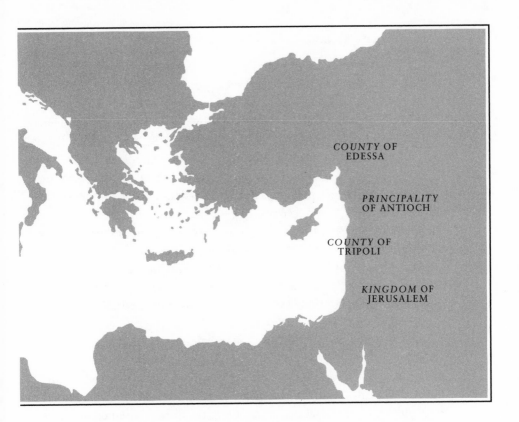

COUNTY OF
EDESSA

PRINCIPALITY
OF ANTIOCH

COUNTY OF
TRIPOLI

KINGDOM OF
JERUSALEM

The *Reconquista* had what might be called cool and hot phases. However deep Spanish Christians' resentment of their political and social subordination, there is plenty of evidence of individual Christians and various Christian groups benefiting economically in the first three centuries after the Muslim invasion, the period of the *pax islamica*. And the nature of the subordination to which Christians and Jews were subjected was, by many standards, relatively mild, since each group was allowed free rights to practise its religion.

In this period one dates the beginnings of that productive intercourse that would yield the translation of so much ancient Greek work into Latin through the intermediary of Jewish and Muslim translators, epitomizers and commentators. But there were different sects of Islam just as there are varieties of all major religions, and productive conversation sometimes faltered. In the period of the fragmentation of authority in small Islamic kingdoms (*taifas*), up to the 1090s, there was much fruitful interchange. When the Almoravids from North Africa managed to achieve hegemony in the peninsula in an attempt to thwart initial Christian successes at reconquest, there was little or no interruption in this interchange. But as the Almohads – Berber Muslims of what is usually called a puritanical streak – displaced the Almoravids in Spain in the mid-twelfth century, they introduced rigorous persecutorial measures against those of other religions and other Islamic sects. It was during their hegemony that one of the greatest Jewish thinkers, the physician and philosopher Maimonides, fled Spain.

The warfare of the reconquest developed certain important character-istics, for example, mutual raiding, including looting, burning and the taking of captives into slavery. But as the Islamic caliphate broke up into *taifas*, whole regions seemed ripe for the taking, and their apparent vulnerability gave a different colour and thrust to at least the Christian side of the warfare. Each of these kingdoms had a number of strategically located cities and fortresses which became the principal objects of the Christian armies. Siege warfare was, therefore, a recurrent pattern of encounter, and it continued to be so in the post-*taifa* period.

Although there were battles at sea and a great deal of piracy and privateering, the main thrust of the Christian reconquest followed the old Roman roads whose junctures were protected by castles that became, if captured, bases for further land expansion. Additionally, conquerors built new castles and refortified captured cities with high and thick castle-like walls to protect their conquests; the distinctive landscape gave its name to Castile (Castle-land).

Not every raid or full-scale attack from either side led to significant resettlement by the conquerors' co-religionists. Down to the twelfth century, if Christians won a victory and captured a small territory it was more common for them to establish their authority over the already settled Christians, Muslims and Jews. Sometimes the Muslims were the majority owing to widespread conversion of the native Christians and/or to the waves of immigration of various Islamic sectaries. Later Christian victories could lead to the wholesale expulsion of the Muslim inhabit-ants, but the operative word is 'could'. In the thirteenth century, the Aragonese conquest of Valencia gave control of a marvellously irrigated country to the Christians. But they needed both the expertise and the labour of the Islamic farmers to exploit the land. The problem, as one might guess, was that leaving the Muslim population in place led to fears, often realized, of rebellion.

The forces deployed in the Christian reconquest were quite varied. Urban militias played an extraordinarily important role in protecting the walled cities and contributing to field warfare as well. Unlike in northern Europe, knighthood in Spain was as common in the towns as it was in the countryside. Because the frontier was both permeable and fluctuating, there were times when the high-born conquerors could impose strong lordship on the dependent rural population. At other, more opportune times for rustics, it was possible to sell one's military labour for the perquisites of knighthood. Peasant-knight was not an oxymoron in twelfth-century Spain. Finally, in areas Muslims abandoned or from which they were expelled, and where Christian princes encouraged settlement from immigrant co-religionists, full freedom, sometimes in return for promises of military service, was often offered to the newcomers. Castile was not a land of serfs.

More professional armies also took the field during the reconquest. Like the crusades to the east which spawned the military orders – the Templars, Hospitallers and Teutonic Knights – Iberia witnessed the creation of celibate monk-knights and sergeants vowed to poverty in the Order of Calatrava (1164) and the Order of Santiago (1170). Indeed, it was almost inevitable that this was so, for the Spanish kings, whatever their general enthusiasm for the international military orders, were usually leery of having funds go to the Holy Land that could be used for the reconquest. As one twelfth-century crusader song written in Iberia or its borderlands would have it, Spain was equivalent to the Holy Land when it came to the task of reconquest.

And yet, crusader forces destined for the Holy Land played an important role in the reconquest. In 1147, crusaders en route for Palestine participated in the siege and conquest of Lisbon. Thereafter they contributed to a number of other victories. But some of their gains were undone after Almohad intervention in the peninsula in the mid-twelfth century. Indeed, every time Portuguese troops, with or without crusader support, made a major advance in the half-century following the capture of Lisbon, it would be countered by some Muslim thrust, recovering lost territory for Islam. In 1189, crusaders on their way to the Third Crusade again intervened with great success, only to have their achievements negated within two years by the Almohads.

Part of the problem on the Christian side was the unwillingness of Christian princes to abstain from quarrels among themselves. Portuguese rulers were trying to establish Portugal as a kingdom independent of its Christian neighbours (achieved by the second third of the twelfth century) at the same time as they were trying to recover territory from Islam. They fought as many wars with other Christian kingdoms as they did with the Almohads. This explains why the Portuguese phase of the reconquest, despite multiple victories in the 1220s and 1230s, was not completed until the mid-thirteenth century.

The back-and-forth nature of warfare described in the Portuguese reconquest was characteristic of the entire peninsula. The frustration inherent in it intensified the violence. There was a great deal of courage on both sides, but, tales of Muslim and Christian chivalry notwithstanding, the level of depravity was very, very high. There were times when barbarism seemed to become a way of life. Enslavement of captives was routine on both sides. Prestige was tied to how many warriors could be captured and either enslaved or ransomed. Where enslavement or redemption of captives was, in the circumstances, not practical, leaders demonstrated their prowess by taking their enemies' severed heads or scalps back to their home bases or displaying them on poles left behind at their retreat from enemy territory. Raids on port towns usually included a depressing catalogue of rape and other forms of terrorism.

The critical encounter in the peninsula as a whole came at Las Navas de Tolosa in the year 1212. Alfonso VIII of Castile (1155–1214) was the victor in the great battle, which followed upon a series of humiliating military losses to the Almohad rulers of central and southern Spain. The Christians contemplated the worst – the possible collapse of their whole enterprise. Alfonso put all his strength into raising a huge force, not just from his Castilian subjects but also with contingents from Aragon and France. A convincing estimate of the size of the force he amassed is 60,000, which would make it one of the biggest, perhaps the biggest field army that Catholic Christians managed to put together in the Middle Ages. To pay for it was an onerous task. The Church in Castile pledged one half of its annual income as a contribution. As a comparison, a normal crusade tax on the Church, that is, a tax for a crusade to the eastern Mediterranean, was ordinarily levied at one tenth of ecclesiastical revenue.

The victory Alfonso won undermined what had been the great Almohad counter-offensive and indeed broke the back of Muslim power in Iberia, helping to make later advances in Portugal permanent, for example. Over the next forty years, there was an almost continuous series of Christian victories in the south and east of the peninsula, none as spectacular as that at Las Navas, but all, like the Aragonese-Catalan conquest of Valencia in 1238, marking the steady expansion of Christian political domination. By 1252, despite Islamic rebellions and minor reversals, the reconquest of Spain was virtually complete. Only the small Muslim client state of Granada in the extreme south remained independent. On more than one occasion, it proved to be a staging ground for attempted Muslim counter-attacks, but although these could be terrifying and lead to troubling short-term setbacks for the Christians, the reconquest was never seriously in doubt after the mid-thirteenth century.

ITALY

One often speaks of the liberty of the Church as a battle-cry, summoning churchmen and worshippers to the vindication of *ecclesia* against the perceived encroachments of its enemies. One could just as accurately speak of the liberty of the city as the motto of the Italian urban republics. By liberty those who defended urban privileges had in mind, first and foremost, *northern* Italy's political independence from the empire and the papacy.

The papacy's hostility to urban independence, particularly Rome's, was ingrained. The establishment of strong bureaucratic government in the papal states seemed at times to be effectively containing the movement for urban independence in central Italy. At other times, the pent-up frustrations of urban oligarchies did threaten social peace, especially in those intervals when the papal court was on the run from the German emperor. Such insouciance on the part of central Italian towns was regarded by papal officials as the equivalent of treason.

For most of the twelfth century, southern Italy and Sicily found themselves, by contrast, under a stable and vigorous central government (the kingdom of Sicily or *regno*) which did not yield independence to the towns. There were, to be sure, nascent movements, as at Messina, seeking recognition of some level of urban autonomy. Despite momentary equivocations, these were met with stern refusals. Thus, the arena where a truly successful fight for Italian urban liberty took place was the north.

Independence – even in the north – was a relative matter. Many twelfth-century communes, as the north Italian city-states are known, continued to have local secular and ecclesiastical lords, and there were serious efforts, especially under Frederick Barbarossa, to recover imperial rights. Politics, on the communes' part, was a mix of diplomacy and open warfare, depending on urban militias, mercenaries and revenues from the public debt to finance them and attempting, in good times, to limit further or, in bad times, at least to prevent the expansion of local and imperial lordship. 'The earliest notable vernacular verses of communal Italy,' writes one historian, 'were passionate patriotic pieces in defence of Lombard liberties against German, Staufer, imperialism' (Jones, 1997, p. 457). Patriotism of this sort put some limits on autonomy, for the need for collective and concerted action *among cities* was widely acknowledged by urban leaders in times of crisis. Groups of Italian city-states would align together in leagues, such as the Lombard Leagues of 1167, 1185 and 1195, and the Tuscan League of 1198. Usually they did not give up sovereignty by doing so, but they voluntarily co-ordinated certain aspects of their foreign policy in order to resist renewed imperial threats to their autonomy.

If the short bursts of imperial pressure inspired the formation of anti-imperial leagues, the long periods of imperial feebleness encouraged something else, namely, the kind of territorial aggrandizement among the city-states that the monarchy's weakness in France in the late eleventh and early twelfth centuries precipitated among territorial principalities like Normandy and Anjou. The difference is that the imperial authority never enjoyed a sustained resurgence of the magnitude of the French Crown in France or, for that matter, of the Hungarian Crown in Central Europe that would re-establish unity. Nor did any single small social configuration of cities in northern Italy gobble up enough others to establish unity in its own name. In the twelfth century, for example, Florence and Milan established real territorial governments, dominating smaller communes and their hinterlands and ultimately incorporating them into their state apparatus, but neither Florence nor Milan became the undisputed hegemonic power of northern Italy.

Much of northern Italy's importance lay in its growing economic power, which in turn affected the social arrangements within the cities and their hinterlands, an issue that will be addressed in chapter 12. Italy in general, not just the north, but the peninsular south and the islands, continued to be notable as the entrepôt of goods, including slaves, from all parts of the medieval world, Catholic, Byzantine and Islamic. It was a great and enormous emporium.

In some cases, like those of Corsica and Sardinia, economic developments depended on relations with north Italian cities. Both Corsica and Sardinia, which remained major sites of transit for slaves in the period, were caught in the political struggle between Genoa and Pisa for domination of the western Mediterranean. (Pisa lost in 1195.) Sicily was different. Some of its kings had strange reputations, particularly Roger II, who was considered a tyrant by outsiders and a bit soft on Muslims, but under his leadership as count (1105–30) and king (1130–54) and that of his royal successors, William I (1154–66) and William II (1166–89), the *regno* achieved the height of its medieval political and economic power. Grain was its principal export, but it was also a producer and consumer of enormous quantities of specialty goods, including silk and quality woollens. A foreboding sign, though, was the fact that carriage of the exports was largely in the hands of northern Italian shippers.

Like the Spanish monarchs, the Sicilian kings were not crusaders in the narrow sense of the word. They did not lead major expeditions to the Holy Land, but they maintained their reputation as successful challengers of Islamic power and continued to protect the sea lanes against the resurgence of Muslim and, for that matter, Byzantine power. Moreover, they carried out raids against Muslim redoubts in north Africa in pursuit of their commercial and political goals. Their credentials as Christian warrior princes were solid. Nevertheless, the situation in the Holy Land was deteriorating, and demanded some sort of intervention, if not from the Sicilians then from elsewhere in the West, if the Crusader States were to survive.

THE CRUSADES AND THE CRUSADER STATES

Western maps of the twelfth century show Jerusalem as the centre of the world (see Figure 12), and the Catholic religious establishment turned it into a shrine where God was perpetually praised in a continuous sequence of processions, masses and alleluias. Jerusalem was also the capital, in more mundane terms, of the Latin kingdom which bore its name. The first ruler, Godfrey of Bouillon, had refused the title king, preferring to think of Jesus as king, and humbly referred to himself as Protector of the Holy Sepulchre. But his brother, Baldwin of Boulogne, in the year 1100, adopted the royal title of king of Jerusalem. Baldwin I (1100–18) was instrumental in working out the political arrangements of the various dominions that made up the Crusader States. These included the kingdom itself as well as the principality of Antioch and the counties of Edessa and Tripoli, the latter only established in 1109.

After a long period of inchoate political and tenurial experimentation, the Crusader States, not surprisingly given the geographical origins of its ruling class, adopted and ultimately canonized the style of governance and political organization typical of north-western Europe, with its fiefs, vassals, ties of homage and fealty, military support system based on knights' service, and so on. Although the crusades were international enterprises, the French element predominated, and French became the common language of most of the upper class. In the aftermath of the conquest of Jerusalem in 1099, this upper class distributed itself in castles in the various domains. Castle-building, in this hostile environment, became one of the great technological achievements of the settled crusaders (see Figure 13).

There were in the immediate aftermath of the First Crusade waves of Europeans, mainly pilgrims, but soldiers as well, who came to the Holy Land. In both cases, unless they died there, only a small fraction of visitors stayed permanently in the Crusader States. New work, fortunately, is beginning to map the precise topography of crusader settlement in ethnically 'pure' Frankish villages and in villages of mixed habitation. But what is certain is that the sheer number of European settlers was still below an optimum level for the protection of the states from a concerted effort at Muslim reconquest.

The crusaders were a minority awash in a sea of eastern Christian and Muslim peasants and townsfolk. The Christians included large numbers of Byzantines, with whom the Catholics had a variety of doctrinal disagreements, like the legitimacy of the *filioque* clause in the creed, but nothing of the order they had with the adherents of various other sects, like the Copts. These the Catholics regarded at best as schismatic, at worst as heretical, for rejecting mainstream teaching on the nature of Christ that had been articulated at the Council of Chalcedon in 451. A notable exception were the Maronites of the mountains of Lebanon, who had held, more or less strictly, to Chalcedonian teaching and, when they resumed contact with Rome by means of the Catholic crusaders, entered into a fruitful alliance that ultimately led to recognition of papal headship and sacramental union.

After some initial enthusiasm, however, most eastern Christians became increasingly hostile to the crusades and the crusaders. The Byzantine clergy felt betrayed that an original agreement to recognize their control of holy places already in their possession was only irregularly honoured; the other Christians, with some exceptions, saw the Catholics as enemies of the true, non-Chalcedonian faith. Moreover, those eastern Christians living in Muslim lands that bordered the Crusader States were in jeopardy during the periods of war, for they were occasionally and quite wrongfully, it appears, suspected of trying to facilitate crusader victories. These suspicions of duplicity and treachery provoked intermittent spurts of persecution. For them, too, the crusades were hardly a blessing.

Like the large kingdoms in the West, the Crusader States seemed given over to succession crises that sapped their ability to work together. The same was characteristic of the Muslim border states until the 1140s and, to a lesser degree, even until the 1180s. It was the internal strife in the Muslim world that allowed the Crusader States to survive even as they seemed to be embarking on a steep downward slope to self-destruction. From 1100 to the end of the twelfth century, the kingdom, merely to concentrate on that polity and neglecting similar succession problems in the other states, had ten rulers, not counting a regent, Conrad of Montferrat (1190–92), whose tenure was cut short by assassination.

Two of the kings, Baldwin I and Guy of Lusignan (1186–7), spent time in Muslim captivity after defeat in battle and had to be ransomed. Seven of the total eighteen years of Baldwin I's rule were also spent gaining control over other Christian lords by military means. His successor Baldwin II (1118–31) had to put down the rebellion of his daughter, Alice of Antioch, who was seeking in 1129 to ally with a Muslim leader, Zangī, to advance her own interests. When Baldwin II died without a male heir, many crusader barons invited Fulk of Anjou, a former pilgrim and the count of the great principality of Anjou in the west, to be king. He accepted and married another of Baldwin's daughters, Melisende, but in taking the throne he incurred the wrath of other barons and of Alice of Antioch as well. To establish his right to rule, therefore, Fulk (1131–43) had to put down at least two rebellions. His son and successor Baldwin II (1143–62), an adolescent at his accession, was obliged to wrest control from his mother Melisende, who was acting imperiously as a kind of co-ruler; he did so in a series of military confrontations from 1150 to 1152.

Of the next five rulers, Baldwin IV (1174–85) was a leper, who was courageous but almost incapacitated by his illness in the last years of his life; he led his final battle while being carried around on a stretcher. Baldwin V, his nephew, was his six-year-old successor; he was probably helped to his death at age seven. One could go on and on with the problems, so many self-generated, including the crusaders' inconsistent but mainly hostile attitude to imperial Byzantine offers of help. The Byzantines had not been widely trusted since the occasion of their failure to support the crusaders at Antioch during the First Crusade (see chapter 7), and the price the emperor desired for renewal of his support was some concession of territory as had originally been agreed on the eve of that crusade. This was a major sticking point. Nonetheless, on several occasions the Byzantines intervened at least indirectly on the crusaders' behalf. A continuing alliance would have been useful to the Christians' cause.

The repercussions of the Crusader States' weakness became manifest in 1144 when Zangī, Alice of Antioch's potential ally, conquered the county of Edessa. Its fall precipitated calls for a new crusade, and the war was eagerly preached by, among others, Bernard of Clairvaux. Unlike in the period of preparations for the First Crusade, however, the Jews were largely spared slaughter; Bernard himself intervened against the vehement anti-Judaism that one of his own disciples was spreading in sermons.

The Second Crusade, 1147–49, brought a German army under Conrad III and a French army under King Louis VII to the Holy Land. But the expedition was futile. In July 1148, to the dismay of the settler barons, the crusaders laid siege to Damascus. The dismay arose from the fact that, though under Muslim control, Damascus was in alliance with Jerusalem and had been so since 1139 in order to counteract Zangī's and his son and successor Nūr al-Dīn's growing power. (Zangī himself had been murdered in 1146.) The failure to take Damascus and the defeat of the crusading armies, blamed by the new crusaders on the treachery of the settler barons, were compounded after the crusade by the capitulation of Damascus to Nūr al-Dīn in 1154.

One can hardly describe the bitter disappointments which the ineptitudes of the Second Crusade generated. St Bernard of Clairvaux, who had worked himself into a frenzy while preaching the crusade and who had bestowed his blessing on the military orders of knighthood, fell into a state bordering on self-pity. To be punished in this way Christendom must deeply have offended God. Bernard, monk that he was, accepted the opprobrium cast upon him as a spiritual gift of suffering.

*

While a crusade brought large numbers of warriors temporarily to the East, day-to-day problems had to be faced by the troops under the command of the various Christian princes, who, as we have seen, did not always act in concert, and also by the military orders, the Hospitallers, Templars and, from 1190, the Teutonic Knights. The European houses of the Hospitaller Order, which had sent funds and recruits to the Holy Land, had spread all over the map, to England, France and Germany, but also to the Low Countries, including Frisia, to Spain and to Slavic lands (Hospitallers were active in Prague by 1169). The network of houses, like that of the Templars, served a useful role in transmitting information and facilitating the exchange of funds between Europe and the Near East for people and institutions that sought the Order's help.

To fulfil their military functions the Hospitallers obtained and manned a number of strategic castles. The same, again, was true of the Templars. Both orders, although a nasty and injurious rivalry was growing up between them, served courageously in the defence of these castles and in other military expeditions. The price they paid was high. At the siege of Ascalon in 1153, forty Templars breached the defences, only to be surrounded and eliminated to a man. The Muslims decapitated the fallen warriors and displayed their mutilated bodies by suspending them from the walls of the besieged city. Even though Ascalon was taken soon after, the middle years of the twelfth century, as we know, saw the continued deterioration of the crusader situation in the Holy Land and many more devastating setbacks than the Templar bloodbath at Ascalon.

Damascus's surrender to Nūr al-Dīn in the spring of 1154 was a major step towards uniting Muslim power in Syria, but it did not solve all problems. Christian attacks were sometimes locally effective, especially in the early years of the reign of King Amalric I (1162–74), and needed to be answered by Muslim counter-attacks. But Nūr al-Dīn's goal was not military equilibrium; he had more in mind. The Egypt of the Fatimid dynasty, a sectarian Muslim dynasty, was weak and, like Damascus before its submission to Nūr al-Dīn, was willing to ally with the Crusader States against their mutual Muslim enemies. In 1168, in bizarre circumstances, which clearly owed a great deal to the mutual suspicions and rivalries among the military orders and the secular princes, the Catholic powers decided to break the alliance with the Fatimids unilaterally and invade Egypt.

Nūr al-Dīn intervened. He sent his lieutenant Saladin, a talented man of the Kurdish lineage which has come to be known, from his father's name, as Ayyubid. His mission was to join with the Fatimids to organize resistance. In 1168–9 Nūr al-Dīn broke the Christian offensive, and in 1169 Saladin, who had become the virtual military ruler of Egypt, deflected a Byzantine attack on the port of Damietta at the mouth of the Nile. The Fatimids, as a dynasty, were not saved by these efforts; they were deposed in 1171. Meanwhile Saladin's victories continued. When the Normans tried to capture Alexandria in 1174, they too were repulsed.

Nūr al-Dīn died in 1174. The Crusader States continued to occupy Saladin's attention but his main interest shifted to the task of consolidating Syrian and Egyptian power. To do so meant to step into Nūr al-Dīn's vacated place in Syria and face any number of Muslim rulers who resented the new Ayyubid ascendancy. For a dozen years Saladin tirelessly and successfully pursued this goal, only later refocusing his efforts on the Crusader States. Victory would be glorious and would cement Ayyubid ascendancy in the Muslim Near East.

At Hāttīn on 4 July 1187 Saladin virtually annihilated Christian forces, numbering as many as 20,000. Nothing and no one seemed to be able to stand against him thereafter. By the tenth of July his forces took Acre. On the second of October 1187, the unthinkable happened. Jerusalem, the centre of the world, fell to the conqueror. The port of Tyre, however, held out and remained in Catholic hands. Nonetheless, the sense of ruin was palpable, as some of the vast number of prisoners were executed and others enslaved or ransomed, if they were lucky.

There was only one thing to do as pleas for help poured in to the West. The aged emperor Frederick Barbarossa took the cross. So did Henry II of England, already in his mid-fifties. Philip Augustus of France, still in his early twenties, was the youngster in whom, it might have appeared, particularly vigorous leadership would inhere. But Henry II died in 1189 and his thirty-something son Richard the Lionhearted completed the English preparations. Here and there (York in England is emblematic) slaughters of Jews resumed. There was no figure of St Bernard's stature to prevent them.

The Third Crusade was, from the Christian perspective, a marvellous, if incomplete success. It was humiliating for Saladin. As we saw in chapter 10, the German imperial army, taking the land route, was less effective than those of the western kingdoms. Frederick Barbarossa's death was bad enough. Most of the army dissolved and only a few hundred knights actually completed the trip to the Holy Land. But this evident failure on the German's part was followed by an amazing series of victories by the other kings of the West.

Richard and Philip set out in July 1190. No love was lost between them. Perhaps the prick that hurt Philip the most was Richard's decision to dump the French king's half-sister and take a new fiancée. In any case, the two rulers seemed almost to be at pains to avoid each other's company *en route*, reaching mutually agreed upon rest points at different times and leaving them separately. Along his way Richard settled some old scores and avenged some dishonours inflicted on his storm-damaged fleet by the Cypriots. So it was Philip who reached the Holy Land first.

In April 1191 the French king began besieging the port of Acre. Supported by an Italian flotilla and Richard's reinforcements, who arrived in June, the crusaders managed to accomplish two tasks: the capture of Acre in July and the containment of Saladin, who was intent on relieving the city. Philip then left for home, to Richard's delight. The latter was never happier than when he ran the whole show. (Back home Philip, in league with Richard's brother John, would gnaw away on any pretext at Richard's continental lands, despite his promise to respect the integrity of a crusader's territory.)

Like Saladin, who executed 200 Templars and Hospitallers after his victory at Hāttīn, Richard took mortal revenge on the captured of Acre. Then, one after another, the English king launched direct but limited attacks on Saladin's forces, inflicting defeat after defeat. Richard did not take Jerusalem, and his tactics, which avoided full-scale confrontation, were not always appreciated by his advisers and allies, but the negotiations that brought the crusade to an end in September 1192 did bring a number of coastal territories back into Catholic hands. Saladin's last year (he died on 4 March 1193) was a gloomy one. To be sure, his reputation as the hero of Islam survived: in Cairo, sugar candies depicting him cutting down a crusader are a favourite confection to this day. But the name of the bogeyman, Richard the Lionhearted, we are also told, came to be used by Muslim mothers to frighten naughty children into good behaviour.

Two consequences of the Third Crusade remain to be mentioned: the foundation of the Teutonic Knights in 1190 and King Richard's fate on his return journey. The Teutonic Knights, as the name implies, were largely an association of Germanic speakers. It too, although to a lesser degree than the Hospitallers or the Templars, became a typical international military order, having houses as far afield as Spain and accommodating the wish of women to join as nuns. Like so many of the new twelfth-century orders, the Teutonic Knights adopted the Blessed Virgin as their patron saint. The Order received Pope Innocent III's approval in 1199.

Originally perhaps only intended as a welfare order for the German wounded and sick in the Third Crusade, the Teutonic Knights were involved in limited military activities in the skirmishes following the crusade. Yet, indicative of the two functions, welfare and warfare, the rule adopted by the Order incorporated chapters on hospitality borrowed from the Hospitaller rule and chapters on prescribed military activities borrowed from that of the Templars. The administration of hospitals did not remain as central to the project of the Teutonic Knights, however, as it did for the Hospitallers.

As to King Richard's fate, his exploits became the stuff of legend and helped rekindle the crusading spirit in the West, but he remained at loggerheads with Philip Augustus. He knew the journey home might be difficult; he did not wish to give Philip any opportunity to seize him by travelling through France, but the French king nonetheless managed to have some of his German allies hold Richard prisoner until February 1194. He was only released upon payment of a king's ransom, £100,000, the equivalent of several years' Crown revenue.

From the moment Richard returned to his own domains in March 1194 until his death in 1199, he took great pleasure in humiliating Philip repeatedly in small battlefield engagements. Virtually all that Philip, with the connivance of Richard's brother, John, had gained during the English king's absence was lost, and not only that. At the Battle of Fréteval in 1194 Richard captured Philip's archives and treasure. In the chaos of a French retreat across the River Epte, Philip was thoroughly soaked, a condition that delighted Richard. Richard fortified his recovered lands with some of the most impressive castles ever built. He seemed unbeatable, but died from an infected arrow wound on 6 April 1199. To the French king's immense relief, he would soon find Richard's successor, his brother John, to be eminently beatable (see chapters 13 and 15).

PART III

THE THIRTEENTH CENTURY

Because of the generous scope of dates given to the 'Renaissance of the twelfth century', 1050–1250, a great many of the issues addressed in Part II will continue to be prominent in the thirteenth century. Yet the thirteenth century also has a certain coherence of its own. It may not have been the 'greatest of centuries', as an American Catholic textbook written in the early twentieth century would have it, but it was typified by the careers of a number of exemplary figures and certain kinds of achievements that earlier generations of scholars thought of as characteristically medieval. It has been called the 'Age of the Cathedrals', the 'Age of St Louis', the 'Age of Thomas Aquinas', even the 'Age of Synthesis'.

To explore the thirteenth century we shall begin with a look at the structure of society and its material and institutional underpinnings. Then we proceed to certain central themes, including the ongoing reform of the Church, the expansion of academic culture, political formations in the great kingdoms, developments in artistic and literary expression, and the continuing political encounter with Orthodoxy and Islam. In the end, our object is to imagine what it was like to have lived and died in the Europe of the thirteenth century.

12

Social Structures

There is no single or simple way to analyse medieval society at the beginning of the thirteenth century. In what follows we will have to look at occupation, wealth and legal status. Attention also has to be paid to issues like people's religious affiliation, age, sex, language, ethnicity and health. All of these helped to determine what the place of an individual or group was in society. There is a danger that the picture will seem static. In reality it was not. The place of a Jewish woman in England in 1290, on the eve of the Jews' expulsion from the kingdom, will turn out to be very different from her position in 1200. To be a communard or member of a sworn association of townsmen in France had something like revolutionary implications at the start of the century; it was little more than a juridical convention at the century's close. Restrictions on lepers were less severe early in the century than they were later on. And so on. The picture about to be sketched in this chapter merely provides the backdrop for changes that will be detailed through other lenses in the chapters that follow it.

*

The principal occupations at the start of the thirteenth century continued to be agricultural. Labourers' formal relationship to the land varied considerably. Some farmers worked allods, homesteads that they owned outright. The rustics of Iceland, Denmark and southern peninsular Scandinavia may be counted among these, as may the mountain dwellers of the Alps, Pyrenees and some of the Mediterranean islands. Often this form of land-holding was associated with the distribution of farms, not in villages but in separate farmsteads or hamlets.

Where villages prevailed, in what has sometimes been called the core of Europe (most of England, France, the Holy Roman Empire, Hungary and Poland), it was more common to hold property either freely by lease or servilely at the lords' pleasure. In both cases, the rustics usually had very secure tenure, sanctioned by what was taken to be immemorial custom. The impression at first sight is one of immutability; yet, there was a vigorous land market. Lessees subleased portions of their properties routinely, and partible inheritance, common among rustics, meant that the parcelling out of holdings repeatedly occurred. One consequence of this was a tendency for some heirs to give up their inheritances, take money instead, and hire themselves out as labourers, migrate to towns or go further afield to regions undergoing massive political transformations, like the Spanish and Baltic frontiers of Christendom. In the borderlands, threats of violence from Muslims or pagans were mixed with enormous numbers of privileges for those who would face the risks and help work the estates being carved out by Christian seigneurs.

Princely, lordly and ecclesiastical holdings varied in size and character from large estates in parts of southern Italy to small, often scattered estates in England and France. Where estates were scattered over a wide region, there were usually attempts to consolidate properties by exchange and purchase. Ecclesiastics were at once the least and the most successful in this regard; the least in the sense that the canon law made it hard to alienate property that had been given to a church, but once permission was obtained to exchange or sell some outlying holding, the very difficulty of further alienation helped preserve the consolidated estates.

To work their estates, lords employed people who were obliged by law to perform manual labour or who freely hired themselves out as workers. Over the course of the thirteenth century in many regions, northern France much more than England, the percentage of free rural labourers rose dramatically. This was in part because many lords saw an advantage in free labour; it was less grudging and more efficient. In part, too, this occurred because inflation, though rarely runaway, was steady in the thirteenth century. Much seigneurial income came from fixed rents, whose value was gradually eroded over the course of the century. It made sense to sell off weak assets like the obligated labour of rustics, who were eager to buy out of it because of the degrading effect it had on their status. But regional variations in the history of the manumission of peasants occurred because of differences in the economies and legal systems of these regions.

Everywhere, however, there was considerable specialization of agricultural labour. Nursery rhymes like 'Little Boy Blue' make it seem as though animal husbandry and agriculture were simple undertakings. In fact, swineherds, cowherds, shepherds and gooseherds all had considerable specialized knowledge passed on to them in apprenticeship. Rounding up nearly feral pigs that had been allowed to pasture in the forests for a season was extremely dangerous and required genuine expertise to do it and remain uninjured. Mastering the trails that led from Pyrenean meadows to the Languedocian plain hundreds of miles away, and were used by transhumant pastoralists, constituted another considerable task. The serious exploitation of marshlands required more than rudimentary knowledge of drainage and dyking techniques. Every generation of olive growers had to pass on the method of preparing the crop and extracting the precious oil. Viticulturalists and grain growers faced problems of plant disease, vermin, crop rotation, storage, and so forth. Their methods appear crude only in retrospect. They could not dust a crop with pesticide as farmers do now, but they knew how to identify diseases in their very earliest stages and to destroy infected plants before the infestation spread.

The same high level of knowledge was required in animal husbandry and domestic labour. Herders recognized common diseases in the very early stages and culled ruthlessly. They were adept at so-called folk remedies for stomach poisoning, a rather common problem amongst animals out to pasture. Disagreeable concoctions with a generous infusion of animal urine got the suffering animals to regurgitate the harmful plants they had ingested. If one turns to domestic occupations like spinning, brewing ale, dairying, bee-keeping and soap-making, often or usually performed by women, one also has to stress the enormous number of craft arcana that had to be learned.

It is certainly true that this knowledge hardly made the rustic population enviable in the eyes of the ruling elite. The image of the peasant was relentlessly negative. They were necessary, it was conceded, or else their betters would have to work the soil; contrariwise, it was a persistent peasant fantasy to imagine a world where prelates and nobles had to plough. Elite clerical writers also sometimes conceded that rustics had a superior chance of getting into heaven because of God's love for the suffering and the poor. But, except for some of the maidens, if the poetry of aristocratic lust can be believed, lower-class rural folk were basically scum, as far as the seigneurial class was concerned.

Of course, not everyone was poor, let alone suffering. Rural society had its prosperous farmers, some of whom supplemented their income by working as reeves or overseers on lordly estates. They went by many titles – stewards, woodwards, haywards – and there was a hierarchy among them. A general supervisor or steward carried substantially more weight in community affairs than the supervisor of the woodlands (woodward) or of the fences and hedges (hayward). The need to keep written accounts, a growing practice in the thirteenth century, meant, too, that stewards commanded in themselves or through modestly trained scribes the power of the written word. All these supervisory positions from steward on down were desirable, and families tried to keep them as a sort of hereditary right, except in those regions where they carried an obligatory or servile taint.

The countryside was peopled with craftsmen as well as agriculturalists. In part, they depended for the materials with which they worked on some of the most despised elements of rural society – those who tanned hides, dug sand, quarried, mined surface coal and made charcoal. Consider the last. Forests – real ones, not the manicured woodlands of modern England, or the carefully trailmarked woods in some Swiss cantons – are gloomy places. The forests of the year 1200 were still extensive and home to wolves, wild boars and, outside of England, bears, but they were also dotted with little endogamous woodland communities whose smoky fires were constantly kept going in the process of making the charcoal necessary for smelting ores. To an aristocrat in a hunting party traversing a forest, the soot-blackened folk of these villages and the 'fire and brimstone' of their surroundings evoked comparisons with the demons in hell.

Of much higher stature in the communities, though again perhaps not very high in the eyes of the elite, craftsmen, like smiths, shared many characteristics with the agriculturally employed population. Leatherworkers or cordwainers might be the owners or keepers of the flocks and herds from which their raw material came. Carpenters' work was seasonal and far less specialized than that of smiths; they doubled as agricultural labourers or small farmers. Rural glaziers also had only occasional work at local abbeys or for local parish churches unless they joined the travelling ateliers involved in the great window-making campaigns accompanying the building of the cathedrals and palaces of Europe.

The miller constituted a special type, part craftsman, part agriculturalist, part merchant. A miller usually worked for someone. Watermills and, from the 1170s, windmills were capital-intensive structures. By and large seigneurs underwrote their construction and hired or created hereditary millers to grind the grain and to keep the equipment in good repair. The millers also sometimes served a middleman function as brokers of rustics' marketable grain. (Much of the grain consumed at home was ground with handmills, to the everlasting exasperation of lords, who claimed monopolies over and a rake off from milling as a price of their investment in the great watermills.) Folklore surrounding the miller came to depict him as a sharp dealer, because of this middleman function and of his opportunities, exploited often enough, to cheat the farmer.

Along with the stewards of great estates, at the apex of the community hierarchy were the mayors and the parish priests. The mayors, sometimes of servile status, were responsible members of the community, assisted by other elders, who helped to co-ordinate village economic activity, such as the payment of taxes and the control of rowdiness and indecency. Typically they acted in the name of the lord who owned the village, but much of their work would have been of little interest to the seigneur as long as he, she or the appropriate ecclesiastical corporation received the levies and the proportion of fines that custom decreed.

The priests were rustics with a basic knowledge of the Catholic faith and a little or enough Latin to say the Mass. A priest might have got his education in a local monastic school or by being tutored individually by a monk or in apprenticeship to the former priest. Priests were made fun of as lechers in stories but their special association with the supernatural, like that of local cunning men and women, meant that they were accorded a certain level of respect. In addition, their office and education, however limited the latter, meant that they were the natural spokesmen for their communities when they needed to negotiate with regional authorities either orally or, more particularly and increasingly in the thirteenth century, in writing.

*

Occupational specialties were even more diverse in towns, and there were strict hierarchies, at least as imagined by municipal authorities. People working with precious metals often ranked at the top. It was they who might have a privileged place in municipal processions. Other metal-workers ranked close behind. Tailors and drapers seem to have been slightly less elevated in social status. The food specialists, like bakers, butchers and fishmongers, trailed below them.

Organization of labour was typically based on guilds, groups of producers or marketers who exercised a putative municipal monopoly over particular goods, putative because there were always black market activities in even the best regulated municipal economies. Craft guilds had a limited number of 1) masters, full members who enjoyed the full range of privileges; 2) journeymen on their way to become masters but who had to establish their expertise in various, sometimes costly ways; and 3) apprentices, the introductory category of young adults or adolescents just beginning to learn their trade. In artisanal households, where manufacture typically took place, family ties often mattered a great deal both in passing on esoteric knowledge, as in the working of precious metals, and in getting access to masterships. There were male guilds, a few female guilds in a small number of towns and, more common than the latter, guilds of mixed membership. Over time, however, two developments occurred. What little female leadership there had been in the guilds declined and mixed guilds tended to exclude women. Jews, of course, even if they practised the crafts or marketing organized by guilds were not ordinarily extended membership.

Corresponding to and overlapping with the guilds were spiritually or devotionally oriented groups which have come to be labelled with the catch-all name of 'confraternities'. They, like guilds, could be organized according to common occupation. But in Italy, where this form of organization was ubiquitous, one finds them organized also according to neighbourhood or parish church or a particular cult. The members prayed together. They pooled resources in order to celebrate their identity by endowing a window or wall painting for a local ecclesiastical or municipal building. They marched in processions together and sponsored teams in municipal sports contests. They feasted together in communal banquets. They shared political goals. Ideally they looked after one another's needs, seeing to the care of orphans of deceased members, monitoring the disposition of property from their estates, making sure that they received proper burial.

The towns were centres of trade and services. Men dominated some areas of commerce and women other areas, as English words like 'fishwife', 'brewster' and 'alewife' suggest. Many of the merchants who engaged in trade were also craftsmen and women. Others were specialists whose full-time occupation was traffic in grain, silk, spices, wine, wool, oil and the like, on a local, regional and sometimes international scale. For the last, the fairs of Champagne, the towns of Flanders, the north

Italian cities and the great ports like Messina, Marseilles, Barcelona, Lübeck and London come to mind.

What might be called the service sector of the economy included a varied but not always large number of townsfolk. Even in big towns, the size of the municipal administration, including the town watch, was small. By the year 1200 there were a number of places in Italy and along the Mediterranean and a few places in the north, like Paris and London, that were well beyond the 20,000 or 30,000 mark in population. They were served by town councils often made up of only twelve men (consuls, jurors, aldermen – the terminology varied), or at least the effective executive committees of these councils were quite small, even if council membership was nominally more extensive. To have a few scribes, tax collectors, a lawyer on retainer and a municipal watch of two dozen mounted sergeants and some foot patrols would have been generous.

The question of the autonomy of these towns has been mentioned in earlier chapters. In northern Italy autonomy was basically absolute, but was nevertheless intermittently challenged by German emperors determined to regain control of resources they thought were theirs by right. Outside of northern Italy, autonomy from seigneurial or episcopal control was only relative. Neither *de jure* nor *de facto*, at least by the year 1200, had the Flemish counts conceded their political control over the vibrant cloth cities that were making them and the burghers rich. Kings in France and England granted limited charters of self-government and fiscal privileges to their towns, but it may be significant that they were extremely wary of extending anything like full autonomy to places like Paris and London, where they had important residences or administrative offices.

Yet, traditional historians speak of a communal movement in regions outside of northern Italy. They mean that, in the course of the twelfth century, a number of Rhineland towns, many northern French ones, and others in western France were engaged in sometimes violent struggles against what they regarded as lawlessness in general and limitations on their freedom of commercial action by their seigneurs. They also resented the fact that certain legal constraints under which they laboured were degrading, almost servile. Similar, if less comprehensive, movements for communal autonomy occurred in southern France and Aragon.

More recently, scholars have fleshed out this picture. Some see the oaths to fight against lawlessness in these communes or sworn associations as an outgrowth or complement of the rural peace movement.

They also see seigneurs' activities in less simple ways. No seigneurs wanted to give up legitimate authority, but they could recognize that changes were occurring that demanded creative responses. Dues and obligations that smacked of rural serfdom could be commuted to an annual lump sum payment or an annual tax denoting subjection to the lord, but which left internal municipal administration and fiscal arrangements fundamentally to the townsmen. Urban dwellers' military obligations might be carefully delineated (where?, when?, under what circumstances?, how much?) – and eventually commuted in peace time.

Fairly frequently, new arrangements were worked out calmly, but sometimes compromise could not be reached and violence ensued. The revolutionary origins of some non-Italian communes and the revolutionary potential of all such social formations were never entirely forgotten. During several urban uprisings of the thirteenth century, critics used the words commune and conspiracy synonymously. Nevertheless, by the end of the thirteenth century, and outside of Italy, to be a communard came to signify full citizenship in a town rather than the status of an urban rebel against lay or ecclesiastical lordship.

Elsewhere the communal movement did not have much success in its angrier creative phase. It was very weak in England, for example, and in some frontier regions it never got off the ground at all because the towns established were given generous charters of fiscal and administrative freedom from the beginning. Villages that banded together as communes in parallel or in imitation of the urban movement seemed intent on making their voice a little stronger in the councils of their princes rather than on obtaining genuine autonomy. And many new seigneurial 'implantations', one name for which is *bastides* (small towns established in the wake of internal colonization in the core territories of Christendom), remained too weak to make the kinds of demands that the disgruntled residents of a city like Cologne could make on their lord.

The number of administrators serving princely rather than municipal interests in towns like Barcelona, London, Paris, Palermo or Krakow, that were becoming or had become capital cities, was increasing, but an observer would not have discerned a horde of bureaucrats. Lawyers and, particularly in Italy, notaries with formal apprenticeship training were coming into prominence. Especially as the Italian or consular form of municipal government, based on ancient Roman precedents being recovered in the law schools, spread to southern France, notaries began to take a more important role in producing and attesting documents.

Yet it would be decades before the notarial system became common in northern continental Europe.

Many of the lawyers and other administrators in princely administrations were clergy. Over time the proportion of laymen among all administrators would rise, but as late as the middle of the thirteenth century some of the most prominent judges in secular courts were clergymen. Of course, virtually all of the officials employed in the papal administration, whether the papal court was resident in Rome or in exile somewhere else, were ecclesiastics. By modern standards the papal bureaucracy was small; by medieval, it was enormous and exploding in size, a fact that helps explain the chorus of complaints about having to deal with the papal court and the stereotype that bribery was the only way to get a quick hearing.

Scholars cannot say for sure how much business was being conducted in 1200 or so, but a pope had to keep in touch with the rulers of the Crusader States and all of the European Catholic kingdoms and major principalities. He had to conduct negotiations with Muslim potentates and the Byzantine Empire. Letters went out to hundreds of archbishops and bishops, to thousands of monasteries and various other institutions and people, like the military orders or pagan princes on the Baltic frontier who flirted with conversion. The precise political configurations had changed by the end of the thirteenth century, but the level of business must have been roughly analogous. By then we know that the annual output of papal letters was 50,000.

As we have seen, some of the major cities and a few minor ones had universities in the early thirteenth century. At this early date it is difficult to determine either the number of teachers or the number of students, but there are indications that these populations, particularly of students, were growing at a rate that was outpacing good cheap housing. Students claimed ecclesiastical status and thus swelled the population of urban clergy and quasi-clergy. But these youths aged thirteen or so upwards were rowdy and kept the municipal watch busy, precipitating endless jurisdictional struggles.

Thirteenth-century towns, even the biggest, often had substantial numbers of people involved in agricultural production, the equivalent of modern vegetable gardening, but also more extensive husbandry, like viticulture and exploitation of marshlands. The Marais district of Paris was once a major area of rural exploitations within the juridical boundaries of the city. It was not always the case that people who exploited such resources could claim citizenship, for citizenship or freemanship was a status closely connected to wealth in that it usually had to be purchased, at least initially; it might be inheritable thereafter. Poor people, in any case, could not purchase it, and thus they were deprived of some of the benefits of town life enjoyed by their betters, such as immunity from certain kinds of (derogatory) taxes or freedom of commerce in the marketplace.

Domestic servants, who were never citizens, were also excluded from the full benefits of urban life. Domestics, often recruited from the countryside, served in the households of every important family, bourgeois or aristocratic, and in those of urban ecclesiastical establishments as well. For lay people, to have a houseful of servants was a badge of honour. The servants received food, lodging and some degree of patronage and support, as, for example, when they needed a dowry in order to marry. But they also encountered the possibility of physical and sexual abuse. In lay households, it is very hard to put a figure on their numbers. Incomplete figures suggest, however, that the number of servants in an ecclesiastical establishment could exceed the number of priests, monks or nuns housed there.

The personal needs of elite urban residents were met not merely by household servants, but by others with more specific skills. The rich had recourse to doctors, although like sick people in many circumstances, they would turn to alternative medicines and healing cults as well. Wealthy women turned to midwives when in labour. Midwives also attended middle- and lower-class women who could afford them. The really poor mother-to-be, if her immediate family did not have money to procure the service of a midwife, might typically turn to female kin and friends for help at birthing time or, again, to local shrines, charms, or tonics that promised help in childbirth.

Wet-nursing was widely practised in the south of Europe, particularly in the north Italian towns. The nurses usually lived in the outskirts of a town and received the child and income and regular visits from a family representative. Why the disparity exists in thirteenth-century reports between the routine employment of wet-nurses in northern Italy and the rarity of their employment elsewhere, particularly in northern Europe, has never been answered satisfactorily. Both northerners and southerners showered affection on their children. Both seem to have believed that they were doing the right thing. Two principles may have been fighting for superiority. Were the benefits of mothers' milk outweighed by the harshness of the urban environment in the life of the infant? More work needs to be done on this issue.

Like birth, death demanded a specialized service, too. Certain women, either as volunteers or for a pittance, came to constitute a kind of caste. They would prepare the dead body for burial by washing it and shrouding it (embalming was rare). These or other women, especially in Latin Europe, also served as professional mourners and wailers, a practice derided in some later sources. Family members of the departed paid or endowed monks and nuns to pray for the deceased. Funeral and burial fees were frowned upon by elite clerical commentators as unseemly, but they were most assuredly being paid. To get value often meant to lay out considerable cash.

All the people discussed so far had something of an honourable place in medieval urban society, even though there might have been those, like priests seeking exorbitant funeral fees, who were prone to abuse it. But there were other categories of urban dwellers whom elite commentators regarded as the detritus of society. These were the beggars, thieves and fences, immigrant day labourers and prostitutes.

Medieval attitudes towards poverty are as complex as those towards sickness. Few people, for example, wanted to be sick. But what did it mean to be sick? On the one hand, the rain fell on the just and the unjust alike. The biblical Job was a just, morally healthy man but he suffered terrible physical illnesses. One's moral state, it seemed to follow, had little to do with one's physical health. On the other hand, the same Bible offered examples of God striking individuals with disease and whole peoples, like the Egyptians, with plagues on account of their sins. To give a concrete medieval example, a leper was to be pitied as a type of the suffering Christ. The biblical Lazarus, considered a leper by medieval commentators, rested after death in heaven, Abraham's bosom (Luke 16:19–31). Yet Aaron's sister Miriam suffered the affliction of leprosy at God's command for presuming to challenge Moses's leadership (Numbers 12). The leper's social death and, increasingly over the course of the century, exclusion from healthy society in thousands of medieval leprosaria or lazar-houses owed much to this vignette.

So it was with poverty. Monks praised it. They typically meant voluntary poverty, signified by a rich person's act of heroic renunciation. But ecclesiastics in general also spoke of the blessed poor, without implying that their status was voluntary. Then, again, there were those whom a later age would call the undeserving poor. Men and women who worked, eked out a living as best they could, yet suffered deprivation, were worthy of pity. Women and men, outside of any religious vocation, who begged for their daily bread, did not work, drank themselves into torpor, hired out their bodies for sex, stole when they could not accumulate enough from begging – these were the undeserving poor, marginal people. They often overlapped in the big towns with new immigrants from the country or from more distant regions. In the 1230s the Bretons of Paris, with their funny-sounding Celtic language or bad French, as native Parisians regarded it, had a nasty reputation as trouble-makers. Every major town in medieval Italy seemed to have its English whore. At least prostitutes, as medical theory would have it, were not good breeders; yet the fact of abandoned children, some almost certainly prostitutes' offspring, others the babies of raped servants, would move ecclesiastics, like Pope Innocent III, to support the establishment of foundling hospitals in Italy in just these years of the early thirteenth century.

*

Society, it must be said, was not supposed to be so complicated. German *ministeriales*, serfs with the powers and authority of knights! And what of the inmates of the military orders? Were they knights or monks? Merchants who specialized in the exchange of goods rather than in the labour of their own hands, was their activity properly to be considered work at all? Worse still were the moneylenders, a lot of whom were Jews. They, so the indictment ran, exploited the poor, elevated themselves by wealth above productive and honourable groups of men and women, and even sold time, which was a gift of God and ought not to be sold. Lend, Christ had said, hoping for no gain in return (Luke 6:35); yet the deniers of Christ, often with the toleration of Christian princes, were disobeying this command. Apologists had answers for some of these problems (perhaps Christ's command extended only to Christians lending to Christians), but it was a messy world.

Things were supposed to be simpler. Christendom was supposed to have three orders: those who prayed, those who fought, and those who worked with their hands. Merchants and their commerce, markets and the cacophony of hawkers, street children at play and cut-purses, jongleurs with filthy songs, were an ugly fact of urban life to ecclesiastical conservatives who endorsed the three orders ideal of Christian society. The twelfth century had been a marvellously creative period, even conservatives might have admitted, save for the growth of towns, of their sinful marginal populations, and of a money economy based on filthy lucre. Bernard of Clairvaux condemned Christians who polluted themselves in money traffic as quasi-Jews. But name-calling was hardly an effective response to the complex changes that had taken place over the past hundred years.

13

The Pontificate of Innocent III and the Fourth Lateran Council

The pontificate of Innocent III, 1198–1216, marks a decisive stage in the history of the papacy and to some extent in the history of the western church and society as well. The pontificate would have been important even if it had not been crowned by the Fourth Lateran Council of 1215, but the Council introduced and ratified enormous changes in ecclesiastical life and had an even more far-reaching effect through the application of its decrees to the secular world. We begin with the background to the great council, including a general consideration of Innocent's rule and the political and religious issues with which he had to deal, and then proceed to a look at the work of Lateran Four and its consequences.

THE PONTIFICATE OF INNOCENT III

Lothario dei Segni ascended the papal throne in 1198 as Pope Innocent III at the age of thirty-seven. He was a scion of an influential Italian noble lineage and it was to be expected that he would rise to some important post in ecclesiastical or secular administration. He had had a splendid education, first in a Roman monastery, then at the schools of Paris, where he studied theology. He had a considerable amount of legal knowledge, too, though whether he was a canon lawyer has recently been questioned. He moved up rapidly in the ecclesiastical hierarchy and became a cardinal in 1190, in his late twenties.

While still a cardinal, Lothario published his most famous book, *On the Misery of the Human Condition*, also known as *On the Contempt of the World*, which was by medieval standards a bestseller. A characteristic passage suggests the tastes of a different age.

Man has been formed of dust, clay, ashes and, a thing far more vile, of the filthy sperm. Man has been conceived in the desire of the flesh, in the heat of sensual lust, in the foul stench of wantonness. He was born to labour, to fear, to suffering and most miserable of all, to death. His evil doings offend God, offend his neighbour, offend himself. He defiles his good name, contaminates his person, violates his conscience through his shameful acts. His vanity prompts him to neglect what is most important, most necessary, and most useful. Accordingly, he is destined to become the fuel of the everlasting, eternally painful hellfire; the food of the voracious consuming worms. His destiny is to be a putrid mass that eternally emits a most horrible stench. (*Two Views of Man*, 1966, pp. 3–4)

These rather pessimistic views of man's destiny did not stop Lothario from pursuing an energetic and, he would have said, virtuous career in the service of God. From the moment of his accession to the papal throne, he pitched himself into the struggles that were plaguing the Church. The premature death of Emperor Henry VI left the Hohenstaufen line of German rulers with a child, Frederick II, as successor. Innocent took the four-year-old boy under his protection at the request of Henry's widow, Constance, the daughter of King Roger II (1130–54) of Sicily. Roger had left a son who ruled after him, William I (1154–66), and this son had left a son as well, William II (1166–89). It was these three men, as we saw in chapter 11, who had brought Sicily to the pinnacle of its political power. The problem was that William II had no legitimate direct male heir, so that his aunt had the strongest claim to Sicily on his death. In fact, an usurper named Tancred, William II's illegitimate son, seized power and for five years tried with the help of barons loyal to him to prevent Constance's accession. It was only after Tancred's death that Constance's husband successfully asserted her rights and, in 1194, assumed the royal title himself as king of Sicily. The young Frederick, therefore, who was the pope's ward, was the putative heir in Germany and, after his mother died in 1198, in Sicily (meaning southern Italy and the island itself) as well. If he became emperor he would also nominally be the ruler of northern Italy.

Innocent III used the opportunity presented by the situation to strengthen papal control over the patrimony of St Peter, the broad swathe of lands in central Italy to which the papacy laid quite disputed claim. He also opposed those who resisted the child Frederick's accession in Sicily, a commitment that commanded his attention for several years as Sicily drifted in and out of civil war and succumbed to a debilitating factionalism. In the end, however, his desire to see Frederick safely on the Sicilian throne was rewarded.

In Germany, the situation that Innocent faced was equally complex, because, despite Frederick's status as Henry VI's son, the German throne was elective, and there seemed no good reason to elect a child, whatever his lineage. 'Woe to thee, O land, when thy king is a child' (Eccles. 10:16) was a favourite medieval text. In the event, in 1198 there was a disputed election of two adult male candidates. Innocent favoured Otto of Brunswick rather than Philip of Swabia, in part because the former promised to ratify papal claims in Italy. But civil strife racked Germany for years, and Philip usually had the upper hand. Following Philip's murder in 1208, Otto seemed secure, but reneged on the promise that he wished he had never given to Innocent in the first place, namely to accept papal territorial and jurisdictional claims in central Italy. In reaction, Innocent excommunicated Otto and engineered the election by dissident German lords of his ward Frederick as German king. It would be many years before Frederick made good his claim, even though he went immediately to Germany and almost never relented in his military pressure on Otto. Indeed, the pope was dead before the definitive resolution of the German situation in the 1220s, but his candidate, Frederick II, did emerge the victor.

If problems in Sicily, Italy and Germany were of near constant concern to Innocent III, he also faced other difficulties that demanded his attention and radical remedies. The crusades of the twelfth century had been uneven in their results, but generally unsuccessful. The loss of Jerusalem in 1187 was a particularly bitter blow. Richard the Lionhearted's crusade, the Third Crusade (1189–92), had gone a long way towards stabilizing the situation, but Jerusalem continued in Muslim hands and the position of the Crusader States remained vulnerable.

The pope, almost immediately after his election, thus authorized a new crusade, for which preparations culminated in 1202. The target of the Fourth Crusade was Egypt, which military forces of the Crusader Kingdom had tried but failed to conquer in the twelfth century. The contract for ships went out to Venice. When the crusaders, including Count Baldwin IX of Flanders, arrived in Venice, they were ill-prepared to pay for the ships, 500 in all. Venetian negotiators persuaded many of them to join in an attack on Zara, an Adriatic seaport that had gone back and forth between Byzantine, Hungarian and Venetian control in the two previous centuries. Meanwhile, a claimant to the Byzantine throne, a popinjay named Alexius, who was a nephew of the reigning emperor, also named Alexius, and the son of a deposed emperor, met with the crusade leaders, made a spirited case for the legitimacy of his claim to the Byzantine throne, indicated his willingness to accept papal supremacy over the Greek Church, and urged them to advance his efforts to gain the throne in return for the empire's support for their expedition to Egypt. Some crusaders demurred on both issues – attacking Zara for the Venetians and installing Alexius. Indeed, some of them, including Simon de Montfort, who was to play an important role in another of Innocent's projects, found the funds to go to the East and prosecute a much reduced expedition against the Muslims.

When the pope heard of the planned onslaught on Zara, he despatched a letter prohibiting it, but it arrived too late to prevent the attack. The majority of the crusaders, therefore, with the papal legate's approval, besieged and took Zara in the autumn of 1202. In July of the next year they landed on the outskirts of Constantinople and along with their Venetian allies launched an attack on the city. In the confused situation, the emperor Alexius III – widely accused of cowardice in the face of battle – fled and restored the throne to his deposed predecessor, the younger Alexius's blind father, who entered negotiations to bring their attack on the capital to an end. While some of the young Alexius's Latin allies pursued Alexius III and began the pacification of substantial Greek territories, he himself entered Constantinople and received the imperial purple as Alexius IV, a condition his Latin entourage imposed on the city before they agreed to remove their camp outside.

Only a few months into his brief reign, rioting and rebellion broke out against Alexius IV. Gangs of Greeks murdered Latins; Muslims in the city for trade suffered at the hands of the westerners; and a terrible fire started by the Latins consumed large portions of the city. Rage among both the Greeks and the Latins centred on Alexius. The sources that depict him as a debauchee may be biased, but there is no doubt that his early and open association with the Latins and his nominal subordination of the Greek Church to papal authority were deeply resented. No love was lost either between Alexius and the Latins. Being robed in the imperial purple went to his head, and he treated his allies with something approaching contempt. Moreover, they feared for their lives as a result of his inability or unwillingness to protect them, and so they recalled the troops who had been pacifying the countryside.

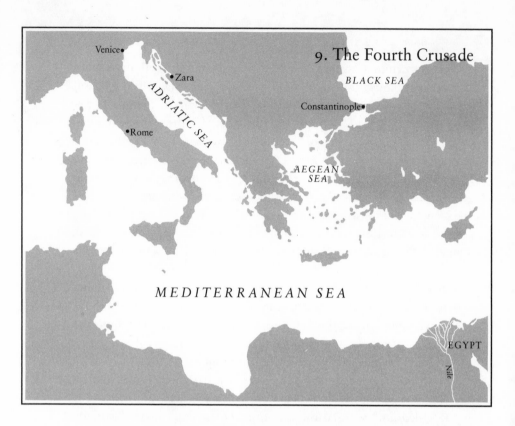

Venice•

•Zara

ADRIATIC SEA

•Rome

BLACK SEA

Constantinople•

AEGEAN SEA

MEDITERRANEAN SEA

EGYPT

Nile

Finally, there was a nativist coup in the city and the new emperor was murdered. The crusaders, from their camps outside the walls, witnessed their hopes for military and financial support, which had already been dimmed because of Alexius's attitude, begin to evaporate before their eyes. They decided to take charge of the situation themselves and on 9 April 1204, following confession and Mass according to the Latin rite, attacked the city. Disaster after disaster plagued them in their skirmishes and assaults. Even nature seemed to be against them; contrary winds made support from the sea nearly impossible. Why they resumed the attack at all after an interruption of a few days is unclear. Certainly, clergy preached the justice of the war: the crusaders and the Venetians had been betrayed, harassed, many killed; the Greeks hated them and were disloyal to Rome; God was testing His holy army, and they must meet the test.

On the twelfth of April they resumed the attack against devastating odds, managing to breach the walls and open the gates of the city, wreaking havoc as they rushed through the streets. When darkness fell, the situation was still uncertain. The smell of burning flesh and the noise of the collapse of buildings weakened by the flames permeated the city as destructive fires spread in the aftermath of the afternoon's murderous street battles. Substantial Greek forces that might have saved the situation for the Byzantines decided instead to abandon the capital. As day dawned, the crusaders and Venetians discovered that they were masters of a smouldering yet still great city. They took their revenge: the spoils of war – reliquaries and relics, cameos and jewels, ornaments and precious icons – would soon find their way to castles and churches in the Latin West. They elected Count Baldwin IX of Flanders as emperor and proceeded to enforce Latin authority over the Greek people and the Greek Church in Constantinople and wherever else they could establish it in Greece, the archipelago and Asia Minor. The pope, who was genuinely dismayed by the fate of his crusading project, decided to accept the outcome as the will of God. It seemed as though the Churches would be definitively united, and there was hope that in the future the Latin empire of Constantinople would provide a base for sustaining the crusader settlements in the Holy Land.

*

Meanwhile, in the heartland of southern France and northern Italy, there was a situation as confounding as the succession crises in Germany and Sicily and the strange course of the Fourth Crusade – heresy. Why heresy was or appeared to the popes as particularly widespread in southern Europe, especially Languedoc, has never been answered with complete satisfaction. Perhaps, as one argument goes, the dioceses in Languedoc were too large for efficient administration, giving dissident groups a chance to flourish there rather than elsewhere. Perhaps the aristocracy in this long-stateless region patronized as leaders of the Church those who supported them in their political squabbles, with little concern as to whether these men would pay much attention to curbing dissent.

What is certain is that, in the twelfth century, several groups or sects of Christians in Languedoc and the neighbouring lands began to claim a more authentic understanding of the faith. They did not all share the same beliefs. Some, like the Humiliati, were insistent on the superiority of the simple life and the necessity to preach the gospel of love even if they maintained their lay status. Yet, the Humiliati were also willing to live in endowed fraternal communities that provided a modicum of institutional control, on the pattern of monasteries, and did not seem to represent too great a breach with Catholic practice. Others wished to renounce all worldly possessions, rejected or at least cared little about institutional life, and also demanded to be allowed to preach, whether they were ordained to do so by the visible Church or not. Those of this persuasion, often called Waldensians after one of the most devout among them, Waldes, a rich merchant turned Poor Man of Lyons, did not all break irrevocably from the Church. Although a blanket condemnation of lay preaching had been imposed in the twelfth century, Innocent III allowed it under local licence and to particular groups. These included the rehabilitated Humiliati, whether lay or ordained, as some were, and also those Waldensians who retained their orthodoxy. Only those Waldensians who stubbornly rejected priestly authority and, over time, much more of the Catholic sacramental system, and penitential theology, including purgatory, came to be regarded as heretics.

Much more serious, in Innocent's view, even than the unrepentant Waldensians were the Cathars, for their disagreement with the visible Church ran deeper. The overwhelming weight of recent research has been to emphasize that not all Cathars were the same, but almost any selection of the various views they held was repugnant to orthodoxy. The range of their beliefs comprehended rejection of the Old Testament and indeed of the traditional unity of God, in favour of dualism. The God of the Old Testament was the God of the visible, created world, a world of evil; the God of the Old Testament was evil. Opposed to him was the God of the New Testament, a spirit unsullied by created matter. Jesus, some sort of manifestation of the good God's will, could not have been a corporeal being. He only appeared to be so and could never have suffered and died, an allegation that undermined the redemptive theology of Catholic orthodoxy, including the central thesis of vicarious atonement: He died and thus paid for *our* sins. Moreover, compounding the Cathars' heresy in Catholic eyes was the fact that they taught their abominable doctrines at least in part through an organized group of teachers; there seemed to be in this sense a competing Cathar Church.

On sexual matters, any similarities between the Cathars and Catholics were more apparent than real. Both prized chastity, and both had people vowed to celibacy, the 'perfect' among the Cathars, monks, nuns and priests among the Catholics. But Cathar perfects spurned sex, not only because they sensed something vile in fleshly yearnings, but also because they detested the idea of reproducing, that is, of imprisoning souls in bodies for another generation. If Catholic theologians found virginity a higher ideal than sexual activity in marriage, they still argued that such activity found its basic justification, some would say its only justification, in reproduction. 'Be fruitful and multiply,' God said in Genesis, pretty good evidence to a Cathar that the Old Testament God was evil.

One of the reasons that Innocent III was willing to reconcile orthodox Waldensians to the Church, and to sanction lay preaching under episcopal licence, is that the orthodox Waldensians found the Cathars' theology repellent and zealously wanted to preach against it and to live exemplary Catholic lives of poverty that would wean the fallen from the heresy. In the same spirit, Innocent promoted St Dominic's efforts to spread Catholic orthodoxy and St Francis's mission to the urban faithful.

Dominic (1170–1221), a Castilian, had been involved in missions to the Cathar heretics in Languedoc since 1206, but had not been particularly effective in his efforts. He hit upon the idea of founding a new order of missionaries, the Order of Friars Preachers, whose principal duties would be to combat the heresy and teach the essentials of the Catholic faith. From the beginning he insisted that recruits to the order be possessed of the high intellectual training necessary to combat non-orthodox interpretations of the Bible, and he required his adherents to take a vow of poverty that, he believed, would promote a way of life that would in itself be exemplary. It would furnish a living answer to heterodox criticisms of clerical magnificence in a world otherwise of great poverty and appalling inequalities between the rich and the vast number of poor. Although Innocent favoured Dominic's struggles, it was the pope's successor who formally approved the new order, familiarly known after its founder as the Dominicans.

Innocent also saw in the movement founded by St Francis (1182–1226), whose rule he approved in 1210, a missionary force comparable to that of the Dominicans. By their poverty, their orthodox preaching of the gospel and their obedience, a necessary precondition to the pope's recognition of the legitimacy of their endeavour, the Order of Friars Minor or Franciscans, also known as Grey Friars, from their plain garb, became something like the shock troops of evangelical Christianity in the early thirteenth century. In the beginning they were more loosely organized than the Dominicans. Their houses, also known as convents, were mere stopping-off points, as the early Franciscans were little more than itinerant mendicants. They were actively in the world and eagerly appealed to townsfolk, including merchants, brokers, artisans, common labourers and prostitutes. They were relentless in their criticism of avarice and self-indulgence and set an austere example of self-sacrifice to the urban laity. But they also, and no one more than their founder, carried with them the gospel of love and forgiveness. In his own time and soon after, there were those who, drawing on the prophecies of a twelfth-century Calabrian mystic Joachim of Fiore (d. 1202), came to regard Francis as a sign or even THE SIGN of a new dispensation, the Age of the Holy Spirit. The belief that at the end of his life he miraculously received on his body the stigmata, the signs of Jesus's suffering, confirmed this somewhat heterodox belief for many.

The St Francis of the Middle Ages ought not to be confused with the nineteenth-century vision of him as a Romantic, a lonely hero standing against conventions, a man who put feelings before the demands of propriety and custom, a perpetual man-child in his awe and love of nature. To be sure, some of the dramatic moments in his life explain his appeal to the Romantics. Francis, the youthful soldier, goes off to fight one more time and has a change of heart; the conversion compels him to renounce the luxury to which the well-to-do Italian merchant's son has been accustomed and, in defiance of his father, to strip naked to formalize the renunciation. Francis's love of nature as God's creation, as expressed in his famous hymn, 'Canticle of the Sun', and in those stories about him preaching to the birds and calming a vicious wolf, fit in well with the Romantics' own obsessions about unity with nature, too.

But Francis was never self-indulgent and always obedient to ecclesiastical, as opposed to paternal, authority; he was absolutely certain that he was chosen as a pillar of the visible Church. Even his personal turn against war and his identification with the gospel of love did not make him, for example, an opponent of the crusades, despite what some commentators have wanted to believe. There is no authentic statement of his condemning the wars, although it is probably true that he would have preferred persuasion or at least that he thought that persuasion might be more effective, as demonstrated by one of the more famous incidents from his life. He accompanied a crusading expedition of 1219, during which he crossed the lines dividing Christian and Muslim forces in Egypt. Taken by Muslim sentries, who thought the poorly dressed man might be an emissary sent to negotiate the Christians' surrender, he was brought before the sultan. Instead of negotiating, he offered to walk unharmed through fire as proof of the supremacy of the Catholic faith. Recognizing their misidentification of the man as an emissary, the Muslims, after some initial uncertainty on how to treat him, finally decided to send the seemingly demented man back to the Christian camp.

It is as difficult to know why the Cathars and their austere doctrines appealed to so many people as it is to know why the Franciscans and their strident critique of the people to whom they were preaching did. Yet there is no doubt that, for example, many urban merchants were attracted to both and were as ready to protect the former from persecution as they were to patronize the latter. Some groups have particularly attracted historians' inquiries and none more so than women. It has been suggested that women relished opportunities in Catharism that were lacking in Catholicism (at least until the Franciscan and Dominican movements seemed to promise them something) and that they became Cathars in greater numbers than men. These assertions still remain open questions, although opinions are strong on both sides.

As for the Franciscans and Dominicans, the situation is also somewhat nebulous. Certainly, a great many women were attracted to the evangelical movement and formed a second order of nuns. Yet, if they thought the roles that they would play would somehow duplicate those played by the men, they soon learned the error of their beliefs. Despite a promise from Innocent III to St Clare, one of Francis's close friends and the founder of the Franciscan second order, the Poor Clares, future popes did not allow the sisters to live as austere a life of poverty as their male counterparts. And the women were never allowed to wander as holy beggars or to preach publicly to heretics or even to do so to plain ordinary sinful townsfolk. Despite these restrictions, women entered the orders in numbers, and women and men who wanted to share something of the evangelical movement without fully becoming friars or nuns came to constitute a third order of lay adherents.

In time, the renewal associated with the evangelical movement might have effected the conversion of Cathars and other heretics, but the pope saw a stumbling block in the refusal of many secular princes to pay more than lip service to bishops' and missionaries' efforts to bring the heretics to heel. No one excited his disgust more than Count Raymond VI of Toulouse, the most powerful baron in Languedoc. Raymond's case was simple enough. He always insisted on his orthodoxy, but he had no desire to disrupt the social life of his domains. It is not clear that he saw the Cathars as a particular problem either. Many were or seemed to be good people, harmless vegetarians who fasted a lot; indeed, the phrase 'good people' (*boni homines, bons hommes,* and their feminine counterparts) was a common popular way of describing them in Langue-doc. Many families were part Cathar, part Catholic. It might be danger-ous to force people to repudiate kin and loved ones and subject them to episcopal censure, fines and imprisonment, backed up by the count's prestige and power. It would destabilize his vast lordships, which stretched from the Atlantic in the west to beyond the Rhône in the east.

Innocent III was a patient man. He cajoled, negotiated, enticed, but he never forgot for one moment what his goals were: the conversion to the Catholic faith of a large and disaffected group of Christians infected with heresy and the protection of the faithful against those heretics who refused to convert. Raymond VI seemed too often indifferent to these goals. And that apparent indifference was maddening to the pope and his emissaries.

The sense of frustration grew over time. When, in 1208, one of the pope's legates whom Raymond VI detested was assassinated, Innocent's relative moderation came to an end. Blaming Raymond VI for engineer-ing the murder, a deed the count always denied, the pope excommuni-cated him, in effect deposing him, and encouraged loyal orthodox Christians to join in a military campaign against him. The material promise was the distribution of his lands to the victors, and the spiritual promise was the bestowal on the soldiers of the same privileges that were granted to militant pilgrims to the Holy Land. The Albigensian Crusade, so-called from the town of Albi, not far from Toulouse, where the Cathars and their supporters were believed to be particularly strong, would be a holy war against Christians, no accident like the one against the Greeks in 1204 to be justified as God's will after the fact, but authorized deliberately against Christian heretics. Some of the military encounters fought at the papacy's behest in defence of its Sicilian policy in the recent past, especially those against Markward of Anweiler, whom Henry VI had made regent of the island kingdom, had an overtone of crusading, but one could still argue that genuine crusades were not being directed against Christians. With the Albigensian Crusade, that could no longer be said.

The war was to drag on for twenty years and its fortunes would profoundly affect the development of the French monarchy, for northern Frenchmen by and large made up the armies that fought in the crusade. In the end, too, though long after Innocent's death, there would be a papal victory, and the missionary and repressive activity necessary to eradicate Catharism would be put in place. But not everyone was persuaded that the extension of crusading to Christian heretics was a good thing. Many would criticize future popes who had recourse to the practice after far less soul-searching than Innocent III.

Not every scholar believes that Innocent III was the greatest of the medieval popes. It is sometimes said, rather testily, that he was just the busiest. As if serious problems in Germany, Italy and Sicily, the strange fate of the Fourth Crusade, the harnessing of the evangelical movement and the confrontation with heresy were not enough, Innocent faced difficult political contests with the French and English monarchs. In both, he showed his characteristic patience and the willingness to resort to a radical solution if the patience did not pay off.

France presented the simpler problem. In 1193, several years before Innocent III's pontificate, King Philip II Augustus married Ingeborg, the Danish king's sister. Almost from the moment they wed he seemed repelled by her. Philip, in a reprise of the behaviour of his namesake Philip I, simply repudiated her. His defenders accused her of rendering him sexually impotent by witchcraft, but to no avail for their legal brief. It was hard for papal diplomats to allow the king to dispense with a wife who was so well-connected, particularly one who seemed so vulnerable as she complained publicly about her ill-treatment in pathetic broken French. The papacy sought to reconcile the couple. Philip wanted no reconciliation. As far as he and some of his ecclesiastical advisers were concerned, the marriage was unconsummated and invalid (the list of justifying reasons grew over time). Compliant bishops confirmed the invalidity of the marriage. Philip therefore took another wife, a Bavarian noble lady, who bore him two children.

The popes (after 1198, Innocent III) continued to demand that the king repudiate his second wife and take Ingeborg back. Every demand was met by refusal, until Innocent decided that he had to act more firmly. In the year 1200 he therefore laid the kingdom of France under interdict, suspending ecclesiastical services. Philip, like any king, had many difficulties facing him when he got word of the interdict. The outcome of one of these was unpredictable, yet boded many possibilities. The English king, John, who was duke of Normandy and lord of most of the other lands of western France, abducted the young fiancée of one of his French vassals in the same year, 1200. If self-help failed and the vassal followed legal practice and appealed to Philip II against John, the French king would be in the enviable position of judging his most serious political rival or, if John refused to be judged, of declaring his lands forfeited.

The interdict made Philip Augustus an unholy king, at least as far as his enemies and those who, enemies or not, recognized the pope's right to discipline him in this way were concerned. How many of his countrymen he alienated is unknown, but whatever the political calculations Philip does not seem to have wanted to put his Bavarian wife aside. He only capitulated after she died in July 1201, and in doing so he received the pope's legitimation of the children of the bigamous marriage. The marriage with Ingeborg was declared valid. Philip never succeeded in getting papal approval for a legal separation. Ingeborg remained in France, a strange and lonely figure, but heroic in her own right and treated with a kind of stand-offish respect until she died in 1236, thirteen years after Philip's own death.

In 1202 Philip Augustus, freed from the interdict, achieved a real coup. John of England had failed to appear in the French royal court to defend himself against his vassal's charge of the abduction of his fiancée. The court declared John's fiefs in France forfeit to the Crown. Before the end of 1204 the French king had – he believed, legitimately – conquered Normandy as well as adjacent lands north of the Loire River and incorporated them into the royal domain. John, needless to say, fell into a foul mood, as did his barons, who mourned the loss of prestige of the English Crown and the loss of ancestral lands on the continent. It was expected that he would do something, sometime, but what and when were not known. In the meantime, John became embroiled in another terrible struggle, this time with the pope.

A strange situation confronted Innocent III in 1205. A delegation from Canterbury arrived in Rome to report that the sub-prior of the monks of Christ Church, Canterbury, had been duly elected archbishop of Canterbury following the death of the incumbent, but another delegation soon told a different story. An election had taken place, but contrary to the law the chapter had not first sought permission from King John to have an election, because the members knew that he preferred a candidate whom they did not want. So John had threatened them into a new election. They had succumbed and chosen the king's friend, the bishop of Norwich, to be the new archbishop. It was now the pope's duty to confirm that second election.

Innocent was unmoved. The illegality of the first election was undoubted; so was that of the second. The liberty of the Church demanded free elections. King John's threats were contrary to the canon law and his coronation oath. Moreover, papal permission was required to transfer a bishop, in this case the bishop of Norwich, to a different see. A bishop was wedded to his diocese, and only the pope, as vicar of Christ, could dissolve the bond between them. Innocent, therefore, quashed both elections and, exercising his rightful powers under the canon law, took the appointment into his own hands. An Englishman at the papal curia, Stephen Langton, a scholar and theologian who was a student at Paris when Innocent III had been there, was picked out for the job and sent to England.

None of the explanations for the pope's behaviour seemed to matter to John, who regarded the appointment of Langton as a deliberate affront and, in the aftermath of his loss of Normandy, an unnecessary humiliation at a very trying time. In retaliation he refused to admit Langton to the realm, seized the possessions of the archbishopric of Canterbury, and exiled those bishops and other churchmen who publicly raised their voices in opposition.

Innocent III responded as he had responded to Philip Augustus's defiance: he placed England under interdict. The suspension of ecclesiastical services would endure from 1208 to 1214. Negotiations were continuous during this period, but Innocent began to lose patience. In 1211 the situation began to change. Welsh revolts against the English began that year, and John, while raising a force to put them down, came upon information that many of his own barons were close to rebellion against him. They had personal grievances against what they believed was his arbitrary rule. There was also the interdict. It may have been getting under their skin; it certainly offered them the pretence of rebelling against an unholy king. And there was the legacy of the loss of the continental lands. Add to this the hints Innocent was giving that he might sanction a French invasion of England and the situation looked grim for John. After all, the pope had used force in the south of France. It was not to be supposed that he would hesitate in England.

John capitulated. A brilliant political move, his modern apologists insist. Less brilliant was the intransigence that had got him in the predicament in the first place. He recognized Stephen Langton as the legitimate archbishop of Canterbury, restored the exiled prelates to their offices and lands, repaid the church for losses incurred in the course of the dispute, and promised in addition to pay an annual tribute of 2,000 marks to the papacy. Finally, he gave the kingdom of England to the pope, receiving it back as a papal fief. Innocent III became John's feudal overlord.

The brilliance of the move cannot be doubted. Innocent got everything he thought was right. John mollified the pontiff, who withdrew his support for any invasion of John's English lands and in fact became an active protector of his new vassal. Meanwhile John undermined at least one ideological justification for rebellion against him; he was no longer an unholy king. While successfully putting down the Welsh insurgency, he also began to make known that he was planning to attack France and reconquer the ancestral lands of the Norman rulers. In a frenzy of diplomatic activity, he induced Otto of Brunswick, the German imperial pretender, to promise to make a second front against the French when the moment came for the attack. In all these preparations, King John had to be very public: English barons needed to be convinced of their king's sincerity and to be persuaded to contribute military taxes, the so-called scutages, to the planned campaign.

In the event, the great two-pronged attack on France, launched in 1214, was a disaster. Philip Augustus destroyed the German forces under Otto of Brunswick at the Battle of Bouvines on 14 July of that year; and John, when he got the news in the camp he had set up in Poitou following his landings in France, decided it was the better part of valour to avoid pitched battle. He retreated to England, where he soon faced an angry nobility in rebellion, a rebellion joined by Archbishop Stephen Langton. The long-term consequences of that confrontation are best left to another time (see chapter 15). But the delight of Innocent III at the resolution of the interdict was now all lost in the rebellion against his new vassal and in his own friend Stephen Langton's siding with rebels. Everything became confused. The treaty which worked out a temporary halt to the rebellion and which we know as Magna Carta (19 June 1215) was, to Innocent, a repugnant document, limiting, as it did, the power of an anointed king without papal approval, even though that king was also the pope's vassal. Langton was recalled to Rome.

THE FOURTH LATERAN COUNCIL

The Rome to which Archbishop Stephen Langton was recalled was preparing for the greatest assembly since the Council of Nicea of 325. More than 400 bishops would be present, 800 other prelates and numerous lay notables. The behind-the-scenes preparation was enormous, for Innocent intended that the council would do its work quickly and efficiently in little more than two weeks, 11 November–30 November 1215, hearing and ratifying decisions already taken in camera, and formally issuing them as seventy canons or decrees. Some of the canons concerned doctrine, others the organization of the church, still others discipline, but even these broad categories hardly cover the wealth of issues that the council addressed, including the Holy Land, the situation in Languedoc, and the disputed German election.

At the opening of the council, the delegates merely received reports on some issues. Innocent had issued the bull for the new crusade, the Fifth, in 1213. Delegates were brought up to date on preparations. With regard to Languedoc, they were informed of the military and religious situation. In 1215 both seemed extremely hopeful. Raymond VI came to the council, seeking reconciliation, but all the cards were in the hands of Simon de Montfort, the commander of the crusading army. He was *de facto* ruler of the region, and his agents were trying to secure *de jure* recognition of his claim as the new count of Toulouse (not that Raymond VI would ever acknowledge its legitimacy). Of the German situation, no resolution seemed possible when representatives of both Frederick II and Otto of Brunswick, the latter recently defeated by the French at Bouvines, stated their cases.

At the second session of the council, on 20 November, the pope-in-council made a series of solemn pronouncements. Raymond VI was formally deposed. Magna Carta was nullified, and all the rebels against King John placed under excommunication, which meant, given Langton's role in securing the charter, that the archbishop was temporarily suspended from his office. Frederick II was recognized as king of the Germans. Important measures were decreed on the crusade, including the suppression of tournaments for three years.

The most solemn pronouncements, of course, were about the nature of the Catholic faith, the incarnation, the trinity and unity of God, the perpetual virginity of Mary, baptism, and the miraculous transformation of the bread and wine of the Eucharist into the true body and true blood of Jesus Christ (transubstantiation). Let heterodox and heretics believe what they would, an authentic Christian was obliged to affirm these doctrines as well as the magisterium of the Roman Catholic Church, outside of which, it was declared, there was absolutely no salvation.

From his time in Paris, Innocent had been involved in the exciting discussions of the nature of Catholic Christianity that are sometimes associated with intellectual reformers in the circle of Master Peter the Chanter. He had, indeed, written a treatise on the mysteries of the Mass while a cardinal, that bears witness to the influence of the circle on his thought. The circle also included a young Stephen Langton. The reformers around the Chanter had delivered over many years a searing critique of some of the practices that had grown up within the Church, including the use of vulgar or popular proofs, like the ordeal, under ecclesiastical licence.

In these rarified intellectual circles, the debate was fierce. If one uses the ordeal as an example, the reformers argued that the received biblical texts prohibited the procedure. One was not to test or try God or believe it possible to force Him to make a miraculous judgement (Deuteronomy 6:16). Then why, rebutted the conservatives, did God sanction the child David's trial by battle against the champion Goliath (I Samuel 17)? It was God's choice, not man's, the reformers replied. And it was well known, they continued, that ordeals of their own time could be in error. Men were condemned to death for murder after ordeals only to have the process compromised by the return of the so-called murder victims from pilgrimage or mercantile voyages. How could a judgement so false be a judgement of an inerrant God? Again, the conservatives had an answer – the ways of God are hidden: the condemned man must have done something warranting his execution or God would not have allowed him to be found guilty. And vice versa, if apparently guilty people went free, it was because the God who sees all in secret recognized their genuine contrition and forgave them openly.

Arguments like these could have remained academic exercises for ever, but the Fourth Lateran Council was the fillip for their impact on society at large. The reformers won: no longer were priests allowed to preside at ordeals. Thus, at one stroke, the connection between the ordeal and the holy was severed. But it was too much of a shock for secular justice. Princes resisted putting the decree into practice. Only Denmark and, in a few years, England seem to have abandoned the ordeal swiftly. Other countries were much slower to act and the ordeal was still being used with or without local priestly sanction in some parts of Europe in the late thirteenth century. In the end, however, it died out as an official judicial process.

The Fourth Lateran Council decreed on many more matters. It strengthened episcopal control over Benedictine monasteries, prohibited the foundation of new orders (a prohibition soon got around), and devised ways to isolate the Jews by making them wear distinctive clothing, for example. The last was also soon modified, in fear that the distinctiveness of Jews might make them easy targets for unscrupulous soldiers preparing for the Fifth Crusade. The council also regulated the use of excommunication and the display and veneration of relics, and clarified the theology of indulgences and, thereby, the doctrine of Purgatory, where souls were punished (purged) pending admission to heaven.

Other decrees required the taking of communion by the faithful and the annual private confession of sins to their priests at Easter. They reiterated the Church's teaching on licit marriages, confirmed the priesthood's duties towards the laity and made clear that the ideal priest was to be sexually pure, sober, and never careless of his cure of souls by being over-occupied with secular matters. But, of course, if any priests or lay persons departed from righteousness into sin, the same conciliar decrees reminded them that 'by true repentance' they could always be restored to the body of the elect and 'through the right faith and through works pleasing to God, can merit eternal salvation'.

INNOCENT III'S LEGACY

Just as with the rulings on the ordeal, many other canons of the Fourth Lateran Council had a chequered history. Germany, an extreme case, was very slow to obey. Civil war and, after the civil war, a renewed struggle between the German king-emperor, Frederick II, and Innocent's successors made papal governance of the Church north of the Alps nearly impossible. Even so, time was on the council's side even in Germany, for the decrees came to be incorporated into the canon law. In more peaceable times, therefore, they were routinely applied to ecclesiastical institutions and persons. Everything depended, of course, on the vigilance of individual bishops and local synods, the effectiveness of local priests, and the ardour of monks, nuns and friars. Backsliding was bound to occur and did occur. There remained a critical reforming spirit alive within the Church that repeatedly sought to renew its devotional and institutional life. But no one could deny that the Fourth Lateran Council was the most important statement of the nature and structure of the Catholic faith since the great ecumenical councils of late antiquity. And it had been Pope Innocent III's work.

Even so, Innocent III did not believe that his labours were over. He was fifty-five or fifty-six when the council concluded, and he began almost immediately to publicize its work, fine-tune its rulings by interpretation and address problems like the still confused English situation, when suddenly and quite unexpectedly he fell ill and died in July 1216. He left a papacy at the pinnacle of its authority and power in the Middle Ages. It remained to be seen whether his successors could maintain the position.

14

Learning

By the year 1200 there were many Latin translations of non-Christian philosophical texts available in the West. Aristotle's works remained of primary interest, but exciting and challenging Arabic and Jewish commentaries on Aristotle, again in Latin translation, were in circulation as well. The challenge of these materials, unmediated by orthodox Christian interpretation, was palpable, and it was not always clear whether the interpretations by academic philosophers and theologians were actually orthodox. Decrees at about this time, imposed at the University of Paris, prohibiting lectures on Aristotle's works of natural philosophy and metaphysics bespoke conservatives' fears of the tainting of Christian doctrine by too clever hermeneutic projects. By about 1240, however, the prohibitions launched at the beginning of the century, if they had ever been effectively implemented, were no longer being enforced, and we find at Paris and at other universities masters lecturing on Aristotle's natural philosophical and metaphysical texts, although still much less often than on his logical and ethical treatises.

The efforts of two men at two different institutions can stand as representative of many early interpreters. First, William of Auvergne. He taught at the University of Paris and wrote on logic and the possibility of the assurance of truth in philosophical speculation, that is, he sought to devise principles whereby it could be possible to determine the truth content of logically coherent propositions. Put interrogatively and as an example: how true was it that a man could never be a jackass, if men and/or jackasses ceased to exist? What truth value was there in a philosophically demonstrable statement that had no real referent? What ensured that logical (Aristotelian) procedures, if properly applied to true propositions (either those garnered from revelation or those regarded as self-evident), would yield true statements? His thoughtful – and not entirely persuasive – discussions of these questions occupied his philosophical career.

William of Auvergne's orthodoxy was unchallenged, as evidenced by his elevation to the bishopric of Paris in 1228, an office he held until his death in 1249. During this time, besides the burdensome routine duties of episcopal office, he was active pastorally in trying to reform prostitutes, served as a close political adviser to the French king and occupied a position on the council of regency that advised the Crown's representatives when the king went on crusade in 1248.

Robert Grosseteste, the second example, was an English supporter of the Franciscans who studied at Oxford and Paris, before becoming a master at the University of Oxford from the mid-1220s to 1235. He, too, addressed the problem of logic and the assurance of truth, doing so with perhaps greater insight than William of Auvergne, although in his case, too, critics maintained that his ruminations were often more interesting and suggestive than convincing. Also like William of Auvergne in France, Grosseteste, following his university career, was an activist bishop in the see of Lincoln until his death in 1253. His consuming passion in these latter years was schemes for the conversion of the Jews.

Theologians and philosophers, in other words, despite their otherworldly mien, were active movers and shakers. It remains one of the truly great unanswered questions of scholarship on the Middle Ages how their theological and philosophical positions, often arrived at early in their careers, informed, perhaps shaped, their later careers in practical administration of the Church and, sometimes, the State. One thing is certain. The rise of many academic types to high positions in the Church, in the aftermath of the decrees of the Fourth Lateran Council and with concern still intense over heresy and other forms of dissent, proves that it was possible to tackle the non-Christian philosophical materials and retain a reputation for orthodoxy. This fact may have been crucial in helping to perpetuate the study of Aristotle and of his post-classical but non-Christian interpreters in the thirteenth century, even though conservative distaste with the practices never abated. Indeed, some conservatives linked together the promotion of such people and the corruption of ecclesiastical life writ large.

The conservatives were perhaps most fearful, on the purely theological level, of seeing their scholastic contemporaries, who loved Aristotle's work, develop intellectually coherent defences of propositions in clear opposition to Christian doctrine. Although those who seemed to do so never left it at that, the critics imagined that the Aristotelians were articulating a theory of 'double truth'. In fact, the Christian Aristotelians argued that where conclusions solely based on reason appeared to differ from divine (revealed) truth, those conclusions had to be rejected or, perhaps better put, had necessarily to be rethought in order to discover a way to reconcile them with revealed truth. Yet, whether rightly or wrongly, the conservatives went after men like Siger of Brabant and Boetius of Dacia, contemporaries of Thomas Aquinas and Bonaventure (on whom, more later), as tolerators or even defenders of the double-truth doctrine.

THE PHILOSOPHICAL GIANTS OF
HIGH SCHOLASTICISM

Roger Bacon was lecturing at Paris in the years 1241–7. The manuscripts of his work indicate his familiarity with Aristotle's scientific and meta-physical treatises as well as a bundle of texts circulating under the name of the *Secret of Secrets*, a pseudo-Aristotelian anthology purporting to be a record of the lore that the philosopher had communicated to his pupil, Alexander the Great. Bacon actually produced a translation/commentary on this collection. More important, he was reasonably well-versed in the works of – to use the latinized form of their names – Avicenna, Avicebron and Averroës, medieval interpreters of the philosopher's thought.

The first, Avicenna or Ibn Sina, was an eleventh-century Persian Muslim, whose views largely penetrated the West through Jewish translations and commentaries. He was the author of works more numerous and more important than those of almost any other contributor to the intellectual legacy of the Middle Ages. His writings on medicine alone would make him exceptional, but in the context of the European learning that we are discussing he was crucial for his effort to harmonize Aristotelian and neo-Platonic views with Islamic revelation. The attempt raised the possibility of parallel attempts in the other monotheistic traditions. But Avicenna also contributed to the specific arguments that occupied Christian scholastics of the twelfth and thirteenth centuries. When Anselm, for example, formulated the ontological proof for the existence of God, his critics responded that the proof, if applied to any object, would posit the existence of the perfect object, than which nothing greater could be conceived. His response was that existence was a necessary attribute of the divinity and not of any other entity, and so the criticism did not have force. He was saying, in a somewhat more imprecise way, what Avicenna had articulated in opposition to Aristotle, namely, that being is a contingency for every entity except God; for God it is a necessity or God would not be God, which is absurd. Whether Anselm could have known of Avicenna's formulation is debatable, but the idea is nonetheless traceable to him.

Avicebron (Solomon Ibn Gabirol) was an eleventh-century Spanish Jewish interpreter. Known principally as one of the most outstanding Hebrew poets, he also wrote metaphysics in Arabic; and since the philosophical treatises are so devoid of anything specifically Jewish, his use of Arabic persuaded western Christians that he too was a Muslim, although some of his ideas persuaded others, like William of Auvergne, that he must have been a Christian. The main body of his metaphysical work became available in a twelfth-century Latin translation, the *Fons vitae* or 'Fountain of Life'. The metaphysical doctrine with which he was most associated, and which had a long afterlife in the West, concerned the relationship between matter and form. For Avicebron, form existed as an emanation of God's will, but by nature it sought its completion in matter. Consequently, granted the completeness of God, form and matter co-existed in God, but the very locution about form somehow seeking its object in matter suggested a wealth of movement, therefore change in the Unchangeable. The proposition may seem on the face of it contradictory, but if in Christian (as well as Jewish) theology God is all-in-all and omnipresent in the mutable world, the mystical conundrum remains: the Unchangeable is infused with change.

Writing in the twelfth century was the third of the great non-Christian thinkers who did so much to shape medieval Christian thought – Averroës (Ibn Rushd). He also came from Spain. A Muslim, his admiration for Aristotle knew no bounds.

I consider that the man was a rule and exemplar which nature devised to show the final perfection of man . . . [T]he teaching of Aristotle is the supreme truth, because his mind was the final expression of the human mind. Wherefore it has been well said that he was created and given to us by divine providence that we might know all there is to be known. Let us praise God, who set this man apart from all others in perfection, and made him approach very near to the highest dignity humanity can attain. (Knowles, 1962, p. 200)

Against religious conservatives within Islam, who were as suspicious of Aristotle's influence as their Christian counterparts, Averroës raised his voice, in defence for example of Avicenna's work, although he disagreed with certain philosophical stances of his predecessor. But even some Muslims who had worked hard to remake Aristotle's philosophy into a body of beliefs compatible with orthodox Islam (by judiciously jettisoning, like Avicenna himself, some key tenets of his thought on occasion) found Averroës's admiration idolatrous.

One of Averroës's propositions which would have a major afterlife in the West was his belief that cause and effect had a necessary not merely habitual relationship. Conservative elements among Islamic theologians saw God's work everywhere; everything had its direct and immediate cause in God's action and will. If God chose to make similar effects follow similar causes, it was because he freely chose to do so. There was no necessity in the sequence; otherwise God, the freest being, would not be free. God could just as freely choose to break the habit. Such propositions distressed philosophers like Averroës who imagined and thought they recognized philosophical coherence in a rational universe, one in which cause and effect were more than merely habitual, but indeed an expression of the divine will. Did this position mean that God was somehow under constraints? Perhaps not, but it led to the accusation from opponents that those who held to the position did imagine a limited divinity. The Christian Averroists themselves would be accused of putting Aristotelian limits on the freedom of God.

Even without access to so many of the works and ideas mentioned above, Roger Bacon would have been a pioneer in scholastic thought in the thirteenth century. He was interested in everything: prophecy and astrology (which he sharply differentiated from magic), alchemy, optics, mathematics, as well as theology, philosophy and natural science. Bacon lived a long time: he was born about 1213 and died in 1291. Many of his late polemical works that defended astrology and urged reform of education, especially of theological education, would get him into trouble and incur condemnation from his Franciscan friends, but his playful and creative mind was characteristic of thirteenth-century scholasticism.

On the theological side, he took issue with the concentration of studies on the *Sentences* of Peter Lombard, to the exclusion of the Bible, from which, after all, Lombard's book largely derived its theology. Indeed, Bacon went further, encouraging his fellow interpreters to return to the unmediated text of the Bible, the original Hebrew and Greek scriptures. If nothing else had been learned in the Jewish–Christian encounter over the text of the Bible in the twelfth century, it was that a knowledge of the original tongues was indispensable for an accurate understanding of God's revelation. Bacon was as good as his word and wrote grammars of the two biblical languages.

Bacon was more typical in his ambivalence towards dialectic. Like many dialecticians, and though a dialectician himself, he did not always find that this quintessential core of the scholastic method satisfied the persistent mystical, Neoplatonic strain of his make-up or his quite remarkable desire, for the time, to encourage experimentation. Of course, his understanding of experimentation and the way he defended his view differed from the approach of early modern exponents of experimentation, which is still dominant today. According to Bacon, experience (or experimentation) is really the handmaiden of deductive truth, to be employed principally to confirm deduced truths.

All of his Christian philosophizing had an end for Bacon – the moral life. Of course, he recognized that moral lives, of the highest calibre, had been lived in the biblical and classical past. The wisdom or inner illumination to live morally had been imparted directly by God, the illuminating principle or agent intellect. Bacon's philosophizing was meant to complement the direct intervention of God.

No less able than Bacon and a good deal more coherent at times was his Franciscan contemporary Odo Rigaud, who studied theology at the University of Paris in the years 1240–45, after which he became a teacher at the same institution. In 1248, he was elected archbishop of Rouen, an office he held until his death in 1275. His career as archbishop was both spectacular and understated. Odo sincerely maintained the public face of his Franciscan humility throughout his life, even though as archbishop of Rouen he became a confidant of the French king, Louis IX, a member of the high court of Normandy as well as that of France, and a presence to be reckoned with in the highest ecclesiastical circles.

Odo and those theologians like him may be thought of, if somewhat inaccurately, as proponents of scientific theology. They wanted to give a philosophical basis to as much of the Catholic faith as possible, always realizing of course that there was an irreducible revealed core that had to be accepted on faith. Odo's approach was to distinguish between *dignitates* and *suppositiones*. The former were principles common to several or all sciences; the latter were principles peculiar to a particular science.

Systematic theology, for Odo and thinkers of his sort, thus had two types of axioms. The first were constituted of generally accepted, rational truths considered to be self-evident to any thinking mind. These did not necessarily arise from, but they were necessarily consistent with, revealed (biblical) truths. The other type of axioms in theology was the articles of faith, which were not evident to reason, but certified by divine, that is, scriptural, authority. Systematic deduction from (or the application of dialectical logic to) the total body of axioms of types one and two would produce demonstrated truths that constituted the full elaboration of the science. Applied to theology, what this meant was that many aspects of Catholic teaching, like that on purgatory, which would have seemed to be floating without any anchor of direct scriptural justification before then, were now seen as deducible from axiomatic propositions and thus part of a coherent body of theology, all systematically interconnected, and also, therefore, more credible doctrinally.

Roger Bacon supported the Franciscans and Odo Rigaud was a Franciscan master. The Franciscan brothers (*fratres*) professed poverty, and the philosophical and theological work of the Franciscans sometimes touched on questions of poverty and seemed to laud what might be called a distinctly fraternal style of living. For both intellectual and careerist reasons, there was considerable resentment towards the mendicant masters among the university masters who were members of the secular clergy. Intellectually the resentment expressed itself in opposition both to the radical celebration of the doctrine of poverty, which implicitly criticized the seculars' mode of life, and also to what some seculars regarded as the friars' hypocrisy, lauding a poverty and humility they increasingly did not practise. But there were also few jobs available in the top echelons of the University of Paris. The friars were rapidly growing in number. The obvious sincerity of the early recruits had deeply impressed the French rulers, Blanche of Castile (the regent from 1226 to about 1234) and her son Louis IX, St Louis, whose piety they profoundly influenced. With royal patronage the friars represented a threat to existing patterns of patronage and preferment.

For all these reasons the seculars tried to put limits on the friars' right to teach. Some critics went further and in not always careful language denounced the two orders, Dominicans and Franciscans, and ridiculed the king's attachment to them and their form of piety. According to one of the critics, Guillaume de Saint-Amour, the most outspoken, it was a travesty to observe Louis IX forsaking royal virtues, including magnificent clothing, to play at being a friar and to count among his closest advisers and friends people who might well have been infected with heretical opinions about a new spiritual age that began with Francis of Assisi.

The struggle against the mendicants at the University of Paris was a doomed one. The Crown protected the mendicants against the violence that sometimes beset them. Its wrath came down hard on Guillaume de Saint-Amour. At the Crown's urging his works came under papal scrutiny and received censure. He himself was exiled from the kingdom of France. And in 1256 two professorial chairs, one for the Dominicans, one for the Franciscans, were established at the University of Paris. The first incumbents were two other giants of high medieval scholasticism, Thomas Aquinas and Bonaventure.

Thomas Aquinas was born in Italy in 1224 and educated in the great Benedictine monastery of Monte Cassino from a very early age, probably five years old. This privileged education at so prestigious a monastery was possible because of Thomas's aristocratic connections. His family was noble and like most noble lineages expected to have at least one influential cleric in every generation. So, Thomas was set on a path that was supposed to lead to the priesthood and a career as a secular clerk.

In his late teens, however, Thomas became attracted to the work and style of living of the Dominicans. The early Dominicans, like the early Franciscans, had no prospects of promotion within the Church. They were service orders, and their vows of poverty meant that no aristocratic lineage was likely to exercise power through the connections of one of their kinfolk to the orders. As has already been intimated, this would change later in the thirteenth century, but it was still basically true when Thomas was expressing interest in joining the order in the early 1240s.

His family, incensed at the prospect of his becoming a poor preacher, restrained him, virtually imprisoned him, hoping to inspire a change of mind, but failed. At the age of twenty the brilliant young man formally joined the Dominican order and embarked on what he probably envisioned as a life's work of preaching. The Dominicans, as we have seen, expected their preachers to contribute to the defence of Christian theology in a manner that would confute heretical interpretations of scripture and of authoritative tradition. To this end, they developed intensive programmes of study in their convents. Thomas Aquinas continued his studies in Paris and in Cologne. In the latter city his master was Albertus Magnus (Albert the Great), a man who had a deserved reputation as a creative and erudite interpreter of Aristotle's works and inspired Thomas to carry on in the same vein.

In 1252, Thomas returned to Paris in the midst of the continuing strife between the mendicants and the seculars, which only a series of ever more determined royal interventions would bring to a conclusion. The end result was the establishment of the mendicant chairs at the university in 1256. As regent master or chaired professor, Aquinas set about to continue works he had already begun and to compose new ones that would give as firm a rational footing to Christian doctrine and the moral injunctions that were believed to follow from it as was humanly possible. And he did so with constant recourse to Aristotle. Never a slavish imitator of the philosopher, he could reject as well as accept his pagan predecessor's ethical insights, but he used the tools provided in the Aristotelian corpus and its accompanying commentaries, daily increasing in number, to provide a philosophical defence of the Christian faith.

Because, in the sixteenth century, Thomas Aquinas's summas seemed to provide an elegant synthesis of mainstream traditional Roman Catholic teaching and furnished polemicists with a considerable number of counter-arguments to the doctrines being put forward by Protestants during the Reformation, Thomas has perhaps been given too much importance in relation to his own time. Thomism – the edifice and mode of argument with which he is associated – was not the be-all and end-all of medieval philosophy and theology. In his own time he was criticized, and he certainly did not offer persuasive arguments on all the matters he treated. Though he tried, neither he, nor anyone, could provide an absolutely coherent philosophical explanation, for example, of transubstantiation, the miraculous transformation of the bread and wine during the Mass into the body and blood of Jesus Christ. That transubstantiation happened was doctrine; how it happens remains a conundrum despite Thomas's best efforts.

In 1277, three years after his death, some of Thomas's philosophical views were condemned out of hand by conservative critics. Later, in the fourteenth century, there would be a massive frontal attack on the whole edifice of what might be called Dominican theology (see chapter 21). Nonetheless, the Thomistic synthesis was extremely impressive, otherwise it would not have animated so many great theologians and philosophers to spend so much time attacking it. Despite the attacks it was steadily influential in the later Middle Ages and has continued to inspire wave after wave of self-identified neo-Thomists.

The Dominican's most important works were the *Summa contra Gentiles* and the *Summa theologiae*, which attempted, in the first case, to provide nothing less than a comprehensive defence of specifically Christian doctrines and, in the second, proofs for the existence of God and philosophical arguments on the relationship of God with fallen humanity. Only partly realizing how much he owed to the pioneering work of Maimonides, for whose work he had enormous admiration, Thomas marshalled his proofs from the domain of observation or sense perception and, of course, deduction. For an object to have motion, for example, it must be moved. For an object to move, it must be moved by an agent. The agent imparts motion by movement, therefore, the agent itself must be moved. The regression is infinite and unsatisfying unless there is a prime mover, a first mover, Who (and the capitalization is deliberate here) does not require any external force to move It/Him. That which moves without an external mover is God.

Thomas, like many of his contemporaries, was also fond of and gave epistemological respect to arguments from analogy. In this case he was as much Augustinian as Aristotelian – perhaps more so. Augustine could delight almost poetically in the threenesses he perceived in nature as a kind of reflection of the Trinity. In the hands of scholastics like Thomas, analogy, linked with direct observation and deduction, permitted powerful statements about the proper nature of political and social life, and especially law, as well as the nature of the Godhead.

Yet it would be wrong to think that Thomas Aquinas believed that the Christian faith and the ethical implications of that faith could stand alone and apart from revelation. Like Maimonides, he acknowledged that some things could not be proved and had to be accepted on faith. What Thomas Aquinas's work establishes or sought to establish is a set of tenets, rationally formulated and thus indisputable, which underpin large parts of the Christian faith, so great a proportion, one might say, that what has to be accepted on the basis of revelation is strikingly narrowed, and indeed is easier for a non-believer to accept as a result.

The downside of this attitude, from the non-believer's point of view, is that failure to accept the Christian faith can be interpreted by believers as an irrational act. There is much in the twelfth- and thirteenth-century scholastic revolution which encouraged a view of the Jews in particular as wilfully refusing to accede to reason and therefore as irrational in their nature, a step on the road to a thoroughly dehumanizing stereotype of them. In fact, the notion that baptism of a Jew could make an authentic Christian raised questions about the coherence of an argument about the 'nature' (therefore, unchanging character) of a Jew. Thomas, whose creative contribution to Christian teaching on the Jews was minuscule, would not have accepted the naturalistic argument of the Jews' unreason, but his work could be marshalled, perversely perhaps, by those Christians who did accept it.

The other mendicant chair was occupied by Bonaventure, also an Italian, the son of a medical doctor. His friends and family had a terrible scare when he was a child of ten in 1227 and suffered a grave illness. The boy and later the man attributed his own recuperation to the saintly founder of the Franciscan Order, Francis himself. His dedication to Francis, the saint, and his order never wavered. He would become minister-general or head of the Franciscan Order and would be the man who brought together all the written materials and collected oral testimony relating to the life of St Francis and wrote the official biography. He also played a fundamental role in temporarily keeping the order from splintering into a strongly reactionary group of those who thought they perceived a softening of Francis's original blueprint for austerity and more accommodationist friars who were reconciling themselves to accepting ecclesiastical offices, establishing permanent convents, and devising ways to institutionalize property-holding without technically violating the vow of poverty. Meanwhile, Bonaventure was involved in the acerbic debates with the seculars who regarded the whole mendicant emphasis on poverty as extreme and contrary to orthodox teaching.

Like Thomas Aquinas, Bonaventure, who studied with Odo Rigaud, did much of his creative work away from Paris and, also like Thomas, the end of his career found him in Italy pursuing work geared to the education of members of the order rather than teaching at a major university. It is wrong, therefore, to think of either man's career in modern academic terms; their fundamental institutional loyalty was to their order not to the university. Yet their teaching became perhaps most influential because of their stints at the University of Paris, even though, in Thomas's case, so much of what he wrote had little to do with his classroom teaching and, in Bonaventure's case, even if it did, the summation of that teaching was not put on parchment while he was actually resident in Paris. The two great men died the same year, 1274.

Bonaventure was a metaphysician and mystic. He grounded his metaphysics in three notions: emanation, exemplarism and consummation. By emanation Bonaventure meant the procession of creatures from the Creator. He defended God's so-called free creation, that is, the Deity's free choice in the forms of creation. Describing what he opposed will make this proposition clearer. Bonaventure dissented from the view that there was a 'necessary emanation' of creation, the natural development or emergence of created forms. To him, this smacked of a process that denied freedom to God, limited God, and therefore invalidated one of the attributes of God. A God circumscribed by necessary emanation would not be God. Consequently, necessary emanation was, in Bonaventure's view, an atheistic process. The much more radical Franciscan theology of the fourteenth century would pursue the general implications of this insight and attack all attempts to limit God's actions by so-called Aristotelian constraints. Bonaventure's followers would see themselves as restoring God's omnipotence.

By exemplarism, Bonaventure meant that all things that are created are echoes of God as the exemplar cause of all creatures. Here, again, Bonaventure is more Platonic (his notion has much in common with Plato's conception of ideal forms) than Aristotelian. These divine exemplar ideals, Bonaventure argued, drawing on the prologue of the Gospel of St John and following Augustine, exist in the Eternal Word of God: 'The Word was made flesh and dwelt among us.' The flesh, in other words, has its divine exemplar in the Word.

Metaphysical essentialism and indeed salvational history are fulfilled by consummation, the return of the created to the creator. It can be conceived, inadequately to be sure, as stages in a journey. And here Bonaventure's deeply mystical streak revealed itself. In a human life, the return is understood as commencing with the creature's recognition of the power and greatness of the Creator, the praise of God. The creature seeks to know this God more, by learning the scripture, the doctrines, the ethical precepts incumbent on the Christian. There comes a point when the creature can go no further, but the Creator acts by divine illumination of the spirit, and spiritual union, reconciliation, consummation occurs.

CONCLUSION

The men who, continuing the work of the twelfth century, built the multiple edifices of high scholasticism were not simply ivory-tower intellectuals. All were at one time masters, but, as we have seen, William of Auvergne and Robert Grosseteste had distinguished ecclesiastical careers as bishops as well and William played an important political role in French royal government. Odo Rigaud was an archbishop, a judge in secular courts, went on crusade, and with his former student, Bonaventure, served on a commission that tried to iron out the differences between eastern and western Christianity. Thomas Aquinas and Bonaventure defended the mendicant orders' celebration of poverty against their critics and thus took part, even while teaching, in a struggle that involved state authorities of the highest rank. Thomas was also called upon by the duchess of Brabant to advise her on her treatment of the Jews, and though he gave her conventional advice, the point is worth making that the great philosopher and theologian was believed to have something important to say about how 'real life' was supposed to be lived. Bonaventure, the great mystic, would die a cardinal, the highest bureaucratic dignity in the Church, saving that of the pope himself. We do no disservice, then, in turning from the academy to the 'real world' in the next chapter, for we will meet our philosophers and theologians there too.

15

The Kingdoms of the North

In a dizzying number of ways, the histories of England and France were intertwined in the thirteenth century. The nobilities of both countries spoke French. The barons of England had, or after 1202 claimed to have, fiefs in France as well. The modes of governance and legal systems had great affinities, in part because French territorial conquests in the west early in the century incorporated regions which had already been influenced by English developments, and the French kings were not averse to improving their administration by selective copying. There was a deep and abiding hatred too. It softened at the highest levels in the mid-century, but re-emerged towards the end and became a characteristic feature of English–French relations for centuries to come.

FRANCE

Paris became the capital of France, because in 1194 Philip II Augustus lost the records of his baggage train in a battlefield defeat at the hands of Richard the Lionhearted. The king thereafter decided to keep most documents and registers of important correspondence at a fixed location. He opted for Paris, an obvious choice as the greatest city in his domains and already an important, perhaps the most important royal residence. The schools of Paris provided the Crown with trained administrators. The city was conveniently near the royal abbey of Saint-Denis, a few kilometres to the north, whose Gothic style was helping to create a European standard and whose scribes were creating the master narrative of French history. In addition, Paris had defensible walls. True, they needed expanding, for the city was growing by leaps and bounds, but

10. England and France in the twelfth century

the walls provided at least psychological comfort in an otherwise very tiny and vulnerable kingdom.

Ten years later, in 1204, this kingdom had been transformed by the annexation of Normandy and the other former Plantagenet lands north of the Loire. Another ten years marked the effective sealing of this annexation with Philip Augustus's victory at the Battle of Bouvines. Thanks to the efforts of Philip's son and successor, Louis VIII (1223–6), the kingdom of the north became the kingdom of the north and the south, for in his brief reign Louis extended Capetian rule south of the Loire in the west and, in the last year of his rule, throughout a large part of Languedoc. In the case of the latter, the king had received the surrender of the rights of Amaury de Montfort, son of Simon de Montfort, the late great commander in the Albigensian Crusade. Simon's victories, which had seemed secure as recently as the Fourth Lateran Council (see chapter 13), suffered innumerable reversals in the years immediately afterwards, largely because of guerrilla warfare on the part of the native population of Languedoc. Indeed, it appeared as though Raymond VII of Toulouse in concert with guerrilla fighters would redeem all the losses endured by his ill-fated father.

Redemption did not take place. When the Crown finally realized the gravity of the situation, it intervened and devoted the bulk of its military resources to conquering the south. The campaign, which took place in 1226, was distinguished by an overwhelming display of royal force in the war-weary region. Battles were few, and the few there were, such as at Avignon, were stunning victories for the Crown. Seeing the handwriting on the wall, southern elites – aristocratic and urban – decided to negotiate for the best possible terms. The young king, who died on the campaign, did not witness the formal settlement, the Treaty of Meaux-Paris of 1229, but it was his victories that assured that this settlement would be favourable to the Capetian dynasty. Large parts of the coastal south were simply annexed to the royal domain. A truncated but still territorially large county of Toulouse remained to Raymond VII, but he was obliged to consent to his daughter and heiress's marriage to a cadet member of the Capetian royal house, thus assuring a Capetian succession. With Raymond's death in 1249 all of southern France, with the exception of Gascony north to Bordeaux (the rump of Plantagenet territories that remained under English dominion), was under French control.

The achievement was all the more remarkable because when Louis

VIII died in 1226, he left as his heir a twelve-year-old boy, his namesake, Louis IX, and, as regent, the boy's Castilian mother, Blanche. She proved to be a tough campaigner and astute diplomat, forestalling efforts to displace her from the regency or to hinder her free exercise of power. As her son came into his own in the 1230s, he demonstrated that he shared his mother's toughness, cleverness in politics and deep piety.

The fundamental problem they confronted, after facing down hostile elements within the kingdom who were still chafing from the authoritarian cast Philip Augustus had left as his legacy to governance, was how to hold together the diverse regions that now made up the kingdom: Normandy, Maine, Anjou, Touraine, Poitou and Languedoc. Most distinctive was Languedoc. Indeed, it was like a foreign country, defeated and therefore hostile, still swarming with closet heretics and supporters of heretics waiting for an opportunity for revenge. Southerners spoke a different language too, Provençal. Their cultural tastes differed from those of the northerners: no tournaments for them. Jews were far more prominent in the Languedocian coastal cities than they were in the urban or rural environments of the north; a few, but enough to evoke the northern conquerors' disgust, even served in princely administrations. Customs invoked in local courts claimed an ancient imperial pedigree, reinforced by the education so many of the administrators and lawyers were receiving at universities, like Bologna and Montpellier, that taught Roman law. The notarial system and the consular form of government were also, at the time, distinctly southern features of life.

The principles applied in running this congeries of principalities were carefully thought out. The Crown retained direct control of conquered areas or at least put cadet princes in rule over them. It maintained direct control over key administrative posts in conquered areas, filling them not with great nobles, but lesser nobles, knights and burghers. These men were paid staggeringly large salaries and were forbidden to have any financial and territorial interests in the areas they administered.

Along with this tight and alien control went a critical concession to the native elites, namely the promise to respect local ways of doing things, local legal customs, and local institutions. The Crown may not have intended the outcome that resulted, but in time it took pleasure in the fact that a wide array of native ways of governance and administration weakened, sometimes even withered away, as what was done in Paris began to set the standard. Moreover, by gradually making positions in the central and high regional administration open to men of talent and loyalty in the provinces, elites of conquered provinces developed a vested interest in the success of the Capetian enterprise. On top of or underpinning all these developments was the continued stress laid on the Crown as the emblem or icon of French unity. It was still possible in the mid-thirteenth century for a Languedocian to speak of journeying to the north as a trip 'to France'. By the end of the century, it was fairly common, partly under the weight of routine administrative usage, to speak of the whole fatherland, *patria*, as France.

The holiness of the Crown and its wearers, who began to be called 'Most Christian', was emphasized by three policies in particular. The first was an aggressive series of campaigns against the Jews. These were designed to put strict limits on the practice of moneylending and pawnbroking and to restrict access to Christians as a market for Jewish products and services. The aim was to make living life as a Jew a humiliation and was supposed to induce Jews to convert. The programme enjoyed modest success, but in the end was less successful than was hoped. An alternative approach was adopted slightly after the century's end – expulsion – which in its way could also be marshalled to emphasize the holiness and purity of the *patria* (see chapter 21).

A second policy, involving heretics, was more problematic. Jews had few active defenders in the Christian community. Heretics had to dissemble after the Albigensian Crusade, and their supporters had to be circumspect. But everyone in authority knew there were many heretics and powerful, if surreptitious, allies. The Church led the way in authorizing systematic investigations into heresy and its support, and the Crown on most occasions fully supported the Church. The Inquisition, unlike the royal Spanish version of the late fifteenth century, was hardly a monolithic institution, but rather a collection of inquiries conducted by bishops and, especially from the 1230s onwards, when the Inquisition came into its own, by Dominicans.

The inquisitors from the mid-century on had the legal right to use torture, but were rather scrupulous and infrequent in its employment, except perhaps in the use of hard imprisonment (shackles and a bread and water diet) as an inducement to confess. They also had, from the mid-century on, the right to hand over converted heretics who relapsed and others who steadfastly and contumaciously refused to recant to the secular government to be burned publicly. These spectacles were deliberate acts of terror, but in numbers or proportions of victims, compared to all those convicted, the medieval inquisitors were far less sanguinary than their Renaissance counterparts in Spain. The inquisitors preferred to punish by imprisonment, which could be hard in order to induce confessions; by fines, which were often crushing; by the public humiliation of wearing signs on their clothing that signalled the wearers as former heretics; and by long penances, especially pilgrimages; or some combination of these.

To the inquisitors, eradication of heresy was a necessary precondition for any successful and beneficial rapprochement between north and south in France. Inevitably, therefore, the Inquisition was resented. Sometimes there were assassinations. Sometimes kings were unsure of whether the inquisitors were overstepping their jurisdiction or were so stirring up hatred in the south that they were jeopardizing the tenuous political stability and integration that had been achieved. Until a final settlement was reached with the English in 1259 to end the war that had begun when King John's fiefs were declared forfeit in 1202, there was always the possibility, too, that an English invasion might precipitate a native uprising in the south. Despite these fears and apprehensions, the French Crown's commitment to orthodoxy and the institutions that were trying to secure it never seriously wavered. In the event, the English gestures proved ineffective, and no general rebellion ever occurred.

One reason for the long-term defusing of local and divisive patriotism was a third policy, pursued with singlemindedness of purpose – crusading in the eastern Mediterranean. The history of thirteenth-century crusading will receive more extensive treatment in chapter 18. Here what is significant to note is the fact that Louis IX seemed to measure his personal worth in terms of his achievement of a Christian ideal of rulership. This meant inducing Jews to convert, supporting the eradication of heresy, and also fighting for Christ. Among the vast majority of southerners, who were orthodox Catholics, the crusade continued to provoke ardour. Failures there had been, certainly, but a determined monarch could inspire support for still another expedition.

Louis IX's two expeditions (1248–54 and 1270) were probably the best planned and best financed of all the crusades. They were also, despite some bright spots from the crusaders' point of view, largely failures. On the first, the king's army was crushed, after a notable victory at the mouth of the Nile in 1249, when it moved a few months afterwards in the spring of 1250 into the interior of Egypt. Louis himself was taken prisoner. Ransomed a few weeks later, the king went to the Holy Land and did his best, with diminished resources, to help fortify the Crusader

States. On the last of his crusades, while besieging Tunis, the king died, and though the expedition enjoyed certain modest successes, despite the uncertainties attending upon his death, it did not do much to forestall the deteriorating situation in the Holy Land.

The crusade was important in supporting loyalty to the French *patria* not merely because it stimulated pride in the French Crown's leadership. After all, the mixed results could easily have undermined the lustre gained by leadership. But the king's failure and capture on the first expedition accentuated certain facets of his character that transformed his rule from the time of his return to France in 1254 until his death in 1270 into a kind of penance.

Before he had gone on crusade he had commissioned investigators of his own, many of whom were Franciscans. Their job was to hear complaints about the government, and on the basis of the information garnered, the king and his mother, who served as regent while he was abroad until her own death in 1252, made many adjustments in the royal administration. After the crusade, Louis reinstituted this system, making it a recurrent feature of administration, and because so many of the records have survived it is possible to get a feel for the impact of the investigations on French society writ large. Poor and rich, men and women, adults and children appeared before the touring investigators. They told tales of abuse, harassment, extortion, non-enforcement of the laws, bribery. The biases of the investigators are clear from the records. They tended to believe the poor rather than the rich, women, particularly widows, rather than men, children and orphans rather than adults. And the government unrelentingly cracked down on malfeasance, bribery, incompetence. It returned large amounts of money and property the king and his advisers felt had come inappropriately into the royal fiscal coffers. It was in these sixteen closing years of Louis IX's reign that his subjects (excluding Jews and heretics) came to regard him as a saint. Even Languedoc was calm.

After Louis IX's death in 1270, the quality of rulership fluctuated. His son and successor Philip III the Bold (1270–85) and his grandson Philip IV the Fair (1285–1314) were very different sorts of kings. Yet both were acutely aware of the lofty heights to which the monarchy had risen in the reign of their saintly predecessor. Somewhat lazy and certainly easy-going, a man who enjoyed hunting and camaraderie rather than supervising government with his father's zeal, Philip III is the less interesting figure in many ways. But he had been with his father on crusade in 1270 and had conducted himself, under very trying circumstances, with credit.

Philip the Bold remained forever a loyal son of the Church. He saw no contradiction between full support of the Inquisition and other papal policies and the grandeur and honour of the French kingdom. To some extent, this attitude undermined the effectiveness of his rule by leading him to pay inordinate attention to foreign policy concerns. His uncle and the late king's brother, Charles of Anjou, had led armies in the pope's support in the 1250s and 1260s which displaced Hohenstaufen rule in Italy and Sicily, and Charles would be able to call on Philip III to support his efforts in Mediterranean politics later in the century. These developments and, in particular, Philip's son's repudiation of them will require detailed investigation later in this book (see chapter 18).

ENGLAND

When Richard the Lionhearted returned from captivity in Germany, he discovered that his brother, John, had conspired with Philip Augustus against him. The king could be brutal to his enemies, as he had shown by his execution of prisoners in the Holy Land. But he could not hold a grudge against his brother. John got off lightly, and when Richard died childless in 1199, he ascended the throne. The circumstances of his accession have already been described, and the chequered nature of his reign, including the civil war towards the end, inasmuch as it responded so closely to issues in French and papal history, has also received considerable attention. The treaty that temporarily ended the civil war between John and his barons in June 1215 has come down to us with the name 'Magna Carta' or 'Great Charter'. Perhaps the name was merely intended to signal the length of the document; but it was easy, in centuries to come, to believe that the Charter was called great because of its solemnization of English liberties.

John did not like Magna Carta, nor did his overlord Pope Innocent III. Sensing an opportunity to undo the mess he had got himself into, the king soon renounced the charter, gathered his forces, and made a concerted effort to regain the military and political initiative. After all, the opposition was not monolithic. The barons in rebellion hated the king, but they agreed on very little else. And many barons were either sitting on the fence or supporting the king's effort to overturn the most humiliating parts of Magna Carta. If John had not died from a bout of dysentery in 1216 and if Innocent III had not been succeeded by a less intransigent pope, Honorius III, in the same year, Magna Carta would not loom so large as it does in English and indeed world history.

John's death was a relief. It meant that barons who were ill at ease with the rebellion could argue that the king's young son and successor, Henry III, was in no way tainted by his father's misdeeds. The triumvirate set up to rule in his name, which included a papal representative, prudently sent the queen dowager into exile, for many traced all of John's troubles to his abduction of her in the year 1200, and she was, in any case, an impolitic figure.

The French – not Philip Augustus, but his son Prince Louis – had dreamed of conquering England under a papal banner, during the period of the interdict. They were predictably upset when Pope Innocent III and John were reconciled, but in the aftermath of John's repudiation of Magna Carta and the civil war that ensued, certain elements were willing to call on Prince Louis for aid, and indeed he launched an invasion of England. The quick action of the regents to try to reconcile the contending English parties would doom the French effort and the invaders would withdraw under a face-saving compromise, but the situation in early 1217 was touch and go for the English.

That year (1217) the regents reissued Magna Carta, though divested of the chapters most offensive to royalists, as a sop to the less intransigent of the rebel party, and also issued a Charter of the Forest to moderate the draconian forest law to which many barons objected. A few years later in 1225, after a few additional modifications, Magna Carta was confirmed once more. This version became the official one and already by the end of the thirteenth century would be copied into books of law as if it were the first statute or fundamental law of the kingdom.

Magna Carta promised liberty to the Church, evidence of the original influence of Stephen Langton, restored as archbishop of Canterbury after John's death. It addressed many specific abuses, such as the king's occasional exercise of his prerogative to force a baronial heiress to marry his choice, even if the man were inferior to her in status. It regulated the collection of feudal revenues, like reliefs and wardships, that the king could collect, sometimes going so far as to fix an amount of payment for all time, an act that assured that inflation would erode their burden. It inscribed certain corporate privileges, like those for the city of London. Even some of the failed chapters, ones excised before the 1225 confirmation, became good law. The suppressed sentence, 'Scutage or aid shall be levied in our kingdom only by the common counsel of our kingdom' (cap. 12), became the underlying principle of licit taxation. But Magna Carta's lasting contribution was its insistence that even a king had to respect the common law.

In chapter after chapter, in memorable but vague language, whose precise meaning would baffle many an interpreter (even revised, the charter was, after all, basically a treaty hammered out in four days during a rebellion), Magna Carta affirmed that 'No freeman shall be captured or imprisoned or disseised or outlawed or exiled or in anyway destroyed, nor will we [the king] go against him or send against him, except by the lawful judgement of his peers or by the law of the land' (cap. 39). 'To no one,' it went on, 'will we sell, to no one will we deny or delay right or justice' (cap. 40). Slightly later, one of the greatest of English law books, conventionally attributed to Henry de Bracton, would sum up these principles in a majestic sentence: 'The king must not be under man, but under God and under the law, because law makes the king.'

These remained lofty principles, even when properly, that is, narrowly, interpreted. Forbearance to sell justice, for instance, did not mean that the judicial process was free; it did mean that there would not be arbitrary changes in fee schedules. And certain writs *were* free, such as the writ of life and limbs, available to a person who had evidence that he was being misused judicially and put in jeopardy of his life because of hate and spite.

John's young heir, Henry III, was destined for a long and eventful reign, 1216–72. He was a religious man, as pious as his continental counterpart Louis IX. Henry represented himself, as his aggressive policy towards the Jews reveals, as a holy king. He believed Jews were crucifying Christian boys and he supported judicially repressive measures against those convicted of doing so. He also launched a very serious effort to get Jews to convert, a project whose success, judging from the extortionate levies on the Jewish communities, was predicated on impoverishing them as a group. As in France, the policy's successes were modest. In 1290, his son, Edward I, went further and expelled the Jews from England.

Henry III's reign was lived in the shadow of Magna Carta. Any move he made that provoked opposition raised the spectre of an appeal against him to the principles of Magna Carta. This is why, despite occasional backsliding, he seems genuinely to have tried to abide by the charter's precepts. Nevertheless his reign was not a political success, and several of the most interesting developments occurred without Henry's active connivance or in opposition to his will. Two of these need to be addressed, the development of trial by jury and the emergence of Parliament.

Trial by jury is the simpler though more curious case. In November 1215 the Fourth Lateran Council decreed the ban on priests participating at ordeals. In many secular judicial systems, however, ordeals were the ordinary mode of proof in criminal cases, and there was widespread resistance to enforcing the papal decree, if priests could be found who were willing to bless the ordeal pools, fires, irons, stones and the defendants. At least for a while, it does not seem to have been difficult to find pliant priests. Yet the regents in England knew that they needed the continuing support of the papacy if they were to re-establish strong government in the aftermath of John's death and the abortive French invasion.

Circuit justices therefore restrained themselves from trying accused felons by ordeal. The problem was that there was no alternative in the cases (the majority) in which grand juries had indicted the accused. The mode of proof for direct accusation was trial by battle, itself an ordeal of a sort that was even slower to capitulate to ecclesiastical denunciation. But a defendant could not be given permission to fight an entire indicting grand jury, which, after all, spoke for the king. On the other hand, the civil side of the law was already routinely using juries to decide disputed questions of seisin of property. Moreover, litigants over the best right, not just seisin, of property, for which the traditional mode of proof was judicial combat, had also been given the option in the late 1170s to switch to adjudication by trial by jury. Finally, grand juries themselves existed on the criminal side of the law. It was no great leap of the imagination for the circuit judges to offer prisoners trial by jury in place of trial by ordeal.

The judges knew this was an innovation. Prisoners were given the option. They did not have to accept trial by jury. And many, choosing to remain in prison, did not accept it, even when cruel treatment in prison was used as an inducement to get them to accept the proffered mode of proof. Sometimes their suffering was heroic and they died under a regime of bread and water (*prison forte et dure*) or heavy weights placed on their chests (*peine forte et dure*). But those who chose this path died unconvicted. Their property could not be confiscated, nor their families disinherited. Most, however, opted for trial by jury for their alleged crimes, which from that point forward took its place as a signal feature of common law procedure.

On the other development, the emergence of Parliament, Henry III's role is ambiguous. Early in his reign the king nourished a desire to reconquer the lands of western France that had once been in the possession of his father. This desire, often expressed by abortive but expensive gestures of support for opposition movements in France, necessarily brought him into negotiation with his barons for monetary assistance. Negotiations took part in aristocratic and joint aristocratic and ecclesiastical councils. At these councils the king's men presented the case for levies, but often there were baronial counter-proposals, including, symbolically, the demand that the king confirm Magna Carta as one part of the price for their support. Loosely, one could call these parliaments, from the French *parler*, to speak, as these were forums where serious speaking took place.

But why could not the king live on his own revenues? Why did he waste so much money on and give so much preferment to his wife's Provençal relatives and to his mother's numerous children from her second marriage and their hangers-on, a group disparaged, somewhat inexactly, as Poitevins (the horde from Poitou)? Why was the king expending such vast sums on refurbishing Westminster Abbey and enhancing the cult of Edward the Confessor? And perhaps the most serious question the barons raised came in the late 1250s: why was Henry pledging to pay for an army to wipe out the pope's Hohenstaufen enemies in Italy and Sicily?

The answer to the last question must make reference to Henry's devotion to the papacy, his rivalry with Louis IX, whose reputation as the most sage and pious Christian ruler clearly galled the devout English king, and the papal promise that Henry's second son would receive the Sicilian crown if the Hohenstaufen were displaced by an English-led army. The barons would have none of it. The intermittent failed attempts to regain the French dominions and the king's extravagance made them issue demands in council for reforms and supervision of government in 1258 in return for a pledge to support the Sicilian enterprise. They also demanded periodic meetings of an enlarged council, including representatives of the shires and the boroughs, the community of the realm (we may call them Parliaments), which would authorize taxation.

The leader of the opposition was a baron, Simon de Montfort the Younger, the youngest son of the conqueror of Languedoc of the same name. He had been denouncing Henry's policies and opposing his requests for subsidies for years. In the brief euphoria following the king's promise to accept the baronial plan of reform, one persistent problem was solved. Henry entered into the conclusive negotiations to end the war with France. The instrument of peace, the Treaty of Paris, was accepted by both sides in 1258 and formally ratified in 1259.

In the event, the barons never granted the funds for the Sicilian enterprise, and the pope turned instead to Louis IX's brother, Charles of Anjou. In England the situation went from bad to worse. In 1261 the pope permitted Henry to renounce his oath to accept the baronial plan of reform, thus frustrating hopes that the Poitevins and Provençals would be forever purged from government and that attempts at heavy taxation would cease. Simon de Montfort and his baronial allies made their attitude very clear in 1263, raising the spectre of full-scale rebellion. A last-minute attempt to redeem the situation was a failure. Both sides asked Louis IX to arbitrate. The barons thought his mandate was narrow, to examine and reach a compromise on individual issues in contention. The French king took a different view and in the Mise of Amiens of 1264 reproached the barons for their attempt to limit the authority of an anointed king. There was only a grudging recognition in the Mise that Magna Carta had the force of law.

Civil war ensued. It was a particularly bloody civil war for English Jews, whom some of the dissident barons and their supporters saw as royal flunkies, insofar as the profits of their money-lending, exacted from their baronial debtors among others, were often appropriated by the Crown. The period of baronial success which followed the civil war was brief, but it was punctuated by the meeting of two parliaments where reforms were instituted. Simon de Montfort's coalition did not hold together, however, and in August 1265 the royalist party led by Henry III's eldest son, Prince Edward, decisively defeated baronial forces at Evesham. There was some guerrilla warfare afterwards, and Jews were often targeted by those barons who postponed their surrender.

Simon de Montfort, however, died at the battle of Evesham, although several of the baronial reformer's ideas survived. There are hints in the sources that even peasants were aware of and saw great benefits in the baronial reforms, which had been articulated in terms of relief from oppression. A popular cult grew up around Simon de Montfort after his death. The Crown, too, though it tried to vilify de Montfort's memory, willingly used parliaments in the future as a forum both to issue statutes to clarify the common law and, in the presence of representatives of the shires and boroughs (the 'common counsel', one might say, recalling chapter 12 of the original Magna Carta), to levy taxes. It came to be accepted as good law indeed that no modification of the common law could be enacted and no taxes could be levied outside this forum. When Edward I, who succeeded his father, tried late in the century (1297) to bypass Parliament in levying taxes, even he, strong and decisive leader though he was, was forced to acknowledge that he could not do so. And for good measure, he also confirmed Magna Carta.

Parliament did not begin in the period of the baronial ascendancy, but the calling of 'the commons', representatives of the shires and boroughs, was new. It was not the case, however, that the 'commons' was necessary for the existence of a parliament or that the commoners, when they were summoned, were all that common. The knights who represented the shires and the knights and burgesses representing the boroughs may have lacked the legal status of nobility in England, but they were all wealthy and elite members of society. Their institutional standing within Parliament was vague. There was little bureaucratic organization among the representatives, although some permanent offices would begin to emerge in the fourteenth century; full institutional development, a real House of Commons, did not arise until the fifteenth century.

There were tasks to which Parliament attended that were dealt with only by the king together with the lords or nobles of the great council, whose composition was also still relatively malleable in the late thirteenth century. The king called on whom he wanted. Like all great royal councils (the Cortes of Aragon, the Parlement of Paris, the Cortes of Castile), the English Parliament was the king's high court. The commons had no role to play in the judicial activities of this high court.

Nonetheless, since the king was the font of justice and could offer private petitioners clemency, pardons and redress against the rigours of the common law, it was natural that representatives of the commons would present petitions, too. Sometimes, unlike the private petitions to which the king was accustomed to responding, the commons' petitions addressed wider, more public matters. The king and great council of lords would act on these petitions. They could reject them, but if they responded affirmatively, they were taken to be statutes, statements of law, sometimes law that modified or clarified the common law. Indeed, as noted, it came to be felt that only a parliament could modify the common law.

The issuing of a statute did not depend on a prior petition from a representative of the commons. Most statutes seem to have originated in the expert or political discussions between the king and the lords. For example, in the 1270s Edward I initiated a campaign to recover royal rights that were in private hands. He insisted that holders of these rights – for example, the right to collect the revenues of a local royal court – show the charters or warrants in which he or an earlier king had granted them the rights. In the course of the campaign it became clear that a great many people did not have such warrants. They argued, most of them honestly, that some of the grants were given verbally at the time of the Conquest or later, and that it should be sufficient that they had been bona fide possessors for a long, long time. Their bitterness was palpable.

By the Statute of Quo Warranto of 1290, a compromise was reached. The standing legal principle on the eve of the issuance of the statute was that time did not run against the king. No matter how long a holder of a franchise held it, if it had originally been the Crown's, then the Crown could recover it unless decisive proof was offered that the Crown had ceded the franchise. Mere long possession did not contravene the king's right. By the statute of 1290, it was decided that any possessor who could show bona fide possession of a royal franchise continually from the time of the coronation of Richard the Lionhearted in 1189 could maintain possession by proprietary right. The year 1189 in legal jargon became the limit of legal memory. It was not the case that the statute overturned the principle that time does not run against the king, it merely asserted that legal time began in 1189. Time immemorial, 'time out of mind', came before.

Parliament, perhaps most importantly, became the forum for the presentation of the Crown's case for its major policies, domestic and foreign. Clergy opened the great sessions with long sermons in which they both invoked the mandate of heaven and adumbrated the king's good causes. Together with the king and the king's men, who went into some details publicly and other details behind the scenes, the propaganda value of these solemn encounters between the king and the 'people' served, if successful, to bind the political nation together – and get it to agree to be taxed. Of course, negotiations were not always successful. Pointed and serious criticisms could be raised, usually directed against the king's men rather than the king himself. This was a perpetual danger in calling these assemblies.

Yet they had to be called. Warfare required money and Edward's wars were numerous. In 1270, still a prince, he had gone on crusade. He arrived in the eastern Mediterranean after the death in Tunis of Louis IX, whom he greatly admired. He spent additional time trying to succour the fragile crusader outposts before returning to England. On the way home, he learned of his father's death in 1272, but Edward, who was delayed in Gascony by a number of disturbances, did not undergo the ceremony of coronation at Westminster Abbey until 1274. Contemporary scribes date his reign from 1272, not the date of his coronation, which until then had been conventional. Constitutional historians take this as a sign that, however significant the coronation ceremony remained, the dynastic principle of right of succession of the *primogenitus* had finally triumphed. It was written into law in 1290. The evidence is similar for France. When Louis IX died in 1270 his son Philip was with him. He could not return to France from Tunis to be crowned at Reims until 1271, but contemporary scribes date his regnal years from the death of his father, not from his own coronation.

Much of the cost of Prince Edward's crusade was paid for by ecclesiastical revenues. His wars as king required the revenues of parliamentary taxation. Wales presented the first challenge. The Welsh prince, Llewelyn ap Gruffudd, refused to do homage to the new king. This was the excuse and legal pretext for Edward's conquest, but the deeper cause was the ethnic hatred between Welsh and English and the inability of the English marcher lords on the Welsh border to control raiding and ambushes. Wales was a formidable terrain. Edward spent the better part of seven years, 1277–84, subduing the country and then assuring its continued subjugation by the construction of some of the most impressive and expensive castles northern Europe had ever seen. In 1284 he celebrated the conquest in the Statute of Wales, which annexed the princedom, and he made his eldest son the new prince.

Edward's relations with Scotland had more mixed results. In 1290 a disputed succession arose in Scotland. The English kings had long claimed overlordship and on occasion had received at least the contested obeisance of the Scottish kings. In the circumstances of 1290, Edward was accepted as the arbiter of the succession dispute, deciding in favour of one John Balliol in 1292, but Balliol later, in part to secure his prestige, repudiated the English overlordship. When he refused to answer a summons for military support while the English were engaged in war with France in 1294–7 (see chapter 20), and even entered into alliance with the French, Edward invaded Scotland.

He crushed Balliol's forces, disgraced him publicly, and assumed direct rule. He took the Scottish coronation stone, the Stone of Scone, back to Westminster Abbey, where it would remain for 700 years. But he had bested a political opponent and his aristocratic supporters; he had not defeated a people. And yet the Scots were not one people. In the south of the country the population might better be described as Anglo-Scottish rather than Scottish, because there had been much settlement of Anglo-Norman nobles and humbler English types in the period since the Norman Conquest of England, much of it with the full support of the Scottish kings. The Highlanders, on the contrary, though deeply divided along what are conventionally termed clan lines, demonstrated a certain ethnic disdain both for the English and for the Anglo-Scots.

Edward realized his misapprehension when revolts erupted and when some of the leading figures were not great aristocrats but rather lower-born men, like that 'brave heart', William Wallace (executed 1305). Edward's anger was rekindled to high intensity when an English army suffered annihilating defeat in 1297 at the battle of Stirling Bridge. Determined on suppressing the rebellion, the English counter-attacked and overwhelmed the Scots in the battle of Falkirk (1298). Nevertheless, Scottish resistance continued. Leadership in Scotland ultimately passed to the aristocratic Bruce family, who would continue the so-called wars of independence. Edward had the determination, but not the time, to do to Scotland, a larger country than Wales, what he had done to its Celtic sibling in the west. There was to be no celebratory English parliamentary Statute of Scotland.

1 The façade of San Bartolomeo in Pantano, Pistoia, Italy

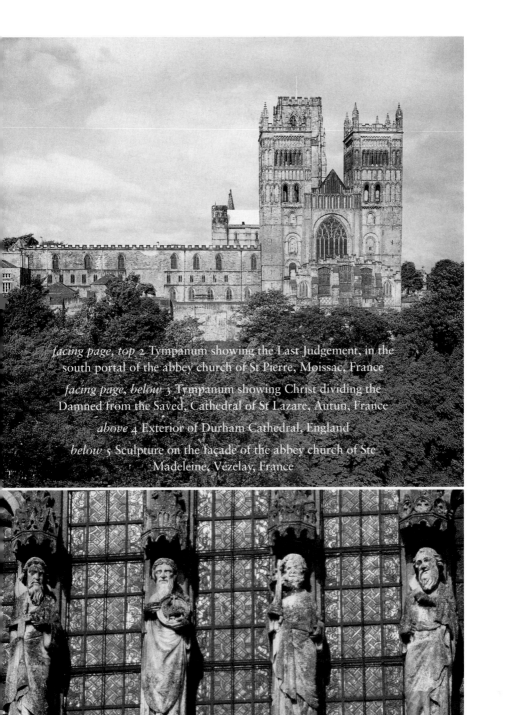

facing page, top 2 Tympanum showing the Last Judgement, in the south portal of the abbey church of St Pierre, Moissac, France

facing page, below 3 Tympanum showing Christ dividing the Damned from the Saved, Cathedral of St Lazare, Autun, France

above 4 Exterior of Durham Cathedral, England

below 5 Sculpture on the façade of the abbey church of Ste Madeleine, Vézelay, France

6 Façade of San Millan, Castile, Spain

7 Interior view of Ste Madeleine, Vézelay

above 8 Rose window, Cathedral of Notre Dame, Chartres, France

left 9 Reliquary in the form of a miniature Gothic church

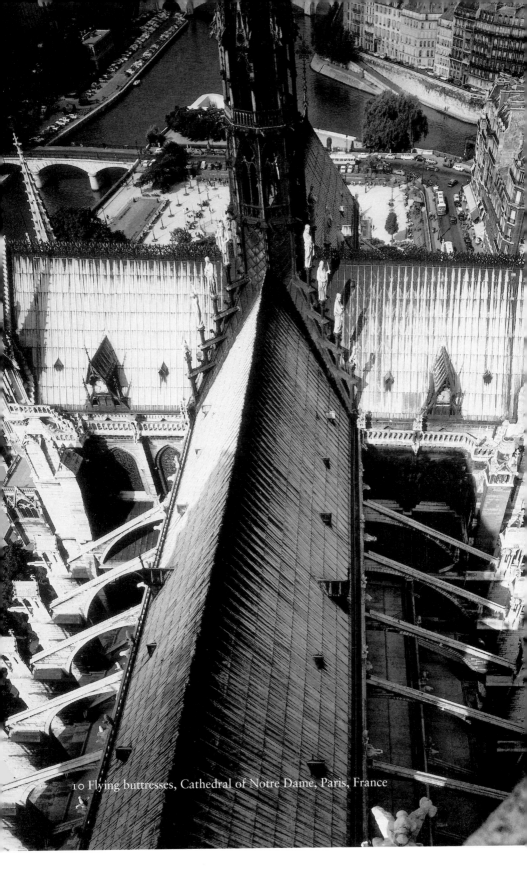

10 Flying buttresses, Cathedral of Notre Dame, Paris, France

11 Exterior of Cathedral of St Etienne, Bourges, France

12 Map showing Jerusalem in the centre, *c*. 1250, from a psalter

above 13 Exterior of Krak des Chevaliers, Syria

below left 14 Interior of the upper chapel, Sainte-Chapelle, Paris, France

below right 15 Centre portal of the west façade of Bourges Cathedral

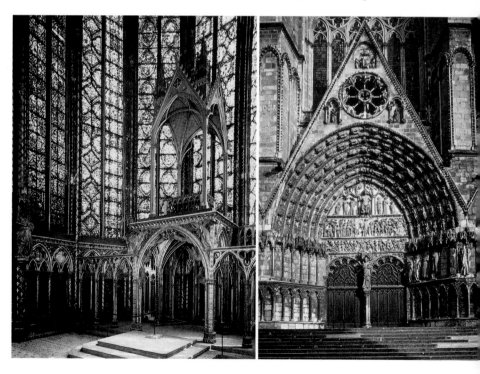

16 Exterior of Burgos Cathedral, Spain

17 West front of Westminster Abbey, London, England.
The towers are an eighteenth-century addition

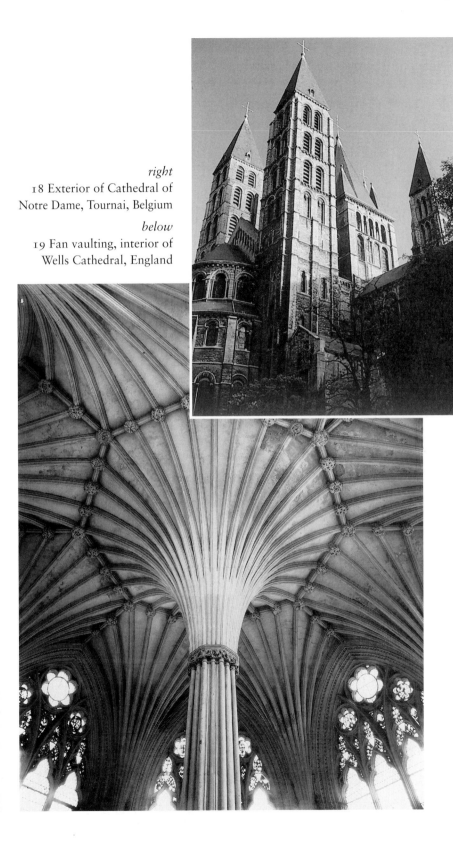

right
18 Exterior of Cathedral of
Notre Dame, Tournai, Belgium

below
19 Fan vaulting, interior of
Wells Cathedral, England

above left
20 Virgin and Child
by Giovanni Pisano

right, above
21 Illumination
showing Abraham
and the Three
Angels, from the
Psalter of St Louis,
1253

right, below
22 A vignette from a
Gothic manuscript
showing monks
singing

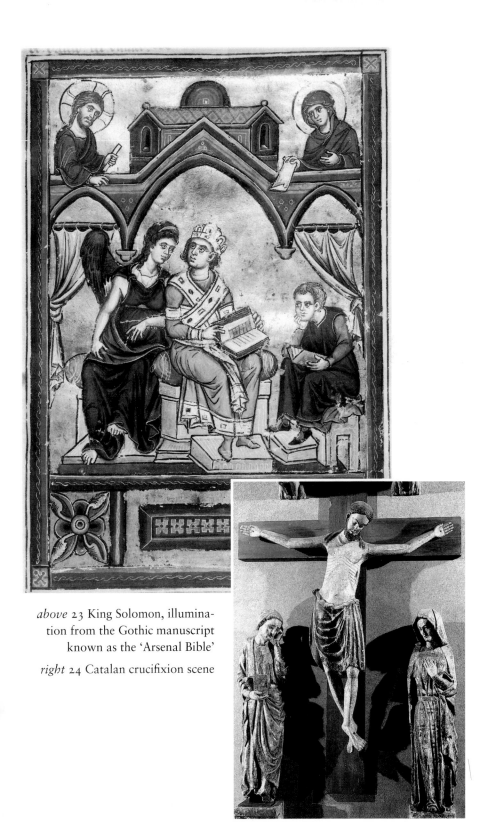

above 23 King Solomon, illumination from the Gothic manuscript known as the 'Arsenal Bible'

right 24 Catalan crucifixion scene

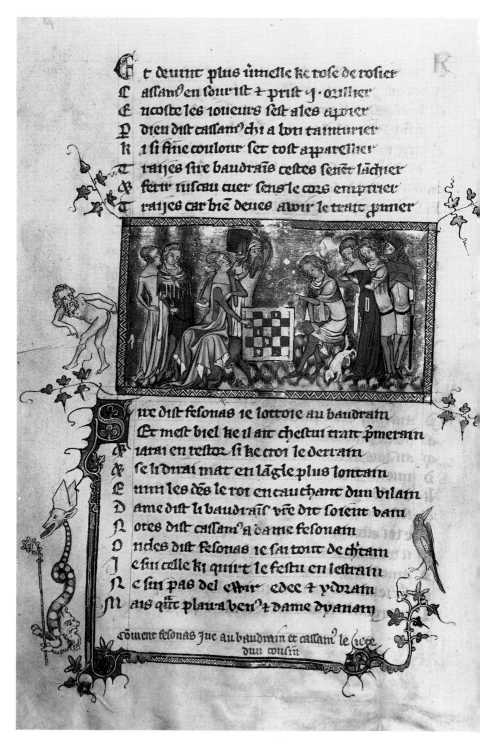

Et deuint plus ūmelle ke rose de rosier
Lassant en sourist ᵵ prist ·i· ouiller
Encoste les iouers sest ales apier
Dieu dist casant᷍ chi a bon taincurier
Ki si sine coulour set tost apareiller
Traies sire baudrais cestes senet lachier
Ferir nuseau cuer sens le cors empirier
Traies car brē deues auoir le traitt pmier

nre dist selonas ie lorroie au baudrain
Et mest biel ke il ait chestui tratt pmerain
Matai en restor si ke croi le derrain
Se li dirai mat en lāgle plus lontain
ꝯmin les dēs le roi en cauchant dun bilain
Dame dist li baudrais vre dit soient vain
Otes dist casant᷍ a dame felonain
Oncles dist selonas ie sai toitt de chtain
Ie sui celle ki quirt le festu en iestrain
Ne sui pas del eſtuir edec ᵵ ydrain
Mais qut plaura ben᷍ ᵵ dame dyanain

ꝯment felonas iue au baudrain et casant᷍ le rege
dun cousin

16

Baltic and Central Europe

The lands of the extreme north (we are speaking of Scandinavia) were characteristically free. Slavery died out in the two centuries following christianization and the containment of Viking raiding. Serfdom was also almost unknown. Partly this was due to the enduring ethos of clan freedom, with the understanding that the clans were composed of free farmers, heirs, as it were, of the great Viking warrior bands. Partly, too, it was due to the absence of the kinds of settlement that might otherwise have made it viable; Scandinavia was dotted with hamlets and individual farmsteads rather than villages. Finally, the low density of population and the ease with which a threatened population could escape to the nearby snowy and forested wilderness undermined attempts to subjugate the population. Only in densely populated continental Denmark in the early fourteenth century, when it suffered a decades-long agrarian crisis, do we see the emergence of a dependent peasantry.

Yet the Scandinavian lands were not oases of equality. There were strong warrior and service aristocracies and a strong Church. From the point of view of the Scandinavian kings, the aristocracies were a problem because they claimed some power over the royal succession, sometimes the right to elect. They also expected to be partners in government. The fundamental problem was the absence of any secure principles of succession, beyond election. This meant that every king, whether in Norway, Sweden or Denmark, who wanted to nominate his successor, use anticipatory succession, or establish the principle of primogenitary succession had to confront rival claimants from within the royal family who were willing to call upon aristocratic support from various factions.

To this extent, the Church was all the more important for royal rule. Time worked to the advantage of churches, which had still been very weak in the twelfth century. Sweden, of course, had offered the most outright resistance to christianization because of the symbolic and

243

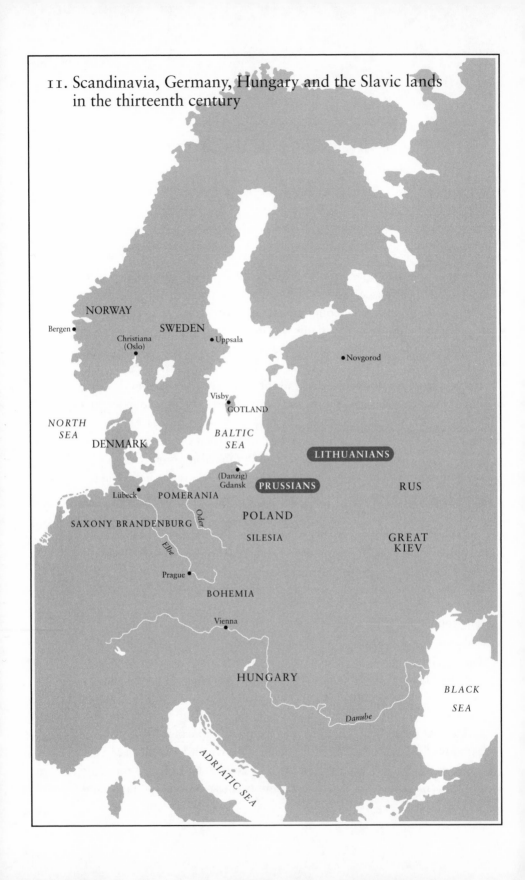

11. Scandinavia, Germany, Hungary and the Slavic lands in the thirteenth century

spiritual importance of the pagan shrine at Uppsala, the prestige its aristocratic protectors enjoyed, and the profits they shared, which were derived from the shrine and the commerce that took place within its 'peace'. It took decades after the formal acceptance of Christianity by the Swedish monarchy to undermine the power of these aristocrats, and how it was done is still not clear, given the thinness of the sources. One argument sees the growing commercial relations with Christian merchants, who, even if they did not refuse to trade with pagans whom they suspected of practising human sacrifice, preferred to deal with Christians.

By the late twelfth century and throughout the thirteenth century, the Church in Scandinavia worked hand in glove with the kings to secure royal rule and establish the kind of peace that would allow ecclesiastical institutions to flourish. Where a combination of ecclesiastical leadership and exceptional rulership – helped on by very long reigns – obtained, the possibilities for economic growth, territorial expansion and internal stability were excellent. This was certainly the case in Norway and Denmark, less so in Sweden.

The Norwegian case is noteworthy. After a series of brief reigns at the turn of the twelfth/thirteenth century, Norway had only three kings for most of the century: Haakon IV (1217–63), Magnus VI Law Mender (1263–80), and Haakon V (1280–99). Dynastic stability was a *sine qua non* for getting aristocrats to see that it was to their advantage to hitch their destiny to that of the Crown. Many of the most formidable heads of families became associated with the itinerant royal court, which in its travels made a terrific symbol of the power of the Crown. At the same time, with the support of the Church, which began to accumulate considerable property and popular loyalty, the monarchs created an elaborate regional administration for the country comprising regulatory, judicial and fiscal districts under the control of approximately seventy key appointees. Local assemblies, *things*, remained intact, but were co-opted in an administrative partnership. In this sense, the Crown was not dependent on the aristocracy for governance. As Magnus VI's epithet 'Law Mender' implies, many of the ordinances and decrees that articulated the rules of this system and the relation of its parts to one another and to the governed were the work of that king and his advisers.

The consequences of a strong administration and a harnessed nobility were widespread advantages in diplomatic and commercial relations.

Norway maintained its hold, jurisdictionally speaking, over Iceland and the North Sea islands. Norwegian stockfish (wind-dried cod) was exported throughout the Baltic region. Bergen, the biggest town, which at its height may have reached 10,000 in population, though this seems a bit exaggerated, emerged as a major entrepôt on the western coast. It also became a sort of royal capital for Norway. The court remained itinerant, but there was a tendency for it to visit Bergen often and to stay resident for relatively extended periods. As southern coastal Norway became more active in trade, however, Oslo arose as a rival centre of Norwegian administration.

In the 1160s, we first hear about the loose Baltic and North Sea association of merchants and merchant towns known as the Hanse. Bergen was to become an important contact point and trading settlement for Hanse merchants. Even so, the Norwegian kingdom's relations with the association were not always good. Leadership of the Hanse rested with the continental German town of Lübeck; it was the soul of Hanseatic self-esteem and was a particular thorn in the side of the Norwegian kings. They tried several times to get control of Lübeck by diplomacy and by force, so as to protect the kingdom from punitive boycotts of grain orchestrated under the town's leadership. The Lübeckers' position was to oppose all measures that were intended to regulate Hanse merchants or to diminish their privileges. Embargoing shipments of grain was one way Lübeckers resisted. Since most of the carrying trade was in non-Norwegian hands, embargo was a very effective way to put pressure on the kingdom.

Norway's neighbour, Denmark, entered the thirteenth century much as Norway had, with a legacy of disorder finally being overcome. The Danes had endured terrible civil wars in the twelfth century, but their country's recovery was astounding, thanks largely to a series of archbishops of Lund, warrior prelates, who used all their influence and power to work with the Crown to establish an environment suitable for the expansion of Christianity. This was not only a domestic imperative. In the twelfth century pagans lived on the continental borders of Denmark. Danes and Germans, sometimes in concert, sometimes not, carried on an enterprise of conquest and conversion. Eventually the Danes created a mini-empire in the Baltic extending as far as Estonia, which they conquered in 1219 and then partially pacified in a series of campaigns justified with a decidedly crusade ideology.

Part of the Danes' success can be imputed to the German emperors' relative lack of concern with matters along the Baltic. It also has much to do with the state of civil unrest in Germany, where the strife over succession in the early part of the thirteenth century and the bitter struggle with the papacy later on (discussed below) made the emperor willing to buy Danish support or at least Danish neutrality by key concessions, including territorial ones. This was not, however, the attitude of Baltic German aristocrats, who did not want to come under an authoritarian form of Danish rulership. It was they who led the resistance.

The well-governed Danish kingdom of the early thirteenth century, the kingdom that could conquer a major stretch of territory in the eastern Baltic and was so well administered that the decrees of the Fourth Lateran Council, including that on ordeals, were enforced quickly and smoothly, was almost in disarray by 1240. German aristocrats came to exercise more and more power in German lands claimed by the Danish kings and in Denmark itself, where they made incursions, by violence and by marriage alliances. Increasingly they ignored or bypassed royal authority. In the event, the Danish aristocracy saw its chance to escape the authoritarian rule of the kings. As in England, they exacted a great charter of liberties, the *hanfæstning* of 1282, which effectively constrained the king's arbitrary powers and confirmed the importance of the Danehof, an institution similar to the English Parliament, as the forum for articulating policy.

The least successful royal experience was in Sweden. To be sure, Sweden was expanding territorially throughout the years of royal weakness, in a pattern similar to Germany's. Towns, island merchant communities, like that at Visby on Gotland, and aristocrats led the way in quasi-crusades with mercantile overtones into southern Finland and, with less success, into Rus' (medieval Russia). The Church, too, managed to deepen its roots in local society, encourage gifts to itself, and articulated the rationale for expansion and internal colonization by an innovative series of building campaigns, including the construction of good forest roads. But little or none of this saved the monarchy from the debilitating succession struggles of the first half of the thirteenth century.

Not until the regency established by Jarl (or Earl) Birger in 1248 was there some hope for stability. In a *coup d'état* he established his twelve-year-old son on the throne as Valdemar I in 1250 and imposed what can only be described as a ruthless regime, suppressing dissent by the free use of capital punishment and the levying of heavy, nearly confiscatory taxes. After Birger's death in 1266, Valdemar ruled alone until deposed in 1275 by his brother and successor Magnus I Ladulås (1275–90), in circumstances that can at best be described as grotesque.

Valdemar became enamoured of his wife's sister and fathered a child by her. Not only was his liaison with his sister-in-law incestuous by contemporary moral and canon law standards, the sister-in-law was also a postulant, the female equivalent of a monastic novice. That is to say, although she was not a fully vowed nun, she was already a daughter of the Church and under its protection. Valdemar went on pilgrimage to Rome to seek papal absolution for his sins. In the hothouse environment of Rome and with the deep stain of incest upon him, Valdemar succumbed to the pope's price for reconciliation.

Sweden had been, as we have seen, one of the slowest countries to destroy paganism. Sweden and Norway were notoriously slow as well in accepting the reforms associated with the Church's victory over lay investiture, such as the celibacy of the clergy, and unlike Denmark had not been particularly swift to enforce the decrees of the Fourth Lateran Council or, for that matter, of the First Council of Lyons (1245), which had furthered the reform of the Church. Now, in the year 1274, the year of the Second Council of Lyons, Pope Gregory X saw an opportunity to strengthen papal leadership of the Church in Sweden. As Innocent III had done with John of England early in the century, Gregory obliged Valdemar to accept papal overlordship of his kingdom and to promise to render annual taxes to Rome as a token.

In Sweden, the news was greeted with derision. Moreover, the resentments incurred in the mid-century during the autocratic rule of Jarl Birger culminated in a coalition of barons seizing power, replacing Valdemar and elevating his brother, Magnus I. Valdemar fought hard to regain the throne, but was defeated in battle and fled to Norway, carrying on his efforts by intrigue and feint until his death in 1302. Magnus succeeded beyond expectations in establishing a stable rule, despite his brother's wearisome machinations. To do so, he had to heed the advice of select nobles, co-opt them, as it were; it is usually said that the mature form of the royal council, the institution within which this co-optation took place, dates from his reign. He was also responsible for improving administration and governance, no doubt in part under the influence of similar developments in Norway. The quality of his work in this regard is indicated by his epithet 'Ladulås', which means 'Barn-Lock'; farmers felt safe from depredations in the best days of his reign. Unfortunately for the groups that benefited from his rule, his work was jeopardized at his death when he left a ten-year-old as his successor. The problems of the early fourteenth century which were to ensue crippled the Swedish monarchy as badly as those which Jarl Birger had temporarily overcome – if not more so.

*

The phrase *Drang nach Osten* or 'Thrust to the East' is the name traditionally given to the movement of Germans and other westerners into central and eastern Europe in the High Middle Ages. 'Thrust', or even an alternate translation like 'Push', does tend to emphasize the violent aspect of a movement that was only intermittently violent. It began by and large with Catholic missionary activity to pagan Baltic and Slavic peoples, and some of this missionary activity was very peaceful. Yet the indigenous peoples, as members of 'heroic' societies that valued conspicuous displays of wealth, were sometimes unimpressed by the public face of humility that the early missionaries bore. Consequently, the missionaries began to adopt practices more likely to attract converts, especially from among the rulers, including ostentatious displays of the wealth of the society from which they came.

The new practices did attract some converts and also some envy. Linguistic barriers aggravated the dissonance of the encounter between Christian and pagan. And the situation was further complicated by the fact that some of the already christianized Slavic allies of the German missionaries had little love for the pagans who had been their traditional rivals. Moreover, missionary activity went hand in hand with trade, then settlement, first temporary, later permanent.

Self-defence on both sides, when violent disputes broke out, exacerbated a situation that became increasingly fractious. When, in the twelfth century, crusade ideology intruded into this mix from the Christian side and when displacement of the indigenous population accompanied permanent settlement, as it did fairly frequently, the *Drang nach Osten* took on the form of recurrent and destructive warfare. The principalities created in the wake of this warfare in the thirteenth century came to be known collectively as 'military states' or 'order states'.

The term 'order states' stems from the prominence of the Order of the Teutonic Knights and the Order of the Sword Brothers, two ecclesiastical associations of monk-knights (they were amalgamated in 1237) that took over the governance of large territories in Baltic Europe with the conquest of Livonia and Prussia. This was possible in part because of the erosion of Danish and Polish power along the Baltic, despite the successes of these kingdoms earlier on. The imposing symbols of the military orders' dominance were the great brick and mortar castles that they erected. These awed the Balts, who at the time of the conquest had not yet mastered the art of making bricks or mortar. Of course, the orders did not manage to create an order state everywhere. The Teutonic Knights, encouraged by King Andrew of Hungary to establish houses in Transylvania from 1211, tried to establish a principality but were expelled forcibly by Andrew for the attempt in 1225. The Hospitallers helped to colonize Slavic villages with Germans in the Czech lands, Silesia and Pomerania at roughly the same time; they were not expelled because they did not try to achieve territorial governance.

It is a commonplace that the *Drang nach Osten*, in its most aggressive and successful military and commercial phases, was the work of princes and towns, ecclesiastics and merchants. Yet the emperors were never completely uninterested in eastern developments. They could at times bring their considerable influence to bear to settle disputes among contending parties. They were particularly concerned when military campaigns in the Baltic east threatened to bring retaliation on the empire from potentially powerful foreign forces, like Poland or the principalities of Rus'. But eastern Baltic problems paled in comparison with those with the Italian communes and the papacy.

This was certainly the case for Pope Innocent III's ward, Frederick II. Hohenstaufen king of Sicily from 1198 and, from 1220, also Holy Roman Emperor, Frederick would come to occupy a unique position in the medieval and modern European imagination as the *Stupor Mundi*, the 'Wonder of the World'. His intellectual interests were wide-ranging: falconology, natural science, political theory. But he had to satisfy his personal interests, as had most other emperors, in the brief intervals between dealing with the seemingly intractable problems of governance in Italy.

The emperor's power base should have been Germany, but Germany itself was decentralized as a result, in part, of Frederick Barbarossa's political reforms in the twelfth century. It became more divided still during Frederick II's rule because of new disputes with the papacy. When Pope Innocent III died in 1216, it was left to Frederick II to settle by force contesting claims to the German royal title with Otto of Brunswick. His success in doing so had another aspect. Future popes were unhappy with the reality of a German king-emperor who was also king of Sicily (southern Italy and the island). They felt territorial pressure on the papal states from both north and south and looked upon every evidence of Frederick's disagreement with papal policy or outright defiance of it as a threat to the liberty of the Church and, therefore, as testimony to the emperor's spiritual corruption. A 'brood of vipers' would be the phrase that papal publicists would ultimately use to describe Frederick and his lineage.

Frederick tried to offer himself as a crusader to help deflect papal censure, but even on this matter it was difficult for him to persuade churchmen and many nobles of his good intentions. He repeatedly postponed fulfilling his vow, and when he finally did so, it was done in a way that antagonized many of the most important leaders in Europe and the Holy Land. In 1229, after denouncing the strategy and tactics of crusaders who were in the field before him, he succeeded in negotiating Jerusalem's return to Christian hands. In so doing he had to make concessions to the Muslims with regard to access to holy sites and agree to limit future fortifications.

Meanwhile, Frederick had secured title to the kingship of Jerusalem through marriage. While on crusade he exercised a nearly autocratic form of rulership in the kingdom, sometimes treating the crusader barons with indifference or contempt. That he was not averse, as the propaganda would have it, to allying himself with Muslims against Christians who violated the treaty recovering Jerusalem, or who just despised his rule, was another point raised against him.

Frederick returned from crusade because forces hostile to him, believing they had papal sympathy, were trying to overthrow his regime in Europe. And so, despite brief truces and temporary reconciliations, the general character of relations between Frederick and the Church turned more and more sour over time. The ultimate confrontation between the pope and the emperor began in the 1240s. Frederick seemed about to attack Rome and capture Pope Innocent IV, when the pope hurriedly took the papal court to Lyons, then on the border of France, where he could rely on the proximity of French forces to protect him. At the First Council of Lyons in 1245, the pope committed the Church to a new crusade under the leadership of the French king, Louis IX, partly as a reward for his good will in the imperial–papal struggle, and he also issued a solemn bull of deposition of Emperor Frederick II.

Frederick used every possible diplomatic means to counter the blow, but to no avail. The French king may have lamented the pope's action, but the pontiff's support for the crusade was of paramount necessity to him, and he did not believe that Frederick had acted properly over the years. In Germany, churchmen loyal to the papacy supported a rival claimant to the throne, with the usual deleterious consequences for civil peace in the kingdom. When Frederick died in 1250, the situation did not noticeably improve, for his heirs were determined to maintain their inheritance. The papacy was as opposed to his heirs' rule, especially the possibility of any one of them uniting again in one person the German and Sicilian crowns, as it was to Frederick's. In the 1250s and 1260s a succession of popes and various aristocratic leagues supported an assortment of claimants to the German throne, including Alfonso X of Castile, half-German through his mother Beatrice of Swabia.

The internal disputes of Germany were compounded by disorder and threats on its borders. Poland's monarchy had been eclipsed in the twelfth century, but the principality of Little Poland, with Krakow as the capital city, enjoyed a considerable resurgence in the first decades of the thirteenth. The recovery was stymied by a new force that sapped not only the Poles' strength but that of several central European Catholic powers as well as of Orthodox and pagan principalities further east – the Mongols. Catholics would name them the scourge of God.

By 1238, when the great Mongol invasion of Europe began, there had already been intermittent raids for fifteen years. Europeans were aware that a great empire was gradually being carved out, but they could scarcely guess its extent until diplomatic contact increased in the mid-century. This Mongol Empire would become the largest contiguous land empire ever created, including at its height China, Persia, the steppe, most of the Russian principalities, a huge chunk of the Near East and a healthy slice of eastern and central Europe.

No one could have predicted this at the start of the Mongol campaign in 1238. Great Kiev, the powerful Rus' principality, was a major force, as was the Rus' principality of Vladimir in the north. Both these Orthodox strongholds had pagan and Muslim enemies to the east, who would also be buffers against the Mongols. No love was lost between the Orthodox principalities and the Catholics, but here again it would have been inconceivable to the Germans that pagan armies from Central Asia could rapidly overcome Muslim and pagan enemies, great Orthodox armies as well as Polish and Hungarian forces.

The unthinkable was realized in a series of stunning campaigns from 1238 to 1241. These ended on a somewhat sour note for the Mongols, with a string of small setbacks, but most of Rus' was already conquered with the exception of the extreme north, the state of Novgorod, 'Lord Novgorod the Great', as it was officially called. German, Polish and Hungarian armies had been annihilated. Mongols penetrated deep into Hungary and even reached the outskirts of Vienna in Austria. The retreat from their advanced lines in 1241 was occasioned by the death of the Great Khan and the recall of his field commanders to Mongolia to help choose his successor. To emphasize their ascendancy, they left mighty armies in readiness and engaged in a series of ruthless raids into Croatia and along the Adriatic Sea.

Much speculation has been focused on the causes of the Mongols' triumph and on whether their successes might have continued if they had decided to carry the war in subsequent years again into central or even western Europe. Certainly the Mongols were not undefeatable. They suffered many defeats, large and small, in the first four decades of the thirteenth century, but always they seemed to bounce back. One advantage they had was the compound bow, but their enemies were not slow in recognizing the utility of the technology, which is one reason successful lightning attacks were so necessary to establish Mongol hegemony. They also had a ruthless policy of reneging on truces and agreements of safe conduct and of sanctioning slaughter, putting males to death in great numbers as an example. The problem was that this policy, effective in the short run and inspiring terror, also stiffened resistance. Knowing that honourable surrender was no guarantee of saving their lives many units fought to the death rather than surrender.

There were other factors, too, that are said to have made the Mongol conquest of central and western Europe unlikely: medieval Europe's great walled cities, its terrain (far less easy to negotiate for horsemen than the steppe), the sheer demographic weight of western Europe in the thirteenth century. But every time these factors are cited, they come up against a powerful counter-argument. The Mongols conquered China, which offered similar, some would say even more formidable, obstacles to steppe and high-plateau warriors. In the end, it is impossible to know what might have been. It was enough that Europeans – western and eastern – thought the end of the world might be upon them, that the biblical avengers, Gog and Magog, were unleashed (Rev. 20:7–8): 'And when the thousand years are expired, Satan shall be loosed out of his prison, / And shall go out to deceive the nations which are in the four quarters of the earth, Gog and Magog, to gather them together to battle: the number of whom is as the sand of the sea.'

If the direct political effect of the Mongol invasions on Rus', outside Novgorod, was catastrophic, the intermittent raids and campaigns, though never again as great or sustained as in 1238–41, were important for other lands. For decades, the Poles had to defend themselves from the Mongols at the same time as they tried to forestall the encroachments of the order states in Livonia and Prussia, and the increasing settlement of Catholic Germans and Jews of German speech in Silesia and in towns elsewhere in the shifting German–Polish borderlands. Polish nobles both benefited from and were disadvantaged by the fluid situation.

The benefits came from the absence of strong authoritarian rule from the centre, both in Little Poland and in Great Poland, whose major city was Warsaw. This is not to say that the rulers of either failed to try to overcome the difficult situation. The ascendancy of Little Poland in the early part of the thirteenth century, although it ended without the establishment of a stable state, was duplicated by the efforts of the princes of Great Poland later in the century. But every effort at creating a powerful state seemed frustrated by internecine strife. The attempt, at the Church's behest, to restore the monarchy with a native dynasty drawn from Great Poland late in the century (1295), for example, was exploded by the almost immediate assassination of the first new king (1296).

The freedom of the Polish nobility allowed it to have its way with lesser social groups like the peasantry. The same may be said of the Church, which remained unified in the thirteenth century despite the political and territorial disunity of Poland as a whole. The Church, too, gained extensive power over its rural dependents. One speaks of the entrenching of serfdom in this region even as it was fading as a major social institution in the West.

The wealth of nobles and ecclesiastics that accrued from the successful exploitation of their estates allowed the flourishing of the most fashionable styles. Gothic architecture began to displace Romanesque in Poland in the thirteenth century in those areas that were safest, that is, furthest from the military problems that plagued the fragmented state. For this was the downside of weak central power. Poland was prey to aggressors, and aggressors exacted a terrible cost by harrying vast tracts of land, reducing their productivity, if sometimes only temporarily. Moreover, in unsettled situations it was not always the case that the nobility formed a coherent group. One lord's weakness was another's opportunity. Only King Wenceslas II of Bohemia's invasion of Little Poland in 1291 and his joining of it with Great Poland very late in the decade finally created the kind of unity that made possible widespread social peace and economic well-being. But by then, the year 1300, the peasantry was virtually in thrall.

Hungary, unlike Poland, seemed to be on the way towards renewed stability in the first third of the thirteenth century. To be sure, both the nobility and the Church had made considerable demands on the Crown, and their rights were recognized in a series of pronouncements, especially the Golden Bull of 1222, which has been compared to Magna Carta in England. There was also considerable alienation of property from the royal fisc in these years. To this extent, although the Crown reached a *modus vivendi* with the Church and the nobility, its authority and power were reduced, especially if the comparison is with the almost mythical days of Stephen I. Nonetheless, under Kings Andrew (1205–35) and Bela IV (1235–70) Hungary attained considerable respect. Andrew was a leader in the Fifth Crusade, which had enjoyed some successes, and the princesses of the royal family became famous for their sanctity. The mendicant movement spread rapidly in Hungary, with the friars becoming the apostles of ecclesiastical and devotional reform. Hungary was a holy Catholic kingdom.

But in Bela's reign, chaos and disaster came with the arrival of the Mongol terror. Army upon army were defeated, thousands of square miles laid waste; massacres and transport of slaves eastwards took place to such a degree as to cause profound depopulation. The infrastructure of the economic system was in chaos and the king sought refuge in the most remote parts of his kingdom, waiting for the final onslaught.

Fortunately it did not come. As we have seen, the death of the Great Khan intervened to the good fortune of Bela IV, who had to witness the devastation, but at least did so in a land from which the Mongol invaders had retreated. Grim determination led subsequently to a massive castle-building programme. Where there were no strong natural frontiers there would now be artificial ones, and villages had to be refounded or restocked with animals and people. Westerners of various ethnic stocks were recruited for the new and revivified settlements.

Even as these efforts to rebuild the shattered country proceeded apace, they came at a cost. All the reconstruction was predicated on the necessity of unity and, to some extent, centralization, certainly the subordination of narrow local and class interests. The Church, having survived the devastation of a pagan enemy, probably saw more wisdom in this than the secular nobility. For the latter, the partnership with the king, unequal though it was, began to break down. Playing on a personal dispute within the royal family, especially between Bela and his son Stephen, in the 1260s (he ruled in his own right as Stephen V from 1270 to 1272), some nobles rose against the king.

The period from Bela's death in 1270 until the end of the thirteenth century saw a tug of war between nobles and king. At those moments of royal ascendancy the Hungarians made a considerable presence on the international stage, as in 1278, when they supported the cause and intervened on the side of the German princes who were resisting the attempt of Ottokar of Bohemia to seize the German throne. At other moments Hungarian politics descended to a deadly farce. Pagan Cumans who fled the Mongols had long sought to find solace among their ethnic Magyar cousins. It was hard for them to overcome Catholic suspicion, and it remained difficult, even after a Cuman troop was raised as the royal bodyguard, to persuade Cumans and Catholic Hungarians to treat each other with mutual respect. The Cumans in particular seemed unwilling at times to live according to the rules of 'civilized' (i.e. Christian) people. Ladislas IV (1272–90), himself the son, by Stephen V, of a Cuman princess, met his death at the hands of Cuman assassins. In the contested succession that followed, the turmoil continued.

Was Bohemia, the other potentially great power in central Europe along with Poland and Hungary, to be different? Yes and no. Because of Bohemian support for Frederick Barbarossa in his struggles, the ruling dynasty, the Premyslides, had received imperial recognition of its royal status in the mid-twelfth century. For the next one hundred years, Bohemia achieved the kind of stability envied by its neighbours. Though technically in the empire, it was nonetheless an independent kingdom, with fixed borders recognized by the emperor and with only nominal obligations expressing its formal dependence on imperial authority. The Bohemian king's voice was heard in elections of the German kings.

Territorial expansion was characteristic of this phase of Bohemia's history, sometimes by negotiation, sometimes by marriage, sometimes by naked conquest. Economic expansion was also typical. Prague entered on that phase of its history that would make it one of the great cities of Europe. Although the economic constriction and chaos of the late medieval and early modern period would make its development chequered, Prague was in the thirteenth century a wealthy and imposing metropolis, the largest in central Europe. Not a bad fate for a town that was probably little more than an assarted village (the name 'Prague' means something like 'burned-over place') in the Central Middle Ages. Other urban settlements multiplied, with the taxable wealth that this implies, and the extraction of silver ore also helped make the Bohemian king one of the wealthiest rulers in Catholic Europe. As the king, in particular Ottokar II (1253–78), grew in power, he made stronger claims of authority that implied a diminution in the freedom of action of the Bohemian nobility. Cowed temporarily, its opportunity for revenge came in the 1270s.

The opportunity was the election of a German king. The imperial situation since the death of Frederick II in 1250 had degenerated into perpetual strife. There was no effective Hohenstaufen candidate for king of Germany after 1254. Richard of Cornwall, the king of England's brother, and Alfonso X of Castile both put forward their candidacies in a disputed election of 1257. The period is called the Interregnum and was marked by strife. But, as usual, political strife, as long as it did not degenerate into perpetually destructive civil war, was not a barrier to economic development; it merely meant that the centralizing or potentially centralizing authority enjoyed far fewer of the benefits of that development – taxation of new towns, expansion to the east, the displacement of vast amounts of trade from the fairs of Champagne to the fairs of Frankfurt.

The Interregnum also offered Ottokar of Bohemia the opportunity of making himself the German king, but the election of Rudolf of Habsburg to the office, thus ending the Interregnum in 1273, meant the rejection of Ottokar of Bohemia's candidacy, a setback that induced him to take up arms to fight for the Crown. The war that ensued was complicated by shifting alliances among the German princes (treachery, Ottokar might say) and also by the hesitation and, in many cases, outright refusal of the Bohemian nobility to support their king. A war of succession thus became a civil war both in Germany and in Bohemia. Ottokar, in 1278, was a casualty of battle. Vaunted Bohemian stability was succeeded by political disarray, although it must be said that the even greater disarray of Poland allowed a later Bohemian king, Wenceslas II, to seize control of that kingdom. It was almost as if the Bohemians saw their future not in a symbiosis with Germans but with the creation of a super-Slavic (Catholic) state.

The irony, of course, for Germany is that the very coalitions that defeated Ottokar promised greater unity and central authority in the realm and created the impression that Rudolf of Habsburg might accumulate the power to subvert the princes' and nobles' prerogatives. This impression was confirmed when Rudolf tough-mindedly put together a swathe of territories, recovered or conquered from Ottokar, as Habsburg property. On Rudolf's death in 1291, the princes acted to prevent further ascendancy by the recently modest noble family of the Habsburgs. In the event, Rudolf's successor, Adolf of Nassau, who was not a Habsburg, tried in other ways to subvert the control of the princes who had brought him to power. As a result, in a subsequent election, the princes renewed their loyalty to the Habsburg claimant, Rudolf's son, Albert of Austria, but only after eliciting the promise that he would not further challenge their status or authority.

*

Baltic and central European history in the thirteenth century is not solely about the vicissitudes of princely, royal and imperial statecraft. But those vicissitudes weighed heavily on that history and cannot be ignored. Most importantly, they contributed to the enserfment, virtual enslavement, of the peasantries and to the grossly ineffective response of Christian polities to the Mongol invasion. Christendom did not save itself. In a curious way, the Mongols saved it. One can only speculate as to what might have happened to the villages and towns of the heartland of Europe if, in the political circumstances of the thirteenth century, the Great Khan had not died in 1241 and the Mongol armies had not rested from their terrifying work.

17

The Gothic World

It is not possible to give a comprehensive account of the cultural practices and artifacts produced in thirteenth-century Europe in a few pages. The following chapter, therefore, tries to indicate some of the more interesting and well-studied aspects of the Gothic world with respect to the visual arts, the Romance tradition in literature, and the aristocratic household.

THE VISUAL ARTS

High Gothic was disseminated widely during the thirteenth century, becoming the dominant architectural style throughout Europe by the century's close. Of course, pilgrims who confined their peregrinations to the architectural sites of the Ile de France, the birthplace of Gothic, or to those of the immediately adjacent regions, would find some of the tallest and most elaborate churches in Christendom to visit. If they were of noble status, they might win access to the Sainte-Chapelle of Paris, the royal chapel (dedicated 1248), with pillars seemingly so thin that the building appeared from within to be constituted of little more than ornately stained glass. Built to shelter the relics of the Passion of Jesus (the Crown of Thorns, among them) which the French monarchy claimed to possess, the Sainte-Chapelle (see Figure 14) was the jewel of Gothic architectural achievement in the capital and gave rise to its own sub-family of imitations.

Less eminent pilgrims would have to content themselves with a vision of the Sainte-Chapelle from afar and concentrate their attentions, if they were interested in great monumental structures, on numerous new and remodelled churches nearby that soared towards the heavens (many were far taller than the royal chapel) and were provided with pointed arches, flying buttresses, lofty spires, an abundant number of stained glass windows, including at least one rose window, and extraordinarily delicate tracery work and sculptural façades (see Figure 15).

Leaving the magnificent cathedrals and monastic basilica, with one or another part of the fabric always under scaffolding (because the building campaigns lasted decades), interested pilgrims would find a host of smaller churches. Every village now had at least one, usually in stone and usually with some sort of structure or decorative embellishment that tied it firmly to the Gothic style. Perhaps there was only one tympanum that bore the mark of Gothic craftsmen's work or one elaborately painted window on the small, spireless building, but the pointed arches, the external buttressing and the sculptural programmes pointed to a kinship with the cathedrals and the great monastic basilica.

Awesome as the architectural accomplishments of High Gothic in the French-speaking lands were, there were rivals in many other regions: the cathedrals of Burgos (see Figure 16) and Toledo in Spain, built in the 1220s, and Léon in the 1250s, for example; exquisite buildings or parts of buildings in the French-German borderlands and the Rhine Valley, such as Trier's Liebfrauenkirche, dated around 1235; the cathedral of Strasbourg, whose nave is exactly contemporaneous; the cathedral of Tournai (see Figure 18), the choir of which was constructed only a few years later; and Cologne Cathedral, splendid already in 1248 though still far from completed.

The dissemination of High Gothic did not entail the eradication of regional differences. A splendid example of High Gothic in England, for example, is the mid-century Westminster Abbey (see Figure 17). It looks backwards towards what English architectural historians sometimes call early *English* Gothic, to emphasize its regional peculiarities, and forward to what they often call Decorated Gothic. Among the differences from continental practices was, in general, the relatively lower popularity and use of tracery and therefore of the rose window (a window outlined in tracery) in England. The buildings of the early Decorated style of the 1250s, 60s and 70s, in particular, still give the impression of the dominance of severe grid-like or rectilinear façades; only in the later Decorated style, towards the end of the thirteenth century and thereafter, do we find experimentation with the curvilinear and with elaborate (technically, flamboyant) tracery. Even so, although it was probably invented in England, German buildings more generally adopted the flamboyant style.

There are other distinctive, if not distinct, emphases in English Gothic, as there are in other regional styles, like the employment of very elaborate mouldings projecting from the tops of walls and columns and the use of heraldic shields as a decorative device. Heraldry, the often intricate abstract and animal images with bold colours that symbolized noble lineages and were used to decorate buildings and shields, came into its own in the thirteenth century all over Europe, but as the English example suggests, it was not the case that heraldic devices were incorporated with other art forms in the same way everywhere.

Some of the most wonderful, in the sense of amazing, developments in Gothic came in the evolution of vaulting. Architectural historians have adopted a dauntingly complex technical vocabulary to categorize the variety of vaulting (tierceron, lierne, net, fan, etc.), which over time became more and more elaborate. All types of vaulting created in fact or created the illusion of additional spaciousness in the large churches (see Figure 19).

The sculptural façades of the buildings and the free-standing statuary of High Gothic have been deemed naturalistic in formal terms. The human beings, animals and plants depicted seem to replicate the impression of volume (three-dimensionality) seen in nature, and the stone is worked in such a way as to imitate the textures seen in life. Proportions harmonize with those found in the natural world. Elongation or shortening, when they take place, are therefore intended to draw attention to particular symbolic messages. Indeed, both the placement of figures and the deliberate employment of distortions from nature contributed to a complex iconography in sculptural arrangements. And the number of scenes depicted in sculptural façades increased substantially during the Gothic period. It has often been said that the intellectually complex nature of these façades is the counterpart of the intellectual virtuosity seen in high scholasticism.

These general observations seem to be appropriate for most of the Gothic world. Again, however, regional variations (we shall use the convenient, but crude, labels of national or ethnic schools) are evident everywhere. Explaining them is not easy. Why do so many examples of German sculpture seem to increase the volume of the figures? The human figures, particularly perhaps the female figures, if given life would be slightly plump and less ascetic-looking than we find elsewhere. A few scholars argue that the German penchant for the more rotund female figure seen so often in sculptural depictions of the Virgin, especially in the rendering of the Virgin and Child, reflects the more emotional, less formal character of German sculpture, but this seems to be an unprovable proposition, and it still begs the question as to why Germans chose a more emotional, less formal style than, say, the Italians.

For Italy also had a distinctive style of Gothic. As one might expect, some of the distinctions relate to the ease with which Italian sculptors integrated certain selected classical characteristics into their work. While classical remains were always available to be copied or to influence medieval Italian workmanship, it was not always the case that medieval Italian sculptures or artists working in other media chose to appropriate them. They may have been more open to classical influence owing to Emperor Frederick II's pronounced classical tastes, but they remained far less enthused by classical models in the thirteenth century than they came to be in the Renaissance. On the other hand, Gothic naturalism, parallel to that seen in France, was wildly popular; the Italians laid particular emphasis on the hip-shot pose, which gave a dramatic, some would say erotic, curvature to the sculpted female body (see Figure 20). Siena, with the two sculptors, father and son, Nicola and Giovanni Pisano, was a major centre of Italian sculptural mastery in the thirteenth century.

Painting in the Gothic style began to appear around the beginning of the thirteenth century. The medium might be glass, cloth (many altar cloths were painted rather than embroidered), walls (frescos), monumental and miniature wood panels, the latter especially common in altarpieces, and, of course, parchment manuscripts. Like the other visual art forms, there were certain universal traits that seemed to link the objects to the same tradition, while at the same time there were distinctive regional styles, similar styles that flourished in different times, depending on the region, and an uneven attachment, also varying by region, to specific media (painted wooden altar-pieces were very common in Germany, but not in a great many other places).

Manuscript painting or illumination, usually given most attention in general books (see Figure 21), occurred nearly everywhere, the pictures often being framed by what appear to be Gothic architectural structures. The borders may also be blended with grape vines and leaves; indeed, the word 'vignette' for a little scene derives from artists' penchant for putting little pictures in the mass of decorative foliage (see Figure 22).

The stylistic idiosyncrasies of the figures within the frame often parallel those already noticed in the sculpture. Two general trends are discernible over the century: the increasing influence of classical models (via Italy and Sicily into Germany) and that of Byzantine painting, with its iconic, ethereal figures, especially after the Latin conquest of Constantinople in 1204. Thanks to traditional contacts and the earlier crusades, Byzantine models had long been available to western Frankish artists. The sack of Constantinople and the continued occupation of the capital until 1261 made the models ubiquitous not only in the Holy Land but in the West. A splendid example is the 'Arsenal Bible' (so-called from belonging to the Arsenal Museum in France), dated about the mid-thirteenth century and believed by some authorities to have been painted in the crusader port of Acre (see Figure 23).

That the French seem to have had a penchant for lavishing painterly attention on the interior spaces of architecturally framed miniatures has been noted repeatedly by art historians, as has the domination of red and blue in their palettes. Some have also seen an exaggerated naturalism, almost a sentimentality, in French Gothic painting. The human, suffering Christ, with twisted body, is a common visual image. It is paralleled in the sanguinary images, bordering on the grotesque, of Christ crucified in Spanish painted sculpture (wooden and stone) and painting (see Figure 24).

Many illuminated manuscripts also have visual marginalia, the interpretation of which has been much disputed. Fairly often the marginalia include quasi-bucolic scenes. At least, the animals – hares and the like – suggest a rustic arena of play or of the hunt but at times the content of the scenes is lewd. If the gestures parallel textual references on the page, then interpretation seems easy. The scene is said to illustrate the text; primacy is traditionally given by the scholar to the text. This choice may be wrong-headed, but is at least defensible.

It is more difficult to judge the relationship – always presuming there is one – between text and image when the image has no obvious echo in the text. Lewd marginal images (see Figure 25), often involving symbolic animals like the ape, and marginal social types of people like jugglers and tumblers, share a page with a prayer. What is implied here? That marginal people, people given over to gross vices, idleness and pleasure haven't a prayer? Or need prayer? If so, whose? Those of the reader/patron of the manuscript or of someone else? Perhaps the images reaffirm hierarchy, in the reader's universe of social discourse. Or perhaps they highlight the seriousness of prayer by contrast with the silliness of worldly pleasures. Or else they are simply supposed to amuse.

ROMANCE

The romance tradition continued to flourish in the thirteenth century. Although the twelfth century saw most romances in verse form, the thirteenth witnessed an upsurge in prose. Indeed, from that time onwards prose came to be the preferred mode of expression for the medieval novel; by the end of the Middle Ages it had become dominant.

At the centre of the romances was a code of behaviour originally associated with the precepts of war and chivalry. But chivalry meanwhile had evolved into a more elaborate set of manners and social postures in the thirteenth century. Still central was the knight's *prouesse*, his fighting ability and spirit, seen as an inherited virtue: birth (*héritage, lignage*) counted profoundly. No matter what conspiracies and circumstances reduced a knight to poverty and subordination in a story or obscured the nobility of his birth in a thirteenth-century romance, it was inevitable in the course of the action that his true knighthood would emerge.

In 'real life', in fact, nobility could be bought. The end of the thirteenth century saw formal acts of governmental ennoblement of commoners even in France, the putative birthplace of chivalry. Elsewhere in Christendom, as we have seen, there were disturbing anomalies – peasant-knights in Spain, *ministeriales* in Germany. The romances, therefore, imagined a less troubled world of social distinctions, one in which, even if a knight was unfairly humbled, time always righted the situation.

As a system of ideal values, as portrayed in the romances, chivalry retained the traditional insistence on kindness and *débonnaireté* (generosity) to widows and orphans and the protection of monks, nuns, the aged and the infirm from the ravages of war. The exemplary knight was a *prud'homme*, one whose violence was tempered by knowledge and practice of the highest (Christian) ethical values, comparable to those of the exemplary monk. However, as with the simplified social categories of the romances that differed so powerfully from the sociology of real life, so, too, the ideals of Christian combat rarely found their mirror image in actual warfare. War was brutal, and innocents were slaughtered. Moreover, though mounted knights always claimed the most prestigious role in the armies, contemporary military forces also consisted of lower-class men, paid soldiers, both mounted and foot, who did an enormous amount of the fighting.

A knight's ingrained, even innate, *loyauté* (loyalty) to his lord motivated him in the romances to undertake *aventures*, excruciatingly long and difficult quests, on his lord's behalf. Inevitably these were complicated by the demands of love, sometimes the troubling love of the knight for his lord's lady. *Courtoisie* required the *chevalier* to walk a fine line between admiration for the lady whom he should not possess and the sexual impulses that sought fulfilment. Even though his masculinity and therefore sexual *prouesse* were clearly represented as admirable when properly disciplined, a knight's failure to contain his carnal drives was often at the centre of romance tales and gave a tragic hue to the stories. The name of Tristan, the courageous and otherwise praiseworthy hero of *Tristan and Isolde*, who consummates his desire for the wife of his lord, King Mark, is understood in French versions of the tale to derive from *triste*, 'sad', although it actually comes from a Celtic word.

The plots of three representative romances will serve to emphasize and elaborate some of the points made above. *Robert the Devil* was originally composed in the late twelfth century, and more than one hundred versions survive, of which fifty are in French. The eponymous hero is the son of the duke and duchess of Normandy. Unfortunately the duchess had been unable to conceive during the early years of her marriage. In her despondency she invokes the devil for help and vows to dedicate her child to the lord of the underworld if he gives her the power to conceive.

The child, Robert, grows up to be extremely strong and extremely wicked, but comes to his senses and seeks an explanation for his corruption. His mother confesses, and Robert sets out on a penitential quest, to atone for his and his mother's sins. Robert, the true knight, takes up a life as a humble menial and fool, in this instance at the court of the emperor of Rome. Yet, despite every effort to play the buffoon in order to hide his *chevalerie*, innumerable adventures befall him, forcing him in turn to display his courage and prowess in war and his inborn chivalry in rescuing and protecting vulnerable women. In the end, Robert overcomes the curse of his dedication to the devil.

Havelock the Dane exists in a long Middle English version. Like so many popular late medieval romances, there is evidence that less elaborate versions were circulating in the twelfth century, and so-called minor versions of this tale continued to circulate in Anglo-Norman in the thirteenth century. In the full story, Havelock's father is killed and his realm is lost. Havelock is taken away and, in a very realistic treatment, lives a life as a scullion in an English lord's household. The English princess Goldeborn (or in her French incarnation, Argentille) has an evil guardian who wants to humiliate and degrade her. He forces her to marry Havelock the scullion. But of course Havelock is of noble lineage, a fact established in an English version by a royal birthmark on his shoulder and in a French version by his ability to blow a note on a great horn. By his knightly prowess, Havelock wins Goldeborn her kingdom of England and also Denmark (he is, after all, Havelock the Dane). They die after living together and ruling wisely for many years as king and queen.

The last of the romances that will be mentioned is the *Knight of Courtesy*, also known as the *Legend of the Eaten Heart*. It concerns the price of illicit love. The knight's world is wonderful, full of songs, feasts and tournaments. The knight himself is depicted as admirable in nearly every respect, and he has wonderful adventures in the name of his lady, in some versions even slaying the proverbial dragon. But, as intimated, their love is illicit, and in various versions of the story the *chevalier* is discovered with his lover either by her husband or, if she is presented as a maiden, by her father. According to one plot line, the knight is killed by the vengeful husband/father, who cuts out his heart. The heart, which the knight had once dedicated to his lady as a token of his love, is instead prepared at the order of the vengeful husband/father as food for the errant lady. When she realizes her cannibalism, she kills herself immediately or, depending on the version of the story, either starves herself or hies to a nunnery. It was such a good story that it just had to be told ('de quoi on doie faire conte') and indeed was told and retold for centuries.

A CULTURAL WORLD: LIFE IN THE ARISTOCRATIC HOME

The term that is used as the title for this chapter, 'The Gothic World', could perhaps be employed in a wider sense to include the peasantry and other so-called lower orders. They, too, visited shrines, modest local ones and the great cathedrals and abbey churches. The stories they enjoyed sometimes parallelled, sometimes borrowed from, and often contributed to the plots and motifs of upper-class literature, relished by the *prud'femme* and *prud'homme*. And yet, there *was* an aristocratic style that separated the Gothic world of the high-born from that of their social inferiors. To some extent the nature of this style of living was common to aristocrats all over Europe in the thirteenth century, but as with everything else there were regional variations. Let us here try to reconstruct a few aspects of aristocratic lifestyles, but away from the traditional core of the Ile de France, in an attempt both to discern the common quality of the experience across regions and to get some sense of the sorts of differences that provincial existence mandated. Poland will serve as a nice example.

In chapter 16, the rise of the Polish aristocracy to prominence in the unsettled political situation deriving from the *Drang nach Osten* and the Mongol threat was discussed. The erosion of Polish royal power liberated the nobility and gave it *carte blanche* in the exploitation of the native peasantry, which was reduced to a peculiarly degraded form of serfdom. But the resources that could be extracted from peasants' surpluses and from the wealth of the towns which supplied armies and benefited, when they could, from the eastern Baltic trade allowed the aristocracy to indulge its fashions – or to over-indulge them, for crippling indebtedness also became characteristic of upper-class life.

Gothic architecture, largely underwritten by aristocratic patronage, became the *sine qua non* for elite self-representation, displacing Romanesque, which had been dominant in Poland in the late twelfth century. To some extent, it was Cistercian foundations, under noble patronage, that carried the Gothic style through Poland. Yet many a Gothic abbey church in Poland would have struck an observer as strange, at least an observer used to western European examples. This is in part because of the relatively widespread use of brick rather than quarried stone in construction.

The power of the Polish aristocrat, largely independent of the constraints of state power, even if the royal court was ostentatious in its own right, was expressed in lavish display and conspicuous consumption. Fast days were occasions for the public display of piety and reverence for the Church, the relics and the saints. Feast days were appropriate for orgies of consumption. From interaction with Danes and intermarriage with western aristocrats, foods favoured among the western nobility became staples of Polish aristocratic diet. One historian concluded that on feast days, like that of Florian, the patron saint of Krakow (4 May), 'consumption was conspicuous and overabundant. Even the poor could count on a generous dole from the royal court, rich burghers, and nobility' (Dembinska, 1999, p. 72). The gift, of course, reinscribed the sense of dependency of the low-born on the high-born and was capable of stoking the resentments of the former towards the latter as well.

Except in small amounts usually produced for sacramental purposes, wine, the aristocratic beverage par excellence, was not directly available in thirteenth-century Poland, because of the unsuitability of the physical environment. But it could be imported. This luxury came from the West or from Hungary in barrels and helped make the great feasts occasions of camaraderie and social bonding, especially among male aristocrats. Such over-indulgent drinking became a pattern, more and more pronounced in Polish aristocratic culture in the later Middle Ages and the early modern period, especially with the introduction of fortified beverages.

Recipes that have come down to us from Polish practices tend to date from manuscripts later than the thirteenth century, but in many cases it does not seem rash to regard them as traditional. At any rate, they give some insight into the gestures of display associated with the aristocratic table and feast. Many of these recipes merely mirror those of the western aristocratic kitchen, although with some substitutions of ingredients because of local necessity (fruit or flower vinegars, for example, in place of tart grape juice).

A great feast, like that planned for Midsummer's Day, 24 June, the Nativity of St John the Baptist, might include fish aspic, 'fare for only the wealthiest of nobles and merchants' (Dembinska, 1999, p. 166). Huge numbers of cast-off fish parts – heads and fins, tails and skins, and the bones, around which there are always gelatinous residues – needed to be boiled down in order to achieve the kind of stock that would firm up correctly. For a major banquet, hundreds of fish parts were required and the cooks would have seasoned the stock heavily, with a variety of common and more exotic herbs and spices. The vinegar in which the flesh of the fish (preferably an oily fish) was poached could have any of a number of seasonings but lavender, a fragrant member of the mint family, was a favourite.

Choosing the flavoured vinegar was important, not merely for the taste it would impart to the poached fish. The choice determined the selection of accompaniments for the fish aspic as well as the decorative display of the food: candied lavender to open and close the meal and lavender sprigs, with their beautiful purple flowers, to garnish other dishes. Or, if lavender was not an option, apple vinegar, apple slices, and sprigs of apple blossom would be appropriate substitutes.

Other flavourings added to the fish stock included the traditional bouquet herbs, like bay leaf, but also onion and garlic, and rarer spices from the East, if they were available. The latter reached Poland from Constantinople, via Kiev, before the Mongol conquests. The minced poached flesh of the fish itself got whipped in with the reduced flavoured gelatinous stock and a miscellaneous mixture of salt, honey and rarer spices, giving the whole concoction an airiness and volume. The finished product would have been taken in shallow pans to the coolest recesses of the lower cellar to help it set, after which it was cut into elaborate patterns, sometimes in imitation of aristocratic heraldry, which was particularly well-developed in Poland. Bright garnishes – chopped hard boiled eggs, for instance – would augment the dish; or some of the aspic, with its own saffron colour (sometimes achieved by the addition of saffron in the cooking), could be put as dollops into halved boiled eggs whose yolks were removed.

Fish aspic of this sort would be only one contribution to the aristo-cratic meal. A feast day, that is, a day without restrictions on the consumption of meat, might have grilled fowl or savoury roasts (plain or marinaded), pastes and spreads made of local fruits, like quince, and, of course, generous portions of wine and good warm bread. A meal that began at five o'clock in the afternoon could go on for hours, for eating was a form of social interaction that, at its most elaborate, required entertainment.

This entertainment sometimes took place beforehand. Prince Henry IV of Silesia loved to organize the classic chivalric pastime, the tourna-ment. Other princes and nobles offered alternative diversions. Perhaps guests were invited to listen to the tale of Walterus Robustus and Helgunda's forbidden love, accompanied by a little music at intervals and still more drinking. Or, in a more pious household, the deeds of a Polish saint might be related. So many, especially of the thirteenth-century female saints, were members of aristocratic lineages that telling these tales amounted to a kind of retelling of family history.

Finally, there was gift-giving, one of the many practices that united the Polish aristocracy with the aristocracies of all medieval principalities. Gift-giving was the expression and reinscription of solidarities within elite groups and between elite groups and their subordinates. From the food doled out to the poor, to the robes and expensive trinkets exchanged by nobles, an abundance of gifts marked the Gothic world. It was possible to forget the Mongols and the Sword Brethren, abased and resentful peasants and mounting aristocratic debt in the social space of the tournament, the feast, the bawdy songs and their maudlin counterparts, and the fun of opening gifts. And all this took place under the satisfying influence of young red wine.

18

Southern Europe

North and south had much in common, as we have seen in the discussion of the Gothic (chapter 17), but the confrontation with Islam gives a particular character to the experience of Catholic life all along the Mediterranean. Even in those regions where the Islamic threat was in retreat, the long experience of confrontation helped shape developments in politics, society and the economy. In regions, like the Holy Land, where Islam was in the ascendancy almost every aspect of daily life depended on Christian leaders' success or failure in some diplomatic or military initiative with regard to the Muslims.

IBERIA

The Castilian Reconquest was more or less complete by 1252, the irritating exception of the Muslim principality of Granada in the extreme south notwithstanding. Christian Iberia entered upon a period of sustained economic growth, largely attributable to the exploitation of the lands recovered from Islamic control. To some extent, the benefit for Christian potentates came by way of the transfer to them of wealth that had once gone to Muslim princes. But there were incentives to economic growth in the newly recovered regions, including the investment of resources formerly mobilized for war into more productive enterprises, like sheep farming and other agricultural ventures, the manufacture of goods for trade, and the building of ships to facilitate trade as well as boats for fishing, defence and privateering.

In Castile, the reign of Alfonso X the Wise (1252–84) was also marked by an extravaganza of cultural productions. The vernacular in Castile had gone a long way towards displacing Latin in all but academic and elite religious life. (The widespread use of Flemish in contemporary Flanders is precisely comparable.) Enormous numbers of works were produced in Castilian, the most famous of which is probably the collection of *Cantigas*, lyric poetry and songs, dedicated to the Virgin Mary. But Castile also produced two long and impressive legal texts: the *Fuero Real*, a royal code of customary law, and the *Siete Partidas*, more a blueprint of an ideal society than a code *per se*. The latter was thoroughly informed by, indeed often copied, the rules and maxims found in Roman law as well as the legal and moral counsels of various other legal and extra-legal sources.

The mid to late thirteenth century also saw Portugal enter upon a new phase in its history, one of decisive economic growth and cultural ferment. Political problems rooted in traditional relations with its gigantic neighbour Castile continued to plague Portugal, of course. The thirteenth century saw a series of border disputes with Castile, especially intense in the late 1240s and in the two decades thereafter, and a set of additional controversies with the papacy, which threatened the stability of the kingdom. Tentative attempts to settle these disputes sometimes compounded the problems. In the event, Portugal's boundaries with Castile remained in dispute until the end of the century, and the papacy at least twice placed the kingdom under interdict because of what it regarded as the bigamous and incestuous marriage of one of the kingdom's rulers, Alfonso III (1245–79). Not until 1279, practically on Alfonso III's deathbed, were problems with the popes more or less settled.

Despite the severity and magnitude of its political problems, Portugal made real strides economically. Castle-building on the Castilian frontier absorbed some of the country's resources, but provided greater peace and security in brigand-ridden regions that had been exposed or underpopulated in the period of Muslim–Christian and Portuguese–Castilian warfare. In the circumstances the Crown sponsored large-scale immigration and resettlement in these regions, and as a result agricultural production increased and small towns took root. Existing urban centres, like Coimbra and Lisbon, also entered a period of significant demographic growth. The country as a whole, by the end of the thirteenth century, was approaching a population of one million.

Internal order was not merely a function of the presence of garrison sites. Portugal, like the other European monarchies, was governed by consensus when it was governed well. The kingdom's parliaments or *cortes* were already meeting with representatives of the towns joining the nobility and prelates by 1254. Perhaps in imitation of Louis IX's rigorous investigations into administrative corruption in France, the Portuguese kings introduced systematic investigations into abuses, beginning in 1258. Sometimes these backfired, generating retribution from over-mighty subjects, which could only partly be checked by the Crown; sometimes the investigations were manipulated in such a way as to make the Crown look better than it was. This was the papacy's interpretation during the high point of its struggle over the Portuguese king's alleged bigamy and incest. Nonetheless this rooting-out of corrupt practices testifies to the gradual emergence in Portugal of a responsible state administration.

Lisbon vied with Coimbra as the administrative centre of the realm and as the site of the university. Established in the late thirteenth century in Lisbon, the university 'migrated' back and forth between Lisbon and Coimbra in the decades to come. Notwithstanding the migrations, intellectual life flourished in Portugal. The *Siete Partidas* was among several works rendered into Portuguese in the thirteenth century and was part of this often royally sponsored cultural efflorescence.

Blocked from the lucrative Mediterranean trading zone by its own geographical position, Portugal oriented itself towards the Atlantic. In the thirteenth century fishermen and traders sailed further and further out into the great sea. Portuguese penetration of the Atlantic would not have colonial consequences until late in the fourteenth century with the exploration and settlement of the Canary Islands and the Azores, but the creation of the Portuguese navy in the thirteenth century, albeit frequently under the command of Genoese captains, made these expeditions possible. Contact with black Africa and with it direct access to African traders in gold and slaves again would not become a major factor in the Portuguese economy until the fifteenth century, but the crusading spirit that was diverted into maritime adventure in the thirteenth century was the foundation for exploration along the western African coast. A final consequence of the increasing oceanic focus of the Portuguese economy in the thirteenth century was the search for new fisheries in the north Atlantic, the full benefits of which were realized only in the fifteenth century with Basque and Portuguese exploitation of cod off Newfoundland in the north Atlantic.

In Castile's other neighbour, the Crown of Aragon, another remarkable monarchy began to take shape under an equally remarkable monarch, James I the Conqueror (1213–76). Still, its beginnings were inauspicious, with regency factionalism rife during the new ruler's youth. The principalities inherited by James were also bitterly divided by ethnic tension, especially that between Aragonese and Catalans. Moreover, while the great victory of Las Navas de Tolosa in 1212 had decisively advanced the Reconquest, there remained much to be done in eastern Iberia. Finally, although the ruling family was thoroughly orthodox, its political sympathies lay with the defenders of Languedoc against the northern crusaders in the Albigensian Crusade. North of the Pyrenees the Aragonese royal family had wide territorial claims which they saw the French encroaching on. They were particularly bitter that James's predecessor, a hero at Las Navas, died fighting the northern French crusaders in Languedoc in 1213.

James, known for his autobiographical *Book of Deeds*, was a deeply pious man determined to bring glory to the principalities he ruled. He was a shrewd prince as well, one who recognized the value of the *cortes* as assemblies in which it was possible to drum up support for his major expeditions, but whose fractious pretensions to autonomy under noble and/or urban control had to be kept in check. The game of checks and balances he played was largely effective, partly because he tended to call the *cortes* into session only when he knew the measures he was seeking support for were popular. Such projects were presented as if they needed immediate and enthusiastic action, and thus avoided drawing attention to other contentious matters.

It helped that James early in his adulthood established himself as a conqueror and thus was both popular and feared. The Balearic Islands – Majorca, Minorca and Ibiza – were Muslim strongholds from which raids on Christian shipping and on coastal cities were launched. In the early 1230s, in a carefully choreographed crusade with an overwhelming force, James invaded and conquered the islands. Soon after, with the support of the *cortes* (1236), he began the conquest of Valencia. It was virtually completed by 1245 despite Muslim (Mudejar) rebellions in the years to come.

Valencia was a jewel, an irrigated paradise. The complex farming practices and the fact that the Mudejar population far outnumbered the Christians made it incumbent on James to rely on his new Mudejar subjects to exploit the land. And the so-called surrender or capitulation charters the Muslim lords agreed to formalized the Mudejar peasants' licit place in now Christian-dominated Valencia. It was not confessional tensions that undermined this *modus vivendi*, though there were such tensions, and one particularly troubling arena of conflict was over how to deal with transgressions of the prescribed boundaries of sexual relations between Christian men and Muslim (and Jewish) women. These tensions paled before the threat posed by successive rebellions, small and large. The Mudejar rebellions were suppressed, and one consequence was that Christian settlers did begin to take up more and more agricultural holdings in Valencia, though the non-Christian population of Valencia continued to be significant for a long while to come.

It was James, ever the conqueror, who chivalrously granted Murcia to Castile after having invaded and won it by arms. This act, though befitting perhaps the ideal of Christian rulership with which James has become associated, had negative consequences for the Crown as well. The one serious issue that James only tentatively had under control was the ethnic rivalries in the country. The conquest of the Balearics, for example, had led to tensions about the distribution of spoils among Aragonese, Catalans and southern French in the vanquishing armies. And the successful conquest of Murcia for Castile embittered many of the largely non-Castilian crusaders who made up the army.

Southern Frenchmen (Occitanians, Provençals) made up such a large portion of James's invasion force of the Balearics because of his territorial holdings in Languedoc. The Albigensian Crusade had concluded in a complete northern and royal French victory by 1229 and with it the beginning of a process of the reimposition of Catholic orthodoxy in the region. Despite occasional native uprisings and posturing from outside powers, including not only Aragon but England, the French Crown managed to hold on and gradually strengthen its control of the south, even – thanks to the work of Louis IX – exciting a modicum of loyalty.

James then began the process of reconciliation with France. In 1258, representatives of James and Louis IX – both crusaders, both pious, and both with analogous visions of ideal Christian rulership – hammered out the Treaty of Corbeil. It drew a line at the Pyrenees between the two kingdoms, yielding James's claims north of the mountains, excepting Montpellier (the geographical origin of James's family), which was permitted to remain in the Spaniard's control. France in return ceded its claims in Catalonia, claims that originated from the French Crown's putative inheritance of Charlemagne's rights in the Spanish Marsh.

James I's reign ended on a somewhat sour note nevertheless, his sure hand beginning to waver. By now, his atavistic ideas on succession, which he insisted allowed him to apportion his lands, in particular those of his conquests, among various children, caused resentment. This resentment was compounded by the ever-simmering ethnic tensions in the kingdom, which struggled to maintain its integrity. Majorca achieved autonomy, for example, in 1276, but the rest of the continental kingdom continued to be closely involved in Mediterranean affairs. Much of its trade was conducted with Mediterranean powers; its navy was a Mediterranean navy by necessity, because of the existence of Islamic raiders from North Africa. But no one could have predicted in 1276, the year of James the Conqueror's death, that the pull of Mediterranean politics would so utterly dominate Aragonese life in the decades, indeed centuries, to come. To tell this story, we must turn to the complicated and fascinating history of the central and eastern Mediterranean polities.

FROM SICILY TO THE LEVANT

In the time of Emperor Frederick II of Hohenstaufen, northern Italy was divided between factions loyal to Frederick and the supporters of the Church. The Ghibellines, Frederick's partisans, take their label from an Italianate version of the word 'Waiblingen', the name of a Hohenstaufen castle. Guelphs, partisans of the Church, are so-called from the German 'Welf', the lineage and war cry of the Bavarian dukes. This simple dichotomy hardly scratches the surface of the complex political situation in northern Italy. There were any number of freebooters faithful to no one but themselves, and even Guelphs could become Ghibellines and Ghibellines Guelphs in certain circumstances. One of the greatest works of literature of all time, Dante's *Divine Comedy*, written in Italian, may be read in part as a commentary on the political strife of the period. The writer's avowedly prescriptive works, like his Latin *De Monarchia*, are explicitly concerned with the overarching political problems and how to correct them – in Dante's view by the restoration of strong imperial authority.

It should be recalled that life was not everywhere and always lived according to political labels, no matter how fierce the strife was and how compelling the loyalties to particular political factions. Reading the *Divine Comedy* as a political commentary is possible, but perhaps not recommended, for it would turn a rich and provocative poem into a flattened and tedious screed. Similarly, while violence and factionalism played themselves out in the Italian cities and to some extent charac-terized urban life, though not to the point of undermining economic growth, the thirteenth century also saw the expansion of the mendicants (especially Franciscans) into every town, bringing with them their con-cerns for the poor, for right belief, for the conversion and reform of prostitutes and Jews, indeed for nothing less than a call for total religious renewal. Something of the sort seems to have occurred as early as 1233, that is, even before the mendicants had achieved their evangelical hegemony. The so-called 'Great Alleluia' swept the region of the lower Po in that year; it seared the land like pietists' exuberance in eighteenth-century Germany or the Great Protestant Awakenings of nineteenth-century America.

As far as political stability goes, though, southern Italy and Sicily were in better shape than the north. Frederick II, besides spending a great deal of time on the island in particular, maintained a gifted group of administrators to deal with governmental problems. The institutions within which they worked were remarkably stable and efficient.

The principal political challenge for the Church was how to control Frederick, how to induce him to act as the popes thought a Christian emperor should act. But Frederick, the 'Wonder of the World' (*Stupor Mundi*), was not a man to accept control by anyone, even the pope. Recognizing that the Church would never be successful in inducing Frederick by peaceful or diplomatic means to modify his policies in conformity with its political agenda, Pope Innocent IV decided to try to remove Frederick from the political scene. Formally deposed in 1245, Frederick nevertheless defied his opposition, retained enormous power and continued to threaten what many churchmen regarded as the liberty of the Church.

It was the emperor's death in 1250 that seemed to provide the papacy with the opportunity to redistribute power in such a way that no single man could ever command at once the resources of Germany, northern Italy, southern Italy and Sicily. Moreover, the desired corollary, so far as the Church regarded it, was that no Hohenstaufen in particular should possess authority in any of these territories ever again. The alternative, again from the papacy's perspective, would provide for the frightening possibility of the revival of Hohenstaufen claims to all of the territories sometime in the future.

The evident reluctance of Frederick II's offspring to accept dis-inheritance motivated the popes to support various non-Hohenstaufen

claimants to the German throne, which, being technically elective anyway, did not *de jure* threaten the inheritance rights of Frederick's children. Sicily was different. Frederick held it by blood right and
presumably could pass it on by blood right. The popes needed in this
case not a candidate willing to stand for election but a designated warrior
determined to destroy the last vestige of Hohenstaufen claims.

They cast about far and wide for a champion and after many false
starts found an effective one in Charles of Anjou, the brother of the
French king, Louis IX. Charles had his brother's grudging support;
Louis preferred a political settlement but none was forthcoming. Charles
was wealthy. He possessed the income from two great fiefs in France,
Anjou and Maine, as well as the income of the county of Provence,
which he came into through his wife, Beatrice of Provence. And he had
the ambition.

In a series of military engagements, culminating in the battles of
Benevento in 1266 and Tagliacozzo in 1268, Charles routed Hohenstaufen forces. Hohenstaufen claims appeared to expire with the deaths
of the last direct male Hohenstaufen claimants, one in battle (Manfred,
Frederick's illegitimate son) in 1266, the other by judicial execution
(Conradin, the great emperor's grandson) in 1268. In Constance
of Hohenstaufen, however, Manfred's daughter, there remained the
possibility of the resurrection of Hohenstaufen pretensions. This Constance married Peter, the son of James I the Conqueror, of Aragon,
who came to the Aragonese throne on the death of his father in 1276.
What was needed for Charles of Anjou, since 1266 King Charles of
Sicily, was time, enough time for memory of the Hohenstaufen era to
fade and for loyalties to the family in Germany, Italy and Sicily to ebb
away.

For a while, it seemed as though time was on Charles's side. But his
initial successes were compromised by a style of rulership that dismayed
even subjects disposed to be loyal. Charles spent little time in Anjou and
Maine; they were administered like other royal provinces of France,
although he rather than the Crown received the surplus income from
the counties. The centre of his ambitions and concerns was the Mediterranean. Where he suspected resistance to his rule he was brutal. His
treatment of Marseilles, the greatest city in his Provençal domains,
reduced the port and its government to abject dependency in the 1250s
and 1260s. The intense economic exploitation of Sicily and southern
Italy led to widespread dissatisfaction, and the tensions between the

Angevin military forces that now dominated Sicily and the local inhabitants were rarely far from exploding point. Added to this was the papacy's apparent distress over some of Charles's actions, particularly his penchant for picking up titles, like senator of Rome, overlord of Albania, suzerain of Tunisia and King of Jerusalem.

Some of the titles had more of show than substance in them. Charles purchased the title King of Jerusalem from one of the many claimants to the throne of that truncated kingdom, and by doing so he became king in (contested) name only. His senatorship was a particular sticking point in his relations with the papacy, and he wisely abandoned it. The overlordship of Albania did give him some leverage in the Adriatic, but it was inevitable that the great maritime power, Venice, would act if it thought its interests were being threatened.

Charles's suzerainty over Tunisia came about as a result of his brother's last crusade (1270). That crusade had been planned under the misapprehension that the Bey of Tunisia would convert if threatened by a major crusading army. The submission of Tunisia would then provide a secure north African staging point for continued Christian expeditions into Muslim lands. In fact, the Bey had not converted and Charles, who arrived at the siege of Tunis just after his brother died from disease, persuaded the army commanders, including his nephew, the new king of France, to abandon the siege and return to France with the pestilence-stricken army. The Bey was willing to make formal obeisance to Charles to expedite the raising of the siege. In the short run this gave Charles and Mediterranean Christians some commercial advantages and religious privileges in Tunisia.

Shallow, temporary and problematic as some of Charles's claims and titles were, his determined rulership in Provence, southern Italy and Sicily, as well as his extraordinary wealth, raised the spectre that he might some day make the claims and titles meaningful. He thought he had found the way to do so by redeeming French arms in Greece. Following the crusaders' conquest of Constantinople in 1204, Franks, specifically a cadet branch of the French royal family, ruled the Byzantine Empire. Their rule was never very stable, however, because hostile Greek forces continued to operate in many of the provinces, and under Michael Paleologus would retake what was left of the much weakened empire in 1261.

By the time Charles became active in the central Mediterranean the Greeks had had what was left of their empire back for almost a decade, but they feared a counter-attack from the West, and this at a time when Muslim forces in Anatolia were also attacking the outposts of the resource-depleted Byzantines. One way to keep the Latins at bay was to reassure the papacy that despite the Greek military reconquest from the Catholic French, Michael Paleologus's intention was to preserve or re-initiate the union of the Churches along the lines of that achieved in the years 1204–61.

Many Greek prelates were vehemently opposed to their emperor's policies, and he felt compelled on occasion to silence them. Islam seemed on the verge of wiping out the Crusader States. If and when that was achieved, the full force of Islamic retaliation would fall on a truncated Byzantium. The abatement of military hostility from western – Roman Catholic – Christendom was absolutely essential for survival. Anything more than this from the Latins could hardly be expected, but it was better than nothing, and the alternative, a war on two fronts, was too awful to contemplate. Was union with the papal church too high a price to pay for the survival of the empire? Those Greeks who continued publicly and stridently to say 'yes' were made to suffer for it.

To the popes, however, Michael Paleologus seemed worth listening to, and in the circumstances Charles of Anjou could scarcely have got the kind of full backing he wanted for an invasion of Greece to re-establish the Latin empire. His dream seemed all the more hopeless in 1274, when Greek prelates sent by Emperor Michael Paleologus to the Second Council of Lyons were ordered to subscribe to the plan that was to be presented there for the union of the Churches. Events in the years after 1274 kept Charles's hopes alive, though. Greek ecclesiastical and popular resistance to union increased in intensity. The emperor resorted to draconian measures, like cutting out the tongues of dissidents who were undermining the process of reunion. Yet the papacy grew restless and suspicious of what it regarded as the Greek emperor's feeble efforts to enforce the union.

With papal support Charles, therefore, began to make secret preparations to invade the Byzantine empire. He would justify himself morally by the need to avenge the expulsion of the French from Constantinople in 1261; he would justify himself legally by the Paleologoi's failure to carry out the agreed-upon protocols of Lyons II. But his preparations were less secret than he wished. A network of spies inhabited Mediterranean political, military and naval circles. Even while Michael Paleologus was pleading his sincerity through emissaries to the

Holy See, he was trying to destabilize Sicily through spies and *agents provocateurs*.

Coincidentally, Charles's exploitative rule in Sicily, and the behaviour of the Angevin forces that were being built up there for the invasion of Greece, were bringing native resentment to the flashpoint. Other interests operating commercially in the Mediterranean, like Aragonese merchants, were also finding Angevin pretensions and interference in their activities distressing. Moreover, in Aragon it became clear, largely through ambassadorial accounts and spies' reports, that conditions might soon be ripe for raising the matter of Queen Constance's claim to Sicily. The French king, fully supporting the family interests of his uncle Charles of Anjou, became suspicious of Aragonese actions, including what seemed to be military preparations. Most historians credit the claim that the Aragonese would certainly have intervened in Sicily sooner or later.

It was sooner, for a native uprising began in Palermo on Easter Monday, 30 March 1282, known as the Sicilian Vespers. The trigger was an Angevin soldier's insult to a Sicilian woman. Bells rang out the rebellion. Angevin troops were killed in numbers, and Charles's forces had to deal with the insurgents, while at the same time trying, more or less successfully, to preserve rule in the other cities of Sicily and confine the rebellion to the island. The papacy saw its hopes of a re-establishment of Latin hegemony in Greece and the vigorous reunion of the churches temporarily suspended. Michael Paleologus died in 1282, without knowing the outcome of these unexpected events.

At this moment, Aragon intervened, ostensibly in the name of the Sicilian people and the Aragonese claim to the Hohenstaufen inheritance. Now, Charles had to fight ill-organized but determined rebels as well as the considerable land and naval forces of the Crown of Aragon. The pope denounced Aragon; the French king fulminated and brought pressure on the pontiff to excommunicate and depose the Aragonese king, in favour of the French king's younger son. Preparations began in northern France to raise an army to invade Aragon in a war that would come to have the status of a crusade against the Christian Iberian kingdom.

Efforts were made to prevent the bloodshed. A plan to have the king of Aragon, Peter III, and Charles of Anjou meet in single combat fell through in a farcical (deliberate?) mix-up of dates. In France the failure to find a way to prevent war was especially exasperating for the royal heir. He, the future Philip IV the Fair, opposed the war. In the days of St Louis his father had married an Aragonese princess, to symbolize the

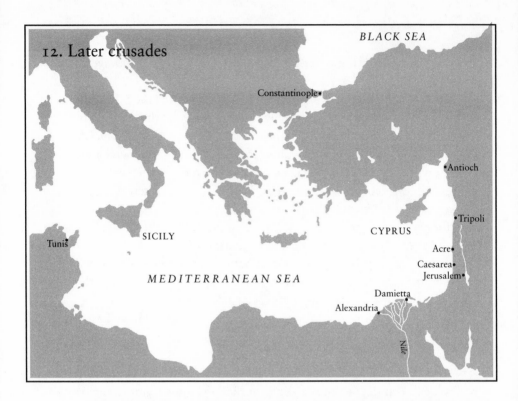

end of tensions between France and Aragon that had been brought about by Louis and James the Conqueror. Philip worshipped the memory of his Aragonese mother and despised his stepmother, a Brabantine, and her entourage, all of whom supported the war. The boy also found solace in the fact that his grandmother, St Louis's widow, despised Charles of Anjou and bemoaned the war against Aragon.

These matters are important because both at sea and overland the French invasion forces were routed in 1285. The French king died on the retreat from the Pyrenees, and Philip IV came to the throne nurturing an abiding dislike for the papacy's propensity to shape French foreign policy, an attitude that would have long-term implications for papal–French relations in the later thirteenth century and beyond. The crusade against Aragon was succeeded by the *status quo ante* on the continent, with drawn-out negotiations meant to save the face of the various contending parties (Philip the Fair's younger brother eventually gave up his claim to Aragon). To a degree, the negotiations were eased by the deaths of so many interested parties in 1285: besides the French king, who perished in the military campaign, others who died that year included King Peter III of Aragon, Pope Martin IV, who had authorized the campaign, and Charles of Anjou himself.

THE COLLAPSE OF THE CRUSADER STATES

The crusades had no dynamic of their own and were inextricably bound up with political developments in Europe. The decision to mount a crusade depended on the enthusiasm that could be turned from investing resources at home into investing them in war and settlement abroad. It must be said that it was far easier to maintain enthusiasm for large and small campaigns alike than it was to bring about settlement. Men might argue whether *passagia generalia*, huge general crusades, were superior to smaller expeditions, *passagia particularia*, or they might argue about whether military command should be unified or divided and about how much autonomy the military orders should have. But in the end, and in scores of expeditions, Catholics sent extraordinary numbers of men and quantities of materiel to the Levant. The crusades may have stimulated the economy of parts of southern Europe, Italy in particular, where a great deal of money was expended, but they were a colossal drain on the wealth of the north. This fact must have been widely recognized, but northerners continued to join the crusading expeditions nevertheless.

Why did thousands of these men not stay in the Holy Land, encourage their womenfolk to settle there, build great cities, new cathedrals, universities, and systematically attempt the conversion of the non-Catholic population they controlled? Although it is certainly true, it is an insufficient explanation to say that the Crusader States had no alternative than to concentrate on war and expend all their resources on defence. If more settlers had come, they would have had the human resources both to resist Muslim counter-attacks and to continue their expansion. The Muslim enemy was very often riven by internal political divisions. The crusaders exploited these, and to some extent that helped preserve the states, but it was not followed up by the kind of sophisticated administration that was commonplace in the thirteenth-century western kingdoms. And the sheer demographic imbalance was never overcome. Yet, if 300,000 Germans could settle in Slavic lands during the *Drang nach Osten*, how was it that nothing close to that number came to settle in the land where, according to their own theology, Jesus the saviour of humankind rose from the dead?

The major expeditions of the thirteenth century, at least those that have not already been discussed (like the Fourth Crusade that culminated in the conquest of Constantinople), can be summarized briefly. Innocent

III had used the Fourth Lateran Council as a forum to seek help in preparations and to drum up additional support for a new expedition. Known as the Fifth Crusade, it is conventionally dated 1217 to 1221. Led by the Hungarian king and the Austrian duke, it deployed its forces against Egypt. In 1219 these forces captured Damietta at the mouth of the Nile after a year-long siege. Despite the victory, the army had been weakened by the episode, and a decision was made to await reinforcements before proceeding inland. Superficially it may have been a wise decision – if the reinforcements had been of sufficient numbers – but the period of waiting gave the enemy time to prepare inland defences up the Nile. In the end these could not be overcome once the army was on the move, even with the help of the newly arrived reinforcements of 1220 and 1221. The commanders ran the risk of losing their entire armies in a retreat that might have turned into a rout. They negotiated a surrender for themselves that preserved the army at the price of returning Damietta to Muslim control.

Some historians continue to number the crusades after 1221, but the system is inconsistent; it is easier to identify them by their leaders. In the period 1228 to 1240 several expeditions went to the East, led by, among others, Emperor Frederick II, Count Thibaut of Champagne and Earl Richard of Cornwall. Frederick's expedition, as we have seen in chapter 16, brought Jerusalem back into crusader hands in 1228 but by agreement. This agreement was not to the liking of crusader barons for two reasons: it did not restrict Muslims from access to their holy places, and it prevented the kinds of refortification that were necessary to maintain military control.

Thibaut and Richard in 1239 and 1240, leading two reasonably big forces, managed to bring some military stability to the Holy Land, largely by exploiting the divisions among Muslim potentates, but neither accomplished the refortification of Jerusalem or left substantial forces permanently in the East to help the situation. The situation was in fact already worsening even as Thibaut's and Richard's armies returned to Europe. In 1244 a new disaster occurred, when Muslim Turks reconquered the city and began to sweep through the Holy Land more effectively than any Muslim force since the days of Saladin.

It was these events that brought Louis IX to the Levant. In 1249, one of the largest crusading armies in history invaded Egypt and captured Damietta, but the scenario in the spring of the next year, when the crusaders moved inland, was depressingly similar to that in the Fifth

Crusade, only this time the crusader army was hacked to pieces and large numbers of men, including the king, were taken captive. To effect their release a huge ransom had to be paid and Damietta returned to Muslim control. Unlike his predecessors, though, Louis did not return immediately to Europe when the hot phase of the expedition was over. He sailed for the Holy Land upon his release and began to channel new monies that arrived from Europe into the refortification of garrison sites, like Caeserea, still in the crusaders' possession. He also financed a contingent of permanent troops after his departure in 1254. It is clear from his actions that westerners recognized the demographic problem bedevilling the Crusader States.

The last of the great crusades was the invasion of Tunisia, described above in the discussion of Charles of Anjou's Mediterranean policies. Its modest success in 1270 in getting Tunisia to accept the commercial hegemony of Charles of Anjou's subjects and, in the event, to remain more or less neutral in the continuing skirmishes in the Mediterranean between Muslims and Christians was more than offset by its lack of accomplishments in the Holy Land. The English prince and future king, Edward I, arrived in Tunisia after Louis IX's death and Charles of Anjou's successful taking charge of the situation. He decided to sail to the East, but his modest forces were unable to do very much, in the absence of the French army which was decimated by pestilence and on its way back home. All his life he wanted to return with a great army to redeem the Holy Land, but events in England always prevented him.

The inevitable – although this is a word that should probably be banned from historical studies – came about in 1291 when the Mamelukes, the Egyptian Muslims, conquered the last crusader outpost, the great port of Acre. Every Teutonic Knight, to the man, died fighting to defend the city. The victorious Muslims took vengeance on all whom they suspected of being Frankish sympathizers, including the Jews of the city. The victors then fortified Acre impressively, using sea sand to fill up the truncated buildings and building on top of the old town. They turned Acre into a citadel. Only some of the Mediterranean islands, like Cyprus, held out. Everywhere else Islam had prevailed. For the Byzantine Empire – or what little was left of it – the handwriting was now on the wall. The remarkable thing is that it held out so long.

PART IV

CHRISTENDOM IN THE EARLY FOURTEENTH CENTURY

19

Famine and Plague

Europe was already beginning to face serious economic problems in the late thirteenth century. Population growth was tapering off, but it had already outpaced proportionate increases in agricultural production. The bulk of the population, therefore, was probably worse off economically in the year 1300 than it was in 1250 or 1200. At the same time, demands on ordinary people, especially peasants in the West, continued to mount as inflation undermined the wealth of the upper classes. The latter benefited from the price inflation in as much as they sold the surplus of their estates at higher prices, but they suffered from the fact that a large part of their income came from rents and obligations that had been fixed in the distant past. To make up for the shortfalls from declining real revenues in fixed rents, they exploited the market for their produce and goods and adopted a much stricter view of their fiscal rights, forcing peasants into positions of dependence and financial obligation that the peasants thought had lapsed, or believed never existed, or which they had managed to wriggle out of over the years.

To compensate for these new demands – when they did not simply refuse to pay them – peasants were forced into debt. With so little in disposable funds, they cut corners on their farms and took the worst kinds of chances against good sense, trying, for example, to bring land under cultivation that was marginal at best. They resorted to poaching and other forms of theft. But still the burden of their debt mounted, without any noticeable reduction in pressure on them from the upper classes to fulfil their fiscal obligations. The countryside, and again one is speaking of the West, became a powder keg. The alternatives were either submission to a new enserfment, perhaps on the degrading mode of eastern Europe, or peasant rebellion.

Urban life was more varied, but many regions, especially Flanders, were entering upon a long period of economic recession. In part, this was because of changing tastes and different trade routes. The Flemish cloth industry depended not only on wool from Flanders and northern France but on fleeces from England. Periodically in the course of the fourteenth century, because of blockades occasioned by war between France and England, English wool was unavailable. This fact, a spur to the development of a native cloth industry in England, had absolutely devastating consequences for the Flemish economy. Even the cloth they did produce was sometimes left for substantial periods unshipped because of war.

Still, fortunes were being made by the greatest families in these urban centres. For war was sometimes as much a boon as it was an evil for the urban economies. One town's destruction, interruption in its commerce, or decline in its production was another's boom times. Leagues of towns sometimes formed that offered regional protection for urban (and hinterland) economic interests. The general situation, however complex, received a massive and altogether detrimental shake-up in the second decade of the fourteenth century.

FAMINE

In the spring of the year 1315 a famine began to affect northern Europe that was more devastating than anything that had occurred over the preceding millennium. The catastrophe began with spring rains that seemed never to stop, and continued all through the summer and well into the autumn. This was followed, so far as one can tell, by one of the worst winters in the history of the Middle Ages (the evidence for the weather patterns comes from contemporary chronicles and from tree-ring studies). The year 1316 was even worse: 150 days of uninterrupted rain. Conditions continued to be deleterious until the end of 1322, with continuously wet summers succeeded by vicious persistent winters only to be followed alternately by other abnormally wet summers or, equally bad, abnormally dry ones.

The immediate consequence was a crisis in the production of crops and, soon after, of draught and food animals. This was compounded by a series of wars throughout the British Isles, northern Germany, Scandinavia, northern France and Flanders – all accompanied by piracy on the seas – that initiated a prolonged distribution crisis. The effect on the production of all major cereals – wheat, barley, oats and rye – as well as on grapes and other crops was nothing short of catastrophic. Selective statistical material indicates a decline in grain production in parts of northern Europe of about one-third during the years of the disastrous weather cycle. Considering that the population of northern Europe was at its medieval peak on the eve of the ecological catastrophe caused by the weather from 1315 to 1322, such a decline in crop yields put the roughly thirty million inhabitants of northern Europe at considerable risk of malnutrition.

The estimated decline of crop yields by one-third is an aggregate figure; the effects on various grains differed. Some could stand soggy soil better than parched soil; for others the reverse was the case. Furthermore, effects varied over regions as well. Nevertheless, nearly everywhere one looks, the combination of weather extremes and the consequences for human labour (it is very hard to plough both sodden fields and those as dry as brick) reduced yields of grains by anything from 12 per cent up to 100 per cent. There were farms where peasants sowed one hundred bushels of seed corn at the beginning of the growing season and harvested less than that at the end.

The ceaseless wet weather of the early years of the Great Famine corrupted the grape harvest to a similar degree. Grapes rotted on the vine or became diseased from the downy mildews associated with excessive dampness. Again, the statistical evidence points to grape production being roughly 80 per cent below normal yields during the famine years. And contemporaries' comments on the small quantities and awful quality of the wine produced from these diseased and stunted grapes are recorded in numerous texts.

The evidence for other kinds of fruit and crop production and what can be extrapolated from the effects of this kind of weather on modern husbandry suggests similar declines in yields. In provinces like Normandy and Devonshire, where the ordinary peasant beverage was very nutritious cider, a pathetic apple harvest, let alone the use of rotting apples in cider-making, must have had disastrous consequences for human health. One can add to this litany of catastrophes the effects of the weather on industrial crops, those that provided products that farmers and estates could sell to manufacturers – flax, for example, from which linen cloth was produced, and woad, which provided the raw material for a blue dye used in the cloth-making industry.

The effects on animal populations were equally severe. It is sometimes said that peasants ate little meat or animal products. This would be true for seventeenth- and eighteenth-century peasants, many of whom were forced into monoculture, but it was not the case in the early fourteenth century. Peasants kept sheep and cows, from which they got milk and made cheese. Cow hides made them money when the cows were no longer needed or were no longer giving milk. Fleeces from the sheep furnished wool, another cash crop. Many peasant families owned oxen. Others had shares in an ox-team, a fact sometimes denied by current scholars but amply documented on the continent. The animals pulled the peasants' wagons and their ploughs, and they were eaten when they got too old to work.

Horses were in widespread use, too. Sometimes they ploughed, sometimes they were used to transport equipment and crops. Sometimes they were ridden, although they were almost never eaten in normal times. There was an elaborate calculation whereby peasants and estate managers decided on the proportion of draught animals to keep, but no one by preference depended on just one sort of draught beast, for fear of disease. Every village, every estate in northern Europe usually had a generous mix of cattle and horses.

Peasants ate large amounts of fish. Fish farms – artificial ponds stocked with carp – were ubiquitous in northern Europe, and although these provided aristocratic fare, some peasants benefited as well. Fishing in mill ponds was also productive, with nearly 10,000 watermills in England, 40,000 in France and a comparable number in Germany. Vast numbers of eels were harvested annually at the mouths of rivers. Finally, villagers harvested the rich schools of fish in the coastal fisheries, especially pilchards, sardine-like fish, and herring.

Peasants and estate managers also kept rabbits in hutches (the peasant way) or in park-like warrens – protected or enclosed areas of waste land on estates. Beehives provided honey and wax. Men and women kept doves and pigeons in dovecotes in their attics or in free-standing buildings on big estates; the really large dovecotes on a great man's estate could house thousands of doves. But the ubiquitous animal was the pig. They were everywhere and they provided nearly everything a Christian man would need: leather, the tallow for soap and cheap candles, grease for cooking and manufacturing, bristles for brushes and, of course, food – ham, bacon, ribs, roasts, maw, sausage.

The bad weather was devastating to the animals and, where capture was necessary, it was a crippling hindrance to the capture of animals.

Freshwater and estuary species of fish died in numbers in the later drought-ridden years of the famine, reducing catches considerably in, for example, East Anglia in England, where fishing in the marshes was an important aspect of life. The fierce weather also often made coastal fishing dangerous and unproductive. Infestation of domestic beehives by vermin was accentuated by the damp weather, even if, like wild hives, the man-made hives themselves were sheltered from the elements by bee-keepers who recognized the natural aversion of bees to dampness. Moreover, the severe winters, to judge from modern experience of bee-keeping, would also have seriously decreased the size of hives and their wax- and honey-making capacity, and the decrease in hive size would itself have negative consequences for the pollinating of fruit crops in the spring. But all these problems with fish, bees, and many other small animals and small animal products were less important perhaps than the effects on herds and flocks.

That is why it was so important for peasants and farmers to keep a variety of animals. Neither horses nor pigs seem to have suffered widespread disease during most of the famine, at least in the early years, while sheep and cattle did. The supply of horses therefore helped ease the effects of the mortality of oxen as beasts of burden. The prevalence and varied utility of the pig helped mitigate the effects of disease on the sheep flocks and cattle herds.

Nonetheless the effects were extraordinary, according to statistical evidence. Flocks and herds were often reduced in size by as much as, or more than, 90 per cent, from the devastating impact of the disease known as Rinderpest and, particularly in sheep, the infestation of the liver by the fluke worm in excessively damp weather. Later, anthrax, judging by surviving descriptions, with its infectious ulcers of the skin, devastated the herds and flocks still further. The historical sources often refer to the cluster of these pestilences by a general term, 'murrain', which means nothing more or less than all-pervasive death. For the animals, far more than for the human victims, who suffered a death rate as high as 10 per cent in heavily populated, particularly urban, areas, the Great Famine was the Great Murrain, the Great Dying.

How did townsfolk and villagers respond to this devastation? In practical terms, there was the predictable tendency to make substitutions – an increase in pork in the diet as the decline in grain, lamb and beef production grew ever more severe; the replacement of oxen by horses in plough teams and cartage. The consequence of the increase of pork in the diet was a drastic decline in the size of the pig herds. In one example, 95 per cent of a herd was slaughtered to make up the deficit in available food from the failure of food crops and the deaths from disease of sheep and cattle. As a result of the shift to more horse power, horses were overworked, and some diseases later in the famine period seem to have affected them as well, increasing prices dramatically for healthy, even if not spectacularly well-muscled animals – old nags that would have sold at bargain prices before 1315.

Surviving healthy animals of whatever species on estates, and wild animals that had escaped disease, became the targets of rustlers and poachers. Venison tended to be more aristocratic fare, but there were scores of forest villages in northern Europe where, either by custom or by special privilege, peasants had access to deer for food and ate a great deal of it. Custom and privilege, however, were intended as much to restrain as reward, for if they permitted peasant hunting, they also limited it. Conditions in 1315–22 encouraged privileged villagers to try to exceed the limits, and in many other villages, where peasants had no rights to hunt the great beasts, the urgent desire for food encouraged poaching. Poaching, in turn, invited reprisals and the escalation of social tensions in village society between lords and their agents – often villagers themselves – on the one hand, and hungry families on the other.

The wealthy escaped the direct effects of hunger, even if their income from businesses and estates sometimes plummeted. In towns they could pay the enormously high prices for foodstuffs; in the countryside they could hold back for their personal consumption as much as they wanted from what little their estates might be producing. The poor, reduced to consuming 'strange diets', did not fare so well; they starved in large numbers, thus lessening their resistance to disease. Mortality was most prevalent amongst the poor, although in towns disease sometimes leaped the barrier of wealth. Well-meaning measures, like price controls, were either ineffective or encouraged those with produce to hoard their goods until price controls were lifted or ceased being strictly enforced. Some major towns like London, Paris and the big cloth centres in Flanders did manage to import grain from southern Europe and distribute it under royal or municipal licence, which helped but did not entirely alleviate the condition of the urban poor. Accusations of cannibalism bespeak the weakening of bonds of community in towns and in some rural areas, too.

All the relevant sources concur that God had caused the famine to punish sinful men and women for their transgressions. It followed that there had to be devotional and penitential responses to the failure of crops, the human mortality, and the terrible diseases that the animals were suffering. Prayers and processions for the return of good weather and the healing of Christendom abounded. There also arose social movements of a less savoury nature that targeted certain groups, like Jews and lepers, as polluted peoples, the toleration of whom provoked God to anger (see chapter 20). Preachers would eventually conclude that the penitential acts had worked, for God did relent in His punishment – after seven horrifying years had passed.

PLAGUE

A little more than a generation later, God's wrath seemed to manifest itself again in a disaster infinitely worse than the Great Famine and one whose impact was felt not merely in the north but nearly everywhere in Christendom and in the Islamic world as well: the Black Death. Despite recurrent doubts among some historians about the precise identification of the disease that struck Europe, the consensus is that it was the plague.

Yersenia pestis, the plague bacterium, is a pathogen carried by fleas. The plague was and is endemic in Asia, but in the Middle Ages it spread twice to the western areas of the Eurasian landmass and North Africa via the fleas on shipboard rats. The first of these pandemics occurred in the sixth century while Justinian ruled the Roman Empire, the second began in 1347.

Yersenia pestis lives in fleas, whose preferred host is the rat, although as the host dies from disease, the flea will seek out another warm-blooded host, like a human being or a cat (or now in America, the prairie dog), feed off and infect it. The disease of plague manifests itself in three forms: bubonic, pneumonic and septicaemic. In the bubonic form, swelling occurs in the lymph glands, most especially in the armpits and crotch, but elsewhere as well. The painful and pus-filled swellings, known as buboes, give their name to this variety of the disease, the bubonic plague. If the buboes suppurate, the stench of the pus is awful. The death rate is high, although it seems reasonably certain, judging from modern pre-antibiotic experience, that a large number of the infected did recover.

Far more likely to lead to death are the pneumonic and septicaemic varieties. As the word pneumonic implies, the disease in this form has pneumonia-like qualities; the lungs (*pneuma*) fill with fluid, and it is possible to pass the disease to a healthy person through these fluids, expectorated or sneezed. The septicaemic variety of the plague is characterized by dark discolorations of the skin coming from the infection of the blood by toxins produced by the pathogen (septicaemia means blood poisoning). These discolorations, together with the dark appearance of some of the buboes in the bubonic form of the plague, contributed to the naming of the disease as the Black Death.

Until the wonder drugs of the twentieth century, there was little that could be done for the victims of this disease. It was soon learned that dispersal of a crowded urban population into the countryside reduced the likelihood of infection, and the rich and middle classes eventually availed themselves of this opportunity during the frequent recurrences of the plague after its initial sweep through Europe from 1347 to 1351. Herbal remedies were tried, to no avail. Relief was offered by lancing the buboes or by blood-letting by hand or by applying leeches. But because the aetiology of the disease was unknown, no very effective measures were taken against the rats and other animals that the fleas infested.

A ship from the Black Sea seems to have brought the plague in 1347 to Italy. From Italy it passed along trade routes into France and by 1348 into England. Meanwhile, it reached Spain either from Italy and France or from North Africa or, perhaps, from both sides more or less simultaneously. In the north of Europe, it entered the Baltic region and the interior parts of Scandinavia and the continent. By 1351 it was in Russia. Even Greenland suffered the scourge because of its commercial contact with Norway.

Remarkably and inexplicably a few regions – parts of Flanders, parts of Poland – escaped the initial wave, but they were not spared when the plague recurred in the 1360s and afterwards. In England between 1348 and 1485 there were thirty-one major outbreaks, and there would be localized outbreaks until well into the seventeenth century. Venice accounted for twenty-one visitations of the disease down to 1630; Florence, twenty by the year 1500; and Paris, twenty-two down to 1596. Indeed, there was never a year from 1347 until 1782 when Europe was not visited in some region by a plague epidemic, although the geographical extent of the affected regions steadily declined, either because the bacterium itself evolved into a less virulent pathogen or because the European population developed greater immunity.

If there were eighty million inhabitants of Europe in 1346, on the eve of the Black Death, it is plausibly estimated that twenty-five million died in the pandemic of 1347–51. And yet, although this book considers the impact only of this initial wave, the recurrent visitations of the plague, and the effects of war and of other diseases, which seem to have increased in infectiousness and virulence, continued to prevent the population from recovering to its pre-plague levels. If the number 100 is used as the pre-plague index of population size in Normandy, then the index stood, at its lowest, not in the 1350s, when it was about 75, but in the 1420s, by which time it had fallen almost to 25. Recovery in Normandy to its pre-plague level of population did not occur before the year 1600. England and Norway, which probably reached their low points in population around 1450, did not recover to pre-plague levels until about the year 1600 in England and 1750 in Norway.

Curiously, historians have been hesitant in ascribing great significance to the plague cycle in European history. Fearing to give credence to a simplistic explanation of historical change, they have preferred to argue that its effects on social and cultural life were somewhat limited. This hesitancy, given the present state of research, seems unnecessary. The plague cycle was the death knell of medieval European civilization. The communities on the other side of the divide, whether called Renaissance or early modern or designated by some more parochial term like Tudor, were radically different from those flourishing before the Black Death.

The demographic crisis was horrendous for the Church. In the first place, the communities in which monks, canons, nuns and cathedral and collegiate chapters lived were particularly vulnerable to the spread of disease. The fleas on the cooling body of one dead monk who succumbed to the pestilence found ready hosts in the members of the community who gathered to wash his body, pray, sing psalms, and otherwise prepare the dead for burial. As evidence accumulates, it becomes ever clearer that these communities suffered higher rates of mortality than the population at large. No generalizations are possible as yet, but a number of religious communities lost as many as 60 per cent of their members, or more.

The first response to losses on such a scale was aggressive recruitment to fill the offices and do the duties the religious and clergy needed to perform – say Mass and prayers for the dead, administer the altars, distribute charity, minister, where appropriate, to the wider lay society, and collect fees. There was a big incentive to laymen to join the clergy.

Pluralism – holding more than one remunerative church office – became ever more common. There were fortunes to be made, presuming always that the labour resources needed to produce income from the property endowments for the offices was available. Prelates – bishops, deans, abbots and their advisers – were of necessity obliged to turn to younger clergy, perhaps promoting them more quickly than usual, and to laymen, some of whom had more interest in achieving wealth than in the pious work of the religious life. A few scholars have also seen a decline in the quality of Latin knowledge and even of handwriting among the clergy after 1350, both because thousands of Latin teachers died in the plague, putting greater burdens of instruction on those who survived to teach the new recruits, and because the length of time devoted to study of the language and mastering the beautiful calligraphy may have declined. Vernacularization, in turn, was given a fillip by the crisis.

Resistance to recruitment in the Church was another factor in the demographic crisis. Inheritance in noble families had always posed a demographic conundrum of sorts, because of the relatively high rate of mortality of adolescent boys and young men in violent games and wars. Despite the masculine rhetoric of heirship, women heirs to fiefs were common in the High Middle Ages. The Black Death and its aftermath put additional pressures on noble families, killing incumbents before they could produce heirs, killing off all or nearly all male and female heirs in many families. In the circumstances, families were torn between the blandishments of ecclesiastical careers, which promised considerable remuneration in a pluralist age, and succession to lay fiefs.

While clergy and nobles scrambled to address their particular problems, they did so in the expectation, at least in the 1350s, that the demographic crisis was temporary. Lords vied with one another to make sure their estates remained productive. This meant trying to keep the productive labour force in place on estates or, where it had been devastated by the plague, to induce workers to replace the lost labourers or take up farms which had lost their tenants owing to plague. The problem was that new workers and tenants realized their bargaining position and demanded higher wages than was customary or requested new and lighter conditions of tenure. Those lords who resisted their demands found their potential workforce drifting to the estates of lords who were less hidebound.

Labour and geographic mobility threatened in the West to bring down the whole servile regime. Resistance was fierce. Seigneurs at times seemed to recognize that it was in their class interest to enforce the servile regime and to cap wages. Legislation in harmony with this recognition becomes common from 1350 onwards, but it was hard to maintain class solidarity in the face of so many individual lords' difficult straits. It made sense to try to keep men and women labourers tied to one's land if one had labourers to keep. The demographic crisis on some estates was so severe, however, that poaching workers from other estates seemed a reasonable strategy, and the surest method of success was to offer higher wages and better tenancies. It was a vicious circle from the seigneurs' point of view.

It is often said that the population relief provided by the Black Death elevated the condition of the peasantry. Marginal lands were withdrawn from cultivation, because the labour was not available to cultivate them. Those who survived the demographic catastrophe accumulated multiple holdings, and a kind of upper class of free peasants emerged in villages. The gap between rich and poor widened, of course, because distribution of these newly available resources was not egalitarian. The already well-off peasant, if he or she survived, managed to accumulate a great deal more tenancies than the very poor survivor. The widening gap probably exacerbated village tensions, even though nearly all peasants who survived were materially better off, albeit to remarkably different degrees, in the immediate aftermath of the plague of the 1350s, than they had been in the early fourteenth century. With fewer mouths to feed and more disposable surplus because urban demand declined, average nutrition improved. And there was the reasonable expectation that the demographic collapse would be reversed.

This optimism was shattered in the 1360s by two major recurrences of the epidemic and a further fall-off in the population. Perhaps more than in 1347–51 it was the 1360s that undermined the emotional world of the High Middle Ages. The years 1347–51 were horrendous in their own right, of course. Historians' identification of bright spots in the economy in the 1350s is not intended to counter the emotional impact of a loss of one-third of Europe's population in so brief a time. But the wide and bewilderingly cruel array of social pathologies of the later fourteenth and the fifteenth centuries could not have been produced in an environment that had only seen the events of 1347–51.

One can imagine a young man in an English village in 1348, suffering the loss of his new wife, their only child, a newborn son, and many of the friends and kin he had known all his life and had come to rely on. By 1355 our young man has remarried, has two children, is more prosperous than he had been at the time of his first marriage. The terrors of the awful year, 1348, have been dampened by the passage of time. Then in 1362 the plague visits his village again. More children die, other friends, other kin follow. Despite all his efforts to rebuild his life, he faces catastrophe once more when the plague hits his village in 1369.

Men and women came to believe, as they had in the long years of the Great Famine, that God was repeatedly visiting them with plague to punish them for their sins. The culmination of human existence came to be imagined and represented in art and dramatic performances as a fearful dance of the plague-dead led by the devil or scythe-carrying skeletons to eternal hell. Refusal to accept the inevitability of this representation manifested itself in the great movement, indeed periodic movements, of flagellants, dancing pilgrims of a sort, who joined in processions in the plague years, sometimes processing barefoot and barely clad for thirty-three days at a time – one day for every year of Jesus's life on earth. They would beat themselves bloody with whips and chains to atone for the sins of mankind in the desire both to bring the pestilence to an end and to inaugurate a moral renewal of the whole Christian world. They aimed at nothing less than the salvation of the world.

As in all times of crisis in the Middle Ages, there were scapegoats too, men and women living in the midst of good Christians, but whose presence polluted the holy community. The pattern was by now an old one. Lepers and Jews had already been targeted in the Great Famine, and Jews had been favoured targets in social crises and periods of religious enthusiasm since at least the First Crusade. Both groups suffered horrendous frenetic violence in the plague years of the mid-fourteenth century.

A new element was gradually added to the mix of prejudice – witches. People regarded as good and bad witches had long been acknowledged to be living in Christian society. There had been plenty of instances when one or another of these, feared or loathed, had been mistreated. But it was the emotional environment of the later fourteenth and fifteenth century that initiated the first elements of a genuine witch-craze, one that would continue for decades upon decades, repeatedly stoked by the religious dissensions among Christians that ultimately would rend the Catholic world.

No historian would argue that violence towards lepers, anti-Jewish massacres and the witch-craze were uniquely the result of the Black

Death and the plague cycle it initiated. Indeed, many would deny that there is any close connection between the witch-craze in particular and the troubling experiences of pestilence and epidemic death. More sober-minded historians have played down the impact of the plague in reaction against the tendency of historians a century ago to see any new development as a direct result of the epidemics. But a simple reactive scholarship of this sort is no longer adequate. The whole matter demands further and deeper investigation. One thing is certain. Europe – Christendom – was never the same after *Yersenia pestis*, or some other equally destructive pathogen, began to do its lethal work in the mid-fourteenth century.

20

Political and Social Violence

A recurring question among many students of the Middle Ages is why the catastrophic natural disasters of the fourteenth century failed to bring anointed rulers, whose duty it was to protect the Christian people, to their senses and end the debilitating wars and selfishly competitive economic practices like embargoes and licensed piracy. The likely answer is simpler than might at first be supposed. In the moral universe of the High Middle Ages, rulers, like everyone else, acknowledged God's role in famine and plague and, also like everyone else, they confessed that the sins of the people were the root cause of God's infliction of punishment. Only virtuous acts would help appease God. But all these rulers believed or said that they believed that the wars they were waging (righteous from their point of view) and the economic policies that played such an important role in military strategy were virtuous acts in themselves. The enemy was always constructed as a swarm of evil-doers. Defeating them was construed as an act that would help appease God and return health and prosperity to the Christian people. A ruler's failure to do his duty in waging a just war would be a damning personal sin and would, therefore, encourage the continuation of divine punishment.

What was true for rulers was true further down the social hierarchy. The violence that began to disrupt the cities and countryside of Europe is characterized by elite sources like royal and monastic chronicles as chaotic, savage and malignant. The perpetrators of that violence, however, saw themselves, whether in carrying out bread riots or revolution, as doing God's bidding, restoring justice to the world. They often claimed to be doing so in the name of their distant but beloved terrestrial king, who, they surmised, would bless their violence as altogether righteous. That is to say, he would bless it, if he only knew the anguish of his people, anguish that malevolent advisers, Achitophels in the language of medieval censure, were hiding from him. The comparison, a standard

slur employed by many who had grievances against constituted authorities, was particularly ugly, for Achitophel was the principal adviser of
Absalom, King David's son, in the Bible and was the man, formerly an
adviser of the king himself, who counselled Absalom to rebel against his
father and to publicly rape the royal concubines as a show of disrespect.
When Absalom later rejected Achitophel's counsel in order to follow
the advice (also evil) of a rival adviser, the spurned councillor returned
to his home and committed suicide (2 Samuel 15–17). A fitting though
reprehensible end, the biblical commentators agreed.

WAR

The fourteenth century opened with a series of wars of succession and
of territorial aggrandizement. In Scandinavia, the worst situation was
in Sweden, where King Birger II (1290–1318) executed two princeling
rivals to his throne, thus propelling the kingdom into a civil war that
lasted almost throughout the second decade of the century. Contempor-
aneously, Danes and Poles joined together in 1316 to invade the Brandenburg lands in order to contain German expansionism into their own
spheres of influence in the eastern Baltic. A double election, that of
Ludwig of Bavaria and Frederick of Austria, to the German imperial
throne in 1314 resulted in a decade of destructive war in that already
war-weary kingdom. Ultimately, Ludwig emerged the victor, but at the
price of arrested economic development, political repression and other
forms of civic regression in Germany.

The period was also one of border wars: Anglo-Scottish, Franco-
Flemish and Anglo-French. For years the English had claimed a vague
overlordship over Scotland, and the Scots at various times resisted. As
English interference became more insistent and more brutal, the Scots
reacted with ever greater violence and brutality themselves. They were
not successful against King Edward I and he was not entirely effective
against them, but they delivered what seemed to be a crushing blow to
his successor Edward II (1307–27) at the battle of Bannockburn in
1314. Because the English were unwilling to withdraw their claims or
concede territory the Scots believed was rightfully theirs, the aftermath
of Bannockburn developed into a prolonged period of guerrilla warfare
in the borderlands of the two kingdoms. This, in turn, precipitated an

almost total collapse of economic production in the war-ravaged regions during the Great Famine.

The Scots under Robert Bruce and his brother Edward Bruce opened a major second front in the savage war by using the small northern islands as a jumping-off point and invading Ireland. They expected an Irish rebellion against that people's English overlords, but like Scotland, if not more so, Ireland was suffering from famine, and no great national uprising took place. The English and Scots, besides inflicting harm on each other, harried the Irish, living off the land by plunder and disciplining enemies of their cause by peremptory and barbaric punishments. The situation, though precarious for the invading Scots, still held promise because the native population of southern Wales rebelled against their English overlords at about the same time, in the wake, that is, of the death of the region's principal English marcher lord at Bannockburn. The power vacuum created by this death and by English commitments against Scotland and in Ireland furnished the Welsh with a unique opportunity. Yet, in the event, the English put down the Welsh rebellion and, helped by a Scottish withdrawal from Ireland, re-established a modicum of control there by 1320. Nevertheless, border raiding and guerrilla warfare, much to English disadvantage, continued in the main theatre of confrontation, the Anglo-Scottish frontier.

The Franco-Flemish situation was just as messy from 1315 until the early 1320s. The issue was the extent of French sovereignty in Flanders: what precisely did it mean to have a tie to the kingdom? How much authority did the feudal dependence of French Flanders give to the royal overlord? What demands, fiscal and otherwise, could the French king legitimately make on the Flemings? Most Flemings thought French pretensions were overweening. The upper class in Flanders was divided as to how much and in what way it should resist, and some elements wanted to reach a compromise settlement. Many nobles, however, were loath to capitulate, and the burghers stubbornly refused to be cowed by the French.

Thus, it was on the battlefields of Flanders that issues were resolved. The French nobility found itself engaged against determined burgher militias and knights of Flanders in a particularly ferocious series of battles, which went very badly for the French in the early phase. The battle of Courtrai, also known as the battle of the Golden Spurs, took place on 11 July 1302. The huge but somewhat ragtag Flemish army, mostly foot soldiers, met and humiliated the cream of French chivalry, taking no prisoners, but slaughtering at least sixty-eight great nobles and, according to one count, 1,100 knights. Their golden spurs, 700 in number, were retrieved from the battlefield corpses and displayed as trophies in a church in Courtrai.

Such savagery (far from the only example on either side) provoked a grim determination among the combatants. The fighting went on intermittently, but always with brutality, for years. The French seemed to achieve the upper hand by 1312 and went so far as to incorporate a territorial swathe of French-speaking Flanders, including Lille and Douai, into the kingdom. But the attempt met vigorous opposition, and more fighting ensued, at least whenever the weather permitted. Some of the more dramatic descriptions of later campaigns describe the contending armies mired in mud while the rains of the famine period incessantly pelted northern Europe. The rains were more helpful to the Flemings precisely because they undermined the French advantage in cavalry. In the end, however, the rain stopped, and though it took considerable time, the vastly superior resources of the French kingdom allowed it to prevail over the burghers and their Flemish baronial supporters. Lille and Douai are still French.

While the English were engaged with the Scots and while the French slaughtered Flemings or got slaughtered by them, the two great kingdoms went to war against each other in 1294. Again, this Anglo-French war was ostensibly a border conflict, since the clash arose out of disputes about jurisdiction in the English-controlled part of south-western France, Gascony. Fortunately for the local population, the warfare was, on the whole, less intense than elsewhere. Although the formal peace treaty was not ratified until 1313, the period of hot war lasted only from 1294 to 1297. In the uneasy truce that followed, each side fought the other indirectly with surrogates, the French by showing amity to the Scots, the English by doing the same with the Flemings, the purchasers of so much of their raw wool in peaceful times.

The war of 1294–7, though of little interest in its military aspects, had two enormous repercussions. First, it caused a dreadful rift in relations between the papacy and the kings of England and France. English anger with the pope, Boniface VIII, who denounced Edward's taxation of the Church without the pontiff's prior consent as an infringement on the liberty of the Church, was relatively short-lived. Eventually, following an enormous amount of diplomatic manoeuvring, the pope conceded that in evident necessity or in an emergency the king did not have to seek papal permission before he levied the tax. Kings protected their subjects – in just wars, they alleged – and they protected the Church. It was inane, perhaps insane, Edward's diplomats argued, to limit their king's prerogatives and his capacity to safeguard the Church in England when the defence of the realm required swift and decisive military action.

Philip the Fair had done the same thing, taxing the clergy without prior papal permission, and Boniface rebuked him in the same way. The outcome was the same – papal capitulation to the royal arguments – but the French king, never particularly solicitous of papal policies since the days of the crusade against Aragon (see chapter 18), looked upon the papacy's diplomatic counter-attacks in the course of the dispute, and the theory of superiority that the pontiff's men articulated early in the struggle, as a calculated attempt to humiliate the Crown of France. Even Philip's victory in the dispute and the pope's generous gesture of canonizing Philip's grandfather, Louis IX, were insufficient to erase the bad memory which the conflict left in the consciousness of the French ruler.

A second consequence of the little war of 1294–7 arose out of attempts to cement the truce. In the period immediately following the cessation of active hostilities a move was made towards permanent peace by arranging a marriage between King Edward I's son and King Philip the Fair's daughter. As it turned out, the marriage of Isabelle, the daughter, to the future Edward II was a disaster. Isabelle did her part and produced potential heirs, but afterwards the royal couple went their own ways, she to a liaison with one Roger Mortimer, a great marcher lord, her husband to the bed of his male lovers or perhaps to some sort of intense but chaste male friendship that has been misconstrued by contemporaries and scholars alike.

Edward II's reign (1307–27), like his marriage, was a catastrophe. Because he rewarded his favourites, was arbitrary and rather limited in his largesse to his 'natural allies' in the high nobility, and was a colossal failure in war (recall the disaster at Bannockburn), he was periodically confronted with baronial conspiracies designed either to wrest control of the government from him, retaining him solely as a figurehead, or to displace him entirely in favour of his eldest son.

Edward II was not a fool, and at times he showed his mettle. Drawing on the deep well of popular respect for their kings that the English of all classes manifested, he articulated a powerful theory of traditional royal authority in the Statute of York issued in Parliament in 1322. Coming at a time when the political nation at large was disgusted by in-fighting among the barons, who had seized power in 1311, Edward's bid for political ascendancy was successful; the circumstances also allowed him the opportunity to execute retribution on those barons who had had the temerity to execute his male lover/dear friend, Piers Gaveston. But the king did not maintain close and effective control of the government thereafter and came again to depend heavily on favourites, who failed to create a strong royal party to sustain their position. That his queen joined one of the factions and plotted to overthrow her husband is indicative of the state of affairs in England. The king's reputation was not helped by being a cuckold or by the awful visitation of the Great Famine of 1315–22.

In 1327, the queen, with her paramour, Roger Mortimer, seized power and forced Edward II to abdicate. He was dispatched in a gruesome murder late in the year. Roger and Isabelle technically ruled in the name of her adolescent son by Edward II, Edward III. The boy, however, despised Roger Mortimer for defiling his father's bed with his mother, for laying violent hands on an anointed king, and for creating the circumstances for his father's murder. In his own *coup d'état* of 1330 the young Edward seized power. Roger Mortimer was executed; Isabelle was eventually shunted off to a convent of Poor Clares.

With hindsight, then, the marriage of Edward and Isabelle, which had been intended to seal a truce, instead created innumerable problems in England while Edward was alive. Isabelle's father, Philip the Fair, lived until 1314. When he died, he was survived by three sons and Isabelle, by then queen of England. One after the other the sons ruled and died prematurely: Louis X (1314–16), Philip V (1316–22), Charles IV (1322–8). None of them left legitimate heirs except Louis X, but his son, born posthumously, died uncrowned after a few weeks.

The French High Court of Parlement chose the son of Philip the Fair's brother to be king in 1328 as Philip VI. There was no formal protest from Isabelle at the time. She counted on support from France to consolidate her own and Roger Mortimer's position in England after their *coup d'état* against Edward II. In fact, the right to the throne of France should have passed to her and through her to her son. It is true that the French had never been ruled by a queen regnant, though queens or queen dowagers had sometimes exercised temporary regencies during a minority or in the absence of a ruler, say, on crusade. And it is certainly true, too, that male aristocrats had no desire to be ruled by a woman. But it was only *ex post facto* that jurists concocted the notion that it was part of the fundamental or constitutional law of France, inherited from the Salian Franks of the early Middle Ages, that no woman could rule in France or even transmit her rights to rule. To enforce this argument the jurists had to extrapolate from inheritance practices prescribed in the completely obsolete laws of the Salian Franks.

After Edward III came into his own, it became clear that the matter of the French succession was still regarded as an open question in England, and in the absence of real amity between the two countries, it was probable that Edward would some day use his claim as a weapon in disputes with France. Indeed, in 1337 he publicly declared his right to succeed in France. The attempt to enforce his claim was the opening act of the Hundred Years War (1337–1453). No attempt can be made here to go into the details of that long war. In a struggle intended to unite the Crowns of France and England, one sees paradoxically the strong stirrings of nationalism. The truces especially contributed to the emerging national hatred between the French and English. The truces were more injurious than the most famous pitched battles, because unpaid or partly paid troops recently discharged took out their frustration and remunerated themselves materially and psychically by oppressing villagers and townsfolk in France, where the war was fought. Some of the English troops were criminals allowed to substitute military service in France for their judicial sentences; they had little chivalry in their ideology. When peasants grew weary of the maltreatment they received, they took savage revenge on the English, but also on their militarily pressured native oppressors, who were also stealing their goods and humiliating their persons.

Still, the worst consequences of the seemingly interminable war did not manifest themselves before the mid-fourteenth century. It was heavy, almost incessant taxation that weighed both countries down in a period that was already showing signs of a severe economic recession. To be sure, the differential impact of the war on the two countries needs to be stressed. Taxation inhibited some aspects of economic growth in England, even if the expenditure of taxes was a stimulus to specifically military industries and military suppliers. But in France, even stimulation of the war-focused industries paled before the destruction wrought by the contending armies and the wandering demobilized troops of the periods of truce. Yet those who mandated that the war be fought thought the price in human and material loss was worth it. Both sides believed their cause to be just.

POPULAR REBELLIONS

National wars exacerbated already existing tensions in society, which themselves eventuated in civil strife. The traditional scholarly consensus is that the first half of the fourteenth century was not half so bad as the second half. This is in some ways a misinterpretation or at least a simplistic generalization, as we shall see when we turn to Flanders and summarize the results of recent research on that region. But before we do so, we need to take a look once more at Flanders' neighbour to the south, the kingdom of France.

In 1320, the famine had not yet abated in northern France when King Philip V made known his intention to lead a crusade to the Holy Land. The fervour the declaration excited was enormous. If anything, this would be the gesture that would reconcile God and the Christian people. Around Lent and Easter, before the Crown could assemble its forces for the expedition (in fact, it never did assemble them), groups of would-be crusaders, many low-born, began to gather in the extreme north of the realm. Their inferior status and the presence of herdsmen among them gave rise to contemptuous references to them as *pastoureaux*, shepherds, men hardly fit for war.

The leaders in this Shepherds' Crusade are a shadowy group, perhaps including some defrocked priests, who justified their taking up of arms as any commissioned crusader preachers would have done. But the contingents, poorly disciplined and bearing grievances against the upper orders of society and the state for failing to raise a crusading army, soon turned their wrath on other Christians. In Paris some of the would-be crusaders attacked the Châtelet, the headquarters of the royal official who governed the city. They continued to garner support from the lower and sometimes middle classes, although their enemies slurred their male supporters as ne'er-do-wells and the women as whores.

Violence spread throughout the kingdom, even into the deep south. Hundreds of Jews, only recently (1315) readmitted for a price to the kingdom after their expulsion in 1306, were massacred at various places or forced to convert. And although a number of princes and, of course, the Crown ultimately brought forces to bear to eradicate the crusade-turned-rebellion, the final remnants of the *pastoureaux* escaped into Spain. It was to be only a minor breather, for there they were efficiently dispatched by troops loyal to the Crown of Aragon.

The uprising of the *pastoureaux* was brief; that of the lower classes in Flanders was not. Social violence of a limited sort had already occurred during the Great Famine in Flanders, because of perceived violations of the moral economy, the deeply embedded view that, despite the profits to be made, the exploitation of less well-off citizens by wealthy ones, particularly in crisis times, was illicit. Hoarding in order to inflate prices artificially was a clear violation of the moral economy. The existence of under-supplied urban markets, the high price of food, and the necessity of lower-class townsfolk to go into debt to meet their minimal material requirements gave rise to suspicions, especially with regard to middle-men. Rumours of river barges full of grain and granaries stuffed to the rafters provoked deadly riots and, then, reprisals against the rioters, as for example in the town of Douai, where the ring-leaders, among whom women figured prominently, had their tongues cut out for having insti-gated the violence.

Incidents of this sort, bloody and disturbing to social peace as they were at the local level, were isolated in the famine years. What happened in Flanders in the aftermath of the famine and the dislocations occasioned by the long series of Franco-Flemish wars and the economic repercussions of the Anglo-French wars (blockades and piracy) were two periods of more sustained social movements that rent the fabric of urban and rural culture, changing it forever. The first was the Peasant Revolt of 1323–8, the second, the movement that culminated in the van Artevelde regime from the 1330s onwards.

The succession of agreements that had brokered the oft-shattered peace between France and Flanders early in the fourteenth century imposed both mandated and unexpected burdens on the Flemish peas-antry. Indemnities intended to placate the ultimately victorious French and redeem captive Flemish nobles fell hard on the rural dwellers already severely hit by natural disasters. In addition, the returned nobles natur-ally set about to bring their estates back into productivity, a process that incurred suspicion and outright hostility from many peasants. However bad the period before 1322 had been, what it had provided, in the deaths of so many Flemish lords and the captivity of so many others, was a relief from or relaxing of traditional seigneurial rents and other forms of exploitation. Moreover, the return of the count of Flanders from captivity in France had a similar effect on the towns, most especially Bruges. The count expected to regain (perhaps to strengthen) his auth-ority and powers and curtail urban privileges, or so it seemed to the lower and middle classes. Revolt flared briefly in the winter months of 1323.

Efforts to contain the violence and reach a negotiated settlement seemed successful at first, but the calm established was more apparent than real. More than two decades of deepening social cleavages between the aristocracy on the one hand and the lower and middle classes on the other came to the surface once again in late 1324. With it came the seizure of power by the lower orders in Bruges from both comital authorities and the urban patriciate, whose position in other towns, too, was increasingly precarious. No attempts by the count to turn the tables seemed to succeed. Indeed, he was captured by the rebels, and thereafter other towns, like Ypres, came under the control of revolutionary governments claiming to represent the interests of the lower classes – weavers' governments, they have been called.

Forces hostile to Bruges, marshalled by the patrician oligarchy in Ghent in particular and its aristocratic allies, counter-attacked, but with little evident success, and the rebellion-cum-civil war persisted. Even Ghent went through a phase in which its weavers tried to orchestrate a coup, although fruitlessly. Through all the vicissitudes of 1324 and 1325, there were incidents of arson, especially directed at aristocratic residences, and there were massacres of suspected and would-be enemies on both sides.

Needless to say, France intervened. The weapons it used were multiple. The Church served by interdicting the rebel regions. The Crown tried to split the rebels, seeking to strike a deal with those who were in favour of releasing the count. This succeeded; it also responded to overtures for a compromise settlement that would forgive some of the leaders of the revolt if they agreed to lay down their arms, allow their fortifications to be razed, and repent of the introduction of new anti-aristocratic modes of governance, like the rebel captains (*hoofdmannen*), who had achieved considerable power in Flanders.

There were a great many rebels who were willing to go along with this. There were many others who were not. In those regions under the control of the latter, a reign of terror ensued. Mass executions took place of those either hostile or simply indifferent to the aims of the rebellion. Particularly targeted were nobles who fell into the extremists' hands. The stories that some of them were forced to execute their own families seem well substantiated. Conditions continued to deteriorate during 1327.

The French then felt they had no choice but to intervene and assembled a huge army. There is little doubt that if the Flemish rebels had concentrated their forces they would have been a match for the French, but they could not be sure where an attack would come from, and they had to be alert for their enemies in Flanders itself who might fight rear actions against them. In the event, a large, but not overwhelming assortment of rebels took up a hill-top position in Cassel in August 1328. The French arrived, having laid waste the lands in their path. Surveying the difficulty of attacking uphill, they delayed, a tactic that proved to be greatly to their benefit, as the Flemish decided to try to annihilate them with a sweep down the hillside which proved disastrous. When the bodies were counted, at least 3,185 rebels lay dead. In the aftermath, their property was confiscated and other rebels taken into custody elsewhere in the county were executed and/or lost their property as well.

The rebels had sought 'a world without corruption', 'a world without privilege' (TeBrake, 1993). At their ideologically most lofty, these were surely the aims of the rebels. On the ground, they sought relief from taxes and the heavy indemnities that had become a recurrent fact of life in Flanders, as France or some set of aristocrats had to be paid off to seal every truce in the long war. Most of the peasants were already free in a legal sense, but they also wanted to prevent the imposition of financial obligations that would have reduced them to a form of financial servitude. Weavers, finally, may have wanted equality, but they would probably have settled for something like greater respect, better wages, more opportunities for advancement, price controls, etc., if the situation had not otherwise got out of hand.

The forces arrayed against the rebels were no less high-minded. They read their enemies' sloganeering as nothing less than a threat to overturn society and hierarchies otherwise sanctioned by God, and they called on the Church to denounce the rebels and their usurpations and to do everything it could to sanctify the violence carried out to re-establish social order. The forces of repression considered themselves virtually equivalent to the holy crusaders of the century before.

The bitterness and hatred had a lingering impact on Flanders. Rebels and their descendants remembered the vicious repression; nobles and patricians remembered their humiliation, the almost ritualistic imposition of violence against their families. No longer was there basic trust among the constituent groups of medieval Flemish society. Indeed, it might be argued that Flemish society ceased to be medieval at all, as all traditional organic metaphors of political co-ordination failed to articulate the real loyalties of real people in Flanders.

This helps explain the other, less violent phase of Flemish revolutionary activity, the establishment of the van Artevelde regime. Ghent had remained 'loyal' to the comital party in Flanders during the troubles, but the loyalty was conditional, in the sense that the city expected its relative autonomy and economic position to be respected by other cities, its hinterland, and the count. No one seemed wholly willing to accept Ghent's vision of itself as the head of Flanders. Nonetheless, the city was in the fortunate position in the 1330s of coming under the inspired leadership of Jacob van Artevelde, who managed to reconfigure internal urban alliances in the face of the count's attempted encroachments on the city's privileges.

International politics also allowed van Artevelde a role. Strategically located for the receiving of imports from England, raw wool mainly, the city's support seemed crucial to the French, who were intent on injuring England's export trade during the opening years of the Hundred Years War. In fact, despite some significant French gestures to the burghers of Ghent, van Artevelde came more and more under the spell of the English, ultimately welcoming Edward III to the city and recognizing his claim as king of France. In other ways, too, partly by playing an international game, partly by his astuteness in local comital politics, and partly because Ghent was supplementing its precarious income from cloth-making by becoming a major grain staple city, van Artevelde brought Ghent to a tentative hegemony in Flanders.

The long-term outcome of this story is beyond the scope of this book. Suffice it to say that the terrifying violence in Flanders in the 1320s and the destabilization and strange political formations of the 1330s and 1340s were early harbingers of what was to come in many places in Europe: rural and urban violence on a scale nearly unimaginable – the French Jacquerie of 1358, the Florentine Revolt of the Ciompi of 1378, and the English Peasants' Revolt of 1381, among them. However, what happened in Flanders was not only the first but the most sustained of all fourteenth-century revolutionary disturbances. Its human cost was also certainly the highest – by several orders of magnitude.

21

The Church in Crisis

The evident failure of Christian princes to bring or impose peace among themselves and between the upper and lower classes within their realms was parallelled by their failure to meet the challenges of the early fourteenth century with the full co-operation of the Church. The multiple strains in relations between the popes and the kings made it difficult to co-ordinate relief in the famine. The papacy, for example, continued to tax the northern Churches during the most intense period of their poverty. Ecclesiastical and royal strife made sensitive and effective responses to popular religious enthusiasm almost impossible. Such movements thus tended to be tarred as heretical and provoked savage attempts at suppression. And there was never really any adequate relief offered to people suffering the various social and economic dislocations caused by the Black Death. Even the bright spot, the 'promise of the fourteenth century' – technological innovation – had its horrifying downside: one of the most important inventions was gunpowder.

THE CRISIS OF CHURCH AND STATE

The Anglo-French war of 1294–7 (see chapter 20) altered traditional doctrines about the taxation of the clergy dramatically. Canonists had long insisted on kings obtaining the prior approval of the pope before taxing the clergy. Both Edward I of England and Philip IV the Fair of France claimed the right to circumvent this procedure in evident necessity. Both insisted that they were fighting just wars and that in military emergencies there could be no delay or their kingdoms and the Church would suffer. The bitter diplomatic wrangling culminated in Pope Boniface VIII's volte-face, and it is clear that he resented his humiliation as much as Philip the Fair, in particular, resented the papacy's interference in what he regarded as matters pertaining rightly to himself.

Boniface VIII (1294–1303) was not a well-beloved pope in any case. He had come to the pontifical throne after the resignation of Celestine V (1294), a hermit with a saintly reputation who had been drafted into the position. Later stories made Boniface into an ogre, who schemed to persuade Celestine that God wanted him to resign. Whatever the truth in tales like this, Celestine did die while under the new pope's protection in circumstances that Boniface's enemies, of whom there were many, found questionable. Vicious struggles with these enemies, including a party of cardinals led by the influential Italian family, the Colonna, further damaged the pope's reputation; many critics accused him of justifying petty wars of family and personal aggrandizement in Italy as crusades.

One of Boniface VIII's most intriguing projects was the celebration of the first jubilee year of the Church in 1300. Pilgrims who visited Rome in that year were to receive indulgences for their penitential acts and, indirectly, their presence would register their devotion to Rome and, by implication, to the pope himself. No one could have predicted how successful the declaration of the jubilee year would be; it exceeded everyone's wildest imaginings. The Holy City was filled with pilgrims and the pope basked in the evident glory of his pontificate, but quick upon the heels of this great success came a much greater failure.

In 1301, Bernard Saisset, the bishop of Pamiers in southern France, was accused of treasonous words against the French king. The bishop set out for Rome, but was arrested, brought north and placed in jail in preparation for a state trial. At every stage the behaviour of the king's officials violated canon law. Indeed, the king recognized as much and in February 1302 allowed the bishop to travel to Rome without putting him on trial for treason. But in December of 1301, that is to say, before the pope became aware of Philip's change of heart, Boniface responded fiercely. Reprising the struggle over taxation, he forbade the French Crown's collection of taxes from the clergy and called a council of French bishops to consider the next step.

Apprehensive about further possible papal censure or even deposition, and already involved in the savage war with Flanders, where many of his chief advisers would soon be killed, the king should have been amenable to compromise, but the tone the pope took with him cut deeply. Propagandists at the French court put out their version of the pope's denunciations in a way that made the pontiff seem almost like a madman. When the French clergy tried to intervene, they were caught in the crossfire: to whom were they loyal? As the situation grew more desperate, Philip's resolve strengthened. He threatened to seize the property of the sees of those bishops who attended the council and the holdings of other churchmen who supported Boniface. Only thirty-three of seventy-nine French bishops had the courage or willingness to defy the king and attend the council. Boniface VIII then published the bull *Unam sanctam* on 18 November 1302, asserting his lordship of the Catholic world.

The pope was very close to deposing the king, but the French acted first, putting together a long list of charges against him, including his illicit election after causing Celestine to resign and many other allegations of heresy and unseemliness. They followed this up by sending a group of determined men to Italy to kidnap Boniface and bring him to trial on these charges in France. Although the pope was only briefly in their hands, the outrage at Anagni, where the attempt took place, indirectly brought on the pope's death, probably from a stroke. From then on the French Crown used its influence on French cardinals as well as on the Italian enemies of Boniface and his supporters to bring the papacy around to its position.

The situation began to stabilize under Pope Clement V (1305–14), who exonerated the French in order to resist their request that Boniface be exhumed and tried posthumously. Other kings and princes looked at the evolving relationship between Philip the Fair and the pope, a Frenchman who was the former archbishop of Bordeaux, with concern. Whether rightly or wrongly they suspected that Clement was intent on furthering French interests. It did not help that he never went to Rome but resided in the papal territory of Avignon, which was, for all intents and purposes except technically, in France. That his doing so initiated the pope's 'exile from Rome', reminiscent of the Babylonian captivity of the Jewish people in antiquity, was a later slur, but the suspicion of excessive French influence remained strong even after Clement's pontificate: there were seven French popes in a row at Avignon and the college of cardinals was dominated by French appointees. Moreover, there seemed in Clement's pontificate itself to be an even stronger piece of evidence of the French Crown's overweening sway, the suppression of the Order of Knights Templars.

Philip the Fair had come to believe that the Templars were, in the lexicon of a bygone age, 'dirty men', that they worshipped the devil rather than Christ, that they dabbled in black magic, and that they routinely committed acts of sodomy. Where he got these ideas has long been debated. To be sure, with the last outpost in the Holy Land gone in 1291, the military orders were open to criticism, but others, like the Hospitallers and the Teutonic Knights, let alone the Spanish orders, survived and did important military work, if never again quite on the scale of the major crusades. Some scholars see an ulterior motive in Philip's hatred. He or his advisers wanted access to the wealth the Templars had accumulated as a result of their status as international bankers or conduits for the transfer of funds. Yet the Hospitallers, who were in this sense bankers too, were not attacked. Of course, the Templars were special in that they had frequently provided financial services as part of the French Crown's treasury. The idea that they might have skimmed off the cream was certainly in the minds of members of the royal court.

Whatever the reasons, in 1307 Philip the Fair authorized the lightning-like and completely unexpected arrest of every Templar in the realm. The method of attack was similar to that which Philip had authorized in the summer of 1306 against the Jews, in which all the Jews of the realm, perhaps 100,000, were arrested under secret orders in a single day. They were imprisoned, their houses ransacked, records confiscated, and after a brief period they were expelled from France. In this case, too, scholars have argued that Philip had money rather than religion on his mind. The same has been argued for Edward I of England, who expelled the Jews of his realm in 1290. But the dichotomy is as false in Philip's case as it has been shown to be in Edward's. Both kings believed the Jews to be enemies within their kingdoms. Both believed that they had committed outrages against Christendom. In Philip's case, he had become convinced, because of certain reports of miraculous happenings, that Jews had stolen consecrated wafers, the body of Christ, and tried unsuccessfully to 'murder' them. Furthermore, both kings seem to have abandoned hope that the Jews could be induced, a few examples to the contrary notwithstanding, to convert to the Christian faith. It was the combination of religious suspicion and the desire for revenue (the appropriation to the Crown of debts owed to the Jews) that combined to justify the attacks in England and France.

The brutal technique used against the Templars thus had a clear and recent precedent in France. Many other princes were persuaded to act against the order, though they did so far less brutally, and not all of them felt that the Templars' crimes and sins were as lurid as the French alleged them to be. Pope Clement V, however, agreed to commission investigations into Templar beliefs and actions and, convicted by the evidence amassed under torture, many Knights Templars were burned as heretics and their order solemnly suppressed at the Council of Vienne in 1312. The order's property was reassigned, usually to its rival, the Hospitallers, but in Portugal to the military Order of Christ, specifically established in 1319 to receive it.

The Avignon papacy, accused of being subservient to the French, endured another slur, namely that the papal court assembled there was given over to luxury, extravagance and simony. It is true that the uncertainty of access to papal and cardinals' revenues in Rome and the papal states forced the displaced prelates at Avignon to try to make up their income in other ways. It is true, too, that the efficient collection of revenue that this necessitated was readily interpreted as evidence of avarice. But by 1350 attitudes had not yet reached the heresiarch John Wyclif's condemnation of Avignon as a 'nest of simony' or the English Good Parliament's description of it (1376) as 'that sinful city of Avignon'; but at a time when famine, plague and political and social violence seemed to be consuming Europe the moral authority of the papacy was probably lower than it had been since the early eleventh century, when it was little more than property available for purchase by one venal Italian family or another.

THE ATTACK ON 'DOMINICAN' THEOLOGY

While the papacy descended further into crisis with respect to its relations with several of the temporal powers who resented its perceived tilt towards French interests, another issue began to disturb the world of Christian theology. The pre-eminently Dominican attempt at scientific theology always had its critics from within and outside the academy. The most radical critique gathered force in the late thirteenth and early fourteenth centuries and goes by the traditional name of nominalism. Although nominalism's ramifications for mathematics and science were very significant in the period, the idea raised the greatest emotional issues in relation to theology and is associated with two distinguished thinkers, John Duns Scotus (*c.* 1266–1308) and William of Ockham (*c.* 1285–1347).

The Franciscan John Duns Scotus, the subtle doctor (*doctor subtilis*), did most of his work during the first decade of the fourteenth century. A Scot, as his name implies, he studied at Cambridge and expounded his views most famously at Oxford and Paris. Though very much an intellectual, he was caught up in some of the most difficult worldly crises of his day. Indeed, he was banished from Paris for supporting Pope Boniface VIII in his struggle with King Philip IV the Fair over the liberty of the Church. After Boniface's death, the Crown relented. John returned to Paris, where he became regent master of theology in 1305 before moving on to Cologne, where he died in 1308. His relics came to be venerated as those of a saint.

John was involved in the centuries-old argument about the nature of universals and their ontological status. He taught that the universal exists in three ways: in the mind of God before creation (*ante rem*), in the individual itself (*in re*), and in the concept (*post rem*). All of these are equally real, partly because of their sequential dependence on God, who is existential reality.

More directly relevant for the issues of this chapter was John's theology. He stresses the will (love) as the royal feature of humankind, a distinctively Franciscan take, as opposed to what has sometimes been asserted about the Dominican or Thomistic position, namely that intellect represented the quintessential aspect of human nature. Of course, this simple statement obscures an infinite number of subtleties of both theological positions, but the traditional Dominican attachment to the Aristotelian mantra that man is a rational animal tended to make critics of Dominican theology focus on the limitations of reason in order to undermine that theology.

Knowledge of the good, for John, is only a condition *sine qua non*; it is not a cause of virtuous action. An action, that is, could not be virtuous if the actor did not know it was virtuous at the time he chose to do it, but mere knowledge that it was virtuous did not cause the actor to act the way he did. For Thomas Aquinas the external law is a reflection of the 'mind' of God and human acts are good, because they are a realization of human nature as originally created by God in His image and likeness and are directed towards man's proper end. For John, on the contrary, only the commandment to love God is concerned with something good in itself. All other acts are good if and simply because they are commanded by God. Acts in themselves, in the strictest sense, are indifferent. Those who read faint heralds of some Protestant doctrines in this summary would not be wrong, although John's philosophical language was so complex, full of neologisms and disjointed that it had far less direct impact on subsequent theology than might be expected.

William of Ockham's influence was of a different order. An Englishman born near London, much of his career was spent at Oxford. Some of what he wrote has profound relevance for science, such as the maxim that goes by his name, Ockham's razor, *entia non sunt multiplicanda praeter necessitatem*, 'entities ought not to be multiplied beyond necessity', which is usually understood to mean that the simplest explanation for an event is always to be preferred to a more complex competing explanation. But in theology William is best known as the most radical exponent of nominalism.

According to William of Ockham, there are no universals or, what amounts to the same thing, if there are, we cannot have knowledge of them, so, in effect, they do not exist for rational discussion. What we know are individuals. It is simply nonsense to speak of a thing being 'known' as present in an intelligible form in the mind of the knower apart from the real existence of the individual. Being itself, insofar as it is a metaphysical concept, is undiscussable rationally, since by definition metaphysical entities are beyond nature (*meta ta physika*) and, therefore, beyond apprehension. No metaphysical knowledge is possible, from which it follows that none of the truths of religion are demonstrable. God cannot be known through the intellect; no demonstrative proof can be given for His existence. This is not atheism: one must, Ockham piously and sincerely insisted, be satisfied with what faith and revelation tell one. There is no easy way to God; belief is an act of will in the absence of comforting scientific proof, and it is therefore even more precious, precisely because reason offers no tools to defend it: 'Blessed are they that have not seen [the biblical Greek can mean "have not known"], and yet have believed' (John 20:29).

Reflections such as these, though radical, were part and parcel of the nature of academic discourse, with its dialectical, not to say combative character. Dominicans would and did come back hard in defence of their contrary opinions, especially the charge that they limited the freedom of God by imprisoning him within the (limited) possibilities of action according to Aristotelian categories. William of Ockham would probably have become a regent master at Oxford, and we would know him more or less simply as that, if the debates had remained simply academic. But this was not to be so.

In a world in which avowedly orthodox philosophers and theologians wanted to prove or at least give probabilistic demonstrations of the truth of, say, transubstantiation, radically nominalist views of William of Ockham's sort were bound to strike some churchmen as verging on heresy. Indeed, certain of William's theological opinions on the nature of transubstantiation were the trigger for an attack on him as a heretic. The matter was too serious to ignore, so William went to the papal court at Avignon to defend himself in 1324. In the course of his stay he was hardly vindicated, but neither he nor the corpus of his beliefs was condemned outright. In time the philosopher might well have been exonerated – but for his views on the proper character of the Franciscan order.

The Franciscans had made 'compromises' with the world which, many critics, some being powerful voices within the order, felt had betrayed the will of the founder. William came to share this so-called 'observant' view, and he was already dismayed by the wealth, ostentation and worldliness of the Church in general and the papal court in particular. He thus came under suspicion while still resident at Avignon in 1327. The animosity he provoked was particularly intense, given his already suspect theological views. The persecution of which he felt himself to be the victim encouraged him to develop an increasingly comprehensive critique of the 'conventual' or anti-observant stance within the order. He moved further towards a decidedly negative appraisal of many more aspects of the visible Church and of the character of its ruler, Pope John XXII (1316–34), who had declared it heretical to believe that Christ and his apostles had never owned property.

The error, according to William, was on the other side, and the theologian began laying stress on the vulnerability of even the supreme pontiff to heresy and on the duty of churchmen of obvious orthodoxy, like himself, to oppose a heretical pope. In the circumstances, William and several other high-ranking Observants fled Avignon for Germany via Italy in 1328, where support for their understanding of apostolic and Franciscan poverty had won the support of the (excommunicated) German emperor of the Bavarian line, Ludwig IV (1314–47). Ludwig's inclinations make sense since he was already involved in a bitter political struggle with John XXII over the apportionment of their mutual rights in Italy. William of Ockham meanwhile broke utterly with the Avignon papacy and supported a pro-Observant anti-pope. For twenty years he also pursued his scholarship and anti-conventual polemic at the Franciscan convent of Munich, dying in 1347. The whereabouts of his remains are unknown, perhaps because his supporters feared that a triumphant papacy would have them exhumed, burned and scattered as those of a heresiarch, a prince of heretics.

THE MYSTICAL TURN OF THE EARLY
FOURTEENTH CENTURY

The Franciscan Observants were not simply involved in a theological and political struggle. They were arguing in favour of an entire way of life – the good life, the holy life. All through Provence, Languedoc and Spain, their followers, especially Third Order Franciscans, tried to live this life, even after Pope John XXII's displeasure became manifest. The Inquisition was deployed effectively to return them to the pope's version of orthodoxy or to wipe them out.

What the Observants and their martyred followers were seeking reflected the quest of many other groups and individuals for holiness. These others were responding to many of the same tragedies that seemed to demand an intensification of that quest: the loss of the Holy Land, the continuing incapacity of Germany to deliver itself from civil strife, Guelph and Ghibelline warfare in Italy, international wars, rebellions, famine, plague, the uncertain moral authority of the Avignon papacy.

Mystical devotion was the fundamentally problematic stream in devotional life. Sometimes it took the form of an extremely learned, even scholastic, reading of biblical and other spiritual texts which went beyond the conventional limits of exegesis. The effort was intended to discern the mystical meanings of both obscure and well-known passages of orthodox works. The esoteric quality of the approach would have made access by ordinary lay people very difficult, but much of the learned speculation and instruction was watered down in vernacular versions or sermons. And many of the greatest authors in the fourteenth-century mystical tradition lived active lives of charity in the world which, by example, gave respectability to the mysticism they preached. One thinks in this regard of Meister Eckhart (c. 1260–c. 1328), a Dominican *magister* (German, *meister*), a professor, and a genuinely decent man.

Pope John XXII condemned him and his works; he regarded them as leading simple souls to unnecessary confusion. But Eckhart retained his stature among less intellectually parochial members of the clergy in Germany and throughout Christendom. This in itself was troubling to the arch-conservatives, according to whom the whole world was infected with heresy and esteem of heretics.

To less apocalyptic observers, the real problem was elsewhere than among the nonconformist university-educated and their elite supporters. All through northern continental Europe, but particularly in the Rhine-land, Flanders and northern France, there were devout, chaste groups of women and to a lesser extent men living in lay communities. These beguines, as they were called, were not obliged to remain in the com-munities to which they had pledged some part of their goods. They could change their minds and leave. In some respects their communities seemed like those of monks and nuns, but the members retained their lay status and they worked at some tasks, like cloth-making, that were not ordinarily undertaken by the cloistered religious. They developed distinctly interesting modes of devotion and spiritual reflection as well, including an abundant literature of mystical piety. Many people recog-nized the beguines' holiness of life. The prayers of the holy women were particularly prized. Sick people often elicited promises from them to prepare their bodies for burial when the time came.

Some Rhineland towns had large numbers of these communities. Occasionally there were complaints. Were there too many beguines? Did their production of cloth compete unfairly with that of more traditional producers? Why was it necessary, a monastic strain of criticism went, to create beguinages when good and holy lives could be lived in traditional monasteries, nunneries and mendicant convents? But the most threaten-ing criticism concerned the mystical devotion associated with the movement.

Mystical tracts had been written long before the fourteenth century and not merely by beguines. Suspicions of the orthodoxy of some of this literature surfaced strongly in the 1270s, but there were only feeble attempts to put the beguinages more firmly under ecclesiastical control. Possibly this was because the French monarchs, especially Louis IX (d. 1270), had favoured them with his philanthropy. The heat was turned up after his death. Around the year 1300, there appeared a mystical tract in vernacular French whose author, Marguerite Porete, was a beguine from Hainaut, a small imperial county adjacent to

Flanders. Known as *The Mirror of Simple Souls*, the work is a dialogue that instructs in contemplation and the achievement of mystical union and marriage with the Godhead and/or Christ.

Even though the number of people who had mystical experiences and, more importantly, had them recorded was small, and almost all of them were conventionally orthodox or made sure the scribes who wrote up their visions said they were, the idea of mystical union always carried with it some notion of the unmediated relationship between a believer and God. The Church could never fully turn its back on the possibility of supernatural visions and immediate ecstatic experiences of the Lord; to do so would be to undermine the claims to holiness of many of the greatest churchmen and women, like St Francis. But prelates and many lower churchmen were suspicious of any experience that obviated the need for the clergy or threatened to undermine dependence on the sacramental system for access to the divine.

Many serious churchmen saw just such a tendency in *The Mirror of Simple Souls*, and the work and its author were burnt in 1310. An indication of the compelling quality of the book is the fact that some copies that escaped the flames were recopied by less anxious orthodox prelates, and the more offending material either deleted or identified for later readers as dangerous. This occurred despite an increasing shrillness against the beguines among other churchmen. The chorus of complaint and fear reached a crescendo at the Council of Vienne in 1312 and in a subsequent canon in 1317. Beguines were accused of antinomianism, an unwillingness to live according to existing norms and law, either those revealed directly (in the Bible) or others sanctioned by tradition and the authority of the Church. Such people were a law unto themselves, not nuns or monks and yet acting like them and writing about matters that they were too uneducated to comprehend.

On the other hand, how could the Church ban lay people from living the decent life in common? The decrees, and still another in 1318, issued by Pope John XXII, seemed to imagine that there were both good communities and bad ones. The good ones could continue if carefully monitored and acceptable to the local episcopal authorities. Bad communities required immediate dissolution, but the actual pattern of destruction is hard to explain. Some houses were suppressed in towns where they were thick on the ground and their economic position may have seemed threatening to traditional producers. Where local support for the beguinages was weak, in other words, they sometimes disappeared. But this was not always the case, because in larger regions (the equivalent of modern Belgium, for example), where just such an economic explanation would seem to predict their demise, the beguinages continued to flourish, albeit under greater episcopal control or in more or less formal association with an established mendicant order.

*

Despite the savagery that sometimes came to the surface in the early fourteenth century and the particularly intransigent attitude of Pope John XXII, the experiments continued. Ordinary men and women across the map of Christendom depended on their priests to help them negotiate with the divine, but sometimes they met the divine face to face. They sought protection from oppression by reminding the authorities of their duty to protect them. When and if the latter failed, they took the law into their own hands – for better or for worse – and justified it by recourse to the law of God, His love of the poor, His interest in justice and mercy. There was a sense of 'promise' in even the darkest years of the fourteenth century, and it sustained many an individual, many a family and many a community. In brief, despite what might look like evidence to the contrary, it seemed that God loved and would never abandon His children.

Epilogue

The siege of Metz of 1324, like any number of sieges as well as pitched battles in the ceaseless wars of the early fourteenth century, would hardly deserve remembering here except for the survival of a description of it that includes the first known reference to the use of cannon in western warfare. No doubt the effectiveness of the novel apparatus against thick walls was quite limited, as the efficacy of all firearms continued to be for decades. But with their rumbling, fire and smoke the new guns inspired fear, even if their killing and wrecking power did not match the promise of the spectacle of eruption. In popular lore, cannons came to be imagined as the devil's craft, spawned in the devil's workshops; the acrid and persistent smell made real the traditional mental and visual representations of hell and its smouldering brimstone.

Like the international style in Gothic architecture and painting two centuries before, the use of cannon and smaller guns in warfare would disseminate throughout Europe. And, as with the international style, there would be local variants on the adoption of this or that aspect of the new technology. Some peoples – one thinks of the Germans – who favoured the pike in infantry warfare added the handgun to their repertory of weapons very willingly and with effect when it became available. Others, like the Swiss, who fetishized the pike as the instrument of their successful fight for independence, were slower to make the transition.

In general, old habits died hard. Cavalrymen in full armour, expressing what they thought were the highest ideals of traditional chivalry, continued to claim pride of place on battlefields even after opposing artillery became mobile and its missiles far more piercing than they had been in the early fourteenth century. Of course, plate armour, rather than simple chain mail, was of some help in sustaining the willingness of cavalry to charge even in the presence of hostile artillery. Nonetheless, a well-known truth bears repeating, namely, the 'modernization' of Europe that took place in the course and aftermath of the upheavals of the early fourteenth century struggled against persistent and strong tendencies to reconstruct society and culture – Christendom – along 'traditional' or 'inherited' lines. The 'old regime', using this term in its broadest possible meaning, was, with all its recent contradictions and agonies, at least familiar. Yet, how long could men and women cling meaningfully to the past? What did the future hold for them – continuity, rebirth or some curious compound of the two? For good or ill, that is not a story that this book can tell.

APPENDIX

Genealogical Tables

RULERS OF AUSTRIA 1000–1350

House of Babenberg

994–1018	Margrave	Henry I
1018–1055		Adalbert
1055–1075		Ernst
1075–1096		Leopold II
1096–1136		Leopold III
1136–1141		Leopold IV
1141–1156		Henry II
1156–1177	Duke	Henry II
1177–1194		Leopold V
1194–1198		Frederick I
1198–1230		Leopold VI
1230–1246		Frederick II
1248–1250		Hermann von Baden
1253–1276	King	Ottokar II of Bohemia

Habsburg Dynasty

1276–1282	Duke	Rudolf I
1282–1308		Albert I
1308–1330		Frederick
1308–1326	Co-regent	Leopold I
1330–1358	Duke	Albert II

RULERS OF BOHEMIA 1000–1350

Premyslid Dynasty

999–1003	Duke	Boleslav III
1003–1035		Vladivoj of Poland
1035–1055		Bretislav I
1055–1061		Spithnjew II
1061–1092		Vratislav II
1092–1100		Bretislav II
1100–1107		Borivoj II
1107–1109		Swartopluk
1109–1125		Ladislas I
1125–1140		Sobjislav
1140–1158		Ladislas II
1158–1173	King	Ladislas II
(Civil Wars 1173–1197)		
1197–1230	King	Ottokar I
1230–1253		Wenceslas I
1253–1278		Ottokar II
1278–1305		Wenceslas II
1305–1306		Wenceslas III
1306–1307		Rudolph
1307–1310		Henry

Luxemburg Dynasty

1310–1346	King	John
1346–1378		Charles

EMPERORS OF BYZANTIUM 1000–1350

Macedonian Dynasty

976–1025	Emperor	Basil II
1025–1028		Constantine VIII
1028–1034		Romanus III
1034–1041		Michael IV
1041–1042		Michael V
1042–1055		Constantine IX
1055–1056	Empress	Theodora
1056–1057	Emperor	Michael VI
1057–1059		Isaac I Comnenus

Ducas Dynasty

1059–1067	Emperor	Constantine X Ducas
1067–1071		Romanus IV
1071–1078		Michael VII
1078–1081		Nicephorus III

Comnenus Dynasty

1081–1118	Emperor	Alexius I Comnenus
1118–1143		John II
1143–1180		Manuel I
1180–1183		Alexius II
1183–1185		Andronicus I

Angelus Dynasty

1185–1195	Emperor	Isaac II
1195–1203		Alexius III
1203–1204		Alexius IV
1204		Alexius V

Latin Emperors

1204–1205	Emperor	Baldwin I
1205–1216		Henry
1216–1217		Peter
1217–1219	Empress (regent)	Yolande
1219–1228	Emperor	Robert
1228–1261		Baldwin II

Lascaris Dynasty (Empire of Nicea)

1206–1222	Emperor	Thoeodore I Lascaris
1222–1254		John III Ducas
1254–1258		Theodore II Lascaris
1258–1261		John IV Lascaris
1259–1261	Regent	Michael Paleologus

Paleologus Dynasty

1261–1282	Emperor	Michael VIII Paleologus
1282–1328		Andronicus II
1328–1341		Andronicus III
1341–1347		John V
1347–1355		John VI

CRUSADER STATES

Principality of Antioch

1098–1111	Prince	Bohemond I
1111–1131		Boehmond II
1131–1163	Princess	Constance (co-ruler)
1131–1149	Prince	Raymond (co-ruler)
1163–1201		Bohemond III
1201–1233		Bohemond IV
1233–1251		Bohemond V
1251–1268		Bohemond VI

Kingdom of Jerusalem

1099–1100	Protector	Godfrey of Bouillon
1100–1118	King	Baldwin I
1118–1131		Baldwin II
1131–1143		Fulk of Anjou
1143–1162		Baldwin III
1162–1174		Amalric I
1174–1185		Baldwin IV
1185–1186		Baldwin V
1186–1187		Guy of Lusignan

County of Tripoli

1102–1105	Count	Raymond of St Gillies
1105–1109		William Jordan
1109–1112		Bertrand of Toulouse
1112–1136		Pons
1136–1152		Raymond II
1152–1187		Raymond III
1187–1233		Bohemond IV
1233–1252		Bohemond V
1252–1275		Bohemond VI
1275–1287		Bohemond VII

County of Edessa

1097–1100	Count	Baldwin I
1100–1118		Baldwin II
1118–1131		Jocelin of Courtenay
1131–1144		Jocelin II

KINGS OF DENMARK 1000–1350

985–1014	King	Sweyn I Forkbeard
1014–1018		Harold, son of Sweyn
1019–1035		Canute the Great
1035–1042		Canute III
1042–1047		Magnus the Good
1047–1074		Sweyn II
1074–1080		Harold the Hen
1080–1086		Canute IV
1086–1095		Oluf I
1095–1103		Eric I Evergood
1104–1134		Niels
1134–1137		Eric II Emune the Memorable
1137–1146		Eric III Lam
1146–1157		Sweyn III Grade
1157		Knud III
1157–1182		Valdemar I the Great
1182–1202		Canute VI
1202–1241		Valdemar II the Victorious
1241–1250		Eric IV Ploughpenny
1250–1252		Abel
1252–1259		Christopher I
1259–1286		Eric V Klipping
1286–1319		Eric VI Maendved
1320–1332		Christopher II
1340–1375		Valdemar IV Atterdag

KINGS OF ENGLAND 1000–1350

978–1016	King	Ethelred II
1016		Edmund II
1016–1035		Canute of Denmark
1035–1040		Harold I Harefoot
1040–1042		Hardicanute
1042–1066		Edward the Confessor
1066		Harold II
1066–1087		William I the Conqueror
1087–1100		William II Rufus
1100–1135		Henry I

1135–1154	Stephen
1154–1189	Henry II
1189–1199	Richard I
1199–1216	John
1216–1272	Henry III
1272–1307	Edward I
1307–1327	Edward II
1327–1377	Edward III

KINGS OF FRANCE

House of Capet 1000–1350

996–1031	King	Robert II the Pious
1031–1060		Henry I
1060–1108		Philip I
1108–1137		Louis VI
1137–1180		Louis VII
1180–1223		Philip II
1223–1226		Louis VIII
1226–1270		Louis IX
1270–1285		Philip III
1285–1314		Philip IV the Fair
1314–1316		Louis X
1316		John I
1316–1322		Philippe V
1322–1328		Charles IV
1328–1350		Philip VI

KINGS OF HUNGARY 1000–1350

997–1038	King	Stephen I
1038–1041		Peter Orseolo
1041–1044		Aba Samuel
1044–1046		Peter Orseolo
1046–1060		Andrew I
1060–1063		Bela I
1063–1074		Salomon
1074–1077		Geza I
1077–1095		Ladislas I
1095–1116		Salomon, nephew of Ladislas I

1116–1131	Stephen II
1131–1141	Bela II
1141–1161	Geza II
1161–1162	Stephen III, son of Geza II
1162–1163	Ladislaus II
1163–1165	Stephen IV, son of Bela II
1165–1172	Stephen III
1173–1196	Bela III
1196–1204	Emeric
1204–1205	Ladislaus III
1205–1235	Andrew II
1235–1270	Bela IV
1270–1272	Stephen V
1272–1290	Ladislaus IV
1290–1301	Andrew III
1301–1305	Wenceslas of Bohemia
1305–1307	Otto of Bavaria
1308–1342	Charles I
1342–1382	Louis the Great

KINGS OF NORWAY 1000–1350

995–1000	King	Olav I Tryggveson
1000–1016		Sven I Forkbeard
1016–1030		Olav II
1030–1035		Sven II Knudsson
1035–1047		Magnus I the Good
1047–1066		Harald III Hardcounsel
1066–1093		Olav III the Gentle
1093–1103		Magnus III Barefeet
1103–1122		Eystein I
1103–1130		Sigurd I the Crusader
1130–1135		Magnus III
1130–1136	(Claimant)	Harald IV Gille
1136–1155		Sigurd II the Mouth
1142–1161		Inge I
1142–1157		Eystein II
1161–1162		Håkon II
1163–1184		Magnus IV
1184–1202		Sverker (Sverre)
1202–1204		Håkon III

1204–1217	Inge II
1217–1263	Håkon IV the Old
1263–1280	Magnus VI Lagabøter
1280–1299	Erik II
1299–1319	Håkon V
1319–1355	Magnus VII (Magnus II of Sweden)
1355–1380	Håkon VI (Håkon I of Sweden)

KINGS OF POLAND

Piast Dynasty 1000–1350

992–1025	King	Boleslav I
1025–1034		Mieszko II
1034–1058		Casimir I
1058–1079		Boleslav II
1079–1102		Ladislas I
1102–1138		Boleslav III
1138–1146		Ladislas II
1146–1173		Boleslav IV
1173–1177		Mieszko III
1177–1194		Casimir II
1194–1227		Leszek the White
1232–1238		Henry I
1238–1241		Henry II
1241–1243		Konrad I
1241–1279		Boleslav V
1279–1288		Leszek the Black
1288–1290		Henry IV
1295–1296		Przemyslav II
1300–1305		Wenceslas II
1306–1333		Ladislas I
1333–1370		Casimir III

THE POPES 1000–1350

999–1003	Pope	Sylvester II
1003		John XVII
1003–1009		John XVIII
1009–1012		Sergius IV

1012	Gregory (anti-pope)
1012–1024	Benedict VIII
1024–1032	John XIX
1032–1044	Benedict IX
1044–1045	Sylvester III (anti-pope)
1045	Benedict IX
1045–1046	Gregory VI
1046–1047	Clement II
1047–1048	Benedict IX (anti-pope)
1048	Damasus II
1049–1054	Leo IX
1055–1057	Victor II
1057–1058	Stephen X
1058–1059	Benedict X (anti-pope)
1058–1061	Nicholas II
1061–1073	Alexander II
1061–1064	Honorius II (anti-pope)
1073–1085	Gregory VII
1080–1100	Clement III (anti-pope)
1087	Victor III
1088–1099	Urban II
1099–1118	Pascall II
1100	Theodoric (anti-pope)
1102	Albertus (anti-pope)
1105–1111	Sylvester IV (anti-pope)
1118–1119	Gelasius II
1119–1124	Calixtus II
1118–1121	Gregory VIII (anti-pope)
1124	Celestine (anti-pope)
1124–1130	Honorius II
1130–1143	Innocent II
1130–1138	Anacletus II (anti-pope)
1138	Victor IV (anti-pope)
1143–1144	Celestine II
1144–1145	Lucius II
1145–1153	Eugene III
1153–1154	Anastasius IV
1154–1159	Adrian IV
1159–1181	Alexander III
1159–1164	Victor V (anti-pope)
1164–1168	Pascal III (anti-pope)
1168–1178	Calixtus II (anti-pope)

1178–1180		Innocent III (anti-pope)
1181–1185		Lucius III
1185–1187		Urban III
1187		Gregory VIII
1187–1191		Clement III
1191–1198		Celestine III
1198–1216		Innocent III
1216–1227		Honorius III
1227–1241		Gregory IX
1241		Celestine IV
1243–1254		Innocent IV
1254–1261		Alexander IV
1261–1264		Urban IV
1265–1268		Clement IV
1271–1276		Gregory X
1276		Innocent V
1276		Adrian V
1276–1277		John XXI
1277–1280		Nicholas III
1281–1285		Martin IV
1285–1287		Honorius IV
1288–1292		Nicholas IV
1294		Celestine V
1294–1303		Boniface VIII
1303–1304		Benedict XI

Papacy at Avignon

1305–1314	Pope	Clement V
1316–1334		John XXII
1328–1330		Nicholas V (anti-pope)
1334–1342		Benedict XII
1342–1352		Clement VI

KINGS OF PORTUGAL 1000–1350

1140–1185	King	Afonso I
1185–1211		Sancho I
1211–1223		Afonso II
1223–1245		Sancho II
1245–1279		Afonso III
1279–1325		Dinis

| 1325–1357 | | Afonso IV |
| 1357–1367 | | Pedro I |

SICILY

Norman Rulers

1072–1101	Count	Roger I
1101–1105		Simon
1105–1130		Roger II
1130–1154	King	Roger II
1154–1166		William I
1166–1189		William II
1189–1194		Tancred

Hohenstaufen Dynasty

1194–1197	King	Henry VI
1197–1250		Frederick II
1250–1254		Conrad IV
1258–1266		Manfred
1266–1268		Conradin

Angevin Dynasty

1268–1285	King	Charles I of Anjou
1285–1309		Charles II
1309–1343		Robert
1343–1381	Queen	Joanna

House of Aragon

1282–1285	King	Peter III
1285–1295		James II
1296–1337		Frederick II
1337–1342		Peter II
1342–1355		Louis

KINGS OF SPAIN 1000–1350

Kingdoms of Leon and Castile united

1035–1065	King	Fernando I
1065–1072		Sancho II
1072–1109		Alfonso VI

| 1109–1126 | Queen | Urraca |
| 1126–1157 | King | Alfonso VII |

Kingdom of Castile

1157–1158	King	Sancho III
1158–1214		Alfonso VIII
1214–1217		Enrique I

Kingdom of Leon

| 1157–1188 | King | Fernando II |
| 1188–1230 | | Alfonso IX |

Kingdoms of Leon and Castile united

1217–1252	King	Fernando III
1252–1284		Alfonso X
1284–1295		Sancho IV
1295–1312		Fernando IV
1312–1350		Alfonso XI

Kingdom of Navarre

1000–1035	King	Sancho the Great
1035–1054		García I
1054–1076		Sancho IV

Kingdom of Aragon

| 1035–1063 | King | Ramiro I |
| 1063–1094 | | Sancho Ramirez |

Kingdoms of Navarre and Aragon United

1076–1094	King	Sancho Ramirez
1094–1104		Pedro I
1104–1134		Alfonso I

Kingdom of Navarre

1134–1150	King	García Ramirez
1150–1194		Sancho VI
1194–1234		Sancho VII
1234–1253		Teobaldo I
1253–1270		Teobaldo II
1270–1274		Enrique I
1274–1307	Queen	Juana I, wife of Philip IV of France

(Navarre was in dynastic union with France 1284–1328)

1328–1349	Queen	Juana II
1349–1387	King	Carlos II

Kingdom of Aragon

1134–1137	King	Ramiro II

County (Contado) of Catalonia

1035–1076	Count	Ramon Berenguer I
1076–1082		Ramon Berenguer II
1082–1096		Berenguer Ramon II
1096–1131		Ramon Berenguer III
1131–1162		Ramon Berenguer IV

Kingdom of Aragon united to Catalonia

1162–1196	Count	Alfonso II
1196–1213		Peter II
1213–1276		James I
1276–1285		Peter III
1285–1291		Alfonso III
1291–1327		James II
1327–1336		Alfonso IV
1336–1387		Peter IV

KINGS OF SWEDEN 1000–1350

994–1022	King	Olof Eriksson
1022–1050		Anund Jakob
1050–1060		Edmund the Old
1060–1066		Steinkel
	(Internal wars 1066–1080)	
1080–1110	Co-regents	Halstan
1080–1112		Inge
1112–1125	King	Philip
1112–1125	Co-regent	Inge
1130–1156	King	Sverker
1150–1160	Rival King	Eric IX
1160–1161	King	Magnus Henriksson
1161–1167		Charles VII
1167–1195		Knut Eriksson
1195–1208		Sverker Karlsson

1208–1216		Eric X
1216–1222		John I
1222–1250		Eric XI
1229–1234	Rival King	Knut Lange
1248–1266	Regent	Earl Birger
1250–1275	King	Waldemar I
1275–1290		Magnus I
1290–1318		Birger II
1319–1365		Magnus Eriksson II

HOLY ROMAN EMPIRE 983–1378

Saxon Dynasty

| 983–1002 | Emperor | Otto III |
| 1002–1024 | | Henry II |

Franconian Dynasty

1024–1039	Emperor	Conrad II
1039–1056		Henry III
1056–1106		Henry IV
1106–1125		Henry V
1125–1137		Lothar II of Saxony

Hohenstaufen Dynasty

1138–1152	Emperor	(not crowned) Conrad III
1152–1190		Frederick I (Barbarossa)
1190–1197		Henry VI
1198–1208		(not crowned) Philip of Swabia
1198–1215		(rival) Otto IV (of Brunswick)
1215–1250		Frederick II
1250–1254		(not crowned) Conrad IV
1256–1271		King of the Romans, Richard, Earl of Cornwall

(the Great Interregnum 1254–1273)

Post-Hohenstaufen Succession

1273–1291	Emperor	(not crowned) Rudolf I of Habsburg
1292–1298		Adolf of Nassau
1298–1308		Albert I of Austria
1308–1313		Henry VII of Luxemburg

1314–1325	Rival King	Frederick III of Austria
1314–1347	Emperor	Ludwig IV of Bavaria
1347–1378		Charles IV of Luxemburg

References

1 Christendom in the Year 1000

Martha Carlin, *Medieval Southwark* (London, 1996), pp. 250–51.

2 Mediterranean Europe

Thomas Head and Richard Landes, eds, *The Peace of God: Social Violence and Religious Response in France around the Year 1000* (Ithaca, New York, 1992), pp. 327–42.

Lester Little, *Benedictine Maledictions: Liturgical Cursing in Romanesque France* (Ithaca, New York, 1993), p. 36.

Jonathan Riley-Smith, *The First Crusaders, 1095–1131* (Cambridge, 1997), p. 51.

3 Northmen, Celts and Anglo-Saxons

John Wright, *The Geographical Lore of the Time of the Crusades* (New York, 1965), pp. 346–7.

The Story of Burnt Njal, trans. George Dasent (New York, 1911), pp. 208–9.

Orkneyinga Saga, trans. Hermann Palsson and Paul Edwards (London, 1978), p. 137.

George Sayles, *The Medieval Foundations of England* (New York, 1961), p. 192.

4 Francia/France

Joseph Strayer, *Feudalism* (New York, 1965), p. 113.

5 Central Europe

Gyorgy Gyorffy, *King Saint Stephen of Hungary* (New York, 1994), p. 89.

Giles Constable, *The Reformation of the Twelfth Century* (Cambridge, 1996).

6 The Investiture Controversy

Ernst Kantorowicz, *The King's Two Bodies: A Study in Mediaeval Political Theology* (Princeton, 1957), p. 46.

H. E. J. Cowdrey, *Pope Gregory VII, 1073–1085* (Oxford, 1998), pp. 504–7.

Robert Moore, 'Heresy, Repression, and Social Change in the Ages of Gregorian Reform', in *Christendom and Its Discontents*, ed. Scott Waugh and Peter Diehl (Cambridge, 1996), pp. 24, 33.

Gordon Mursell, *The Theology of the Carthusian Life in the Writings of St Bruno and Guigo I* (Salzburg, 1988), p. 256.

Theodore Evergates, 'Aristocratic Women in the County of Champagne', in *Aristocratic Women in Medieval France*, ed. Theodore Evergates (Philadelphia, 1999), p. 105.

7 The First Crusade

Riley-Smith, *First Crusaders*, p. 33.

The Penguin Book of Hebrew Verse, ed. and trans. T. Carmi (Harmondsworth, 1981), pp. 372–3.

Fulcher of Chartres, *A History of the Expedition to Jerusalem, 1095–1127*, trans. Francis Ryan, ed. Harold Fink (New York, 1969), pp. 121–2.

Alan Murray, 'Walther, Duke of Teck: The Invention of a German Hero of the First Crusade', *Medieval Prosopography*, 19 (1998), 35–54.

8 The World of Learning

Bernardus Silvestris, *Cosmographia*, trans. Winthrop Wetherbee (New York, 1973), p. 69.

Abelard, 'The History of My Calamities', in *The Letters of Abelard and Héloïse*, trans. Betty Radice (Harmondsworth, 1974), p. 75.

Stephen Jaeger, *The Envy of Angels: Cathedral Schools and Social Ideals in Medieval Europe, 950–1200* (Philadelphia, 1994), p. 239.

Medieval Woman's Guide to Health – The First English Gynecological Hand-book, trans. Beryl Rowland (Kent, Ohio, 1981), p. 139.
Kantorowicz, *King's Two Bodies*, p. 104.

9 Cultural Innovations of the Twelfth Century: Vernacular Literature and Architecture

Raoul de Cambrai, trans. Jessie Crosland (London, 1926), pp. 43–4.
William Paden, 'The Figure of the Shepherdess in the Medieval Pastourelle', *Medievalia et Humanistica*, 25 (1998), pp. 1–14.
Raymond Cormier, *One Heart, One Mind: The Rebirth of Vergil's Hero in the Medieval French Romance* (University, Mississippi, 1973), pp. 86–7.
John Harvey, *English Cathedrals* (London, 1961), p. 44.

11 Political Power and Its Contexts II

Philip Jones, *The Italian City-State: From Commune to Signoria* (Oxford, 1997), p. 457.

13 The Pontificate of Innocent III and the Fourth Lateran Council

Two Views of Man: Pope Innocent II, On the Misery of Man; Grannozzo Manetti, On the Dignity of Man, trans. Bernard Murchland (New York, 1966), pp. 3–4.

14 Learning

David Knowles, *The Evolution of Medieval Thought* (New York, 1962), p. 200.

17 The Gothic World

Maria Dembinska, *Food and Drink in Medieval Poland: Rediscovering a Cuisine of the Past*, trans. Magdalena Thomas (Philadelphia, 1999), p. 72.
Dembinska, *Food and Drink in Medieval Poland*, p. 166.

20 Political and Social Violence

William TeBrake, *A Plague of Insurrection: Popular Politics and Peasant Revolt in Flanders, 1323–1328* (Philadelphia, 1993), chapter headings.

Suggested Reading

1 Christendom in the Year 1000

Guy Bois, *The Transformation of the Year One Thousand* (Manchester: Manchester University Press, 1990)

Christopher N. L. Brooke, *Europe in the Central Middle Ages, 962–1154* (New York: Longman, 1975)

Léopold Genicot, *Rural Communities in the Medieval West* (Baltimore: Johns Hopkins University Press, 1990)

J. A. Raftis (ed.), *Pathways to Medieval Peasants* (Toronto: Pontifical Institute of Mediaeval Studies, 1981)

2 Mediterranean Europe

Thomas Head and Richard Landes (eds.), *The Peace of God* (Ithaca: Cornell University Press, 1992)

Frederick C. Lane, *Venice: A Maritime Republic* (Baltimore: Johns Hopkins University Press, 1973)

Robert S. Lopez and Irving Raymond, *Medieval Trade in the Mediterranean World* (New York: Columbia University Press, 1955)

G. A. Loud, *The Age of Robert Guiscard: Southern Italy and the Norman Conquest* (Harlow, England: Longman, 2000)

Joseph F. O'Callaghan, *A History of Medieval Spain* (Ithaca: Cornell University Press, 1975)

3 Northmen, Celts and Anglo-Saxons

Theodore M. Andersson, *The Icelandic Family Saga: An Analytical Reading* (Cambridge, Mass.: Harvard University Press, 1967)

Peter Foote and David M. Wilson, *The Viking Achievement: The Society and Culture of Early Medieval Scandinavia* (New York: St Martin's Press, 1990)

Ruth Karras, *Slavery and Society in Medieval Scandinavia* (New Haven: Yale University Press, 1988)

P. H. Sawyer, *Kings and Vikings: Scandinavia and Europe, A.D. 700–1100* (New York: Methuen, 1982)

Frank M. Stenton, *Anglo-Saxon England* (Oxford: Clarendon Press, 3rd edn, 1971)

Patrick Wormald, *Legal Culture in the Early Medieval West: Law as Text, Image and Experience* (Rio Grande, Ohio: Hambledon Press, 1999).

4 Francia/France

David Bates, *Normandy Before 1066* (London: Longman, 1982)

David Bates, 'West Francia: The Northern Principalities' in *The New Cambridge Medieval History*, vol. III (Cambridge: Cambridge University Press, 1999)

Marc Bloch, *The Royal Touch: Sacred Monarchy and Scrofula in England and France*, trans. J. E. Anderson (London: Routledge & Kegan Paul, 1973)

A. W. Lewis, *Royal Succession in Capetian France: Studies in Familial Order and the State* (Cambridge, Mass.: Harvard University Press, 1981)

5 Central Europe

Erik Fugedi, *Kings, Bishops, Nobles and Burghers in Medieval Hungary* (ed. J. M. Bak) (London: Variorum, 1986)

Karl J. Leyser, *Rule and Conflict in an Early Medieval Society: Ottonian Saxony* (Bloomington: Indiana University Press, 1979)

Karl J. Leyser, *Medieval Germany and Its Neighbors* (London: Hambledon, 1982)

Timothy Reuter, *Germany in the Early Middle Ages, 800–1056* (London: Longman, 1991)

6 The Investiture Controversy

Uta-Renate Blumenthal, *The Investiture Controversy: Church and Monarchy from the Ninth to Twelfth Century* (Philadelphia: University of Pennsylvania Press, 1988)

Giles Constable, *The Reformation of the Twelfth Century* (New York: Cambridge University Press, 1996)

C. H. Lawrence, *Medieval Monasticism: Forms of Religious Life in Western Europe in the Middle Ages* (London: Longman, 1989)

Ernst Kantorowicz, *The King's Two Bodies: A Study in Mediaeval Political Theology* (Princeton: Princeton University Press, 1997, reprint)

Gerd Tellenbach, *Church, State and Christian Society at the Time of the Investiture Contest*, trans. R. F. Bennett (Toronto: University of Toronto Press, 1991)

7   The First Crusade

Robert Chazan, *European Jewry and the First Crusade* (Berkeley: University of California Press, 1987)

Carl Erdmann, *The Origin of the Idea of Crusade*, trans. Marshall W. Baldwin and Walter Goffart (Princeton: Princeton University Press, 1997)

Jonathan Riley-Smith, *The First Crusade and the Idea of Crusading* (Philadelphia: University of Pennsylvania Press, 1986)

Jonathan Riley-Smith, *The First Crusaders, 1095–1131* (Cambridge: Cambridge University Press, 1997)

Jonathan Riley-Smith, *Hospitallers: the History of the Order of St. John* (London: Hambledon press, 1999)

8   The World of Learning

Robert L. Benson and Giles Constable (eds.), *Renaissance and Renewal in the Twelfth Century* (Cambridge, Mass.: Harvard University Press, 1982)

James Brundage, *Medieval Canon Law* (London: Longman, 1995)

Marcia Colish, *Medieval Foundations of the Western Intellectual Tradition, 400–1400* (New Haven: Yale University Press, 1997)

Alexander Murray, *Reason and Society in the Middle Ages* (Oxford: Oxford University Press, 1978)

Hilde De Riddler-Symoens (ed.), *Universities in the Middle Ages*, vol. I of *A History of the University in Europe* (Cambridge: Cambridge University Press, 1992)

Beryl Smalley, *The Study of the Bible in the Middle Ages* (Oxford: Blackwell, 3rd edn, 1983)

9   Cultural Innovations of the Twelfth Century

Peter Dronke, *The Medieval Lyric* (New York: Cambridge University Press, 1977)

C. Stephen Jaeger, *The Origins of Courtliness: Civilizing Trends and the Formation of Courtly Ideals, 939–1210* (Philadelphia: University of Pennsylvania Press, 1985)

Gustav Kunstler, *Romanesque Art in Europe* (Greenwich, Conn.: New York Graphic Society, 1968)

William D. Paden (ed. and trans.), *The Medieval Pastourelle* (New York: Garland Pub., 1987)

10   Political Power and Its Contexts I

John W. Baldwin, *The Government of Philip Augustus: Foundations of French Royal Power in the Middle Ages* (Berkeley: University of California Press, 1986)

Robert Bartlett, *England Under the Norman and Angevin Kings, 1075–1225* (Oxford: Clarendon Press, 2000)

Horst Fuhrmann, *Germany in the High Middle Ages, c. 1050–1200*, trans. Timothy Reuter (Cambridge: Cambridge University Press, 1986)

Karl Hampe, *Germany Under the Salian and Hohenstaufen Emperors*, trans. and intro. Ralph Bennett (Oxford: Blackwell, 1973)

11   Political Power and Its Contexts II

Jean Richard, *The Latin Kingdom of Jerusalem*, trans. Janet Shirley, 2 vols. (Amsterdam: North-Holland Pub. Co., 1979)

Jonathan Riley-Smith, *The Crusades: a Short History* (New Haven: Yale University Press, 1987)

Daniel Waley, *The Italian City-Republics* (London: Longman, 3rd edn, 1988)

Kenneth Baxter Wolf, *Christian Martyrs in Muslim Spain* (Cambridge: Cambridge University Press, 1988)

12   Social Structures

Edith Ennen, *The Medieval Town*, trans. Natalie Fryde (Amsterdam: North-Holland Pub. Co., 1979)

Robert Fossier, *Peasant Life in the Medieval West*, trans. Juliet Vale (New York: Blackwell, 1988)

Paul Freedman, *Images of the Medieval Peasant* (Stanford: Stanford University Press, 1999)

Barbara A. Hanawalt, *The Ties That Bound: Peasant Families in Medieval England* (New York: Oxford University Press, 1986)

Michel Mollat, *The Poor in the Middle Ages: an Essay in Social History* (New Haven: Yale University Press, 1986)

13   The Pontificate of Innocent III and the Fourth Lateran Council

Christopher Cheney, *Pope Innocent III and England* (Stuttgart: Hiersemann, 1976)

C. H. Lawrence, *The Friars: the Impact of the Early Mendicant Movement on Western Society* (London: Longman, 1994)

Mark Pegg, *The Corruption of Angels: the Great Inquisition of 1245–1246* (Princeton: Princeton University Press, 2001)

Jane Sayers, *Innocent III: Leader of Europe, 1198–1216* (London: Longman, 1993)

Walter Wakefield, *Heresy, Crusade and Inquisition in Southern France, 1100–1250* (London: G. Allen & Unwin, 1974)

14   Learning

Jacques-Guy Bougerol, *Introduction to the Works of St. Bonaventure*, trans. José de Vinck (Patterson, NJ: St Anthony Guild Press, 1964)

M.-D. Chenu, *Toward Understanding St. Thomas* (Chicago: H. Regnery Co., 1964)

John Marenbon, *Later Medieval Philosophy: An Introduction* (London: Routledge & Kegan Paul, 1987)

F. E. Peters, *Aristotle and the Arabs: the Aristotelian Tradition in Islam* (New York: New York University Press, 1968)

Fernand van Steenberghen, *Aristotle in the West: the Origins of Latin Aristotelianism*, trans. Leonard Johnston (Louvain, Nauwelaerts, 2nd edn, 1970)

15   The Kingdoms of the North

D. A. Carpenter, *The Reign of Henry III* (London: Hambledon Press, 1996)

William C. Jordan, *The French Monarchy and the Jews: From Philip Augustus to the Last Capetians* (Philadelphia: University of Pennsylvania Press, 1989)

Jean Richard, *Saint Louis: Crusader King of France*, ed. Simon Lloyd and trans. Jean Birrell (Cambridge: Cambridge University Press, 1992)

G. O. Sayles, *The King's Parliament* (New York: Norton, 1974)

16 Baltic and Central Europe

David Abulafia, *Frederick II: a Medieval Emperor* (London: Allen Lane, 1988)
Robert Bartlett, *The Making of Europe: Conquest, Colonization, and Cultural Change, 950–1350* (Princeton: Princeton University Press, 1993)
Philippe Dollinger, *The German Hansa*, trans. and ed., D. S. Ault and S. H. Steinberg (Stanford: Stanford University Press, 1970)
Peter Jackson, 'The Mongols and Europe' in *The New Cambridge Medieval History*, vol. V (Cambridge: Cambridge University Press, 1999)
Birgit Sawyer, *Medieval Scandinavia: From Conversion to Reform, circa 800–1500* (Minneapolis: University of Minnesota Press, 1993)

17 The Gothic World

Jean Bony, *French Gothic Architecture of the Twelfth and Thirteenth Centuries* (Berkeley: University of California Press, 1983)
A. Gasiorowski (ed.), *Polish Nobility in the Middle Ages: Anthologies* (Wroclaw: Zaklad Narodowy im. Ossoli'nskich, 1984)
Roberta L. Krueger (ed.), *The Cambridge Companion to Medieval Romance* (Cambridge: Cambridge University Press, 2000)
Emile Mâle, *The Gothic Image: Religious Art in France of the Thirteenth Century*, trans. Dora Nussey (New York: Harper, 1958)
David Robb, *The Art of the Illuminated Manuscript* (South Brunswick: A. S. Barnes, 1973)
J. W. Sedlar, *East Central Europe in the Middle Ages, 1000–1500* (Seattle: University of Washington Press, 1994)

18 Southern Europe

Thomas Bisson, *The Medieval Crown of Aragon: a Short History* (Oxford: Oxford University Press, 1991)
R. I. Burns (ed.), *The Worlds of Alfonso the Learned and James the Conquerer: Intellect and Force in the Middle Ages* (Princeton: Princeton University Press, 1985)
Jean Dunbabin, *Charles I of Anjou: Power, Kingship and State-Making in Thirteenth-Century Europe* (London: Longman, 1998)
Steven Runciman, *The Sicilian Vespers: a History of the Mediterranean World in the Later Thirteenth Century* (Cambridge: Cambridge University Press, 1958)

19   Famine and Plague

Guy Bois, *The Crisis of Feudalism, Economy and Society in Eastern Normandy, c. 1300–1500* (Cambridge: Cambridge University Press, 1984)

William C. Jordan, *The Great Famine: Northern Europe in the Fourteenth Century* (Princeton: Princeton University Press, 1996)

Millard Meiss, *Painting in Florence and Siena after the Black Death* (New York: Harper and Row, 1964)

Philip Ziegler, *The Black Death* (New York: Harper and Row, 1969)

20   Political and Social Violence

Richard W. Kaeuper, *War, Justice and Public Order: England and France in the Later Middle Ages* (Oxford: Clarendon Press, 1988)

D. Nicholas, *Town and Countryside: Social, Economic and Political Tensions in Fourteenth-Century Flanders* (Bruge: 'De Tempel', 1971)

D. Nicholas, *The Metamorphosis of a Medieval City: Ghent in the Age of the Arteveldes, 1302–1390* (Lincoln: University of Nebraska Press, 1987)

W. M. Ormrod, *The Reign of Edward III: Crown and Political Society in England, 1327–1377* (New Haven: Yale University Press, 1990)

Jonathan Sumption, *The Hundred Years War: Trial by Battle*, 2 vols. (London: Faber, 1990–99)

21   The Church in Crisis

Marilyn McCord Adams, *William Ockham* (Notre Dame, Indiana: Notre Dame University Press, 1987)

Marilyn McCord Adams and Allan B. Walter (eds.), *The Philosophical Theology of John Duns Scotus* (Ithaca: Cornell University Press, 1990)

Bernard McGinn (ed.), *Meister Eckhart and the Beguine Mystics* (New York: Continuum, 1994)

Francis P. Oakley, *The Western Church in the Later Middle Ages* (Ithaca: Cornell University Press, 1979)

Joseph R. Strayer, *The Reign of Philip the Fair* (Princeton: Princeton University Press, 1980)

Index

Abelard, Peter 117–18, 123
Accursius, Master; *Glossa Ordinaria*
    127
'Achitophels' (royal advisers) 302–3
Acre 174, 175, 263, 285
Adalbert of Prague, St 71
administration: investigations into
    corruption 232, 273; municipal
    187, 188; *see also* governance,
    institutions of *and under individual
    states*
Adolf of Nassau, Holy Roman
    emperor 258
adultery 135
Aethelred II, the Unready, king of
    England 58
Africa: North 23, 29, 30, 169, 296;
    west coast 273
agriculture 8–10, 21–2, 182–3,
    189–90, 289, 290–91; assarting
    9–10, 11, 14; Britain 47; Burgundy
    61; Castile 271; Germany 68;
    Hungary 74; Iceland 40, 42;
    Mediterranean Europe 21–2,
    23–4; specialization 23–4, 182–3;
    technology 9–10; in towns
    189–90; two- to three-field
    transition 8–9; warfare reduces
    productivity 47; *see also* animal
    husbandry; dyestuffs; food supply;
    grain; land; wine production
Albania 279

Albert of Austria, Holy Roman
    emperor 258
Albertus Magnus (Albert the Great)
    119, 221
Albigensian Crusade 160, 204–5,
    209, 228, 274, 275
Alexander II, Pope 90
Alexander III, Pope 148, 155
Alexandria, Egypt 174
Alexius I Comnenus, Byzantine
    emperor 107, 109, 172
Alexius III, Byzantine emperor 197
Alexius IV, Byzantine emperor 197–8
Alfonso VIII, king of Castile 166
Alfonso X the Wise, king of Castile
    252, 257, 271–2
Alfonso I, king of Navarre and
    Aragon 112
Alfonso III, king of Portugal 272, 273
Alice of Antioch 171
allegory 114, 136
'Alleluia, Great' 277
alliteration 115
allods 15, 145, 181
Almohads 163–4, 165, 166
Almoravids 163
Alps 22, 95, 181
altar cloths and altarpieces 262
Althing (Icelandic assembly) 41, 42
Amalfi 31–2, 35
Amalric I, king of Jerusalem 173
Amaury de Montfort 228

America, North 38–9
Amiens, Mise of 238
Anagni 316
Andrew, St 109
Andrew, king of Hungary 250, 255, 284
Andrew of St-Victor 117, 120
Angevin dynasty and empire 56–7, 147, 152, 158, 160, 176; *see also individual kings*
Anglesey 45
Anglo-Saxons 43, 45, 49; *see also* England (Anglo-Saxon dynasty)
animals and animal husbandry 8–9, 183, 290, 291–3; draft 8–9, 290, 291–3; Mediterranean Europe 21, 22; northern Europe 38, 59, 62
Anjou 56–7, 62, 147, 152, 158, 278
Anne, princess of Kiev, queen of France 63
Anselm, archbishop of Canterbury 123–4, 151, 215–16
Anselm of Baggio (Pope Alexander II) 90
anthrax 293
antinomianism 324
Antioch 109, 169
Apennines 21
apocalyptic movements 102
apple growing 291
apprentices 186
Apulia 35
Aquinas, Thomas 119, 179, 220–23, 319–20
Aquitaine 136, 152, 158
Arabic language 22–3; translation into Latin 116, 121, 125, 213, 216
Aragon 273–6; communal movement 187; cortes 239, 274; crusade against 281–2, 306; and France 275, 281–2, 306, 309; learning at court 119; reconquest of Valencia 164, 166

architecture 137–42, 259–61; brick 250, 267; Byzantine influence at Amalfi 32; funding 141–2; Gothic style 138, 139–42, 226, Figs. 8, 10, 11, 14–19, (Decorated) 260–61, Figs. 17, 19, (High) 140, 141, 259–61, (phases) 140, (regional styles) 260–62, 254, 267; interruption of building 141, 142, 260; itinerant craftsmen 184; patronage 141–2; in Poland 254, 267; Romanesque style 138–9, 254, 267, Figs. 1–7; rotunda of St-Bénigne, Dijon 58; Spain, Muslim influence in 24
Aribert, Archbishop of Milan 89–90
aristocracies 12–16; admission to 146, 264; and Church 56, 85, 103–4, 141; Corsican 33; culture, and popular culture 137; education 131; incomes 11, 182, 267, 289; Irish traditional 46; jurisdiction 13–14; and kings 14, 52–3, 147, (charters of liberties) 233–4, 247, 255, (*see also* Magna Carta *and under* emperor, Holy Roman; England; France; Hungary; Poland; Scandinavia); land holdings 182; lifestyle 266–70; and peasantry 13–14, 294, 310–11; plague and 298; and towns 18, 188; *see also* feudalism *and under individual countries*
Aristotle 121–2, 213–15, 216–17, 221, 320
Arles 25
Árpádian dynasty of Hungary 74
Arsenal Bible 263
Artevelde, Jacob van 310, 313
Arthur of Brittany 159
Arthurian legends 135, 136
artillery 327–8
artisans 17, 62

arts, seven liberal 119
arts, visual 199, 259–63, 300, 327;
   see also architecture; frescos;
   manuscripts, illuminated; sculpture
Ascalon 110, 173
Asia Minor 107, 108, 148, 199
assarting 9–10, 11, 14
assemblies, Scandinavian 41, 42,
   245
associations, sworn (communes) 181,
   187–8
assonance 114–15, 130
astrolabe 117
Atlantic Ocean 273
Augsburg 74
Augustine of Hippo, St 100, 113, 121
Augustinian (Austin) canons 94, 116,
   122
Austria 68, 253, 284
Autun cathedral Fig. 3
auxilia, feudal 14
'Ave Maria' (prayer) 95
Averroës (Ibn Rushd) 216–17
Aversa, county of 35, 36
Avicebron (Solomon Ibn Gabirol)
   216
Avicenna (Ibn Sina) 215–16
Avignon 25; battle of 228; papacy
   316, 318, 321, 322
Ayyubids 174
Azores 273

Bacon, Roger 215, 217–18
baillis (French officials) 159
Baldwin IV, count of Flanders 59–60
Baldwin V, count of Flanders 59, 60
Baldwin IX, count of Flanders 199
Baldwin I (Baldwin of Boulogne),
   king of Jerusalem 108–9, 169,
   171
Baldwin II, king of Jerusalem 171
Baldwin III, king of Jerusalem 171
Baldwin IV, king of Jerusalem 171

Baldwin V, king of Jerusalem 171–2
Balearic Islands 25, 34, 274, 275
Balliol, John, king of Scotland 242
Baltic region 143, 182, 243–9; Black
   Death 296; brick castles 250;
   Danish power 246–7, 250, 303;
   map 244; missionary work 189,
   246, 249; Polish power 250, 303
banalities 12
banditry 47, 157
banking 317
Bannockburn, battle of 303, 304,
   306
Barcelona 187, 188
Bari 32
barons see aristocracies
barter 17
Basil II, Byzantine emperor 35
Basque language 22
bastides 188
Bec, ducal abbey of, Normandy 150,
   151
Becket, Thomas, archbishop of
   Canterbury 154–6, 158
bee-keeping 183, 292, 293
beggars 191, 192
beguines 323–5
Bela IV, king of Hungary 255–6
Benedict IX, Pope 29–30
Benedictine order 22, 94, 115, 211,
   220
Benevento, battle of 278
Berbers 23
Berechiah ha-Nakdan 132–3
Bergen 246
Bernard of Clairvaux 96, 112, 123,
   172, 193
Bernard Silvester 114
berserkers 42
Bertha, queen of France 64
Bertrade de Montfort, queen of
   France 64
Bethlehem 110

Bible: Arsenal 263, Fig. 23;
Cistercian 116; *Glossa Ordinaria*
117; romance draws on 135;
scholarship 116, 117, 120, 218;
Vulgate 116, 129
Billungs, March of the 68, 72
biography 114
Birger, Jarl, regent of Sweden 247,
248, 249
Birger II, king of Sweden 303
bishops: German, under Henry IV
91–2; inquiries into heresy 230;
Irish 46–7; itinerant, Scottish 47;
and Jews 106; lay investiture *see*
Investiture Controversy;
philosophers 214, 225; symbols
and responsibilities 2; temporal
power 18, 46–7, 143
Black Death 295–301
Blanche of Castile, regent of France
219, 229, 232
Blois-Champagne, counts of 60–61
Boethius 121
Boetius of Dacia 215
Bohemia 255, 256–8
Boleslaw I, king of Poland 73
Boleslaw II the Bold, king of Poland
92–3
Boleslaw III the Wry-Mouthed, king
of Poland 93
Bologna, university of 118–19, 229
Bonaventure 220, 223–4, 225
Boniface VIII, Pope 305–6, 314–16,
319
book production and trade 115–16,
118
Bordeaux 228
bot (nature of injury, legal term) 50
Bourges 64; cathedral Figs. 11, 15
Bouvines, battle of 160, 208, 228
bow, compound 253
Brabant, duchess of 225
Bracton, Henry de 235

Brandenburg 303
brewing 183, 186
Brian Boru, king of Dál Cais, and
dynasty 46
brick architecture 250, 267
British Isles 44–51; map 39; smaller
islands 44–5, 46; *see also* England;
Ireland; Scotland; Wales
Brittany 56, 59
Bruce family 242; Edward 304;
Robert, king of Scotland 304
Bruges 59, 310–11
Bruno, St 95, 98
brutality 166, 264, 304, 305, 308,
311
Burgos, cathedral of 260, Fig. 16
Burgundy 61, 136
burial 105, 186, 191
Byzantine Empire: customs duties 28;
Charles of Anjou plans to invade
280–81; and Crusader States 170,
172, 285; and crusades, (First)
105–6, 107, 108, 109, 172,
(Fourth) 31, 197, 198–9, 263;
decline 79, 285; espionage 280–81;
Frankish rule 199, 279; and
Hungary 74; Italian dependencies
27–8, 32, 34–6; Kievan alliance
with 63; Michael Paleologus' rule
279, 280–81; naval activities 169;
Otto II's connection 70; painting
263; and papacy 189; Roman
heritage 34–5; Turkish attacks on
280; *see also* Constantinople

Caesarea 285
Cagliari 34
Cairo 175
Caithness 47
Calabria 23–4, 35, 36, 70
Calatrava, Order of 165
Cambridge, university of 119, 319
Canary Islands 273

cannibalism 266, 294

cannon 327

canon law 116, 127–8

canons and canonesses 94, 97, 116

Canossa, Henry IV's penance at 92

Cantabrian mountains 21

Canterbury: appointment of archbishops 49, 206–7; Becket's shrine 137, 155, 158; Christ Church 206

Cantigas, Castilian 272

Capetian dynasty 54, 56, 63–5; Burgundian line 61; cadet princes in conquered areas 228, 229; touching for scrofula 54, 156–7; *see also* France (kings) *and individual kings*

capital punishment 154, 247

capitanei 89

Capua 36

cardinals, college of 88

Carinthia 68

Carolingian era 13–14, 66, 114, 115

Carthusian order 94, 95–6

Casimir I the Restorer, king of Poland 73, 92

Cassel, battle of 312

castellans 13, 56, 57

Castile 119, 164, 166, 239, 271–2

Castilian language 129–30, 271–2

castles: brick, Baltic 250; in Crusader States 170, Fig. 13; 11th-century proliferation 13, 29, 57; in Hungary 76, 255; in Iberia 164, 272; of military orders 173, 250; of Richard I the Lionhearted, in France 176; in Wales, of Edward I 241

Catalonia 166, 274, 275

Cathars 160, 200–201, 203–5; *see also* Albigensian Crusade

cathedrals: building of 141, 142, 179, 184, 260; schools 116–17, 119

cattle 292, 293

Celestine V, Pope 315, 316

Celts 45, 46–8

central Europe 5, 8, 17, 66–79, 249–58; map 67; *see also individual states*

centrifugal forces 52–3

cereals *see* grain

Cevennes 21

Chalcedon, Council of 170

Champagne 60–61, 136; trade 62, 186, 257

chanson de geste 130–32, 136

charcoal burning 62, 184

Charlemagne 66; legends of 130, 131

Charles IV, king of France 307

Charles of Anjou 233, 238, 278–82

Charroux, Council of 26

charters of liberties 187, 247, 255; *see also* Magna Carta

Chartres, cathedral of 117, 141, Fig. 8

childbirth 8, 190

children 111, 186, 190–91, 192

China; Mongol invasion 252, 253

chivalry 13, 100, 264, 327

Chrétien de Troyes 135

Christ, Order of 318

Christendom 1, 30, 66

chronicles *see* historiography

Church: architecture 138–42, 259–62, Figs. 1–8, 10, 11, 14–19; aristocrats and 56, 85, 103–4, 141; Becket affair 154–6, 158; and beguines 323–5, 324–5; canon law 116, 127–8; condition in 1000 18–19; East-West relations 30–31, 104, 170–71, 197, (prospects of reunion) 30–31, 37, 199, 225, 280, 281; and famine 295; fourteenth century crisis 314–25; funding of building 141–2; Greek, (in southern Italy) 35, 36, 37,

Church – *cont.*
(*see also* East-West relations
above); in Greenland 39; healing
cults 190; Inquisition 230–31,
233, 332; in Ireland 46–7; jubilee
year (1300) 315; jurisdiction
154–5, 156; kings' relation to 49,
56, 69, 75, 78, 86, 149, (*see also
under* papacy *and individual
monarchs*); land holdings 69, 182;
language use 31, 129; lay
preaching 200; liturgy 19, 31,
101–2, 170; Magna Carta and
234; missionary activity 18–19,
71, 249; Muslim attitudes to 24,
161–2, 163, 171; and mysticism
322–3, 324–5; and philosophy
113–14, 214; and plague 297–8;
pluralism 298; reform 1–2, 64, 85,
93–7, 112, 151, (Cluniac) 1, 55,
58, 94, (*see also* friars; Lateran
Council, Fourth; papacy
(reforming popes)); Russian 63, 75;
in Scotland 47; and slavery 11, 41;
and state 49, 75, 78, 101, 148,
314–18; Syriac liturgy 31; taxation
of 166, 305–6, 314–15; territorial
dioceses 46–7; *see also* bishops;
clergy; councils, Church; friars;
monasticism; papacy; theology;
and under Hungary; Poland;
Scandinavia; Slavs; warfare
Cid, El 130
cider production 291
Cinarca, counts of 33
Ciompi, Revolt of the 313
Cistercian order 94, 96–7, 115, 116,
267
Cîteaux, abbey of 96, 116
citizenship, purchase of 190
civilians (masters of Romam law)
127
clans 43, 47, 242, 243

Clare, St 203
Clares, Poor 203, 307
classical culture 114–15, 135, 262,
263; *see also* Aristotle; Plato
Clement II, Pope 30, 87
Clement III, anti-pope 93, 97
Clement V, Pope 316, 318
clergy: education of 298; legal and
administrative work 49, 189;
married 85, 90, 91, 248; power in
towns 18; *see also* bishops; friars;
monasticism
Clermont, council of 98, 104
climate 20–21, 22, 290, 305
Clontarf, battle of 46
Cluny, abbey of 1, 98, 116; reform
movement 1, 55, 58, 94
Cnut the Great, king of Denmark,
Norway and Ebgland 43, 50,
77
Coimbra 272, 273
coinage 43, 48, 77
Cologne 106, 188, 221, 319;
Cathedral 137, 142, 260
Coloman, king of Hungary 78
Colonna family 315
combat, trial by 150, 153–4
communal movement 181, 187–8
communion 31, 211
compass, magnetic 32
complexions (medical concept) 125
Compostela, pilgrimage to 137
confession 211
confraternities 186
Conrad II, Holy Roman emperor 75,
89
Conrad III, Holy Roman emperor
146, 172
Conrad of Montferrat, regent of
Jerusalem 171
Conradin, grandson of Emperor
Frederick II 278
consensus, government by 10, 272

Constance, Empress, wife of Henry VI 195

Constance of Hohenstaufen, queen of Aragon 278, 281

Constantinople: First Crusade reaches 108; Iaroslav of Kiev's failed attempt to take 63; patriarchate 30–31, 104; Peasants' Crusade reaches 107; sack by Fourth Crusade 31, 197, 198–9, 263; spice trade 269; Venetian merchants in 28

conversi and convers(a)e (monastic lay workers) 95–6, 97

Copts 170

Corbeil, treaty of 275

Cordoba 23, 161–2

cordwainers 184

Cornwall and Cornish language 48

coronation 86, 241; Capetian ceremonial 54–5, 63; Stone of Scone and 242

corporate privileges, Magna Carta on 235

correspondence, official 129–30, 189

Corsica 32–3, 168–9

cortes 239, 272–3, 274

corvées 12

councils, Church: of French bishops, 1302 315, 316; southern French, and Peace of God 25, 26; see also Chalcedon; Clermont; Lateran Council, Fourth; Lyons; Vienne

councils, municipal 187

councils, royal: English 49, 238, 239; Swedish 248

countryside 8–16, 25–7, 181–5, 289, 296, 298–9; see also agriculture

courtly love 134–5

courtoisie 265

Courtrai, battle of 304–5

courts, judicial 13–14, 17, 49–50, 151; ecclesiastical 154–5, 156

courts, royal and aristocratic 49; itinerant, Norwegian 245, 246; literary culture 120–21, 136–7

crafts 17, 62, 183, 184, 186

Creed 31, 170

crime 308; see also theft; murder fine; underworld

Croatia 8, 74, 79, 253; map 67

Crusader States 110–12, 161, 169–76, 283–5; collapse 280, 283–5; establishment 110–12; map 162–3; and papacy 189, 196; 13th-century crusaders' support 231–2, 241, 285; see also Antioch; Edessa; Jerusalem; Tripoli

crusades: First 100–112, (Byzantine failure to support at Antioch) 109, 172, (Crusader States set up by) 110–12, (genesis) 98, 100–105, (Jerusalem captured by) 98, 110, 112, (map) 101, (Peasants' Crusade) 105–8, (Princely Crusade) 108–12, 151; Second 157–8, 165, 172; Third 148, 159, 165, 173–4, 174–5, 196; Fourth 31, 196–9, 263, (map) 198; Fifth 202–3, 209, 250, 255, 283–4; later 284–5, (1228–40) 284, (1249) 214, 231–2, 251, 252, 284–5, (1270) 231, 232–3, 241, 285; Albigensian 160, 204–5, 209, 228, 274, 275; Aragonese 281–2, 306; burial of crusaders 105; clergy on 202–3, 225; economic effect 141, 166, 283; and Iberian Reconquest 165; ideology and Drang nach Osten 246, 249; penitential vows 103, 104; prestige of king's participation 156, 158; return home 112; settlement in Holy Land 170, 283; Shepherds' 309–10

Cumans 78, 256

customs, French legal 229
customs duties 28
Cyprus 175, 285
Czech lands 8, 250; map 67

dairying 183, 292
Dál Cais, kingdom of 46
Dalmatia 22
Damascus 172
Damasus II, Pope 30, 87
Damietta 174, 231, 284, 285
Danehof (parliament) 247
Danelaw, England 48, 49
Dante Alighieri 276
David, Welsh cult of St 47–8
death 105, 186, 191, 195, 300
debt 12, 267, 289
defence, local 49, 164, 226, 228,
  304
Denmark: Baltic empire 246–7, 250,
  303; and England 43, 48–9, 50,
  58, 149; institutions of government
  43, 247; justice; trial by ordeal
  210; land holdings 181; maps 39,
  244; and Norway 44; Polish
  lifestyle influenced by 267;
  population 8; in 13th century 243,
  245, 246–7; see also Scandinavia
Desiderius, abbot of Montecassino
  97–8
Devon 291
dialectic 122–3, 218
Dictatus Papae 91
diet 22, 267–9, 292, 293–4, 299
dignitates and suppositiones 219
Dijon; abbey of Saint-Bénigne 58
diplomacy 145, 189
disease: animal 183, 293; human 8,
  20, 109, 191, 294; see also plague
display, conspicuous 249, 267–70
disseisin, writ of novel 153
distribution, 14th-century crisis in
  290

doctors 111, 190
Domesday Book 150
Dominican order 19, 201, 203, 230;
  theology 220, 221–2, (see also
  Aquinas, Thomas)
Dorylaeum, battle of 108
Douai 305, 310
dovecotes 292
drama 300
Drang nach Osten 249–58, 267, 283
drapers 185
droughts 21
Dublin, Viking kingdom of 46
Duncan I, king of Scotland 47
Duns Scotus, John 319–20
Durham Cathedral 138, Fig. 4
dyestuffs 24, 62, 291

East Anglia 293
Eaten Heart, Legend of the 266
Eckhart, Meister 322–3
Edessa, crusader state of 109, 170,
  172
education 131, 217, 226; of clergy
  185, 201, 298; see also learning;
  schools; universities
Edward the Confessor, king of
  England 43, 50–51, 58, 149, 237
Edward I, king of England 241–2;
  confirms Magna Carta 239; expels
  Jews 235, 317; and papacy 305–6,
  314–15; and Parliament 239; and
  Philip IV of France 305–6; Statute
  of Quo warranto 240; wars 238,
  241–2, 285, 303
Edward II, king of England 303–4,
  306–7; proclaimed prince of Wales
  241
Edward III, king of England 307,
  308, 313
eels 292
Egypt 110, 173–4, 196, 231, 284,
  285

Eleanor of Aquitaine 152, 154, 157, 158

Elne, Council of 26

Emich, count of Flonheim 106–7

Emma, queen of England 58

emperor, Holy Roman: and aristocracy 69, 71–3, 87–8, 143, 145–6, 146–7, 258; and *Drang nach Osten* 250; election 196, 209; extent of empire 68; as heir of Roman Empire 34; and papacy 127, 143, 161, 211, 247, (Henry III) 30, 85, 87, (Henry IV) 87, 91–3, 97, 98, 105, 196, (Hohenstaufens) 147–8, 155, 195–6, 209, 211, 250–52, 276, 277–8; theological position 66, 85–7, 99; succession disputes 196, 209, 303; *see also* Germany; Hohenstaufen dynasty; Investiture Controversy; Italy (emperors' power); Ottonian dynasty; *and individual rulers*

encastellation 13, 29

Enéas (romance) 135

England 48–51, 148–56, 233–42; Anglo-Saxon dynasty 43, 45, 49, 50–51, 58, 149, 237; architecture 138, 260–61, Figs. 4, 17, 19; aristocracy, (and king) 49, 237–41, 306, (and king John) 207, 208, 209, 233–4, 234–5, 238, (land holdings) 182, (Normanization) 149–50, 226; Black Death 296, 297; Church 42, 49, 151, (courts) 154–5, 156, (*see also* papal relations *below*); coinage 43; constitutionalism 148–9, 235; council, great 49, 238, 239; Danelaw 48, 49; Danish kings 43, 48–9, 50, 58, 149; ethnic groups 149–50, 151; exchequer 151; famine 307; and Flanders 290, 305, 313; and France 226, 308, (kings' lands in) 147, 152, 158, 160, 228, (Kings' loss of lands) 175, 176, 205–6, 207, 208, 228, 233, (wars) 238, 242, 303, 305–8, 310; governance 48–9, 151, 152, 226, 238, 239; invasion of Ireland 304; Jews 150, 174, 181, 214, 235, 238, 317; justice 49–50, 150, 151, (church courts) 154–5, 156, (common law) 152–4, (juries) 152–3, 153–4, 236–7, (trial by ordeal) 210–11, 236–7; kings, (and church) 49, (and Parliament) 237–41, (*see also under* aristocracy *and* France *above*); knighthood 13; law 49, 150, 226, (common) 149, 152–4, 155, 240, (forest) 234, (king bound by) 235, 240, (Statute of Quo Warranto) 240; learning 115, 119, 123–4, 214, 215–16, 217–18, 319, 320; literature 132, 265–6; map 226; Norman Conquest 51, 149; papal relations 151, 206–8, 234, 305–6, 314–15; Parliament 237–41, 318; Peasants' Revolt 313; population 5, 297; Scots wars 241–2, 303–4, 305; slavery 10–11; taxation 235, 238, 239, 305–6, 308, 314–15; towns 187, 188; villages and land holdings 181–2; and Wales 47, 207, 208, 241, 304; *see also individual rulers and towns*

Enlightenment 134, 156

entertainments 132, 137, 209, 229, 269

environment, Mediterranean 20–22

Epte, River 176

Ereghli, battle of 108

escheat (reversion of fief to lord) 16

espionage, Byzantine 280–81

Estonia 246

Esztergom, archbishopric of 75
Etienne Garlande, chancellor of
    France 157
Eudes II, count of Blois-Champagne
    60–61
Eulogius (martyr of Cordoba) 162
evangelical movement *see* friars
Evesham, battle of 238
excommunication 2, 27, 127, 204,
    209, 211; pope's and patriarch's
    reciprocal 30–31, 104
experimentation, scientific 218

fables 132–3
Faeroes 40
fairs 61, 186, 257
falconry 20, 250
Falkirk, battle of 242
family size 8
famine 8; as divine punishment 295,
    302, 309; Great, 14th-century
    290–95, 305, 309, 310, 322, (in
    British Isles) 304, 307, (papacy
    and) 314, 318, (scapegoats) 300
farmers, free 25, 183–4
Fatimids of Egypt 173–4
fealty 14, 60, 170
feast days 86, 267–70
Fécamp, abbey of 58
feudalism 15, 25, 134, 147, 170;
    king's revenues from 159, 234–5
feuds 29, 41, 47, 50
fiefs 15–16, 298
filioque controversy 31, 170
Finland 247
fish aspic 268–9
fishing: in mill-ponds 62, 292; river
    and sea 20, 38, 56, 246, 273, 292,
    293
fishmongers and fishwives 185, 186
flagellants 300
Flanders 59–60, 289–90, 310–13;
    counts' power 60, 64, 187,
310–11; crusading movement 105;
    and England 290, 305, 313; famine
    294, 310; and France 303, 304–5,
    310, 311, 312; imperial and French
    59–60; land reclamation 59;
    languages 59–60, 129–30, 272;
    maps 39, 144; Peasant Revolt
    310–13; plague 296; towns 59, 68,
    187, 311; trade 59, 186, 290, 305,
    313; van Artevelde regime 310,
    313
flax cultivation 62, 291
Flemish language 59–60, 129–30, 272
fleur-de-lys 157
Florence 29, 168, 296, 313
Florian, feast of St 267
food supply 8, 185; *see also* famine
forests 9, 62, 184, 234
formariage 12
Fortune, steppe peoples and 74
foundling hospitals 192
fowling 20
France 24–7, 52–65, 156–60,
    226–33; and Aragon 275, 281–2,
    306, 309; architecture 138–40,
    141, 259–60, Figs. 2, 3, 5, 7, 8, 10,
    11, 14–16, 18; aristocracy 13, 18,
    103, 182, (and kings) 52–3, 56,
    60–61, 61–2, 64, 147, 157, 231,
    (rivalries) 25, 56, 61–3, (*see also*
    individual names); famine 290, 291,
    309; farming 62; fragmentation 52,
    53, 56, 60, 61–3, 66; Francia,
    concept of 53; geographical extent
    53, 68, 228, 229–30; governance
    and administration 27, 52–3, 64,
    69, 159, 226, 229–30,
    (investigation) 232, 273; heresy
    160, 199–201, 203–5, 209, 229,
    230–31, 233; identity 53, 230,
    232; Jews 25, 55, 62, 172, 229,
    231, (expulsions) 230, 309, 317,
    (massacres) 105, 159, 309; kings

54, 63–5, (authority) 60, 145–6,
147, 156, (coronation ceremonial)
54–5, 63, (co-rulers) 55, 63, 64,
155, (domain) 54, 157, 159, 160,
(emblem of unity) 230, (sanctity)
54, 156, 157, (*see also individual
kings*); knighthood 13; late
Carolingian period 53; law 226,
229, 308; learning 115, 116–18;
literature 130–2, 133–6, 136–7;
maps 53, 226; Paris as capital 226,
228, 229; plague 296; population
5; rebellions, popular 309–10,
313; regional diversity 229;
Romance dialects 22; Scots alliance
242, 305; southern 24–7, (*see also*
Languedoc); taxation 159, 308;
towns 18, 62, 56, 187; villages and
land holdings 181–2; *see also
individual kings, regions and
towns and under* England;
Flanders; papacy
Francis of Assisi, St 201–3, 223, 324
Franciscan order 19, 201–3, 219–20,
223, 232, 277; Observants 321–2;
scholarship 217, 218, 219–20,
319–20; Third Order 203, 322;
women, Poor Clares 203, 307
Frankfurt 257
Frederick I Barbarossa, Holy Roman
emperor 146–8, 155, 167, 174,
250, 256
Frederick II, Holy Roman emperor
195–6, 250–52, 262, 276–9, 284;
minority 195–6; Otto of
Brunswick's rival claim 196, 209,
250; and papacy 195–6, 209, 211,
251–2, 276, 277
Frederick of Austria, Holy Roman
emperor 303
Frederick of Staufen, duke of Swabia
146
freemanship 190

French language 170, 226
frescos 139, 262
Fréteval, battle of 176, 226
friars 19, 201–3, 205, 219, 255, 277;
lay adherents 203, 322; learning
115, 217, 218, 219–20, 221,
319–20; poverty 201, 219–20,
223, 225; *see also* Dominican
order; Franciscan order
Frisia, Hospitallers in 173
fruit growing 183, 189, 291
Fuero Real (Castilian legal text) 272
Fulbert, bishop of Chartres 60
Fulbert, canon of Paris 117
Fulcher of Chartres 110
Fulda monastic library 116
Fulk of Anjou, king of Jerusalem 171
Fulk Nerra, count of Anjou 57
funerals 191

Gaeta 32, 36
Galen, texts attributed to 125
Gallo-Roman people 25
Garde Frainet, Provence 24–5
Gascony 228, 241, 305
Gaveston, Piers 307
Genoa 27, 28–9, 32, 34, 169, 273
Geoffrey Martel, count of Anjou 57
Geoffroy, count of Anjou (husband
of Empress Matilda) 152
Germany 66–73, 143–8, 246–7,
250–52, 257–8; agriculture 68;
aristocracy 69, 71–3, 87–8, 143,
145–6, 146–7, 258; art and
architecture 261–2, 263; civic
regression, 14th-century 303; civil
wars and unrest 66, 92, 146, 247,
257, 322; expansion 68, 143, 147,
246, 283, 303; extent of emperor's
rule 68; Hanse 246; and Hungary
52, 75, 78, 143; land holdings 68,
145; learning 116, 119; literature
136; maps 67, 144, 244; marcher

Germany – *cont.*
  regions 68; *ministeriales* 143, 145,
    192, 264; monasticism 77, 94; and
    Mongol invasion 253; Ottokar II
    of Bohemia and 256, 257; and
    paganism 66, 246; and papacy
    209, 211, 161, (*see also* Investiture
    Controversy); particularism 52–3,
    143, 145–6, 250; and Poland 52,
    71, 73, 92–3, 254; population 5,
    68; towns 17, 68; *see also* emperor,
    Holy Roman *and individual rulers*
Geza, Grand Prince of Hungary 75
Ghent 59, 311, 313
Ghibellines 276, 322
gift-giving 269–70
Gisela, queen of Hungary 75
glass: Gothic window- 139, 140, 141,
    260, 262; Venetian industry 28
Glossa Ordinaria 117
Godfrey, duke of Lorraine 87–8
Godfrey of Bouillon, ruler of
    Jerusalem 110, 169
Godwin, earl of Wessex 50, 51, 149
Golden Bull (Hungary, 1222) 255
Golden Spurs, battle of the 304–5
Gorze, abbey of 77, 94
Goslar 88
Gothic style 259–63, Figs. 14–25;
    classical models 262, 263;
    dissemination 327; painting
    262–3, Figs. 21–3, 25; regional
    styles 260–63, 327, Figs. 17, 19,
    20, 24; *see also under* architecture;
    sculpture
Gotland 44, 247
Gottschalk (leader in Peasants'
    Crusade) 105
governance, institutions of: consular
    188, 229; Scandinavian 41, 42, 43,
    245; *see also* cortes; councils,
    royal; parliaments; *and under*
    England; France

Grail legends 136, 137
grain: cultivation 59, 61, 62, 169,
    183; in Great Famine 291, 294;
    trade 42, 169, 246, 294, 313
Granada 166–7, 271
Gratian; *Concordance of Discordant
    Canons* (*Decretum*) 116, 127–8
Greece, Fourth Crusade and 199
Greek culture in Italy 35, 36, 37
Greek language: ancient 113, 120,
    121, 163, 213, 215; Biblical 218;
    medieval, in southern Italy 35
Greenland 38, 39–40, 41, 296
Gregory VII, Pope 1–2, 87, 91–3, 94,
    103; and lay investiture 1–2, 87,
    88, 90, 91–3
Gregory X, Pope 248
Grosseteste, Robert, bishop of
    Lincoln 214, 225
Gruffydd ap Llywelyn (Welsh leader)
    48
Guelphs 276, 322
guerrae (internecine violence) 103
Guido of Velate, archbishop of Milan
    90
guilds 17, 141, 186
Guilermo of Volpiano 58
Guillaume de Lorris 136
Guillaume de Saint-Amour 220
Guiscard, Robert 36
guns and gunpowder 314, 327–8
Guy of Lusignan, king of Jerusalem
    171
Gwynedd, princes of 45
Gyula, Hungarian prince 76

Haakon IV, king of Norway 245
Haakon V, king of Norway 245
hagiography 114
Hainaut 323
hanfæstning (Danish charter of
    liberties) 247
Hanse 246

Harald Fairhair, king of Norway 40
harbours, silting-up of
    Mediterranean 20
Harold Godwinson, king of the
    English 51, 149
hasidim (pious Jews) 107
Haskins, Charles Homer 83
Hastings, battle of 149
Hâttîn, battle of 174, 175
Havelock the Dane 265–6
haywards 184
heads, severed, as trophies of war
    166
healing cults 190
Hebrew language 120, 121, 132–3,
    213, 216, 218
Hebrides 45
hell, representations of 327
Heloise 117–18
Henry II, Holy Roman emperor 71,
    73, 89
Henry III, Holy Roman emperor 30,
    85, 87–8, 89–90
Henry IV, Holy Roman emperor
    87–8, 98, 105; and Investiture
    Controversy 87, 90, 91–3, 97, 98,
    105
Henry V, Holy Roman emperor 87,
    98–9, 146, 152
Henry VI, Holy Roman emperor 146,
    195–6
Henry I, king of England 151–2
Henry II, king of England 152–6,
    158, 159, 174; invention of
    common law 149, 152–4, 155
Henry III, king of England 234–41;
    and Magna Carta 234–5, 236,
    237; and Parliament 237–41; trial
    by jury developed under 236–7
Henry I, king of France 54, 59, 61,
    63–4
Henry IV, prince of Silesia 269
Henry the Lion, duke of Saxony 147

heraldry 261, 269
heresy 170, 318, 321; burnings 55,
    230–31, 324; in France 55, 160,
    199–201, 203–5, 229, 230–31; *see
    also* Cathars
heroic ethos 131, 132
Hildebrand *see* Gregory VII, Pope
Hildegard of Bingen 124
Hippocratic texts 125
historiography 115, 121, 130, 140,
    226, 290
hoarding 310
Hohenstaufen dynasty 146; and
    papacy 147–8, 155, 195–6, 211,
    250–52, 276, 277–8; *see also
    individual rulers and under* Sicily
Holy Land 30, 59, 137, 170; *see also*
    Jerusalem
homage 14, 170
Honorius III, Pope 234
honour 16, 41–2, 54
horses 9, 74, 292, 293, 294;
    improved collar 9, 10
horticulture 21–2, 23–4, 189–90
Hospitallers 111–12, 173, 175, 250,
    317, 318
hospitals 17, 111, 192
hostels, pilgrim 77, 137
Hruodland (Roland) 130, 131
Hugh, Abbot of Cluny 1
Hugh Capet, king of France 54, 55
Hugh of St-Victor 117
Huguccio (canonist) 128
Humiliati 199, 200
humiliation, public 211, 230, 231
humoral theory 125
Hundred Years War 308
hundreds (English administrative
    units) 49
Hungary 73–9, 255–6; aristocracy
    and Crown 255, 256; Árpádian
    dynasty 74; castles 76, 255;
    Church 74, 75, 77, 78, 255;

Hungary – *cont.*
  crusades in 77, 105–6; and
  Germany 52, 75, 78, 143; Golden
  Bull 255; government 66, 76; and
  Kiev 63; law 76–7, 78; maps 67,
  244; 'Mirrors of Princes' 76;
  Mongol invasion 253, 255;
  paganism 66, 75, 256; and
  Pechenegs 76; and Poland 76;
  population 8, 74; royal succession
  75, 77–8; unity and centralization
  78, 255–6; villages and land
  holdings 181–2; violence 66, 78;
  wine trade 268
hymns to Virgin Mary 95
Hywel the Good (Welsh leader) 47–8

Iaroslav the Wise, prince of Kiev 63
Iberia 22–3, 24, 161–7, 271–6;
  architecture 24; Black Death 296;
  castles 164, 272; Church under
  Islam 24, 161–2, 163; climate 21;
  convivencia 24; cultural
  development 271–2; ethnic groups
  24, 274, 275, 276; Franciscan
  Observants' followers 322;
  government 272–3; Hospitallers in
  173; Jews 24, 163, 164; knighthood
  164–5, 264; learning 119, 121,
  163; literature 24, 130; military
  orders 165, 173, 317, 318; Mudejar
  population 274–5; Muslim rule
  22–3, 24, 25, 163–4, 166, (see also
  Reconquista below); *pax islamica*
  163; population 5; Portuguese fight
  for independence 165–6, 272;
  Reconquista 162–7, 182, 271, 274;
  Romance dialects 22; sculpture
  263, Fig. 24; seafaring 164, 273;
  serf-knights 165, 264; settlement
  165, 182, 272; slavery 166; *taifas*
  163, 164; *see also* Aragon; Castile;
  cortes; Portugal

Ibiza 274
Ibn Rushd (Averroës) 216–17
Ibn Sina (Avicenna) 215–16
Iceland 38–43, 181, 246
Ile de France 15, 56, 259
impotentes 25
imprisonment, hard 230, 237
Imre, Hungarian prince 75, 77
incest 55, 248, 272, 273
indigo production 24
indulgences 211, 315
inflation 182, 235
Ingeborg of Denmark, queen of
  France 205, 206
inheritance: of fiefs 15–16, 298;
  ministeriales' rights 145; partible
  182; primogeniture 150, 158, 241;
  serfs' rights 12; under-age heirs 16;
  women's 16, 234, 298
Innocent III, Pope 194–212;
  background 194–5; and crusades
  196, 197, 199, 209, 283–4,
  (Albigensian) 160, 204; death 234,
  250; and England 206–8, 233,
  234; and foundling hospitals 192;
  and Fourth Lateran Council
  209–11, 283–4; and France
  205–6, 208; and Frederick II
  195–6; and friars 201–3, 205; and
  heresy 160, 199–201, 203–5;
  interdicts 205, 206, 207; legacy
  211–12; *On the Misery of the
  Human Condition* (*On the
  Contempt of the World*) 194–5;
  student in Paris 194, 207, 210;
  Teutonic Knights approved by
  176; treatise on mysteries of Mass
  210
Innocent IV, Pope 251–2, 277
Inquisition 230–31, 233, 322
interdiction 27, 205, 206, 207, 234,
  272
internecine violence 103

Investiture Controversy 73, 85–99; Alexander II and 88, 90; Anselm of Canterbury and 151; background 85–8; English attitude to 49, 151; Germany and 69, 92, 143; Gregory VII and 1–2, 90, 91; Henry IV and 87, 97, 98–9, 105; learning stimulated by 113, 127; and Milan 88–91; Nicholas II and 88; Scandinavian reaction 248; Urban II and 97, 98; Victor III and 97–8; violence over 89, 90–91, 93, 97

Ireland 38, 41, 45, 46–7, 304; map 39

Irnerius, Master 127

iron tools 9

irrigation 21–2

Isaac, martyr of Cordoba 161

Isabelle of France, queen of England 306, 307–8

Islam and Muslims: Avicenna reconciles Greek philosophy with 215, 216; Balearic Islands ruled by 25, 34, 274; conversions to 23, 164; and Corsica 33; and Crusader States 171, 280; decline of power begun 79; Genoese and Pisan war against 28, 29, 32, 34; Hospitallers and 111; in Iberia 21–2, 22–3, 24, 25, 161–7; internal strife 171; and Jerusalem 102–3, 250, 284; and Jews 23, 24, 163, 285; medicine 111, 125, 215; merchants 197; metaphysics 216; Otto II defeated by 70; as pagans 102; and papacy 189; piracy 24–5, 33, 169; in Sardinia 29, 34; sexual relations with Christians 275; and Sicily 35, 36, 37, 161, 169; and urban culture 23

Italy 27–30, 31–2, 167–9, 250–52, 276–79; aristocracies 35, 85, 182; art and architecture 32, 138, 141–2, 262, 263, Figs. 1, 6, 20; castles 29; crusading movement 105, 175; emperors' power 66, 69, 70, 88, 143, 168, 187, (Frederick I Barbarossa) 147–8, 167, 250–52, (Frederick II) 276–9; English whores 192; friars 277; Guelph/Ghibelline warfare 276, 322; islands of 32–7; learning 118–19; literature 168; Lombard lords 35–6; map 67; population 5, 187; Romance dialects 22; silk production 24; simony 85; slavery 168; southern see Sicily and southern Italy; towns of northern 18, 23, 27–9, 167–9, 186, (and emperor) 147–8, 167, 168, 187, (leagues) 168; trade 31–2, 37, 168, 186–7; wetnursing 190–91; see also individual states and papacy

Jacquerie 313

James I the Conqueror, king of Aragon 274–6, 278

Jean de Meun 136

Jerusalem 102, 103, 169, Fig. 12; First Crusade captures 98, 110, 112; Crusader State 110, 169–70, 250, 279; Saladin captures 148, 174, 196; Frederick II negotiates return to Christians 250, 284; pilgrimage to 57, 59, 77, 102, 137

Jews: of Acre 285; administrators 145; Avicebron 216; Christian clergy protect 106, 172; crusades and 105, 106–7, 159, 172; expulsions 230, 235, 309, 317; Fourth Lateran Council and 211; guilds exclude 186; hasidim 107; Hospitallers and 111; humiliating treatment 211, 230; and Islam 23, 24, 163, 285; Khazar conversion to Judaism 76; learning 117, 119,

Jews – *cont.*
120; literature 106–7, 132–3;
liturgy 106–7; massacres 159, 174,
309; moneylending 192, 230, 238;
as scapegoats 295, 300; scholars of
St-Victor consult 117, 120;
scholastic view of 222–3, 225;
sexual relations with Christians
275; translators 163, 213, 215; *see
also under* England; France; Iberia;
Sicily
Joachim of Fiore 202
John, king of England 159–60;
accession 233; and barons 207,
208, 209, 233–4; and Innocent III
206–8, 234; Magna Carta 208,
233–4; and Philip II of France 175,
176, 205–6, 208, 228, 233; wife
205–6, 234
John XVIII, Pope 34
John XXII, Pope 321–5
John of Jerusalem, Order of
St (Hospitallers) 111–12, 173,
175, 250, 317, 318
John of Salisbury 117, 155
jongleurs 133
journeymen 186
jousting 132, 209, 229, 269
jubilee year, first papal (1300)
315
juries, English 153–4, 236–7; grand
152–3, 236
justice 13–14; barons and 13–14;
church courts 154–5, 156;
clergymen as judges 189;
compensation 50; English 49–50,
150, 151, 152–4, 235, 236–7; fees
for 235; serfs' right to 11; students'
immunities 118; violence as means
of restoring 302; *see also* juries;
ordeal, trial by
Justinian, plague of 295
Justinianic corpus 121, 126–7

Khazars 76
Kiev, principality of 63, 252, 269
kings and kingship: acclamation 55;
advisers' distancing from people
302–3; anointing 49, 54, 85–6, 99,
156; authority increases in France
60, 145–6, 147, 156, 230;
constitutionalism 148–9, 235; co-
rulers, anticipatory succession 55,
63, 64, 155, 156, 158; elective
146; feudal rights and revenues
234–5; ideology of, and just war
100; king's peace 50; lay nature of
authority 86–7, 99; liturgical 86;
Louis IX's Christian ideal of 231;
miracles 54, 156–7; and papacy
55, 305–6, 314–18, (*see also*
Investiture Controversy); and
parliaments 237–41; sanctity 156,
157, 230; petitions to 239–40;
theology of 85–7; theory of
traditional 306; *see also individual
dynasties and kingdoms*
Knight of Courtesy, The 266
knights and knighthood 13, 14,
164–5, 170, 264–5; idealized 13,
135, 137; serfs with power of 143,
145, 165, 192, 264
Koppány (Hungarian leader) 75
Krakow 188, 252, 267

La Grande Chartreuse 95
labour: agricultural 23–4, 182–3,
298–9; artisans 17; ban on Sunday
19; Black Death affects status
298–9; slavery 10–11;
specialization 8, 9, 17, 23–4,
182–3; in towns 17, 191, 192
labour services 12
Labrador 38
Ladislas I, king of Hungary 78
Ladislas IV, king of Hungary 256
lais 132–3, 135

laisses 130

Lance, Holy 109

land 15–16, 181–2; allods 15, 145, 181; church 69, 182; confiscation 69, 76, 147; in Hungary 76; marginal 289, 299; ownership 15–16, 17, 145, 181–2, (transfer of) 15–16, 182; reclamation 59, 68, 189

Landnámabók (Book of Settlements, Icelandic) 38

Lanfranc, archbishop of Canterbury 150

Langton, Stephen, archbishop of Canterbury 207, 208, 209, 210, 234

languages: increasing use of vernacular 129–30, 298, (*see also* literature, vernacular *and individual languages*)

Languedoc 23, 24–7, 183, 228, 229, 322; heresy 199–201, 203–5, 209, 229, 230–31; under Louis IX 232, 275

Las Navas de Tolosa, battle of 166, 274

Lateran Council, Fourth 19, 208–11, 236, 247, 283–4; implementation of canons 211–12, 247, 248

Latin language 22; Church use 31, 129; classical literature 113; poetry 114–15; translations, (of Arabic and Hebrew texts) 116, 125, 213, (of Greek texts) 113, 120, 121, 163, 213, 215

laudes regiae 86

lavender, culinary use of 268

law: academic studies of 115, 119, 126–8; canon 116, 127–8; Castilian 272; Icelandic 42; and labour crisis in Black Death 299; notaries and municipal 188–9; Roman 22, 121, 126–7, 188, 229,

272; Welsh 48; *see also under* England; France; Hungary

lay preaching 200

leagues of towns 168, 290

learning 113–28, 213–25; at aristocratic courts 119, 120–21; Aristotelian 121–2, 213–15, 216–17, 221, 320; bishops and 214, 225; and classical culture 113; curriculum and scholarship 121–8; dialectic 122–3, 218; dissemination of ideas 115–16, 118; friars and 115, 217, 218, 219–20, 221, 319–20; institutional setting 115–21; Investiture Controversy as stimulus 113, 127; Jewish 117, 119, 120; law 115, 119, 126–8; medicine 119, 124–6; monastic 115–16, 119, 120; women 119–20; *see also* philosophy; schools; universities

leather 184, 292

Lebanon, Maronites of 170

Lechfeld, battle of the 73–4

Leo IX, Pope 1, 30, 36, 85, 87

Léon, cathedral of 260

lepers 181, 191, 295, 300

lewdness in painting 263, Fig. 25

libraries 116, 121

life and limbs, writ of 235

lighting, artificial 139

Lille 305

Limoges, Council of 26

linen textiles 62, 291

Lisbon 165, 272, 273

literature, vernacular 15, 121, 129–37; audience 136–7; Castilian 130, 271–2; *chanson de geste* 130–32, 136; classical influence 114–15; courtly love 134–5; fables 132–3; Flanders 272; poetry 132–3, 133–5, 168; romance 134, 135–7, 264–6; stylistic innovation

literature – *cont.*
114–15; women's contribution
120, 132, 133; *see also under*
France; Germany; Italy
liturgy: Christian 19, 31, 101–2, 170;
Jewish 106–7
Livonia 249, 254
Llewelyn ap Gruffudd 241
logic 121, 122, 213, 214, 218, 222
Lögrétta (Icelandic law-making body)
42
Loire valley 62
Lombard, Peter; *Sentences* 116, 218
Lombards in Italy 23, 35–6, 168
London 187, 188, 235, 294;
Westminster Abbey 237, 260, Fig.
17
lords *see* aristocracies
Lorraine 87–8
Lothar III, Holy Roman emperor 146
Louis VI, king of France 64–5, 140,
157
Louis VII, king of France 140, 154,
155, 157–8, 172
Louis VIII, king of France 228–9
Louis IX, king of France (St Louis)
179, 229–32; advisers 214, 218;
and beguines 323; canonization
232, 306; crusades, (1248–54)
214, 231–2, 251, 284–5, (1270)
231, 232, 241, 279; death 241,
279; and England 231, 234, 237,
238; and friars 219, 220, 221; and
heresy 230–31; investigates
complaints 232, 273; and Jews
230, 231; kingship, ideal of 231;
Languedocian loyalty to 232, 275;
Psalter of Fig. 21; and Sicilian
succession 278; widow of 282
Louis X, king of France 307
loyalty 25, 60, 108, 264–5
Lübeck 187, 246
Lucca 23–4

Ludwig IV of Bavaria, Holy Roman
emperor 303, 321
Lund, archbishopric of 246
Lyons 251; First Council of 248, 251;
Second Council of 280

Macbeth, king of Scotland 47
Mâcon, counts of 61
Magdeburg 97
Magna Carta 208, 209, 233–4,
234–5, 238; confirmation 234–5,
236, 237, 239
Magnus I Ladulås, king of Sweden
248–9
Magnus VI Law Mender, king of
Norway 245
Magyars 73–9; *see also* Hungary
Al-Mahdiya 29, 32
Maimonides (Moses ben Maimon)
120, 164, 222
Maine 59, 147, 150, 152, 158, 278
Mainz 106
Majorca 274, 276
Malaspina family 33
Malcolm III, king of Scotland 47
maledictions, liturgical 26–7
Mamelukes 285
Man, Isle of 45, 46
Manfred, son of Emperor Frederick II
278
manumission 11, 182
manuscripts, illuminated 141, 262,
263, Figs. 21–3, 25
Manx people 45
Marcabru, *pastourelles* by 133
marcher regions 14; German 68, 72;
Welsh 241
Margaret of Antioch, *Life* of St 134
Marie de France 132, 133
markets 8, 17, 49
Markward of Anweiler 146, 204
Maronites 170
marriage: Alfonso III's as bigamous

and incestuous 272, 273;
ceremonies 14; clerical 85, 90, 91,
248; dynastic 57, 63, 70;
formariage 12; Fourth Lateran
Council on 211; heiresses' 16, 234;
serfs' 12, 134
Marseilles 25, 187, 278
marshlands, exploitation of 183, 189
Martin IV, Pope 282
martyrs 71, 104, 106–7, 161–2
Marxist interpretation of feudalism
15
Mary, Blessed Virgin *see* Virgin, cult
of
Massa, William, marquis of 33
mathematics 217
Matilda, Empress, queen of England
152
Matilda of Tuscany, duchess of
Bavaria 98
May, Isle of 45
mayors 185
meat in diet 292, 293–4
Meaux-Paris, treaty of 228
medicine 115, 124–6, 190; Arabic
125, 215; nursing of pilgrims 111;
and plague 296; Salerno institution
124–5; in universities 119, 125;
women's contribution 120, 124,
125
mediocres 25
Mediterranean Europe 20–37,
271–85; *see also individual states
and regions*
mêlées 132
Meles of Bari 35
Melisende, queen of Jerusalem 171
mercenaries 35, 44, 264
merchants 18, 186, 192, 203
Messina 35, 167, 187
metalworking 62, 141, 185, Fig. 9
metaphysics 213, 216, 224
Metz 106, 327

Michael Paleologus, Byzantine
emperor 279, 280–81
midwives 190
Mieszko I, ruler of Poland 69, 70, 71
Milan 88–91, 168
military orders 111–12, 189, 192,
249–50, 317; Iberian 165, 317,
318; *see also* Hospitallers;
Templars, Knights; Teutonic
Knights
military states 249, 254
militias, urban 164, 304
millenarianism 102, 134
mills 62, 184–5, 292
mining 68, 184, 257
ministeriales 143, 145, 146, 192, 264
Minorca 274
mints 17, 43
miracle plays 48
miracles 26, 54, 55, 95, 109, 137,
114
'Mirrors of Princes' 76
Moissac, church of Fig. 2
monasticism: architecture 141;
aristocratic patronage 72, 103,
141; asceticism and austerity 94,
96, 201–2; Cluniac influence 1, 55,
58, 94; expansion 93–7; Fourth
Lateran Council and 211; in
Hungary 77; lay workers and
adherents 95–6, 97, 190, 203, 322;
learning 115–16, 119, 120;
libraries 116; new orders 94–7,
115, 211; nunneries 94, 96–7, 120;
plague and 297; plundering by
Norsemen 45, 46; prayers for dead
191; serfs barred from 12; *see also*
friars; military orders; *and*
Benedictine, Carthusian, Cistercian
and Premonstratensian orders
moneylending 192, 193, 230, 238
Mongol invasions 252–4, 255, 258,
267

Montecassino, abbey of 97, 220
Montfort, Simon de, the Elder 197, 209, 228
Montfort, Simon de, the Younger 238–9
Montpellier 275; university of 119, 229
morality 191, 218, 300; moral economy 310
Morosaglia, Council of 33
mortality 8, 294
Mortimer, Roger, 1st Earl of March 306, 307
Moses ben Maimon (Maimonides) 120, 164, 222
mountain environment 21, 22
mourners, professional 191
Mudejars 274–5
Munich; Franciscan convent 322
Munster, Ireland 46
Murcia 275
murder fine 150
murrain (animal pestilences) 293
Musat, Muslim chieftain of Sardinia 34
mysticism 224, 322–5

Nantes 57
Naples, duchy of 35
Narbonne 25
nationalism 308
Navarre 22
navies 28, 29, 164, 273, 276
Neoplatonism 113
Newfoundland 38
Nibelungenlied 136
Nicea 107, 108
Nicholas II, Pope 88
Nicholas V, anti-pope 322
Nitra 106
Njal, Saga of Burnt 41–2
nominalism 122, 318–22
Norbert of Xanten, St 97

Norman kingdom in Italy and Sicily 35–7, 87
Normandy 57–9; Capetian rivalry 60, 62; co-rulers 55; dukes' power 14, 60; and England 50, 51, 58, 149, 152, 158; French annexation 147, 160, 206, 228; Great Famine 291; Odo Rigaud as member of high court 218; plague 297; population 297
Norsemen: and British Isles 44, 45–6, 46–7; in Iceland 38–43
North Sea islands 246
Northern Europe 38–51; see also individual countries
Norway 43–4, 243, 245–6; Church 42, 43–4, 248; Danish rule in south 43, 44; Greenland trade 296; and Iceland 38, 42, 43, 246; Kievan marriage alliance 63; maps 39, 244; plague 296, 297; population 8, 297; trade 42, 296; see also Norsemen; Scandinavia
Norwich, bishop of 206, 207
notaries 188–9, 229
Novgorod 253
nunneries 94, 96–7, 120
Nūr al-Dīn 172, 173, 174
nuraghi (Sardinian defensive structures) 34
nutrition 8, 299

Occitanians 275
occupations 181, 182–7, 188–9, 189–91
Ockham, William of 319, 320–22
Odilo, abbot of Cluny 77
Odo Rigaud, archbishop of Rouen 218–19, 223, 225
Olaf II Haraldson, king of Norway 43
Olaf Tryggvason, king of Norway 42
olives and olive oil 22, 183

Olof Eriksson, king of Sweden 44
ontology 122–3, 123–4, 215–16,
    319
optics 217
Orange 25
ordeal, trial by 152–3, 154, 210–11,
    236–7, 247
order, keeping of 185, 187, 189
order states 249, 254
oriflamme 140
Origny, nuns of 131
Orkney 45, 46
Orkneyinga Saga 45–6
orphans 111, 186
Orseolo, Peter, king of Hungary 78
Orseolo, Pietro II, Doge of Venice 28
Oslo 246
Ostmark 68
Otto I the Great, Holy Roman
    emperor 68, 69, 70, 73–4
Otto II, Holy Roman emperor 70
Otto III, Holy Roman emperor
    70–71, 73
Otto of Brunswick 196, 208, 209, 250
Otto-Guillaume, count of Mâcon 61
Ottokar II, king of Bohemia 256, 257
Ottonian dynasty 66, 69, 70, 88–91;
    see also individual members
outlawry 153
oxen 9, 292, 292, 293, 294
Oxford, university of 119, 214, 319,
    320

paganism 19; Baltic and Slavic 66,
    73, 79, 246, 249; Islam seen as
    102; *see also under* Hungary;
    Poland; Scandinavia; Sweden
painting *see* frescos; manuscripts,
    illuminated
palaces 70, 184
Palermo 188, 281
papacy 29–30, 189; administration
    189; anti-popes 97, 98, 148, 322;

Avignon 316, 318, 321, 322;
    college of cardinals 88; and
    Crusader States 189, 196;
    diplomacy 189; elections 88, 91;
    and France 55, 157, 205–6, 208,
    281–2, 305–6, 314–16; and Greek
    church 30–31, 104, 197; and
    Hohenstaufens, (in Sicily) 237,
    238, 250, 277–8, (*see also under*
    emperor, Holy Roman);
    interdiction of states 205, 206,
    207, 234, 272; and Italian cities'
    independence 167; Italian families'
    influence 79; and military orders
    189; and kings 55, 305–6,
    314–18, (*see also* Investiture
    Controversy); moral authority
    declines 318, 322; and Normans in
    Italy 35, 87; patrimony of St Peter
    195; reforming popes 30, (*see also*
    Gregory VII; Leo IX; Urban II);
    taxing of churches in famine 314;
    warfare 87; *see also* emperor, Holy
    Roman (and papacy); Investiture
    Controversy; *and individual popes*
Paraclete, monastery of, Champagne
    117–18
Paris: Breton community 192; capital
    city 226, 228, 229; Châtelet 309;
    church building 141, 259, Figs. 10,
    14; expansion 226; in Great
    Famine 294; kings and 141, 187;
    Marais district 189; Notre Dame,
    cathedral of Fig. 10; Parlement of
    239; plague 296; population 187;
    royal administration 188, 226;
    Saint-Denis, abbey of 115,
    139–40, 226; Sainte-Chapelle 259,
    Fig. 14; schools 117, 194, 226; St-
    Victor, Abbey of 116, 117, 120;
    trade 62; treaty of (1259) 238;
    university and schools 119, 213,
    219–20, 221, 226, (Innocent III at)

Paris – *cont.*
194, 207, 210, (other scholars)
117, 214, 215, 218, 221, 223, 319;
walls 226, 228
Parlement of Paris 239
parliaments: Danehof 247; English
237–41, 318; *see also* cortes; Paris
(Parlement of)
parody, literary 135
pastoureaux, rebellion of 309–10
pastourelles 133–4
pasturage 21, 62, 183
patarini (Milanese reform party) 90,
91, 93
patronage 136–7, 141–2, 203
Paul, St 121
Pavia 89
pawnbroking 230
pax islamica 163
peace, king's, in England 50
Peace of God movement 25–7, 52,
93–4, 102, 187; aristocratic
support 25, 26, 55, 103; similar
movement in Corsica 33
Peasant Revolt, Flemish 310–13
peasants: 14th-century problems 289,
294, 298–9; free 10, 12, 25, 183–4,
299; lifestyle 266; rebellions,
274–5, 289, 310–13; Spanish
peasant-knights 165, 264; *see also*
serfs
Peasants' Crusade 105–8
Pechenegs 76
peine forte et dure 237
penance, public 155, 231, 300
'perfect', Cathar 200
Peter, St 109
Peter III, king of Aragon 278, 281,
282
Peter the Chanter, Master 210
Peter Damian, Cardinal 87
Peter the Hermit 105, 107
Peter Lombard; *Sentences* 116, 218

petitions to king 239–40
Philip I, king of France 54, 63, 64,
157
Philip II Augustus, king of France
147, 158–60, 229; and English
kings, (Richard I) 156, 175, 176,
226, 233, (John) 159–60, 175,
176, 205–6, 208, 228; marriages
205, 206; on Third Crusade 159,
174, 175
Philip III the Bold, king of France
232–3, 241, 279, 281
Philip IV the Fair, king of France
232, 233, 282, 307; and England
305–6, 314–15; expels Jews 317;
and papacy 281–2, 305–6,
314–16, 319; suppression of
Knights Templars 316–18
Philip V, king of France 307, 309
Philip VI, king of France 307
Philip of Swabia 196
philosophy: Bacon on 217; church's
attitude to 113–14, 214, 225;
classical 113–14, 121–2, 124,
213–15, 224, (*see also* Aristotle);
main proponents of high
scholasticism 215–24; and
medicine 124; metaphysics 213,
216, 224; and theology 121–4; in
universities 119
physicians 111, 190
pig keeping 183, 292, 293
pigeons 292
pilgrimage 137, 138; to Canterbury
137, 155, 158; to Holy Land 57,
59, 77, 102, 137, 170; hostels and
hospitals 77, 111, 137; to Rome
30, 77, 137
piracy 42, 45–6, 56, 290, 302, 310;
in Mediterranean 25, 28, 29, 33,
164
Pisa 27, 28, 29, 32, 35, 169; war
against Muslims 29, 32, 34

Pisano, Nicola and Giovanni 262
Pistoia; San Bartolomeo in Pantano
    Fig. 1
plague 295–301, 322; cycle 296,
    297, 299–300, 300–301
Plantagenet lands in France 147,
    159–60, 175, 176, 205–6, 228,
    233
Plato 113–14, 224; *Timaeus* 113–14,
    124
plough, heavy 9–10
pluralism, clerical 298
poaching 289, 294
poetry: *chanson de geste* 130–32,
    136; Germanic languages 136;
    Hebrew 106–7, 216; Italian
    patriotic pieces 168; *laisses* 130;
    Latin 114–15; lyrical and love 132,
    133–5; Muslim influence on
    Spanish 24; peasant maidens in
    183; rhyming techniques 114–15,
    130; by women 120, 132, 133
Poitiers, council of 26
Poitou 13, 57, 152, 158, 208, 237
Poland 69–70, 92–3, 254–5,
    267–70; architecture 254, 267;
    aristocracy 254, 267–70; Baltic
    possessions 250, 303; Bohemian
    control 255, 257; Boleslaw I
    founds kingdom 73; Church 70,
    71, 73, 254; and Denmark 267,
    303; and Germany 52, 71, 73,
    92–3, 268–70, 254, 303; Great
    Poland 254, 255; and Hungary 76;
    and Kiev 63; lifestyle 267–70;
    Little Poland 252, 254, 255; maps
    67, 244; Mongol invasions 252,
    253, 254, 267; paganism 73;
    plague 296; population 8; serfs
    254, 255, 258, 267–8; villages and
    land holdings 181–2
Pomerania 250
Poor Clares 203, 307

popular culture 137
popular movements: millennarian
    and apocalyptic 102; and reform
    93–7, 112, 314; *see also* Peace of
    God movement
population 68, 74, 243, 289, 297;
    increase during period 5, 8–10;
    urban 17, 187
Porete, Marguerite 323–4
pork 293–4
Portugal 5, 165–6, 272–3, 318; *see
    also* Iberia
potentes 25
poverty 191–2; friars and 201,
    219–20, 223, 225
Prague 106, 173, 256–7
Premonstratensian order 94, 97
Prémontré, monastery of 97
Premyslide dynasty of Bohemia 256
price controls 294
priesthood 12, 185, 211
prison forte et dure 230, 237
prose romances 136, 264–6
prostitution 191, 192, 214
Provençal language 133, 229
Provence 24–7, 275, 278, 279, 322
provosts 18, 64, 159
Prussia 71, 249, 254
purgatory 211, 219
Pyrenees 21, 22, 181, 183, 275

quadrivium 119
Quo warranto, English Statute of 240
Qur'an, Latin translation of 116

rabbits 292
Rainulf (Norman mercenary leader)
    35
Rambam *see* Maimonides
ransom of captives 14, 171, 174,
    231, 285
Raoul de Cambrai, Song of 15, 131
Rashi (Rabbi Solomon ben Isaac) 120

Raymond VI, count of Toulouse 203–4, 209
Raymond VII, count of Toulouse 228
Raymond of Saint-Gilles 110
rebellions, popular 78, 289, 302, 309–13
recession, 14th-century economic 289–90, 308
record-keeping 184, 226
reeves 18, 49, 184
reform see under Church
Reformation 221
Regensburg 106
Reims, cathedral of 54, 55
relics 30, 102, 137, 199, 211, 259; Holy Lance 109; Peace of God movement uses 25, 26, 27
relief (feudal payment) 16, 234–5
reliquaries 141, 199, Fig. 9
'Renaissance of twelfth century' 83
rents 182, 289
representation, popular 238, 239, 273
Rhineland 17, 68, 106–7, 187, 323; see also individual towns
Richard, earl of Cornwall 284
Richard I the Lionhearted, king of England: accession 159; castle-building 176; as crusader 148, 156, 159, 174, 175; and Philip II of France 156, 175, 176, 226, 233; return from crusade and death 159, 175, 176, 233
Richard II, duke of Normandy 57–8
Richard of Cornwall 257
Richard of St-Victor 117, 123
Rigaud, Odo, archbishop of Rouen 218–19, 223, 225
Rinderpest 293
Robert II the Pious, king of France 54, 55, 61
Robert I, duke of Normandy 59

Robert II, duke of Normandy 150, 151
Robert the Devil (romance) 265
Roger I, count of Sicily 36
Roger II, king of Sicily 36, 169, 195
Roland, Song of 130, 131, 157
Roman empire, heritage of 22, 23, 34–5, 70, 113, 126–7
Romance languages 22
Romance of the Rose 136
romance tradition 134, 135–7, 264–6
Romanesque style 138–9, 254, 267, Figs. 1–7
Romanticism, 19th-century 134, 202
Rome 23, 29–30, 70, 167, 279; pilgrimage to 30, 77, 137; synods 30, 88
rose windows 140, 260, Fig. 8
Rouen 58, 62, 105, 150
Rouergue, Council of 26
Rousillon 26
Rudolf of Habsburg, Holy Roman emperor 257, 258
Rumania 74; map 67
Rus' 247, 250, 252, 253, 254, 296
Russian Church 63, 75

sagas 39, 41–2, 136
Sagrajas, battle of 103
sail, lateen 31–2
St Albans, Abbey of 115
St David's, bishopric of 47–8
Saint-Denis, Abbey of 115, 139–40, 226
Saint-Pierre-le-Vif, monastery of 94
saints 109, 255, 269
Saisset, Bernard, bishop of Pamiers 315
Saladin 148, 173–5, 196
Salerno medical instition 124–5
Salian Franks, law of 308

salt 28, 74
San Millan, church of, Castile Fig. 6
Sancerre 61
Santiago, Order of 165
Sardinia 22, 29, 32, 34, 168–9
Sardo (Romance dialect) 22
Sarolt, 'The White Lady',
    Transylvanian princess 75
scalps as trophies 166
Scandinavia 38–44, 243–9;
    aristocracies 243, (and kings) 243,
    245, 247, 248; assemblies 41, 42,
    245; Black Death 296; church 19,
    42–3, 43–4, 243, 245, 247, 248;
    14th-century wars 290, 303; and
    Germany 143; Iceland settled from
    38, 43; kingship 243, 245, 247,
    248; land holdings 181; maps 39,
    244; Normans originate in 57;
    paganism 243, 245, 246;
    population 5, 8, 243; settlement
    pattern 243; social structure 243;
    trade 38, 42, 44, 245, 296; see also
    individual countries
scholasticism 121–4, 213–25; and
    medicine 125–6; proponents of
    high 215–24
schools, cathedral 116–17, 119
science, natural 217, 250
Scone, Stone of 242
Scotland 47, 241–2, 303–4, 305
scribes 184
scrofula, touching for 54, 156–7
sculpture: Byzantine bronze relief 32;
    Gothic 140, 260, 261–2, 263, Figs.
    20, 24; Romanesque 32, 138–9,
    Figs. 2, 3, 5
scutage 208, 235
seafaring 20, 31–2, 273; see also
    navies
Secret of Secrets 215
Sefer Hasidim ('Book of the Pious')
    107

seisin of property 153, 236
Sénonais region 94
Sepulchre, Holy 102, 104
serfs 11–12; Black Death and 298–9;
    central European 254, 255, 258,
    267–8; debtors become 12;
    freedom for assarting 10, 12; land
    holdings 182; manumission 11,
    182; mayors 185; ministeriales
    143, 145, 192, 264; Polish 254,
    255, 258, 267–8; rights and
    liabilities 11, 12; in Scandinavia
    243; in southern France 25
Sergius I, duke of Amalfi 32
servants, domestic 190, 192
service sector 187
settlement patterns 181–2, 243
settlements, new: in Baltic region
    182; crusaders', in Holy Land 170;
    in Hungary 255; in Iberia 165,
    182, 272; in Slavic lands 283; see
    also assarts; towns (new)
sexual relations 134, 190, 192,
    200–201, 275
sheep 292, 293
shepherdesses, idealized 133–4
Shepherds' Crusade 309–10
sheriffs 49, 151, 152
Shetlands 45
shipbuilding 33, 271
shires 49
Sicilian Vespers 281
Sicily and southern Italy 34–7; and
    Byzantine Empire 34–6; Charles of
    Anjou's rule 233, 278–9, 281;
    climate 21; economic success 169;
    environment and productivity 22;
    Greek church and culture 35, 36,
    37; Hohenstaufen dynasty 146,
    195–6, 250, 277, 281, (pope
    displaces) 233, 237, 238, 250, 278;
    Jews 35, 36–7; Muslims and 35,
    36, 37, 161, 169; Norman rule 32,

Sicily and southern Italy – *cont.*
35–7; silk cultivation 23–4;
strength of central government 23,
167; visual arts 263
siege warfare 164
Siena 262
siesta 22
Siete Partidas (Castilian legal text)
272, 273
Siger of Brabant 215
Silesia 250, 254
silk production 23–4, 169
silver mining 68, 257
simony: 1, 85, 87, 89, 90, 318
skraelings (migratory peoples of
Greenland) 39
slavery 10–11, 25, 41, 50, 243;
enslavement of captives in war
164, 166, 174; manumission 10,
11, 182; trade 28, 32, 168
Slavonic, Old Church 31
Slavs 8, 173; and Church 19, 31, 71,
249; Germans and 68, 69, 143,
147, 283; map of lands 244; *see
also individual peoples*
Slovakia 8, 74; map 67
smiths 184
soap-making 183
social structures 8–16, 181–93;
complexity 192–3; three orders
ideal 192
Solomon ben Isaac, Rabbi (Rashi)
120
Solomon Ibn Gabirol (Avicebron)
216
Spain *see* Aragon; Castile; Iberia
Speyer 106
spice trade 269
spinning 183
'Stabat Mater' (hymn) 95
state, 14th-century crisis of church
and 314–18
state formation 52–3, 146

Statute of Quo Warranto, English
240
steel production 62
Stephen, king of England 152
Stephen I, king of Hungary 74–8,
137
Stephen V, king of Hungary 256
stewards 184
Stirling Bridge, battle of 242
stockfish 246
story-telling 266, 269
Strasbourg, cathedral of 260
students 189
succession: anticipatory 55, 63, 64,
155, 156, 158; Hungarian royal
75, 77–8; James I of Aragon's
ideas on 275–6; primogeniture
150, 158, 241; Scandinavian 243,
247
Suetonius; *Lives of the Twelve
Caesars* 114
sugar cane 24
Suger, abbot of St-Denis 140, 157
suicide 106–7, 113
Sunday; ban on labour 19
suppositiones and *dignitates* 219
Sweden 43, 44, 243, 245, 247–9,
303; church 44, 243, 245, 247,
248; and Kiev 63; maps 39, 244;
paganism 44, 243, 245, 248;
population 8; trade 44, 245; *see
also* Scandinavia
Sweyn Forkbeard, king of Denmark
43
Switzerland 68, 327
Sword Brothers, Order of the 249–50
swords, doctrine of the two 101
synthesis, 13th century as age of 179
Syriac liturgy 31

Tagliacozzo, battle of 278
taifas (Iberian small kingdoms) 163,
164

tallages 12

Tancred (Norman crusader) 108–9, 110

Tancred, king of Sicily 195

tanning 184

Tarsus 109

taxation: collection 64, 185; commutation of service to cash 188; rebellions against 78, 312; in Sweden 247; in towns 190; *see also* scutage *and under* Church; England; France; papacy

technology 9, 31–2, 253, 314

Templars, Knights (Order of the Temple of Solomon) 111–12, 173, 175, 316–18

Teutonic Knights 173, 175–6, 249–50, 285, 317

textiles: beguines' production 323, 324; painting on 262; *see also* linen; silk; wool

Thanet, Isle of 45

theft 191, 192, 289, 294

theology: Bacon on 217–18, 217; nominalism 318–22; and philosophy 121–4; scientific, 'Dominican' 218–19, (attacks on) 318–22; Trinity 122, 123, 222; universities and schools 119, 194

Theophano, regent of Holy Roman Empire 70

Thibaut, count of Champagne 284

things (Scandinavian assemblies) 41, 42, 245

Thuringia, March of 68

timber 33, 40, 62

Toledo, cathedral of 260

tools 8–9, 62

torture 230, 231, 237, 318

touching for scrofula 54, 156–7

Toulouse 25, 228

Touraine 57, 158

Tournai, cathedral of 260, Fig. 18

tournaments 132, 209, 229, 269

Tours 57

towns 16–18, 23, 185–91; administration 18, 187, 188; agricultural production in 189–90; charters 187; citizenship purchased 190; courts of justice 17; expansion 8, 56, 59, 68, 182, 226, 247; fourteenth century problems 289–90; friars in 201; guilds 17, 141, 186; labour force 17, 191, 192; land tenure 17; leagues 290; libraries and book production 116; markets 17; merchants 18, 186, 192, 203; militias 164, 304; mints 17; new 8, 17–18, 188, 257, 272; political power in 17, 18, 23, 187, 311; population 8, 17, 187; plague 296; privileges 12, 17, 187; representation in parliaments 239, 273; taxation and feudal obligations 188, 190; and trade 8, 17, 23, 62, 186–7; underworld 191, 192; walls 226, 228, 253; *see also under* England; France

trade: Atlantic 273; Brittany 56; Flanders 59, 186; Hungary 268; Iceland 38, 42; Iberia 273, 276; Ile de France 56; middlemen 192; missionary activity and 249; Poland 268; *see also individual commodities and under* Champagne; Italy; Scandinavia; towns

transhumance 183

translation *see under* Latin language

transport 17, 56; *see also* seafaring

transubstantiation 221, 321

Transylvania 76, 250

Traù (Trogir) 28

tree-ring studies 290

Trier 106, 260

Trinity 122, 123, 222

Tripoli, county of 170
Tristan and Isolde, legend of 136, 265
trivium 119
Trogir (Traù) 28
Trotula (woman physician) 125
troubadours 133
Troy legends 135–6
Truce of God 26, 52, 93, 102
Tunisia 232, 241, 279, 285
Turks 280, 284
Tuscany 23, 168
Tyre 174

Ukraine 74
Unam sanctam (bull) 316
undertakers 191
underworld, criminal 191, 192
unity, ideal of 47–8, 71, 78
universals and their ontological status 319
universities 118–19, 125, 189, 229; *see also under* Bologna; Cambridge; Coimbra; Lisbon; Montpellier; Oxford; Paris
Uppsala, pagan sanctuary at 44, 245
Urban II, Pope 97, 98, 103–5, 157

Valdemar I, king of Sweden 247–8
Valence 25
Valencia 21–2, 164, 166, 274–5
vassalage 13
vengeance 41–2
Venice 23, 27–8, 196–7, 279, 296
venison 294
Vézelay, church of Figs. 5, 7
Victor III, Pope 97–8
Victor IV, anti-pope 148
Victorines 117, 120
Vienna 253
Vienne, Council of 318, 324
vignettes 262, Fig. 22
Vikings *see* Norsemen

villages 10, 17, 50
Vinland Sagas 39
violence, political and social 52–3, 66, 90–91; 14th-century 302–13, 318, 322; *see also* rebellions; warfare
Virgin Mary: crusaders' visions of 109; cult of 94–5, 96; new monastic orders and cult of 115, 176; sculpture of 261–2, Fig. 20; vernacular poetry in praise of 133, 272
Visby, Gotland 247
visions 109
viticulture 183, 189, 291
Vladimir, principality of 252
Volkmar (leader in Peasants' Crusade) 106–7
Volsungssaga 41

Waldensians 200, 201
Wales 47–8, 207, 208, 241, 304
Wallace, William 242
walls: frescos 139, 262; town 226, 228, 253
Walter the Penniless (Sansavoir) 105, 107
Walterus Robustus and Helgunda, tale of 269
wapentakes (administrative units) 49
wardships 16, 159, 234–5
warfare: brutality 166, 264, 304, 305, 308; church and 87, 100–102, 202–3, 225; compound bow 253; criminals in armies 308; fourteenth century 303–8, 327–8; funding 166, 237–8; economic effect 47, 62, 290; guns and transformation of 327–8; idealization 264; internecine, *guerrae* 103; just 100, 102, 103, 104, 198, 302, 312, 314; liturgy of war 101–2; pikemen 327; rules

100, 253; siege warfare 164; trophies 166; *see also* crusades

warrens 292

Warsaw 254

watch, municipal 187, 189

water power 62

water resources, strife over 34

watermills 62, 184, 292

wealth: disparity 299; display of 249, 267–70

weavers, Flemish 312

Welf, duke of Bavaria 98

Wells Cathedral Fig. 19

wergild 50, 77

Werner of Bolland 145

Westminster Abbey 237, 260, Fig. 17

wetnursing 190–91

Wight, Isle of 45

William I the Conqueror, king of England 149–50, 154; as duke of Normandy 59, 63–4, 149

William II Rufus, king of England 150–51

William I, king of Sicily 169, 195

William II, king of Sicily 169, 195

William, marquis of Massa 33

William of Auvergne 213–14, 216, 225

William of Volpiano 58

windmills 184

windows: rose 140, 260, Fig. 8; *see also* glass

wine production and trade 22, 61, 62, 183, 268, 291

witan (English great council) 49, 50

witchcraft 77, 300–301

witenagemot (English high court) 49–50

woad cultivation 62, 291

women: Cathar 203; guilds and 186; inheritance of fiefs 16, 234, 298; learning 119–20; literature by 120, 132, 133; and medicine 120, 124, 125; monastic orders and 176, 203; mortality in childbirth 8; occupations 183, 186, 191; religious 94, 96–7, 116, 120, 176, 203; sexual relations with Muslim or Jewish 275

woodlands 9, 62, 184, 234

wool and woollen cloth 42, 62, 169, 292; English trade with Flanders 290, 305, 313

Worms 106; Concordat of 99, 146

writing 184, 185

Wyclif, John 318

Yersenia pestis (plague bacterium) 295

York 174; Statute of 306

Ypres 59, 311

Zangī (Muslim leader) 171, 172

Zara 28, 196–7